The Sage Dictionary of
Qualitative Management Research

Acknowledgement

This dictionary is a companion to a complimentary title, *The Dictionary of Quantitative Management Research*, edited by Luiz Moutinho and Graeme Hutcheson, that will be publishing shortly. Luiz is the Series Editor for both volumes and his early contribution to this edition is acknowledged.

The Sage Dictionary of Qualitative Management Research

Compiled and edited
by
Richard Thorpe
Robin Holt

SAGE Publications
Los Angeles ▪ London ▪ New Delhi ▪ Singapore

© The editors and contributors 2008

First published 2008

Apart from any fair dealing for the purposes of research
or private study, or criticism or review, as permitted under
the Copyright, Designs and Patents Act, 1988, this
publication may be reproduced, stored or transmitted in
any form, or by any means, only with the prior permission
in writing of the publishers, or in the case of reprographic
reproduction, in accordance with the terms of licences
issued by the Copyright Licensing Agency. Enquiries
concerning reproduction outside those terms should be
sent to the publishers.

SAGE Publications Ltd
1 Oliver's Yard
55 City Road
London EC1Y 1SP

SAGE Publications Inc.
2455 Teller Roads
Thousand Oaks, California 91320

SAGE Publications India Pvt Ltd
B-1/I1 Mohan Cooperative Industrial Area
Mathura Road, New Delhi 110 044

SAGE Publications Asia-Pacific Pte Ltd
33 Pekin Street #02-01
Far East Square
Singapore 048763

Library of Congress Control Number: 2006940707

British Library Cataloguing in Publication data

A catalogue record for this book is available
from the British Library

ISBN 978-1-4129-3521-0
ISBN 978-1-4129-3528-9 (pbk)

Typeset by C&M Digitals (P) Ltd., Chennai, India
Printed in Great Britain by The Cromwell Press Ltd, Trowbridge, Wiltshire
Printed on paper from sustainable resources

Contents

List of Figures and Tables

Figures

Tables

List of Contributors

EDITORS

Richard Thorpe is Professor of Management Development and Deputy Director of the Keyworth Institute at Leeds University Business School. His interests include: performance, remuneration, and entrepreneurship, management learning and development and leadership. He has sought to develop these interests at all the institutions in which he has worked. His early industrial experience informed the way his ethos has developed. Common themes are: a strong commitment to process methodologies and a focus on action in all its forms; an interest in and commitment to the development of doctoral students and the development of capacity within the sector; a commitment to collaborative working on projects of mutual interest. He is currently the President of the British Academy of Management and a member of the UK's ESRC Training and Development Board.

Robin Holt is a Reader in Strategy and Ethics at the University of Liverpool School of Management. He has an abiding interest in questions of being and identity that emerge from our wealth creating activity. He has published in *Organization Studies, Human Relations* and *Research Policy* and is currently co-authoring a book on *Strategy without Design: The Efficacy of Everyday Detours*.

CONTRIBUTORS

Fran Ackermann is a Professor based in the Department of Management Science at the Strathclyde Business School. Her research has predominantly focused on messy complex problems, in particularly strategy making, with a preference for action research. Along with Colin Eden she has developed an approach called Journey Making which has as its foundation cognitive mapping. As such she has considerable experience in using the technique for strategy making and capturing/analyzing rich qualitative data.

Mats Alvesson is a Professor of Business Administration at Lund University, Sweden. He has published extensively on organizational culture, qualitative methods and critical theory. His recent books include *Postmodernism and Social*

Research (Open University Press, 2002), *Studying Management Critically*, edited with Hugh Willmott (Sage, 2003), *Knowledge Work and Knowledge Intensive Firms* (Oxford University Press, 2004) and *Changing Organizational Culture* (Routledge, 2007, with Stefan Sveningsson).

Lisa Anderson is a Lecturer in HRM at the University of Liverpool Management School. Her research interests centre on action learning and management and leadership development, particularly in the SME sector. Other areas of interest include social learning, especially how language use in groups helps to create critical reflection.

Elena Antonacopoulou is Professor of Organizational Behaviour at the University of Liverpool Management School and Director of GNOSIS, a dynamic management research initiative. She is also a Senior Fellow of the Advanced Institute of Management Research. Her principal research interests include change and learning processes in organizations. Her work is published in *Organization Studies, Journal of Management Studies, Academy of Management Review*. She serves on the editorial board of *Organization Science, Academy of Management Learning and Education Journal Society, Business and Organization Journal* and *Irish Journal of Management*.

Tore Bakken is an Associate Professor at the Norwegian School of Management BI in Oslo. He completed his sociological thesis on systems theory at the University of Oslo. His current empirical work includes a study of risk in food production, and an examination of the notions of mind and social reality in John Searle's philosophy of language and Niklas Luhmann's sociology of autopoietic systems.

Pat Bazeley provides training, assistance, time out (and good food) to researchers at her retreat at Bowral, Australia. She has expertise in making sense of both quantitative and qualitative data and in using computer programs for management and analysis of data. She also enjoys experimenting with new ways to integrate analysis of text and numeric data.

Emma Bell is a Senior Lecturer in Organisation Studies at Queen Mary, University of London. Prior to this she worked at the University of Warwick and Manchester Metropolitan University. She has published articles in *Journal of Management Studies, Human Relations* and *Organization* and is the co-author of a book with Alan Bryman, *Business Research Methods* (2004).

Robert Blackburn PhD is Director of Research, Faculty of Business and Law, HSBC Professor of Small Business Studies and Director of the Small Business Research Centre, Kingston University. He is editor of the *International Small Business Journal* (Sage) and Vice President of the *Institute of Small Business and Entrepreneurship*. His academic output is prolific and his books include

Researching the Small Enterprise (with James Curran) (Sage, 2001) and *Intellectual Property and Innovation Management in Small Firms* (ed. Routledge, 2003).

David M. Boje holds the Bank of America Endowed Professorship of Management (awarded September 2006), and is past Arthur Owens Professorship in Business Administration (June 2003–June 2006) in the Management Department at New Mexico State University. Professor Boje is described by his peers as an international scholar in the qualitative areas of narrative, storytelling, postmodern theory and critical ethics. He has published nearly 100 articles in journals, including *Management Science, Administrative Science Quarterly, Academy of Management Journal, Academy of Management Review* and the *International Journal of Organization Studies.*

Ulrik Brandi is a doctoral student at the Learning Lab Denmark, The Danish University of Education. He is a student in the Doctoral School of Organizational Learning (DOCSOL) and his project is on organizational learning and change and the relation between the two. His empirical field is public organizations and his theoretical sources of inspiration draw on pragmatism and neo-pragmatism.

David Bricknall had a career as a solicitor in industry before deciding to pursue a PhD in order to try to understand and make sense of what he had been doing. His current research interests are the strategic exploitation of technology and the intuitive nature of strategic decisions.

Jane Broadbent is Deputy Vice Chancellor at Roehampton University. She has a range of refereed publications aligned to management and accounting change in the public sector. Recent research (with Richard Laughlin) includes a project to study Performance Management in Higher Education Institutions. A study of the Private Finance Initiative has resulted in a range of academic and policy inputs and an on-going three year collaboration with colleagues in Australia.

David Buchanan is Professor of Organizational Behaviour at Cranfield University's School of Management, UK. He holds degrees in business administration and organizational behaviour from Heriot-Watt and Edinburgh Universities. Research interests include change agency, change management, research methods, and organization politics. Current projects include a study of links between corporate governance and organizational performance in healthcare.

John Burgoyne is Professor of Management Learning in the Department of Management Learning in the Management School, University of Lancaster, of which he is a founding member, and Professor of Management Learning at Henley Management College. A psychologist by background he has worked on the evaluation of management development, the learning process, competencies and self-development, corporate management development policy, career formation, organizational learning, knowledge managing, the virtual organization and leadership.

Bernard Burnes is Professor of Organisational Change in the Manchester Business School. His research covers organizational change in its broadest sense. This includes the history, development and current state of organizational change, organizational and inter-organizational behaviour, leadership, strategy, and culture.

Catherine Cassell is Professor of Occupational Psychology and Director of Postgraduate Research Programmes at Manchester Business School. She has a long term interest in, and commitment to, the use of qualitative research techniques in management and organizational research. Together with Gillian Symon she has published a number of books and articles in this area and co-edits *Qualitative Research in Organizations and Management: An International Journal.*

Peter Checkland worked in R&D in ICI for fifteen years, after which time he led the action research team at Lancaster University which produced the SSM approach to real-world problems. This work has been recognized in four honorary doctorates, medals from the UK Systems Society and the OR Society, and a 'Most Distinguished Contributor' award from the British Computer Society.

Robert Chia is Professor of Management at the University of Aberdeen and Visiting Professor at Strathclyde University Graduate Business School. He was a senior editor of *Organization Studies*, and is a member of the international advisory board for *Journal of Management Studies* and *Management Learning*. His research interests revolve around the issues of strategic leadership and foresight, complexity and creative thinking, contrasting East–West metaphysical mindsets and critical cultural studies. He is the author of three books and numerous international journal articles, as well as book chapters.

Ian Clarke is Professor of Marketing at Lancaster University Management School and Senior Fellow of the EPSRC/ESRC Advanced Institute of Management Research (AIM). His main research interests lie in decision-making and sensemaking processes within senior management teams and their impact on strategy processes and practices.

Jean Clarke has now completed her PhD in Entrepreneurship and is now a Researcher at Leeds University Business School. She completed her MSc in Occupational Psychology in the University of Sheffield in 2004. She has an interest in visual methods, particularly visual ethnography and the use of moving images. She is also interested in ideas in the area of relational constructionism and relating them to the field of entrepreneurship.

Gail P Clarkson is a Lecturer in Organisational Behaviour at Leeds University Business School, The University of Leeds, UK. Gail's research is focused on gaining a deeper understanding of how managers can engage employees in employment relationships that will enhance individual and organizational performance and well-being. A second stream of research is related to the development and validation of research methods.

Stewart Clegg is a prolific publisher in the leading academic journals in management and organization theory as well as the author of many books, one of the most recent of which is *Power and Organizations* (with David Courpasson and Nelson Phillips, Thousand Oaks, CA: Sage, 2005, Foundations of Organization Science series).

Ian Colville has a first degree in psychology, and a masters and PhD in management. He is fascinated by what people do, and this explains his abiding interest in organizing and sensemaking. He is married with three daughters, who collectively transcend sensemaking.

Robert Cooper is a visiting professor in the Centre for Culture, Social Theory and Technology, Keele University. He writes mainly on the general theme of social and cultural production. He has published widely on the relationship between technology and modern organizing, on technology and mass society, and on the social and cultural aspects of information.

Joep Cornelissen is Professor of Corporate Communications at Leeds University Business School. He previously worked at the Amsterdam School of Communications Research, University of Amsterdam. His research interests include the management of corporate communications and the use of metaphor in management and organization theory and practice. He is author of *Corporate Communications: Theory and Practice* (Sage). His research articles on metaphor have appeared in *Academy of Management Review, Organization Studies, British Journal of Management, Journal of Advertising Research, Human Relations, Psychology and Marketing* and the *Journal of Management Studies*.

Anne-Marie Cummins is Lecturer in Sociology and a Fellow at the Centre for Psycho-Social Studies at the University of the West of England and the UK editor of *Organisational and Social Dynamics*. She works as an independent consultant and has acted as a staff member on national and international Group Relations conferences.

Ann Cunliffe is the Albert & Mary Jane Black Endowed Professor of Economic Development, Department of Organizational Studies, The Robert O. Anderson School of Management, The University of New Mexico. Her publications include articles in *Journal of Management Studies, Organization Studies* and *Human Relations*. In 2002 she received the Breaking the Frame Award from the *Journal of Management Inquiry* for the article 'that best exemplifies a challenge to existing thought'. She is currently Associate Editor for *Management Learning* and on the editorial boards of *Organization Studies, Human Relations*, the *Scandinavian Journal of Management* and the *Journal of Organizational Change Management*.

Ardha Danieli is a Lecturer in Qualitative Research Methodology and Organizational Analysis at Warwick Business School. Her research is concerned with issues of social and economic inclusion, with a specific interest in equality, diversity, gender and disability. Her work has been published in *Personnel Review*, *Disability and Society* and *Communities and Nations*.

Barry Davies is Associate Dean for research at the University of Gloucestershire Business School. He studied at what are now the universities of Bolton, Central Lancashire, Lancaster, and Cranfield. He researches into retail environments and their effects on customers, decision support in marketing and issues in globalization. Probably a pragmatist, he uses a variety of approaches in his work.

Lex Donaldson is Professor of Management in Organizational Design in the Faculty of Business of the University of New South Wales, Sydney, Australia. He has a PhD from the University of London. He is the author of seven books on organizational theory, organizational structure and management. In addition, he has written numerous journal articles.

Fraser Dunworth is a Consultant Clinical Psychologist, Head of CAMHS Psychology and Clinical Lead for North Derbyshire CAMHS. In a previous career he was an actor, director and writer. His research interests are in how young people and their families experience mental health issues.

Mark Easterby-Smith is Professor of Management Learning at Lancaster University. He has written extensively on management research methodology and organizational learning. From 2003–2007 he was a senior Fellow of the UK's Advanced Institute of Management (AIM) research initiative. His current research covers the links between organizational learning and dynamic capability, the competitive strategies of successful multinationals operating in the China market, and the way high technology companies attempt to learn from their customers.

Bente Elkjaer is a Professor in organizational and workplace learning at the Learning Lab Denmark, The Danish University of Education. She is the head of the Doctoral School of Organizational Learning (DOCSOL) and the current editor-in-chief of *Management Learning*. Her research interest is to develop an understanding of organizational learning based upon pragmatist philosophy (John Dewey) and sociology (Anselm Strauss).

Boris Ewenstein did this work as a Research Associate at the Tanaka Business School, Imperial College, London. He now works as a consultant for McKinsey and Company in the Berlin office. His research interests include organizational knowledge and knowing, the process of reflexivity, and the sociology of formal and informal learning.

Jason Ferdinand is a Lecturer in Management at the University of Liverpool Management School. His research interests include managing knowledge, economic and industrial espionage, and piracy. The majority of his work is framed by dialectical materialism and conducted through ethnographic investigation.

Jason has a particular interest in the application of Marxist theory in trans-disciplinary research projects.

Bent Flybjerg is Professor of Planning, at Aalborg University, Denmark and Chair of Infrastructure Policy and Planning at Delft University of Technology, The Netherlands. He was twice a Visiting Fulbright Scholar to the USA, where he did research at UCLA, UC Berkeley, and Harvard University. His most recent books in English are *Making Social Science Matter, Megaprojects and Risk: An Anatomy of Ambition* and *Rationality and Power: Democracy in Practice*. His books and articles have been translated into 17 languages. Bent Flyvbjerg is currently doing research on power, truth, and lying. Further details at http://flyvbjerg.plan.aau.dk.

Steve Fox is Professor of Social and Management Learning at Lancaster University. He is interested in interdisciplinary research and theory spanning social, organizational and management learning.

Jeff Gold is Principal Lecturer in Organisation Learning at Leeds Business School, Leeds Metropolitan University. He is the co-author of *Management Development, Strategies for Action* (with Alan Mumford), published by the Chartered Institute of Personnel and Development in 2004. The fourth edition of his textbook on *Human Resource Management* (with John Bratton) was published in 2007 with Palgrave Macmillan.

Ian Greenwood is Lecturer in Industrial Relations and Human Resource Management in the Work and Employment Relations (WERD) Division of Leeds University Business School, University of Leeds, UK. His current research interests include: workplace skills; the industrial relations of team working; community unionism; the impact of restructuring in the steel industry.

Michelle Greenwood is on the faculty in the Department of Management, Monash University, where she teaches and researches in the area of business ethics. Her specific fields of interest are ethical issues in HRM, stakeholder theory and social and ethical auditing. Michelle's research has been published in international journals and she currently serves on the editorial board of the *Journal of Business Ethics*.

Mauro F. Guillén is the Dr Felix Zandman Endowed Professor of International Management at the Wharton School and Professor of Sociology in the Department of Sociology of the University of Pennsylvania. His work has to do with the social and cultural context in which organizations operate. His current research deals with the internationalization of the firm, and with the impact of globalization on patterns of organization and on the diffusion of innovations. His most recent books are *The Rise of Spanish Multinationals* (Cambridge University Press) and *The Taylorized Beauty of the Mechanical* (Princeton University Press). He is also the author of *The Limits of Convergence: Globalization and*

Organizational Change in Argentina, South Korea, and Spain (Princeton University Press, 2001) and *Models of Management* (The University of Chicago Press, 1994).

Evert Gummesson is Professor of Marketing and Management at the Stockholm University School of Business, Sweden. His research interests are services, relationships, networks and qualitative methodology. His book *Qualitative Methods in Management Research* has been reprinted and revised continuously since 1985. Since 2000 he has published ten articles and book chapters on methodology and theory development.

Mark Hall is a Lecturer in operations and project management in the Department of Management at the University of Bristol. He has researched and published on a range of topics related to operations and project management, including public sector culture, sustainable development, risk behaviour and quality management. He holds a PhD in international management and cultural theory.

Karen Handley is a Senior Lecturer in the HRM and Organisational Behaviour department at Oxford Brookes University. Her business research interests include management learning, client-consultancy projects and relationships, and communities of practice. She has recently completed an ESRC-funded project, *Knowledge Evolution in Action: Client-Consultancy Relationships* (http://www.ebkresearch.org/). Before joining academia, Karen worked in the financial services industry and as a management consultant at PriceWaterhouseCoopers.

Elaine Harris is Professor and Head of Department of Accounting and Finance and Head of Leicester Business School's Graduate Centre at De Montfort University. She teaches Research Methodology and Project Management and has developed a framework for project risk assessment, based on action research. Elaine is currently Chair of CHA, Secretary of the MCA, and a member of ACCA's Research Committee.

John Hassard is Professor of Organizational Analysis at Manchester Business School (University of Manchester) and Senior Professorial Research Associate at the Judge Business School, University of Cambridge. His main research interests lie in theories of organization, critical management studies, and the empirical analysis of industrial change. On these subjects he has published 12 books and more than 100 research articles.

John Hayes is Professor of Management Studies, Leeds University Business School. He has published ten books and over 60 papers. His latest books are *Interpersonal Skills at Work* (Routledge, 2002) and *The Theory and Practice of Change Management* (2nd edn. Palgrave, 2007). His research interests focus on cognitive style and processes of change and development in organizations. Professor Hayes has worked as a consultant for a number of organizations including British Gas, British Petroleum, Delphi, Lucas, ICI, NHS, Reckitt and Coleman, Glaxo, British Telecom, Nestlé, the RAF, the US Army and the Yorkshire Bank.

Tor Hernes is Professor of Organization and Management at the Norwegian School of Management BI in Oslo, where he is Head of the Department of Innovation and Economic Organization. His main interest lies with process theorizing. Drawing inspiration from the work of Alfred North Whitehead, his current project consists of developing a theoretical framework to account for processes of organization and innovation.

Vivien Hodgson is Professor of Networked Management Learning in the Department of Management Learning and Leadership at Lancaster University Management School, Lancaster, UK. Her research interests are related to the students' experiences of learning in higher education and management learning, particularly in the context and use of technology supported open and collaborative learning approaches. Further details available at: http://www.lums.lancs.ac.uk/dml/profiles/143/

Heather Höpfl is Professor of Management at the University of Essex. She has a long-time interest in organizational symbolism and narratives. In the 1980s she worked as a tour manager for a touring repertory company and is a former chair of SCOS. She is currently co-editor of *Culture in Organizations*. Her recent publications have been concerned with aesthetics, narratives and mythologies.

Masahide Horita, having formerly worked at Durham Business School, is currently Associate Professor at the Department of Civil Engineering, University of Tokyo. His areas of interest include decision-making, public management, problem structuring methods and collaborative argumentation.

Shelby D. Hunt is the Jerry S. Rawls and P. W. Horn Professor of Marketing at Texas Tech University, Lubbock, Texas. A past editor of the *Journal of Marketing* (1985–87), he is the author of numerous books, including *Foundations of Marketing Theory: Toward a General Theory of Marketing* (M.E. Sharpe, 2002), *Controversy in Marketing Theory: For Reason, Realism, Truth, and Objectivity* (M.E. Sharpe, 2003), and *A General Theory of Competition: Resources, Competences, Productivity, Economic Growth* (Sage, 2000). One of the 250 most frequently cited researchers in economics and business (Thompson-ISI), he has written numerous articles on competitive theory, strategy, macromarketing, ethics, relationship marketing, channels of distribution, philosophy of science, and marketing theory.

Phil Johnson was, until recently, a Reader in Management and Organization at Sheffield Hallam University. Now he is Professor of HRM at Sheffield University. He has published mainly in the areas of research methodology, epistemology and organization studies. His current research is into alternative forms of organizational governance.

Jong Jun is Professor Emeritus of Public Administration at California State University at East Bay and Visiting Professor at Leiden University in the Netherlands. He received his PhD from the University of Southern California and is a fellow of the US National Academy of Public Administration. He has published numerous books, symposium issues, and over 50 articles in professional journals.

Panagiotis Kokkalis is a Senior Lecturer in Strategy at Manchester Metropolitan University Business School, UK. The focus of his research is on tacit knowledge in organizational settings. He has presented a number of research papers at international conferences including the British Academy of Management, and the European Academy of Management.

Ann Langley is Professor of Strategic Management and Research Methods at HEC Montréal. She obtained her PhD in administration at HEC in 1987. Her empirical research deals with strategic decision-making, innovation, leadership and strategic change in pluralistic organizations and notably in the healthcare sector. She has a particular interest in qualitative and process research methods.

Richard Laughlin is Professor of Accounting at King's College London, University of London. He has a range of publications most of which are related to method-ological issues and to understanding the organizational and human effects of changes in accounting, finance and management systems in organizations and soci-ety, with a particular emphasis on the public sector. Recent research projects include studies of performance management in higher education institutions and the pri-vate finance initiative in the UK and public–private partnerships in Australia.

Stephen Linstead is Professor of Critical Management at The York Management School. He co-edited *The Aesthetics of Organization* (Sage, 2002) with Heather Höpfl and co-founded the *Art of Management and Organization* series of confer-ences. His current interests include post-punk music and organization, *The Clash*, Georges Bataille and the political aesthetics of Jacques Ranciere.

Karen Locke, PhD, is W. Brooks George Professor of Business Administration at the College of William and Mary's School of Business. Dr Locke's work focuses on developing a sociology of knowledge in organizational studies and on the use of qualitative research for the investigation of organizational phenomena. Her work appears in journals such as *Academy of Management Journal, Organization Science, Journal of Organizational Behavior, Journal of Management Inquiry* and *Studies in Organization, Culture and Society*. She has authored *Grounded Theory In Management Research* and co-authored *Composing Qualitative Research*. Dr Locke also serves as an associate action editor for *Organizational Research Methods* and as a member of the editorial board for the *Academy of Management Journal*.

Robert MacIntosh did a PhD in engineering management at the University of Strathclyde before transferring to a business school post. He currently holds a Chair in Strategic Management at the University of Glasgow and his two main areas of research interest are strategic change and the methods which underpin practice-relevant management research.

William Mackaness is a Senior Lecturer in the Institute of Geography, School of GeoSciences, at the University of Edinburgh. His research interests are in automated cartography, and the role of visualization in qualitative reasoning. Automated cartography explores ideas of constraint-based reasoning. Visualization and cognition are key research themes in the delivery of information over mobile devices which forms a third area of research.

Donald MacLean graduated in Physics from Strathclyde University, received his PhD in optoelectronics from the University of Cambridge and spent ten years working in the optoelectronics industry. In 1991 he began lecturing in strategic management and is now a Senior Research Fellow at the University of Glasgow. His interests lie in the development of alternative conceptions of strategy, leadership, organization and management.

Allan Macpherson is a Senior Lecturer in HRM and Organizational Behaviour at Liverpool University's School of Management. He has worked on a number of research projects using qualitative methods concerned with management development, network learning and the evolution of business knowledge in small firms. Current research is focused on the use of objects that mediate collective learning in small firms and barriers to collective learning.

John McAuley is Professor of Organisation Development and Management in the Faculty of Organisation and Management, Sheffield Hallam University. He is Head of Programmes: Research Degrees. He has published in the areas of change management, organization behaviour, organization theory, research methods and the work of professionals.

Sara McGaughey is a Professor of International Management at the Strathclyde Business School, University of Strathclyde. Her research explores processes within international entrepreneurship, strategy and knowledge management across borders, and her interest in methods of representation, such as dramas and cartoons, crosses these fields. Sara has a forthcoming book on narratives and international entrepreneurship, and her work has been published in journals including *Academy of Management Review, Journal of Management Studies* and *Journal of World Business*.

Hugh McLaughlin is Director of Social Work and Social Policy at the University of Salford. Hugh is a qualified social worker and before entering academia was an Assistant Director of Social Services. He has published in the fields of management, child care and more recently in the fields of social inclusion and meaningful service user involvement in research.

Reijo Miettinen (PhD in Social Psychology) is Professor of Adult Education at the University of Helsinki. He is Vice Director of the Center for Activity Theory and Developmental Work Research, University of Helsinki. He has directed since 1995 a research group that studies innovation networks, producer-user interaction, and the free/open source development model (FOSS) in software development, and the as well as other forms of internet-mediated distributed knowledge production.

Eamonn Molloy is a University Lecturer in Technology and Operations Management at the Saïd Business School, University of Oxford and a Fellow of Green College, Oxford. He holds a PhD in Science and Technology Studies from the University of Lancaster and is interested in theories of technology, organization, practice and agency.

Stephanie J. Morgan, BSc, MSc, PhD, Chartered Psychologist, is Director of Crosslight Management Ltd and an Associate Lecturer at Birkbeck, University of London. She consults and carries out research on various aspects of work including outsourcing, staff motivation, customer service, technology-related change, and managing diversity. She has a special interest in qualitative methods and the use of technology in research.

Alan Murray lectures in Accounting and Corporate Social Responsibility at Sheffield University's Management School. His research focuses on the interaction between financial markets and the social and environmental aspects of business. He sits on the executive committees of the British Accounting Association and the British Academy of Management.

Sara Nadin is a Lecturer in HRM/Organisational Behaviour at the University of Bradford's, School of Management. She obtained her PhD from Sheffield University's Management School in 2004 and has published in the areas of qualitative research methods, gender, the psychological contract, and small businesses.

Ajit Nayak is a Senior Lecturer in Strategy and International Business at the Bristol Business School, University of the West of England, UK. His research interests are 1) creativity, innovation and change, 2) ontological, epistemological and methodological issues in organization studies, 3) self and identity in the workplace, and 4) entrepreneurship, corporate governance and Indian elites. Ajit received his PhD entitled 'Creative Management: A Decentred Perspective' in 2004 and has published in Organization Studies.

Wilson Ng holds a UK Research Council's Robert's Fellowship in Corporate Governance at Leeds University Business School. He has an MA and PhD in Management Studies from Cambridge and an MBA from London University. Wilson conducts company research on the growth and development of family-controlled firms in Europe and East Asia using both a case study and a mixed methods approach.

Cliff Oswick holds a Chair in Organization Theory and Discourse at the University of Leicester. His research interests focus on the application of aspects of discourse to the study of organizations and organizing. He has published work in a range of international journals, including contributions *to Academy of Management Review, Human Relations, Journal of Management Studies, Organization,* and *Organization Studies.*

Krsto Pandza is Senior Lecturer in Technology and Management at Leeds University Business School. His research activities centre on understanding the role of technology and operations in creating and sustaining a competitive advantage in technology-intensive organizations. He is especially interested in the role of managerial agency within dynamic organizational phenomena, specifically exploring how managers deal with uncertainties associated with the future, and this explains his interest in Delphi methodology.

Mike Pedler works with people in organizations on learning processes and practices. He is known for his work on action learning, the learning organization and leadership development. He is Professor of Action Learning at Henley Management College and holds Visiting Professorships at the Universities of York and Lincoln. He edits the journal *Action Learning: Research and Practice.*

Luke Pittaway is the Director of the Enterprise and Regional Development Unit and Director of Research for the White Rose CETLE at the University of Sheffield. His research focuses on business-to-business networking, entrepreneurial behaviour and entrepreneurship education. He also engages in the practice of enterprise through his involvement in a university spinout company, two family businesses and the development of a social enterprise led by students at the University of Sheffield (Sheffield SIFE Ltd).

Marlei Pozzebon is Associate Professor at HEC Montréal. She holds a PhD in administration from McGill University. Her research interests are the political and cultural aspects of information technology implementation, the use of structuration theory and critical discourse analysis in the information systems field, business intelligence and social responsibility, the role of information technology in local development and participatory practices.

Robert W. Putnam, PhD., is a partner and co-founder of Action Design, a firm that educates leaders and agents of organizational learning and change. He is a co-developer of action science, an approach to inquiry that emphasizes knowledge for action. He earned his doctorate in Counselling and Consulting Psychology from Harvard University. He holds a BA in Political Science from Syracuse University and was a Woodrow Wilson Fellow.

Annie Pye began her academic career working with Professor Iain Mangham from whom she learnt much about the role and relevance of dramatic performance in understanding organizational performance. She is Professor of Leadership at the University of Exeter where she continues to research and write about senior executive teams running complex organizations.

Julia Rouse is interested in the relationship between small business and social structures, particularly the structures of class, region and gender. Her research includes various longitudinal studies of the experiences of small business owner–managers, employing both qualitative and quantitative methods. Julia currently works as a Senior Research Fellow in the Centre for Enterprise at Manchester Metropolitan University Business School.

Mark N.K. Saunders BA, MSc, PGCE, PhD, FCIPD, is Professor of Business Research Methods and Assistant Dean (Research and Doctoral Programmes) at Oxford Brookes University Business School. Mark undertakes research on trust and justice perspectives on the management of change and research methods. He is co-author of six books including *Research Methods for Business Students,* now in its fourth edition.

Julie Schönfelder is Head of Branding at the Siemens Networks Headquarters in Germany. She completed her PhD in marketing with a focus on branding at Manchester Metropolitan University, England. She has published in the areas of branding and research methods and appears as a guest speaker at international conferences in these areas.

Brian Simpson has held senior roles in employer relations and mainstream human resources alongside commitments in teaching. He is currently Deputy Director of Human Resources at Manchester Metropolitan University, and for the past ten years has had responsibility for management and organizational development.

David Sims is Professor of Organizational Behaviour, Cass Business School, Associate Dean, and Director of the Centre for Leadership, Learning and Change. His research interests are in living, leading, thinking, learning and storying. He has applied these interests to topics as diverse as why people get angry in organizations, middle managers' motivation, agenda shaping, consulting skills and mergers.

J.-C. Spender served in experimental submarines in the Royal Navy, studied engineering at Oxford (Balliol), worked as a nuclear submarine reactor engineer and as a merchant banker with Slater-Walker Securities. His PhD thesis (Manchester Business School) won the Academy of Management's 1980 A.T. Kearney PhD Research Prize, later published as *Industry Recipes* (Blackwell, 1989). He served on the faculty at City University (London), York University (Toronto), UCLA, and Rutgers and was Dean of the School of Business and Technology at SUNY/FIT before retiring in 2003. Now researching, writing, and lecturing widely on strategy and knowledge management in US, Canada, and Europe, with Visiting Professor appointments at Cranfield, Leeds, and Open Universities.

Andrew Sturdy is Professor of Organisational Behaviour at Warwick Business School, University of Warwick, UK. He has a particular interest in critical approaches to work and organizations including the study of management ideas and knowledge.

Alexander Styhre (PhD, received from Lund University) is a Professor in the Department of Technology Management, Chalmers University of Technology, Gothenburg, Sweden. Alexander is interested in the use of knowledge in organizations and has conducted research in the automotive, pharmaceutical, and construction industries. His most recent book is *The Innovative Bureaucracy* (Routledge, 2007).

Peter Svensson is Associate Professor of Business Administration at Lund University, Sweden. His research interests include marketing work, knowledge production in business life, marketing/management knowledge, qualitative method, discourse theory, critical social theory and its relevance for marketing and management studies.

Gillian Symon is Senior Lecturer in Organizational Psychology at Birkbeck, University of London. Her main research interests lie in the areas of technology and organization, where she has applied a rhetorical approach to examining their mutual social construction, and in the promotion of qualitative research in general. For more details about Gillian's work see: www.bbk.ac.uk/manop/ orgpsychology/staff/symon/symon.shtml

Scott Taylor is currently working as a Lecturer in Management in the Department of Accounting, Finance and Management, University of Essex. His research centres on the tensions and conflicts that people feel in workplaces or through work. He is particularly interested in religious or spiritual influences on work, smaller companies, and post-structural analytical approaches.

Torkild Thanem is an Assistant Professor in the School of Management and Economics, Växjö University, Sweden. Torkild was formerly a Research Fellow in the School of Business, Stockholm University, and he has been a Visiting Scholar at the University of Oregon and Stanford University. Torkild's research focuses on the organization and non-organization of space and embodiment in urban planning and health promotion, and his work has been published in *Culture and Organization*, *Organization Studies* and *Organization*.

Russ Vince is Professor of Leadership and Change in the School of Management, the University of Bath. The focus of his research is on management and organizational learning, leadership and the management of change. Russ is Editor-in-Chief of the international academic journal *Management Learning*.

Tony Watson is Professor of Organisational Behaviour at Nottingham University Business School. His interests cover industrial sociology, organizations, managerial and entrepreneurial work and ethnography. Current work is on the relationship between the shaping of the 'whole lives' of managers and entrepreneurs and the shaping of the enterprizes within which they work.

Elke Weik is a Lecturer at the Centre for Critical Management Studies of the University of Leicester. She works in the field of organization theory, but relates much of her work to social theory and philosophy as well. Her current research includes studies on process theory and philosophy as well as an empirical project on the institutionalization of birth practices in Germany.

Hugh Willmott is Research Professor in Organization Studies, Cardiff Business School. Current research projects are connected by a common theme of exploring the relevance and application of poststructuralist understandings of agency, power and change for studying diverse aspects of management and organization. He has published 20 books and numerous papers in leading social science and management journals and currently serves on the editorial boards of the *Academy of Management Review, Organization Studies* and *Journal of Management Studies*. Further details can be found on his homepage: http://dspace.dial.pipex.com/town/close/hr22/hcwhome

Julie Wolfram Cox holds the Chair in Management at Deakin University, Australia. Julie received BA (Honours) and MA (Research) degrees in psychology from the University of Melbourne and holds a PhD in Organizational Behaviour from Case Western Reserve University in Cleveland, USA. Her research interests include critical and aesthetic perspectives on organization theory and research, particularly organizational change.

Martin Wood is Senior Lecturer at York Management School, University of York, and was previously a member of faculty at both Exeter and Warwick Universities. As an educator and researcher Martin has continued to explore the ideas and problems of management and organization studies as they relate to process-oriented social and political theory. His current research looks at leadership in relation to philosophical issues of identity and difference.

Carol Woodhams is a Reader in Human Resource Studies at Plymouth Business School. Her primary research interests include examining equal opportunities within small- to medium-sized enterprises, debates of human resources and disability equality and the impact of disability equality legislation. She is a Chartered Fellow of the CIPD.

Mike Zundel is currently a Doctoral Researcher at Manchester Metropolitan University Business School. His research focuses on practice perspectives in organizational settings and he has presented his work at international conferences such as the British Academy of Management and the Organization Studies Summer Workshop. He has previously worked for Hewlett-Packard and IBM in Germany.

What is Management Research?

Why do we inquire into activities of wealth creation? At its most general, this inquiry is defined by its aim: to become more aware of and find meaning in, social experience. From such awareness comes the possibility of influence, both within the institutional structures and objects we encounter, create and use, and over our own development in terms of character and conduct. Using this influence we can satisfy what Alfred Whitehead (1929a: 14, 23) calls our three-fold urge: 'to live, to live well, to live better'; and so to transform life into a potentially good and better life. Managerial research is a particular and increasingly important form of such influence; its concerns being those aspects of social life that are broadly concerned with the production and distribution of material wealth through some form of social organization, whether an entrepreneurial venture, a corporation, a public department, a profession, an occupation, and so on. Often the term 'management' relates to an improvement in performance, however this may be determined, but the root of the word comes from the French *main* meaning 'to handle and direct something', whether it is simply the taking and application of decisions, or more broadly, a concern with the possible effects of such decisions. As a practice of handling action, management has become increasingly pervasive, touching many sections of many societies, almost like a transformational force akin to how engineering came to pervade the nineteenth century. What is handled can include a multitude of things, from physical objects and production and distribution spaces to human emotions such as dissent or expectation. In covering all manner of such objects, procedures and actions, managers are not restricted to a particular craft or locale – they can practise their skills across many different organizations in many different places. Once the preserve of private companies, management initiatives are now experienced in a myriad of organizational conditions: voluntary organizations, government offices, schools, prisons and international advisory bodies to name a few. Developments in communication, production and distribution technologies have served to catalyse this institutional a range. They have made possible a division of labour, a separation of agency and ownership, and a geographical reach that has meant this production and distribution of goods, services and knowledge rarely occurs in one place under the auspices of a single person. Our products are made by many hands and machines, our services can be delivered from remote places, our organizations can be owned and influenced by many different interests and our knowledge arises from many sources. With this separation between imaginative judgements, planning, ownership and execution comes an increasing need for co-ordinating wealth-creating effort across activities, times and spaces, and hence a need for managers. As economies grow in terms of net product, as material expectations rise, as managerial behaviours become increasingly sophisticated, and as the shareholder form of such economies becomes increasingly the norm, these management activities are becoming ever more pervasive.

While there is broad recognition of the basic nature and extent of such management activity, and so its being an area of our personal and social lives worthy of study, what is far less certain is how we should understand, present and judge it. It is to pursue this understanding, presentation and judgement that the field of management research is devoted, a field that, from tradition, has been occupied by a number of disciplines from the social sciences. So to understand what we mean by managerial research we have to understand both what we mean by social science and why management as an activity is amenable to such scientific study. Among those who study managers, the activity of management and the wider organizational structures and effects complicit with managerial endeavour, agreement across the disciplines has proved difficult to reach. Psychologists, sociologists, mathematicians and anthropologists each have their own setups in the field of management studies, setups whose own traditions, paradigms, worldviews and tools cast the character and influence of management and managerial problems in particular forms. So where some researchers emphasize an overtly technical understanding of management as though it were akin to social engineering or eugenics, others emphasize its inherently political nature. Whether managers are akin to caliphs, architects, or technicians is open to constant debate. Some may deem the role inherently praiseworthy where others remain suspicious of or antagonistic to its influence. Similarly, where some researchers might argue that what they are studying are individuals and the cognitive patterns associated with subjective judgement and decision-taking, others regard the appropriate unit of analysis to be wider, sometimes objectifying forces, such as the structural influence of foreign direct investment, or the influence of non-negotiable cultural traditions. This variety of perspectives and approaches in the field can make any attempt to locate the edges of management research activity a messy one. This is why Whitehead's identification of the three-fold urge informing human inquiry is instructive. What defines a field is not so much common methods or units of analysis, but its influence on human problems. The influence he envisages coming from any form of broadly scientific activity is not despotic in its nature, but a self-control emerging from the capacity to see things anew, to envisage how the world is and so how it can be both different from the way it is, and better. It is this ability to see things anew that Whitehead argues as the root of good science, irrespective of the field or discipline. For a social science this ability involves researchers recognizing the intimate relationship between their perspectives and the experience of the ongoing problems people have. Social science involves researchers in an internal and ongoing relationship with the human experiences that form the raw material for the data by which they make sense of the social world. From a management research perspective, these problems can be those of managers and their colleagues, or those under the influence of managers, including the researchers themselves, or those in the thrall of management as an idea or even ideal. As life goes on, so the problems change; they are not fixed, universal or entirely tractable, and as social scientists the researcher's job is to reflect and attempt to make sense of this. It is only by recognizing this complicity with the phenomena they research that management researchers can realize the kind of influence that Whitehead talks about, because it is only from this recognition that management can be understood in terms of its potential rather than a formally defined field.

Take, for example, the problems that first prompted Frederick Taylor to associate inquiry into managerial life with a science. These included the problem of how to better control growing organizational size; how to instil order into workers and how to rid the influence of greed from investment cycles. Each of these problems was experienced by Taylor within a specific milieu, a shop or factory, set within a wider economic sector such as retail or steel manufacture, and within the even wider environs of the USA and international economies. Hence Taylor's problems were both local and global; there were immediate concerns of payment schedules set against the equally pressing backdrop of the changing demographics, technologies and economic aspirations of an increasingly internationalized workforce. His response was to insist management activities adopted clear and consistently applied methods (time and motion studies, psycho-physiological testing), planning (simple hierarchical structures, rationalized production systems) and standardization (task separation, common parts) (Guillén, 2006: 4). These responses meant factories became better organized and as a result more efficient as more units were produced with less material and labour. Yet the responses were also problematic. Far from enabling us to live better, Taylor's solutions were felt by some to be retrograde, confining the rhythms of work to the steady and monotonic pulse of a machine. For example, the heirs to the British Arts and Crafts movement grouped in associations such as the Industrial Research Fatigue Board thought the solutions of scientific management cheapened human life by ignoring the vital contribution humans made to the nature of products. Emotional and social well-being was being traded for supposed efficiency. In responding to his problems, Taylor was simply creating new problems: the growing urban workforce was abandoning the skills associated with self-sufficiency and creativity in exchange for a wage economy that tied them into a wider culture of dependency and idiocy. Swapping apprenticed crafts for repetitive tasks meant there was little room for personal engagement with and even interest in what was being produced. In turn, the self-management and group ownership solutions advocated by these exponents of Arts and Crafts were criticized for being anachronistic in tone and impractical in effect; and so the inquiry into desirable forms of production went on to try to reconcile drives for efficiency with problems of boredom, alienation and absence. With each arrival at a solution comes an invitation for new, critical departures.

Viewing this from Whitehead's perspective suggests that what matters is not that these early management researchers failed to find a lasting solution to their problems, but that as problems were met with solutions new problems arose warranting new insights. What defines managerial research activity is not the provision of definitive solutions that look to set habitual and seemingly natural limits to what we do and say, but the continuing interest in how an awareness of what we do and say can transform our practices of material wealth creation by posing alternatives – either reforming existing practices or creating alternate ones. It is as a result of providing such contrasts that researchers are able to distinguish how we live now from how we might live well and live better. If all social science does in providing explanations is to fix meanings concerning what exists, it quickly degenerates because of what Whitehead called fatigue; the ennui arising from repeated attempts at explaining 'the base matter' of life un-enlivened with any concern for why that life matters and in what ways it can be lived differently.

So to avoid fatigue the field of management inquiry and its associated disciplines needs to concern itself with problem-solving activities and hence the distinct and alternate perspectives that ensue when attempts are being made to solve these problems. It is in this spirit that we have edited this dictionary. The inclusion of different worldviews, methodologies and methods reflects the range of disciplinary influences, each of which serves in some way to encourage and assist researchers in their inquiry. Taken as a whole, the variety might appear bewildering. With each worldview and methodology come different background emphases, different techniques to be learnt and different data to be 'collected'. Yet in our experience this 'critical mess' of views, methods and data (Gartner and Birley, 2002) is the stuff of doing good research. Judging appropriate moves in the field requires a familiarity with different views, methods and data because from such familiarity come skills of discernment and hence the ability to go on and do research that matters and in ways that broach both alternate forms of practice and new practices. One common thread around which much of this variety is wound in this dictionary, however, is the term 'qualitative'. The entries cover largely non-statistical approaches to data collection and analysis. The definitional split between qualitative and quantitative research enjoys widespread currency among the social science community, and in using the term in our dictionary title we continue to accept it as one that endures.

Yet perhaps too much is made of these being opposing approaches. For example, we would argue that the logic or framing that defines the research questions of social scientists using structured equation modelling is the same as that of those using discourse analysis, or semiotics; relevances are identified, categories assigned, theories are proposed that researchers believe will create a particular truth, and audiences are spoken to, irrespective of the methodologies or even worldviews adopted. What does distinguish the approaches is the manner in which experiences are highlighted and how they are sifted. Quantitative work tends to limit its range to finding out what exists from a perspective of distance (isolating variables) and of averaging phenomena through numerical proxies, whereas qualitative work looks to find what exists by involvement and hence accepts the ensuing messiness and difference of using rich descriptions. Both approaches are prescriptive in so far as comparisons are made with other situations (both real and imagined), yet where quantitative approaches seek legitimacy in causal weightings of significance, qualitative work uses exemplary stories or cases. Qualitative work typically requires researchers to involve themselves with those they are studying in some way; a dialogue is created, whether cursorily and at some physical remove (as in short telephone interviews or postcards, for example) or through sustained engagement (as in participatory research). There are of course exceptions: archive work in business history, for example, is often conducted without such direct engagement, though data analysis is still conducted from a narrative text. Similarly, some quantitative work also involves engagement, the collection of survey data being an obvious example.

The distinction is useful in so far as it suggests differing views as to what management research is for. Those exclusively using quantitative methods will tend to emphasize the importance of getting accurate representations (data) of what we mean by the social that can be analyzed for patterns from which theories concerning managerial activity can be stated and then re-tested for robustness, both in different conditions and over time. What are significant for the researcher using quantitative approaches are the patterns that can or cannot be established between isolated variables. Qualitative work also shares a desire for scientific rigour in making accurate representations, as well as being minded to focus on the problems being experienced by managers and their organizations. Yet it remains distinctive in its approach to delivering on these aims. Quantitative research tends to be oriented to large groups of problem situations – such as understanding how to organize wealth-creating institutions so as not to materially disadvantage critical constituent interests – and there are common elements that are few and significant enough to isolate as separate phenomena on the assumption that the propositions by which they are explained afford possible orientations towards possible futures. Yet these propositions are nothing more than tendencies, ones that often pertain in fairly strict *ceteris paribus* conditions, of the kind: increasing regulatory surveillance reduces scope for malfeasance (Knight, 1921: 8). Fluctuations, modifications and accidents are excluded, and it is these that qualitative work picks up on, arguing that much is missed by way of understanding, and hence influence, if the only views and approaches being used are those that require an explicit limiting of what constitutes scientific engagement. To get at the exceptions, the outliers, and to convey the depth and richness of managerial and organizational life, qualitative research places more emphasis on words than numbers; it requires research converse with the researched in some way, and that attention is given to the experiences as they are experienced as much as to the manner in which experiences can be abstracted and compared. A branch of qualitative research labelled under the term 'action' approaches take this engagement one stage further, working to establish collaborative inquiry, often using managers themselves as collaborators and sharing the collection and analysis of data to ensure the implementation of findings.

If we were to map out in some way the objectives of managerial research covered by both quantitative and qualitative approaches, then, broadly speaking, these would occupy either end of a dimension that ranged from reporting what exists to an active involvement with trying to improve upon what exists. The social theorist Walter Runciman suggests this range can be parsed into four related activities: reportage, explanation, description and evaluation (Runciman, 1983; Schatzki, 2005b), with quantitative approaches typically (though not exclusively) bunching around reportage and explanation, and qualitative extending across all four.

Reportage

Reporting events offers what Runciman calls a primary understanding; the use of established words to present what exists and what happens. Here there is no attempt at explaining the social world, only recounting observed phenomena in standard 'factual' terminology using analytic definitions. So reporting on the corporate governance structures of a particular firm might, for example, involve: listing the company officers; drawing an organogram of who is responsible for what; outlining the regulatory frameworks and the actions required to comply with such, and so on. There is no attempt to explain why the governance system is in place, or to describe what life is like living with the system, or to suggest improvements to it. Reportage involves breaking a phenomenon into elemental parts in order to have a clearer understanding of how those parts are made up, how they relate to one another, and how they are influenced by other phenomena.

The problem with limiting management research to reportage is that it is notoriously difficult to avoid the use of words that carry with them assumptions as to why one event or experience is of significance and others are considered peripheral, or even go unnoticed. Facts, notably those associated with social science, are not uncontested in the way that they can simply be reported; in the main they are observer-dependent phenomena; to exist they have to be experienced by subjects. As Searle (2005) remarks, this observer-dependency does not preclude the possibility of having an objective science of these facts because we can still make true and false claims concerning such phenomena. What it does preclude, however, is equating physical facts (phenomena existing independent of human intentionality such as water) with social facts (phenomena that arise from, or have arisen from, the interestedness to human beings). So, to go back to the corporate governance example, the reporting of regulatory structures will require the researcher to identify significant parties to such structures, primary among which will be shareholders. Shareholders exist because of a widespread web of existing activity and tradition in which the idea of having owners who are removed from daily managerial activity, who have the mobility to divest and re-invest, and who have an interest in maximizing capital returns, has become a sensible and even desirable condition. Reporting on the existence of shareholders carries with it an attempt to define them: for example, as those who carry the residual risks associated with wealth-creating activity. Yet no sooner are words such as 'residual', 'risk' and 'wealth' used than the definition begins to become contentious. Are longer-term shareholders different from short-term ones in terms of the quality of the risks they carry and the kinds of ownership they exert? Don't others, such as employees with pensions, also carry residual risk without being shareholders? Is the risk accepted by shareholders extendable to those who have pledged to buy shares at some point in the future? To approach questions such as these it is not sufficient to simply report on events and define terms. As we have already argued, what is of interest to management researchers are not formal definitions per se – which are never absolute – but what gives rise to the fact of phenomena like shareholders. To report on the existence of shareholders is to invoke an entire grammatical background of word use by which the *activity* of shareholding has come to make sense. The meaning of the word is indistinct from its use within this wider grammar, meaning any sustained effort to report events inevitably slips into explanation, description or evaluation.

Explanation

Explanation is the lifeblood of scientific research. It realizes what Runciman calls a second-order understanding, in which the facts stemming from observations and experience are interpreted in some way by aligning them with presuppositions and theoretical ambitions. What is disputed is the character of such alignment; specifically whether the explanation of social phenomena can operate causally from which emerge law-like connections between actions, the intention 'behind' the action and the generative conditions of the intention itself. Why we humans think, say and do things has been explained with reference to conscious, unconscious or subconscious mental states, reasons, beliefs, norms and principles, structures, dispositions, communal agreement, rules, habitus, grammar, social structures. A scientific explanation will typically err towards a dispassionate identification of elements held in some form of serial alignment. It is out of these recognized patterns that theories can be built, and then tested through their application to other phenomena. Those theories that are continually able to fit these other phenomena come to be general or even grand theories whose truth status no longer requires constant verification and that gradually become part of the background assumptions by which future research is conducted. Most social science does not aim for theories that provide such a level of law-like coverage and predictability (Schatzki, 2002). Even economics recognizes the need to constantly absorb apparent contradictions between its assumptions and observed phenomena (recognizing goods of ostentation, for example, as those for which demand rises because of a high price) and accepts that some of its theories, like its curves, run almost asymptotic to the world (as indicated by the frequent use of *ceteris paribus* conditions).

Another indication of the distinct nature of social science is that where laws are created they are typically embellished with literary effect. So we have, for example, the political scientist Roberto Michels identifying 'The Iron Law of Oligarchy'. The adjective 'iron' is an implicit acknowledgement that the theory itself is a rhetorical creation: its insight (in this case, the tendency for elite groups to always emerge from within institutions, no matter how radical and egalitarian the framing ideas of the institution) is suggestive, rather than exhaustive and predictive, precisely because it retains its connexion to the open-ended phenomena under investigation. Michels' law arose from an impressive and sustained analysis of a number of political parties in pre-First World War continental Europe. From these cases came an explanation as to why revolutionary and worker parties became apologists for policies that contributed to the expansionist aspirations of an imperialist and demonstrably anti-working-class German empire. Once formed, the parties became increasingly absorbed into institutional politics, and so to the demands of compliance and representation from which skilled elites emerge. The predictive element of the theory is such that were the conditions of the cases to be found experienced by human beings elsewhere, then the emergence of such elites would be likely. The law has an 'iron' quality not because the phenomenon is inevitable in all cases, but that in some it is very likely and the effect has an 'iron-like' grip on those experiencing it.

Again, to go back to Searle's (2005) point about the nature of social facts, the reason social laws work is not because they predict events, so much as convey tendencies that resonate with those who might have, or are currently, or even are about to, experience them. To understand a simple social performance of the kind: person X is performing action A because of reasons 1 and 2, and requires an assessment not only of the collective intentional framework distinguishing the type of action being undertaken, along with the physical form and range of the tools being used, but also an evaluation of what counts as a correct or sensible performance. It is a mistake of management researchers if they assume their categories capture the social world as it is because the world in which they are interested is human, and hence not easily reduced to abstract planes, fixed entities and stable relations. No matter how abstracted, the data of managerial research carry with them the residue of volition, of judgement, and hence the possibility that they could have been, and could be in the future, different (Ghoshal, 2005). What are being explained in social science are not objects and their relations but objects that are assigned what Searle calls 'status functions':

> … where the objects cannot perform the function in virtue of their physical structure alone, but only in virtue of the collective assignment or acceptance of the object or person as having a certain *status* and with that status a function. (Searle, 2005: 7–8, emphasis in original)

Ascribing status functions fundamentally casts the nature of the phenomena being dealt with – human being–action–object arrangements – as non-predictable. As Schatzki (2002) argues, those who claim explanations are in fact law-like in the same way as the second law of thermodynamics are wrong, but not because there is inadequate fit between the law and phenomena (exceptions can always be empirically observed), but because fundamentally human action is not predictable and so it makes no sense to attempt to divine the kind of predictive, tight theories common to explanatory modes in natural science. Any achievement in social science, whether reportage, explanation, description or evaluation, is never complete; what Cooper (2005) calls the 'aboriginal potential' of human life always spills over the edges of these grammatical containers. To study managerial life effectively requires that researchers acknowledge the empirical existence of will. So in looking to explain managerial life they must avoid the presumption that the experience of being a human being can be pinned down to the perspective a researcher might have on this human being (Callon, 1999).

This is not, however, to abandon theorizing, but to understand the concepts and theories generated by social scientists as useful ways of punctuating and understanding experience rather than covering it. The French social theorist Pierre Bourdieu, for example, uses an abstract and universal concept he terms the 'field': a unified social space whose elements are the forces of power such as prevailing interests that impose themselves upon people as they occupy the field, and the struggles that ensue as people with differentiated means confront one another on the field. Fields, it is argued, can exist as different forms (there are fields of power, and more specific fields associated with politics, or education) and across different societies (the French fields are distinct from Chinese ones), yet the field (in conjunction with other concepts such as *habitus*, which Bourdieu uses to refer to those basic dispositions of character that we have and carry through our lives) allows a social scientist like Bourdieu to explain the relational conditions by which the interests of any one individual or group come to be distinct among others, without being confined to those conditions (Bourdieu, 1998: 31–34). Bourdieu's concepts and theory can be argued against, but as social theory, and so any critique might be centred upon the clarity of his concepts (how can a field be a unity without being itself grounded in wider, unifying social forces?) or the theoretical implications (with so much emphasis on social structures, is there any room for individual judgement?). Bourdieu is suggesting concepts such as his are useful when trying to explain the practical problems faced by all people and groups when, in social conditions, they attempt to demonstrate the desirability of their interests. Others might have different concepts or even homonyms with different meanings and emphases – the sociologist Norberto Elias, for example, also uses the concept *habitus* but argues for a less 'structural' interpretation of what it means to be unthinkingly disposed to do something in a certain way. What matters, then, is that theoretical explanation resists the tendency to assume concepts somehow reveal and then represent the social world, when their explanatory power rests with their helping us to describe and redescribe it in potentially novel ways.

Description

As well as reporting and explanation, social science is engaged with what Runciman calls descriptions, where the researcher aims to try to realize what those being studied thought of both themselves and the events in their lives. Descriptions don't aim to convey the quality of the experiences directly, they still rely on concepts to account for and compare it. The aim is to grasp in some way what it is like to be the people under investigation and to go through the experiences as they go through them. This requires an imaginative effort on behalf of the researcher to appreciate meanings and understandings from within the field. Usually associated with ethnomethodology (small-scale or micro-interpersonal practices) and ethnography (larger-scale, culturally bound practices), the concern is for a richly textured and typically ongoing investigation that looks to interpret meanings and understandings associated with the actions, events and mental states under investigation, rather than explain them. Schatzki (2005b) calls this a practical under-standing; the researcher is looking to act in ways that those under investigation can appreciate. This can even extend to being able to participate somehow in their spontaneous or unreflective habits; a direct comprehension of what it means to practically engage in their lifeworld. It also requires of the researcher an acceptance that they are themselves versed in a specific practice of inquiry; social science is first of all a practice, and only second an intellectual endeavour, involving researchers in submitting to the traditions and values whereby others within the prac-tice recognize that it is research that is being done (Piore, 2006). To describe others' practices requires some form of reflexive engagement with the actions and thoughts that make up one's own practice because only then can some form of blending take place sufficient for the researcher and the researched to become complicit with each others' experiences.

In addition to being self-reflexive, the associated difficulty in description is appreciating the veracity, integrity and scope of the accounts given by those being studied. It also assumes that respondents themselves know the reasons for their actions or whether, as is often the case, they might need help to make sense of and articulate the views they hold, how they were formed and how they might be changed. Typically, more is required for a description to be authentic than simply repeating verbatim the account of those involved. Inherent within any account of experience are ambiguities associated with the rise and fall of things being studied (employees and employers don't always remain in post, firms go bust or merge with others bringing new dynamics and values into play, research access can be closed off and so on) and with the nar-rative demands of researchers having, in effect, to tell stories. According to the literary theorist William Empson (1947: 48), this persisting ambiguity of meaning and understanding arises because when studying other human beings what is apparently said and done need not be what was actually said or done, or be entirely what was said or done, or even be accepted as what was said and done. There could have been possible indecision about what was meant; the delib-erate intention to mean a number of things; the fact that statements and events can be read with different meanings; and the fact that the practice of research can itself change the nature of experiences under observation. Researchers have to acknowledge and negotiate all of these, while recognizing the double bind that these types of ambiguity might equally apply to their own writing, conversations and presentations. This sense of ambiguity is not something to be avoided necessarily, but worked at. This pushes the demands of description away from those associated with dispassionate rigour and towards what Latour (2005: 135) calls giving 'vigorous accounts' free from the comfort of empty, technical abstractions.

Evaluative

In becoming immersed in these accounts there are moments when the evaluative backgrounds informing both the practice of research and those being researched come to the fore. This is brought out most clearly when considering the difference between instrumental and expressive action. Typically, explanations and descriptions of what motivated someone to act in the ways they did accord with identifiable reasons whereby an action is undertaken in order to bring about a state of affairs. In considering these reasons and aims, some form of evaluation as to their desirability becomes possible; consideration of the instrumentality of the action gives way to consideration of the expectations and values inherent within it. To understand the desirabil-ity of the act is to understand how its outcome contributed in some way to human well-being. This awareness of contribution takes the researcher from a concern with how social meaning arises (conceptual clarity and explanatory structures) towards a concern with the relation between meaning and flourishing. The problems being addressed are not just those of what, why and how phenomena occur, but whether the occurrence is acceptable.

Evaluative analysis exposes research to the vagaries of historical and social relativism. What counts as a contribution to well-being in one era or society might be considered somewhat ineffective or damaging in another. The Christianized and patrician provision of homes, schools and credit systems favoured by many early industrialists in the UK, for example, might be regarded less favourably in a social climate suspicious of tithed belief systems. That Robert Owen found good reasons for building worker communities around his factory at New Lanark was tied into his wider evangelising concerns with encouraging temperance, diligence and rectitude, into his oscillating feelings of self-confidence, and into his being accepted to a greater or lesser degree by his peers as an individual whose business activity constituted a worthy and worthwhile enterprise (Podmore, 1906/1971). To analyze the activity of Robert Owen requires that researchers understand and tease out the multiple criteria and standards of the practices of industrialism and philanthropy by which such improving action can be assessed. As already mentioned, not all of Owen's actions can be assessed instrumentally. In addition, there were expressive actions that evoke an attitude that cannot be explained or described with reference to outcomes. Robert Owen did not create *New Lanark* simply because he wanted to make profits or secure a better and more god-fearing life for his workers. The enterprise was also a direct expression of belief – a sentiment. To evaluate expressive action requires the researcher to recognize the difference between conditions of rationality (the criteria and standards by which outcomes can be assessed in the light of prevailing norms, values, rules, and so on) and conditions of intelligibility (the criteria and standards that transcend historical and social context in so far as they are shared by researcher and researched alike). As with descriptive achievements, evaluation requires the researcher to develop a sympathy with the researched that is distinct from that of being simply an observer. Here the practical understanding has an ethical hue, hence its being *phronetic*, an ability to appreciate how the goods being pursued constitute the right goods. To understand Robert Owen is to evaluate his idea of the good, as well as describe and explain it.

	Reportage	Explanation	Description	Evaluation
Question type	What exists or happened	Why does it exist or happen?	What was the experience like?	Was it desirable?
Informing spirit	Clarity	Coherence	Comprehension	Improvement
Adverbial mode of inquiry	Inquisitive	Systematic	Imaginative	Ethical
Aim of inquiry	Representation	Objectivity	Depth	Progress

By discussing Runciman's distinctions between reporting, explanation, description and evaluation we are suggesting that management research should not be idealized as being one type of activity above all others, but an amalgam of these four, the mix and admixture of which the researcher has to broker. The entries in this dictionary constitute one tool for doing this, affording introductions on the views and approaches others have taken, and taken on, so as to report, explain, describe and evaluate what is significant about wealth-creating activity.

Why a Dictionary?

Dictionaries are about words, not things, which are typically the concern of encyclopaedias. This is a dictionary about words used in a specific social scientific practice: management research. As a subject field dictionary it does not limit itself to descriptive and lexical entries, but also has a normative purpose: it aims to suggest to the reader the ways in which they might say and do things *in order to* engage with the practice of management research. The difference between general words and scientific ones is typically understood as being one associated with the source of meaning. Defining general words involves finding and citing uses of those words in literature or everyday speech. The dictionary establishes the common sense attributed to the word in ordinary language. Scientific words are different because their role is not only to make sense, but to do so in a way that sustains the coherence of a discipline. Hence not every use is accorded the same weight; and expert influence is brought to bear on the correctness of use. It is through such an imposition of meaning that the inquiries, by which the disciplinary tradition lives, are given clarity (Landau, 2001: 33). Understanding the distinction between different types of interview, or between grounded and non-grounded approaches, allows researchers to recognize one another in their actions, and so engage in critical inquiry without having first to agree on basic definitions or risk always talking at cross purposes. Yet as the entries here make plain, no matter how definitive a statement is made about the meaning of a term, there is a latency of meaning. Words are nothing without their being spoken, written and heard in a myriad of different ways, and their categorization is an upshot of this use, not a precursor or blueprint. Dictionaries have to acknowledge this inherent ambiguity of language in so far as the more refined and detailed the attempt to reveal the skeletal essence of a word the more enigmatic its meaning. In other words, they have to absorb what the American artist Bruce Nauman calls the paradox of definition – words, in their most unadorned form are at their most absent. Hence these entries are adorned with discussion.

The need for a more discursive approach is especially pressing when, as in our dictionary, the focus is not just upon a specific scientific field, but upon actions undertaken within that field and the values informing these actions. The words defined in this dictionary are typically verbs or adverbs in so far as the entries elaborate on what has been meant by a specific research practice or set of values informing the practice. In this regard, management research is no different from any other practice in so far as meaning is negotiated within the activities, norms and material conditions of which the practice consists. The words, even the most basic, elicit a variety of meanings. For example, the root word for the whole dictionary – manager – can be defined within the practice of management research as a formal office occupied by an agent defined by a set of duties, or as a type of person who, to paraphrase the poet John Betjeman, has 'clean cuffs', a 'slim-line briefcase' and a 'company Cortina'. Reference can also be made to specific managerial activities, such as issuing instructions, presenting numerical summaries of performance, motivating employees, and so. Yet what holds the distinctiveness of the word 'manager' together is the assent each of us gives as practitioners to these definitions being legitimate associations with the word 'manager', as opposed to closely related organizational figures such as a leader, apprentice or entrepreneur, or ostensibly more distinct figures such as a nun, or therapist. There is no common essence to all the activities that make up management practice, and as practitioners managers can of course be leaders, pupils and entrepreneurs, and can be associated with those in other practices such as nuns or therapists. Wittgenstein (1953: §67–68) likens the understanding we have of such words to spinning a thread; as we use the word 'manager' we twist fibre on fibre, use on use, 'And the strength of the thread does not reside in the fact that some one fibre runs through its whole length, but in the overlapping of many fibres.' The fibres of management are varied, some more commonly used than others, and there is nothing outside their continued use to prevent them being unravelled. The definition cannot be fixed.

So just as for the words 'manager' and 'management', so for the words often used in the research of the activities they describe. To understand the distinction between constructionist and constructivist approaches to management research, for example, reference has to be made to the way in which the former arose from within sociological disciplines and the latter from those of social psychology. While both approaches assume the reality we experience to be constructed by that experience in some way, one emphasizes the influence of structural fields (such as laws or institutional procedures) whereas the other emphasizes cognitive or behavioural patterns (such as mini-max reasoning or defensiveness). The distinction, however, becomes hard to sustain when, for example, researchers begin to use the term 'social constructivism', in which cognitive and behavioural patterns in thought and action are explicitly linked to wider objectifying structures. The language of the discipline is on the move and there is no exhaustion to such movement; there are always novel ways in which words, even scientific ones, can be used. So although the normative element of a special-field dictionary is strong, the dictionary cannot provide exhaustive definitions; the Scholastic urge to define meaning according to classified essences such as *genus* (the class of things to which it belongs) and *differentia* (what distinguishes it within that class) always runs up against exceptional and novel use.

Here our dictionary, while it deals with words, is what Umberto Eco (1984: 68) calls a 'disguised encyclopaedia' because with each entry comes an array of non-criterial, suggestive knowledge that extends well beyond any hierarchical classification of genus and species. Ambiguity is part of meaning. Sentence-based entries giving examples of what is meant by a particular word vie with more formal definitions of nomenclature, even within individual entries. So the entries reflect the senses that many different researchers associate with the activities and values they are writing about; the entries invite curiosity in a subject, rather than stand as the last words upon it. Each entry is a discussion of how the various threads of the specific method, methodology or worldview have been woven, unwoven and rewoven within the practice of management research. They reveal both the scope of the practice and the curiosity and insight it has excited in those who practise it. The purpose of the entries is to be *read* as accounts of how management researchers have investigated both managerial life and how, through organization, that life can be lived differently.

Dictionary structure

Each entry is approximately 1,000 words in length. This we considered concise enough to be read in a single sitting but broad enough to cover the significant elements of the method, methodology or worldview, along with positions of critique. Each entry begins with a brief definition of the word, followed by a discussion of the actions, thoughts and values by which the activities and approaches described by the word have found, and continue to find, uses in research practice. Towards the end of many entries there is a further section (often brief) introducing the potential for, and critiques of, such uses. Where the entry simply considers the nature of an outlook or an approach this last section has been omitted. So while each entry begins like a dictionary with a definition (albeit a discursive one), it ends up being encyclopaedic in nature. In addition, as editors we have tried to keep the style of each entry faithful to that of its writer. While this may make continuous reading of the dictionary problematic, requiring the reader to adjust from entry to entry, we think the style of writing conveys, perhaps in very subtle ways, what is meant by the outlook or approach. This is especially germane to qualitative work, where the manner and structure of writing are influential components of the knowledge being conveyed.

The references are contained in a single bibliography at the end of the dictionary. They have been used to inform the writing of the entry, but are also intended as good starting points should the reader wish to pursue the subject further. We have tried to keep the bibliography manageable in length, so the sources used by each author are not in any way exhaustive of each subject. Notwithstanding, the citations cover both seminal pieces as well as those papers and studies whose approach and claims are novel and arresting. We have also tried to ensure cited references are in accessible as well as authoritative journals and books. As well as avoiding duplication, another benefit of creating a single bibliography is that we ensure the reader has reference to pieces by authors other than those used in the entry from which they were initially reading. Where two citations of the same paper or book were used, but with different dates and/or publishers, these have been merged into one reference, but with the individual details preserved.

We have inserted cross-references into each entry. The cross-references are designed to suggest to the reader related outlooks and approaches, as well as those that we feel are in stark or interesting contrast. Cross-referencing in this active manner affords the reader a sense of there being other methods and approaches, some of which are sympathetic and others more critical. Where the actual cross-referenced term is used in the entry, the symbol (q.v.) is adopted; elsewhere we have used square brackets containing the cross-referenced entry/ies in italics.

The entries have been listed alphabetically, without thematic grouping. We felt, for example, that dividing the book into method, methodology and worldview sections would give the impression of these being somehow distinct arenas of concern. Moreover, there were many entries that we felt could happily sit in more than one such thematic section, leading to possible frustration when using the book.

Where there is not an entry covering something in which the reader is interested, the index should be consulted. So while there is no entry on 'covert research', for example, the index will point the reader to those entries that discuss it, in this case these would include the entries on: 'ethics', 'ethnography' and 'participant observation'. Similarly, while there is no entry on empiricism, the entry on 'positivism and post-positivism' provides a short overview and critique.

It is in the nature of any discipline that a number of terms are used interchangeably. Hence we also use the index to list those terms that, where they might not be explicitly mentioned in the text, are nevertheless associated with the entry (one example being the association between the entry on 'postmodernism' and the term 'poststructuralism' which is linked to the entry page despite the entry not actually containing the term).

In some cases, rather than have a single entry, there are two, three, or four entries providing alternate perspectives. We felt this multi-voiced approach would afford the reader a richer appreciation of the outlook or approach by introducing them to some of the outlooks and approaches using more than one author. To reflect the fact they remain distinct, we have not given the entries the same title, but have indicated through cross-referencing where their companion entries can be found. The companion entries include:

Table 1   Companion entries

Action learning	action research	action science	
Causal cognitive mapping	cognitive mapping	composite mapping	repertory grid technique
Interviews	interviewing	interviews – electronic	interviews – group
Interviews – group	focus group		
Drawings and images	projective techniques	visual data analysis	
Metaphor	projective techniques		
Complexity theory	complexity theories		
Practice theory	practise-centred research		
Participant observation	field research	ethnography	
Process philosophy	process research		
Existential phenomenology	phenomenology		

A

ACCESS

Definition

Social science methodology texts, especially those aimed at students, often include chapters or sections of prescribed advice on gaining access that vary in length from the virtually non-existent (De Vaus 2001; Ghauri and Gronhaug, 2002) to short sections within chapters (Bryman and Bell, 2003; Easterby-Smith et al., 1991; Gill and Johnson, 1991; Hussey and Hussey, 1997; Jankowicz, 2005; Riley et al., 2000; Robson, 2002; Silverman, 2000; Whitfield and Strauss, 1998) to rather longer sections in chapters (Saunders et al., 2003) and finally whole chapters (Gummesson, 2000).

The format and context of these limited accounts tend to be similar. Access is usually regarded as requiring most consideration within research designs where the researcher expects to spend a significant amount of time with the same research subjects or where a range of research subjects (i.e. individuals or groups) are to be included in the project. It is, therefore, not unusual to see more extensive discussions on access in texts on qualitative research methods (Berg, 2001; Lofland and Lofland, 1995). In more general methodological textbooks, discussions on access are often to be found within chapters that consider ethnographic research. So, for example, Bryman and Bell (2003) discuss access within their chapter entitled 'Ethnography and participant observation', while Gummesson (2000), in his book *Qualitative Methods in Management Research,* devotes the whole of his second chapter to issues of access. Discussions of access within this context are often concerned with not just 'getting in' but also 'getting on' (Buchanan et al., 1988); that is, with managing relationships during the research process and the difficulties and benefits that the identities of researchers and researched can create for accessing information and opinions.

Discussion

The inference within these texts is that structured research designs are associated with a decreased need for attention to access. For example, Saunders et al. (2003: 117), argue that gaining access is 'less applicable where you send a self-administered, postal questionnaire to organisational participants'. The authors acknowledge that some access issues do apply to the construction of 'pre-survey contact and the written request to complete the questionnaire' (Saunders et al., 2003: 117) which will be used by the respondent to decide whether to grant you access to their individual opinion. In support of this they cite Raimond (1993: 67), who argues that 'provided that people reply to the questionnaires, the problem of access to data is solved'. In our opinion, however, this advice undermines the difficulties inherent in access even for a short interview (Danieli and Woodhams, 2005) and marginalizes implications of non-response bias within structured methods.

An alternative context that frames discussions on access can be found within research ethics (q.v.) (see Bryman and Bell, 2003; Hussey and Hussey, 1997; Robson, 1993; Saunders et al., 2003) [*field research; participant observation*]. Here the discussion is likely to be related to factors of informed consent, protecting respondents from harm, confidentiality and anonymity. Again, these issues tend to be seen as more significant in qualitative research and organizationally based research where the researcher is going to spend a significant amount of time in the organization. These issues are, of course, relevant to all types of research irrespective of the research methods used, but this is rarely pointed out. And given the location of this advice within textbooks, it is unlikely that researchers conducting remotely administered questionnaire-based survey research or one-off face-to-face interviews will consult them.

A common theme of concern that informs advice on research access focuses on the feasibility of the proposed investigation (see Buchanan et al., 1988; Easterby-Smith et al., 2002; Marshall and Rossman, 1989; Riley et al., 2000; Saunders et al., 2003). The main concern here is the likelihood of researchers being able to gain entry to organizations and whether they are likely to be given access to the type of information they will need in order to answer their research questions. Here we are more likely to see discussions of the research topic and the difficulties this creates for 'getting in' to organizations. These discussions are often replete with advice on the kinds of strategy that researchers might use to ensure they are not refused access by gatekeepers. Nevertheless, because of the limited reflection on access by experienced researchers, the advice tends to be uniform and to rely on few sources. It focuses on physical access, that is 'getting in', selling the value of the research to the participants, talking down sensitive aspects of the research while talking up the credibility of the researcher or research team.

In brief, the typical advice includes locating a gatekeeper who has the power or authority to grant formal entry to the research site and/or respondents. Advice on how to find this power figure includes using directories, asking the person who answers the phone within the target organization for the name of an appropriate person, approaching third parties for referrals or going through a 'broker' figure (such as a personnel manager) (see Buchanan et al., 1988; Easterby-Smith et al., 1991; Jankowicz, 2005; Saunders et al., 2003). In our experience, this advice underplays the role of the initial contact (the person who answers the phone), who often performs a highly effective access rebuff role in their own right (Danieli and Woodhams, 2005). Once contact has been made, it is stated, researchers must ensure that they maximize the relevance of their research to their target organization, offering them something useful (a report is suggested) in return for access. They should also try to avoid an access request 'that appears to concentrate on aspects associated with non-achievement or failure' (Saunders et al., 2003: 123). Once again, our reflections, informed by our research experience (Danieli and Woodhams, 2005), demonstrate that in certain circumstances, this advice does not apply. Finally, it is agued that establishing credibility is highly significant. Strategies to help create credibility include: expressing the research project clearly in initial contacts (Healey, 1991), demonstrating that the researcher is knowledgeable about both the topic being investigated and the organization they are attempting to access, and that they conform to the dress code appropriate to the research site.

Prospects

Gaining access to organizations to conduct research is a major hurdle to researchers (Bryman, 1988). Yet, while its importance is frequently recognized, it remains underdiscussed and theorized within methodology texts (see also Buchanan et al., 1988; Gummesson, 2000). In a recent piece reflecting on securing research access on a sensitive topic (Danieli and Woodhams, 2005), we were only able to find one book dedicated to the topic (Brown et al., 1976) and very few informed academic accounts within organization studies on how it was achieved.

It is surprising, given the importance of access to data within the research process, that so few reflective accounts of access experience are published. It is likely that, with the increased emphasis on data protection, problems of achieving access will increase. It is to be hoped that the body of reflective literature in this area will be expanded to account for some of the nuances that are found within this multidisciplinary area and that these publications will penetrate a broader base of sources of advice delivered to novice researchers.

Carol Woodhams, Ardha Danieli

ACTION LEARNING

Definition

Action learning originates with Reginald Revans (1907–2003), Olympic athlete, student of nuclear physics, educational administrator and professor of management. Revans's pragmatic philosophy and commitment to experiential learning in the face of intractable social and organizational problems draw on both John Dewey and Kurt Lewin. With other contemporaries, such as W. Edwards Deming, Stafford Beer and the Tavistock researchers, Revans sought the improvement of human systems for the benefit of those who depend upon them. The philosophy of action learning is based on a fundamental pragmatism about what can, and must, be done now, and a deeply humanistic view of human potential. Action learning can be seen as part of a wider family of action-based approaches [*action research; action science; mode 2*] to research and learning, distinguished by the primacy it gives to those actually facing the problems in question, and its scepticism on the views and advice of experts of all kinds.

A prime difficulty in researching action learning is the lack of an agreed definition. As Weinstein notes, 'it means different things to different people' (1995: 32). Revans eschewed any single definition, citing many principles,

but defining only 'what action learning is not' (1993/1998: 87 *et seq.*). Willis has assembled some 23 of these principles of action learning, and examined a sample of cases in the USA against this 'Revans' Gold Standard' (Willis, 2004). An alternative to this search for a single definition is pursued by Marsick and O'Neill (1999), who define three sub-categories of action learning: scientific, experiential and critical reflection. Action learning does not follow a single, agreed approach but is best described as a discipline or practical philosophy embracing a variety of practices around a core of shared values. Action learning appears to have spread more as an 'ethos' or general way of thinking about learning and teaching, than as a specific set of practices (Pedler et al., 2005: 64–5).

Discussion

In management education and research, action learning emerged in opposition to traditional business school practice. In 1965, Revans resigned his Chair at Manchester following negotiations over the new Manchester Business School, which he describes as a victory for the 'book' culture of Owens College over the 'tool' culture of the then College of Technology, later UMIST (Revans, 1980: 197). He favoured the latter as being closer to the needs of industry and objected to the importation of USA business school practice, describing the MBA as 'Moral Bankruptcy Assured', anticipating a continuing critique of this approach to management education (e.g Mintzberg (2004)). Action learning has been a recognized innovation in action research, organization development and management education since major UK initiatives undertaken by Revans in a consortium of London hospitals (1965–66) and the General Electric Company (1975) (Casey and Pearce, 1977; Clark, 1972; Wieland, 1981; Wieland et al., 1971).

Action learning can also be seen as part of a wider growth of interest in 'action approaches' to management and organizational research. Building upon Brooks and Watkins's six 'action inquiry technologies'

(1994), Raelin (1999) proposes action learning as among 'the burgeoning action strategies that are now being practised by organization and management development practitioners around the globe' where 'knowledge is produced in service of, and in the midst of, action'. He contrasts these with positivist approaches that separate theory from practice (1999: 115, 117).

In the last forty years interest in action learning has waxed and waned without ever becoming mainstream. It has been controversial, especially because of the championing of practitioners over the ideas of experts and teachers. Unsurprisingly, given the dominance of the MBA in UK Business Schools, interest in action learning has been strongest among practitioners, with periodic assertions that it has finally 'come of age' (Levy, 2000). However, there has been growing interest from academics for two main reasons: (i) because of the increasing demand for practitioner-oriented postgraduate programmes, and (ii) because of a quest for a more critical business and management education.

Action learning is one of a cluster of 'context-specific' teaching and learning methods that have grown in relation to other approaches to management and leadership development (Horne and Steadman Jones, 2001; Mabey and Thomson, 2000). Some surveys of management development practice have suggested that the use of action learning has grown substantially, alongside coaching and mentoring (Horne and Steadman Jones, 2001; Thomson et al., 1997).

In contrast to the great attention given to theories of learning in professional and managerial education, the power of action learning stems from its philosophy of action and emphasis on practice (q.v.) or praxis. Revans's attempt at a 'praxeology', or general theory of human action, sets out to create a unity of action and learning and also to connect the actor with the wider, collective context of action (1971: 33–67). This rests on the three overlapping systems of alpha, beta and gamma, which deal respectively with the external world (third person), with oneself (first person), with other practitioners (second person) (1982: 724). These can also be translated as categories of learning: *personal* – what has the researcher learned about their own practice?; *practitioner* – what has been learned about the practice which is useful to other practitioners?; and *organizational* – what has been learned in the wider system or network of stakeholders in which the researcher and the problem are located (Coghlan and Pedler, 2006: 137)? An adequate theory of action learning must take account of the contextualized and situated nature of human actions and activities. Thus, action learning sets themselves may be viewed as activity systems and members of sets as 'actors-in-complex-contexts' (Ashton, 2006: 28).

The current practice of action learning frequently departs from Revans's foundational principles (Revans, 1998). These principles are both diluted, for example by the use of the term to describe 'task forces' which report findings rather than take action on organizational problems (Dixon, 1997), and variously criticized; for throwing the baby (of teaching) out with the bathwater (McLaughlin and Thorpe, 1993); for being too rational and for neglecting the role of emotions and politics in learning (Vince and Martin, 1993) and for needing a component of 'critical theory' (q.v.) if action learning 'is not to be selectively adopted to maintain the status quo' (Willmott, 1994: 127). It is important to note that these criticisms are made in the context of aspirations for action learning as a promising means for the developing of a more critical management education (Burgoyne and Reynolds, 1997; McLaughlin and Thorpe, 1993; Reynolds, 1999; Rigg and Trehan, 2004; Vince and Martin, 1993; Willmott, 1994, 1997).

Prospects

A leading challenge to current practice comes from critical theorists. Given its protean nature, action learning is easily adapted to serve local agendas, but how can it avoid the trap being 'selectively adopted to maintain the status quo' (Willmott, 1994: 127)? Willmott and others call for a more critical action learning which goes beyond 'ordinary criticality' to a social and organizational critique. A critical action learning would distinguish between effective practice, reflective practice and critically reflective practice (Burgoyne and Reynolds, 1997: 1) or, as Reynolds and Vince (2004: 453) put it, 'Do ideas brought into action-based discussions help to question existing practices, structures and associated power relations within the organization?' This would be especially valuable in management education, currently seen by these writers as very uncritical of the status quo.

Whether this mission can be fulfilled by an action learning which puts its trust in peers and emphasizes the 'art of the possible' is an open question. A critical practice of action learning would not only bring Revans's 'insightful questions' (1983/1998: 6) to bear on 'existing practices, structures and associated power relations', but would also aim to change them for the better. This is a 'big ask', but the fact that such hopes are pinned here can be taken as evidence of the emerging maturity of action learning.

Mike Pedler

ACTION RESEARCH

Definition

Action research may be defined as an informed investigation into a real management issue in an organization by a participating researcher, resulting in an actionable solution to the issue. It is a method by which the researcher may bring new knowledge to organizational members, and discover a workable local theory of benefit to the organization, which may also inform the research community. The researcher may be an employee of the organization or may be independent. However, what distinguishes action research from other field study methods is

the concept of an intervention, involving the researcher in an active role with other organizational participants in bringing about some change, however small, in the working of that organization [*action learning; mode 2*]. A more passive approach to observing organizational change may be framed as ethnographic (q.v.) or case study research (q.v.) [*ethnomethodology*].

Discussion

Action research was first used by Lewin (1946) and Whyte (1955) to explore social issues, and then used in educational research (Elliott, 1991; Halsey, 1972). It has been adopted within the field of management by Argyris and Schön (1978b) as an appropriate research method for organizational learning [*action science*]. Models of action research are closely related to Kolb's (1986) experiential learning cycle, and to systems thinking (Checkland, 1981; Flood, 2001) [*soft systems methodology*]. The focus of action research is upon the practice of management (the action), but what distinguishes it from business consultancy is the role of theory, both to inform the action and to theorize from an analysis of the effects (research) of that action. Eden and Huxham (2002) present 15 characteristics of action research, expanding on these essential concepts.

Whyte (1991) edited a collection of work by action researchers, but the methodology has attracted criticism (some fair and some not), preventing widespread publication of such work in top management journals. Authors who have become well known for action research include Heller (1986), Chisholm (1998), Coghlan (1998). Examples include work on new management accounting practices (Kasanen et al., 1993), risk assessment of strategic investment projects in decision-making (Harris, 1999) and IT in organizational change (Scholl, 2004). Sage launched its *Action Research* journal in 2003 and published a review article of action research literature in volume 2 issue 4 in December 2004.

Prospects

Common problems and criticisms encountered in action research are:

- An apparent lack of prior theorizing, mostly due to the newness of the phenomenon being studied, is often claimed by novice researchers who may not have fully conceptualized the issue or read much work outside their core discipline.
- The role of the researcher as participant in the action research process may lead to undue influence of the outcomes by the researcher [*field research; participant observation*]. This is an obvious challenge due to the overt nature of an action research intervention, but can also impinge on other studies such as case study research (Scapens, 2004).
- The validity of findings from studies which often cannot be replicated, due to the context and the timing of the phenomenon observed. Difficulty in building robust theory from a single intervention in a single organizational setting, which follows on from the issues of validity in terms of the value added to the published body of knowledge. Again this can be levelled at case study research, especially single cases, as well as grounded theory.
- Responsibility for the impact of the outcomes of the research, where action may have been taken before it can be properly evaluated. There is an important ethical issue here for the researcher and collaborators to be clear about before entering the field.

Strategies for rising to the challenges and overcoming common problems include:

- Developing an awareness of relevant literature, not just from a single discipline, as many natural management phenomena do not relate closely to a discrete body of knowledge. Previous research on the topic may only offer partial insights, but drawing upon other disciplines may offer alternative ways of conceptualizing the research problem. This can be daunting for an individual researcher, but when operating within a wider research community the benefits of team-working can include access to related bibliographies.
- Personal skills development and training in the use of action research techniques can help to overcome issues around the role of the researcher, especially reflexivity (q.v.) [*ethics*]. Results should reflect the shared understandings of participants, not just the researcher's views. For external action researchers, background research on the organization and the participants is important for the researcher to become aware of characteristics of the organizational setting. Researchers working in their own organization may have to stand back from existing values and beliefs and adopt a more critically independent mindset.
- Good data collection and feedback mechanisms which draw on the tacit knowledge of participants so that they can make sense of results can help to ensure internal validity. When analysing and writing up the research it is important to give all the actors in the study a voice, and not to assume consensus where none exists. Explicit reporting of the research process is required to help outsiders to understand the methods adopted and follow a similar process in another organization or context. This often leads to a dilemma of the comparative length of the research methods section of the paper or thesis, especially where there is an overall constraint on word length. However, as action research is often criticized for its non-replicability and context specificity of results, it is necessary to both describe and evaluate methods in the text. Theory can be built through meta-analysis. What is lost from any lack of generalizability can be compensated for by extra relevance and value to practitioners, and contribution to practice-based theory, especially where results compare well with other studies (whether action research based or not).

Adopting these strategies can help action researchers to overcome many of the arguments, though action research will still have its critics. Sponsors of research are aware of governmental agendas to increase the relevance of funded research to business organizations to help them compete in the global marketplace, so the adoption of action research may grow.

Elaine Harris

ACTION SCIENCE

Definition

Action science is for creating knowledge people can use to improve practice. It proceeds in conjunction with educating practitioners and intervening in organizations. Action science engages people in reflecting on their own behaviour and on the consequences of their behaviour for the social systems in which they participate [*action learning; action research; mode 2*].

Discussion

The term 'action science' was first used by Torbert (1976: 166), who envisioned 'a science useful to an actor at the moment of action'. Torbert and associates have pursued this vision through what he now calls developmental action inquiry (2004).

Argyris (1980) provided a critique of normal behavioural science and outlined an action science that would produce knowledge that can be implemented and would contribute to building alternatives to the status quo. He pointed to the action research of Kurt Lewin as an early model. Schön (1983: 319) suggested that an action science 'would aim at the development of themes from which practitioners ... can build and test their own on-the-spot theories of action'. Argyris et al. (1985) placed action science in the context of the philosophy of science, compared it to

examples of normal social science, and offered research on how people learn to improve their practice as interventionists [*positivism and post-positivism*].

What counts as 'science' in the realm of social research is subject to debate. Some approaches disavow the label. The name 'action science' announces an intention to be assessed by the features of rational deliberation in science: 'responsibility to the evidence, openness to argument, commitment to publication, loyalty to logic, and an admission, in principle, that one may turn out to be wrong' (Scheffler, 1982: 138) [*phronetic organizational research; realism; relativism*]. The radical claim is that these features can be realized among human agents in the action context, where 'commitment to publication' translates to making one's reasoning testable in the relevant public.

The theory of action approach (Argyris and Schön, 1974, 1978a, 1996) is the framework for much theory, research, and practice under the name of action science and the terms are often used as synonyms (e.g. Argyris and Schön, 1989, 1996; Friedman, 2001; Raelin, 2000; Senge, 1990). The theory of action approach distinguishes espoused theories of action, those that people believe they follow, and theories-in-use, the theories of action that can be inferred from actual behaviour. People are usually unaware of gaps between their espoused theories and their theories-in-use. To interrupt this unawareness, people must reflect on what they actually do and say. This leads to a fundamental methodological principle of action science: to use actual behaviour, such as conversation (q.v.), as data. This principle applies both in the action context and to research texts, which often include transcripts of tape-recorded conversations (e.g. Argyris, 1982, 1993; Putnam, 1990, 1991; Torbert, 2000).

The use of conversation as data leads to methodological similarities with socio-linguistic analysis (e.g. Donnellon, 1996) [*discourse analysis*]. Ethnographic (q.v.) methods for studying rules of social interaction are also relevant to action science (Argyris, D. 1985). But research in these traditions normally intends only to describe the world, not to change the world. Action research that combines the use of conversation as data with intervention (e.g. Kristiansen and Bloch-Poulsen, 2004) might be considered action science despite not being situated within the theory of action approach.

Action science focuses on learning and change involving shifts in perspective, assumptions and values as well as in behaviour, what Argyris and Schön (1974) termed double-loop learning. This focus differentiates action science from approaches to 'usable knowledge' that address techniques people can apply within their current values and assumptions. Double-loop learning requires reflecting critically on the often tacit reasoning embedded in one's action. This emphasis led Senge (1990) to see action science as helping people become aware of the mental models underlying their behaviour. Many of the challenges facing organizations today, for example the shift from functional to matrix and project-based organizations, require double-loop learning by many individuals to manage successfully.

Action science focuses both on individuals and on the behavioural worlds they create and that constrain them. A key feature of a behavioural world is the quality of discourse: what can be said and what remains unspoken, norms for accepting or rejecting arguments, deference and face-saving routines. Prevailing norms of discourse routinely limit inquiry and learning in organizations and other social settings. Action science engages practitioners in identifying patterns that inhibit organizational inquiry and in improving the quality of inquiry (Argyris and Schön, 1996). A methodological device for displaying such patterns and identifying leverage points for changing them is the action map, a diagrammatic representation of initial conditions, actions, consequences, and feedback loops (Argyris, C., 1985; Argyris et al., 1985).

Argyris et al. (1985) suggested that action science is a critical theory (Geuss, 1981).

Critical social science, like normal science, makes empirical claims, for example about the prevalence of certain patterns of behaviour in organizations and their impact on the quality of inquiry [critical realism]. What is distinctive of critical social science is that it also makes normative claims, criticizing what exists from the perspective of what might be and offering the possibility of bringing about the desired state. A critical theory (q.v.) justifies its normative stance through the method of internal criticism. That is, it shows those to whom it is addressed that its normative stance is implicit in their own beliefs and practices and how their current behaviour is inconsistent with their own value commitments.

Action science is proving useful in educating practitioners in a variety of professions while also building knowledge for practice. Putnam R.W., (1990, 1991) worked with an organizational consultant learning to use a new approach with clients. Rudolph et al. (2006) address how medical instructors can debrief trainees more effectively. Peppet and Moffit (2006) focus on how negotiators can learn from experience by testing negotiating theories in their own practice. Witherspoon and Cannon (2004) apply the perspective to executive coaching. Friedman and Berthoin (2005) offer an alternative approach to intercultural competence that suggests how individuals can learn in the midst of cross-cultural interactions. Educators and researchers in management development, work-based learning, and human resource development often draw on action science (Raelin, 1999, 2000; Watkins and Marsick, 1999).

Perhaps the most fully-realized presentation of an organizational intervention from an action science perspective is Argyris's (1993) account of his work with a professional service firm. Friedman et al. (2004) describe a year-long project with a programme that helps schools work more effectively with students characterized by chronic failure. In recent years Argyris has emphasized integrating behavioural and technical change in organizations, for example the behavioural aspects of innovations in managerial cost accounting (Argyris and Kaplan, 1994; Moingeon and Edmondson, 1996). Smith (1996) analyzes how behaviour affects strategy formulation and builds theory for improving strategic conversations.

Prospects

Perhaps the biggest challenge to broader use of an action science approach is educating researcher/interventionists who can do the work. Most graduate programmes educate scholars to conduct descriptive research. Professional schools educate practitioners to intervene with individuals and social systems. There are few opportunities to learn how to do both and to combine them as intervention research. Addressing this challenge was a primary reason that we wrote *Action Science* over two decades ago (Argyris et al., 1985). We are gratified that the work is indeed spreading, as is partially (and incompletely) indicated by the references cited here. There is much still to do.

Robert W. Putnam

ACTIVITY THEORY

Definition

The founder of activity theory, a Russian psychologist, Lev Vygotsky (1979, 1986), was prompted by the schism in psychology during the early 1900s between a focus on physiological and biological functions, and individual mental life on the other. He could accept neither the biological reductionism represented by behaviourism nor the mentalistic and idealistic psychologies that regarded the mind as a self-sufficient entity opposed to the material world. According to Vygotsky, human consciousness and actions are mediated by the cultural means of artifacts. The basic types of such mediating means are signs and tools. An individual, he argued, internalizes the use of language and tools during socialization by participating in shared activities with other

humans. The human consciousness, therefore, has social origins and is constantly reconstructed through participation in artifact-mediated human activities [*constructivism; social constructionism; structuration theory*]. Accordingly, the activity-theoretical approach regards *retooling*, the shared creation of artifacts used as means of reflecting on, and the practical transformation of, activity, as a key to changing practices and learning (Vygotsky, 1979) [*action science*].

Discussion

Vygotsky redefined the traditional object of psychology – actions and consciousness of an individual – by emphasizing their social origins. His colleague and follower A.N. Leont'ev (1978) developed the theory to cover those social or collective activities characterized by a division of labour (Leont'ev, 1978). On the basis of Leont'ev's work, Yrjö Engeström (1987) formulated a model of an activity system (Figure 1).

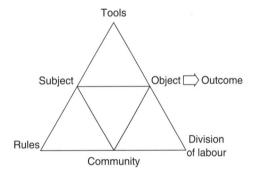

Figure 1 *The Structure of Human Activity (Engeström, 1987)*

Its elements are the subject and the object of activity, the tools, as well as the division of labour and rules of a community of actors. An object and motive of activity is both given and projected, the 'why of an activity' and a horizon for practical actions. It is realized in the construction of products and services that constitute the outcome of the activity.

Consequently, the shared reconsideration of the object of activity is vital for the change of an activity. In Engeström's theory of expansive learning, the internal contradictions are the starting point for developmental change. On the basis of this theory, the foundation of an interventionist research approach called *developmental work research* was elaborated in the 1980s (Engeström, 1991). In the 1990s, a specific version of it, an intervention method called *change laboratory*, was developed (Engeström et al., 1996).

In the methodology of activity theory interventions are used both to study the conditions of change and to help those working in organizations to develop their work. In empirical studies, qualitative methods are used. Typically, participant observation, interviews and the recording and video-taping of meetings and work practices are combined. In the change laboratory pieces of data (for instance in the form of video (q.v.) excerpts) are used as a 'mirror' in the laboratory sessions to enhance critical reflections of the work practices. The communities studied use the model of an activity system as a means of analysing the history of their activities to uncover the developmental contradictions of their activity. The community studied then forms an hypothesis for possible solutions along with a description of the 'zone of proximal development' for the development of the activity. The community then designs new tools and organizational solutions to move forward in this zone.

Prospects

Activity theory has been adopted and developed thus far primarily in the confines of psychology and education. The international community of activity theorists and representatives of the socio-cultural approach is ISCAR, International Society for Cultural and Activity Research. The journal *Mind, Culture, and Activity* is perhaps the most important publishing forum of the community. Activity theory was introduced to management studies in the 1990s to analyze organizations as activity systems (Blackler, 1993, 1995). Many

of the activity theoretical studies have focused on the work of the public sector (Kerosuo and Engeström, 2003; Miettinen and Virkkunen, 2005; Puonti, 2004) but firm activities and innovations (Hasu, 2000; Toiviainen, 2003) as well as scientific work (Saari and Miettinen, 2001) have been studied. Among the challenges of the approach are how to use and develop it in the study of networks of activities, specifically internet-mediated virtual activities. Further challenge lies in the study of activities organized in rhizomatic or mycorrhizae-like fashion having very light centralized superstructures but intense involvement and horizontal interaction at the ground level, such as the disaster aid teams of the Red Cross [*process philosophy*]. They may have temporal discontinuities and their activity is episodic, but at the same time they are resilient and self-sustaining.

Reijo Mietinnen

ACTOR-NETWORK THEORY

Definition

Originating in studies of science, technology and society (STS), actor-network theory (ANT) – or the 'sociology of translation' (Callon, 1986; Latour, 1999a) – is an increasingly popular method used within a range of social science fields.

Issues of power are of central concern for ANT [*critical theory; dialectic; Marxism*]. It is argued, in particular, that power is effected through the production and reproduction of a network of heterogeneous 'actants', this term being employed to suggest that both humans and non-humans be included in the analysis. Forces of the social and the technical are to be accounted for through a process of 'generalized symmetry', a method that employs a common analytical vocabulary for interpreting such phenomena. In this accounting process any *a priori* separation of the social and the physical world is prohibited (Callon,

1986). Thus, the actor-network (a purposively oxymoronic term) is realized through the common 'enrolling' of human and non-human participants into a network through processes of negotiation and translation.

Discussion

When we seek to translate the ANT approach into the sphere of management and organizational studies, we are involved in the analysis of alliances or networks that 'initiate and maintain the superordination of individuals or groups over others' (Grint, 1998: 142). We are thus reminded that many actors are locked into networks that exist outside the focal organization. In addition, managerial networks take recourse not just to the network of peer managers and the control over material resources with the organization, but also, for example, to the resources of the legal system and domestic sources of support, which are 'invisibly meshed into the organization's disciplinary mechanisms' (Grint, 1991: 149). As Latour (1987) demonstrated similarly in the field of STS, scientists physically isolated from the rest of the world in their search for knowledge are actually highly dependent upon a large array of supportive networks outside the laboratory.

In accounting for such processes, the character of the actor-network emerges as a contingent phenomenon. As noted, actor-networks are relentlessly produced and reproduced. The point here is not whether the actants of a network are social or technical, but, as Latour (1987: 140) points out, 'which associations are stronger and which are weaker'. In a later discussion Latour (1992) gives the 'mundane' example of hoteliers attempting to discipline their guests to leave room keys at the reception desk, instead of retaining them when going outside. He explains that to effect this practice the hotelier adds various elements to the key, including a verbal request, an inscription on the key and, if these fail, the practice of increasing the weight or size of key so that it becomes difficult to carry around. As the entities enrolled in the network have their own strategic preferences, the problem for the 'enroller' therefore is to ensure that participants adhere to the enroller's interests rather than their own. (Another basic example of the utility of ANT is offered by Grint (1998) when he considers the ways in which differing formations of office or classroom furniture appear to generate different 'cultural resonances'. He outlines how discrete rows of desks facing the front imply a hierarchical approach to work and school, whereas a circle of chairs in a classroom, or a communal 'hot desk' in an office, has 'quite different connotations about the role of power and equality' (1998: 111)) [*affordances*].

The conceptual tools underlying the ANT approach therefore enable us to study the assembling and stabilization of diverse human and non-human entities within diffuse socio-material systems (Hassard et al., 1999; Law, 1999). The use of these tools has been part of a movement away from a formal-functional emphasis on organization as an entity towards the study of processes and practices of organizing, and importantly socio-technical organizing (Bloomfield and Vurdubakis, 1999; Calás and Smircich, 1999; Hull, 1999; Lee and Hassard, 1999; Newton, 2002) [*practice theory; practise-centred research*]. ANT has been used by writers to examine a wide range of research issues within management and organization studies, but notably with regard to studies of information systems and information technology (see Bloomfield and Vudubakis, 1994, 1999; Bloomfield et al., 1992; Bowker et al., 1996; Hine, 1995; Vidgen and McMaster, 1996).

ANT gains much of its notoriety through advocating a socio-philosophical approach in which human and non-human, social and technical factors are brought together in the same analytical view. In attempting to comprehend complex social situations, ANT rejects any sundering of human and non-human, social and technical elements. In a much cited article, Michel Callon (1986) warns, for example, of the dangers of 'changing register' when we move from concerns with the social to those of the technical. The methodological philosophy is that all ingredients of socio-technical analysis be explained by common practices. It is this common analytic view that proves to be the challenge for many social science researchers for whom the human takes precedence as a unit of analysis.

John Hassard

AESTHETICS

Definition

Aesthetics is a field of philosophy that deals with form, beauty and ugliness, and the sensuous and symbolic dimensions of existence such as art, music and culture. The meaning of aesthetics covers forms of art and design; sensuous cognition (aesthetic understanding) or how what we know and believe connects to what we see and feel; and beauty, appreciated as a comprehensible 'intellectual feeling' capable of discrimination between the good and bad in form. The idea that aesthetics might be relevant to the study of management developed most dramatically in the 1980s as an offshoot of the study of organizational culture [cross-cultural research] and symbolism. Culture studies emphasized shared meaning and drew attention to the importance of communication in the process of establishing it; cultural fit was increasingly seen as being important to strategy and competitive advantage. Understood aesthetically, this fit involves meanings associated with products and commodities coupled to the development of a 'feeling intelligence', intuitive knowing; and to how greater refinement, or connoisseurship in appreciating beauty can be achieved [dramaturgy; drawings and images; projective techniques; representations; social poetics; space; video; visual data analysis].

Discussion

Studies of symbolism and symbolic processes in organizations drew on ideas developed in cultural and media studies, art criticism,

architecture, design, semiotics (q.v.), physical anthropology and philosophy to understand the significance of the material and visual environment to processes of sense-making (q.v.) and meaning-making in organizations. An important part of culture changes and corporate turnarounds in the 1980s and 1990s was often the visual redesign of corporate image and symbolic 'corporate identity', which was intended to express the values of the new culture in concrete terms – uniforms, dress codes, décor, shopfronts, logos, letterheads, catalogues, buildings, and advertising included. Much of the initiative in taking this work to a deeper level was done by members of the Standing Conference on Organizational Symbolism (SCOS), culminating in two important books in 1990 – Barry Turner's edited *Organizational Symbolism* (De Gruyter) and Pasquale Gagliardi's edited *Symbols and Artifacts* (De Gruyter). Gagliardi's introduction is classic, as is his later contribution to the *Handbook of Organization Studies* (Gagliardi 1996; 2nd edition 2006). Another early and seminal contribution was Ramirez's *The Beauty of Social Organization* (1991).

The understanding of aesthetics in organizational life broadened considerably in the 1990s, aided by further seminal contributions from Strati (1992, 1999) and Linstead and Höpfl's edited collection (2000). It now encompasses *aesthetic theory* – discussion of the basic concepts found in classical and modern philosophy including thinkers as diverse as Aristotle, Kant, Hegel, Schiller, Freud and Lyotard, and also art critics such as Jencks, and their relevance to organizational life in general, including establishing criteria of the beautiful; *aesthetic processes* – which concentrates on developing a sensuous methodology of researching organizational life, as well as taking sensuous experience into account in terms of its effects on other organizational processes such as sense-making, motivation, identity, culture and leadership, innovation and creativity; *aesthetic organizations* – which looks at arts organizations and cultural industries to see how they are or could be managed, drawing practical lessons and role models (such as the orchestra conductor as leader); *aesthetic modes of analysis* – specifically considering how ideas and concepts drawn from the arts can be applied to the analysis of organizations, such as the metaphor of organizational theatre, and also used to improve their functioning or stimulate change in consultancy interventions [*metaphor*]; *crafting aesthetics* – which looks at the practical issues of creating and developing an aesthetic, including negotiating between competing aesthetics, for a group or organization; *aesthetic pedagogies* – using art and aesthetic methods in training, therapeutic regimes, professional education and management development; *aesthetics and ethics* – which looks at the connections between truth, beauty and goodness, taking into account questions of form, morality and spirit and may draw on a wide range of cultural traditions [*affordances*]; and *radical aesthetics* – where aesthetic modes of representation are specifically used for political purposes to challenge the status quo and explore alternatives, including alternatives to capitalism.

Historically, three threads in modern aesthetics can be discerned, and these are all present in the aesthetic approach to organization: first, the idea that art imitates reality – that by seeing more accurately through art our attention can be drawn to aspects we may otherwise overlook and gain greater insight into what is true (realism) (q.v.), or alternatively that art tries to imitate subconscious fantasy, thereby gaining insight into our otherwise concealed psyche (surrealism); second, the idea that art gives us intimations of the transcendent ideal, often in a spiritual sense, and acts as inspiration in this way (idealism or romanticism); and third, that aesthetic processes are in use by everyone constantly and are an important part of reality production in everyday life and our common sense (mundane aesthetics). With the rise of the global media, the increasing importance of information, the proliferation of images and simulated reality (simulacra) in cultural transmission, consumption and identity formation, there is also a focus on virtuality and the role of aesthetics in virtual organizations and communities (postmodern (q.v.) aesthetics) [*deconstruction*].

Much of the research in this area is conducted and presented in non-standard forms and arenas, often in performance. The (US) Academy of Management recently experimented with an Academy Arts section for visually presented research, and an official Fringe for performance-based research; the Art of Management Conferences takes place every two years to provide an arena for alternative research; the Art, Aesthetics and Creativity in Organizations Network (www.aacorn.org) is a closed network of scholars, artists, consultants and others that runs a website with links and resources for anyone interested in doing both theoretical and applied work on the connections between aesthetics and organization and their practical consequences. Useful recent print resources include a special issue of *Human Relations* on 'Organizing aesthetics' (Strati and Guillet de Monthoux, July 2002); a special issue of *Organization Studies* on theatre and organization (Schreyogg and Höpfl, 2005); Adrian Carr and Phil Hancock's *Art and Aesthetics at Work* (2003); Pierre Guillet de Monthoux's book *The Art Firm* (2004); Lotte Darso's *Artful Creation* (2004); and Pat Kane's best-selling *The Play Ethic* (2004).

Prospects

As a developing area, the field is characterized by a proliferation of debate. Key issues for the field include how to avoid mystification of its work through elitist, connoisseur languages; how to avoid an over-concentration on objects and artefacts at the expense of socially negotiated meanings and relations; how to avoid absorption in the emotional dimensions of creating new forms of research at the expense of failing to interrogate and develop core concepts; how to avoid over-knowledging, or emphasizing, the cognitive dimensions of aesthetics; how to avoid research outputs being functionally simplified, commodified and turned into kitsch (Linstead, 2002b). The aesthetic approach is nevertheless here to stay and is recognized as being important across the range of management disciplines – marketing, organizational

25

design, organizational theory and behaviour, innovation and new product development and strategy all included.

Stephen Linstead

AFFORDANCES

Definition

The concept of affordances stems from and plays a principal role in Gibson's (1979) work in ecological and environmental psychology. The concept concerns what the environment offers its inhabitants – what it provides, furnishes or affords. In other words, it suggests that the environment – and the material surfaces, objects and artefacts comprising it – afford, suggest and make themselves available to certain uses and users while constraining others. Thus, it is central to the commitment in ecological and environmental psychology to an ontological realism and materialism. Although research on affordances is dominated by work in ecological and environmental psychology, it has also been taken up by researchers in engineering, computer science and cognitive science, in medicine, ergonomics and disability studies, and, more recently, in science and technology studies as well as in management and organization studies.

Discussion

Affordances may be both functional (or objective) aspects of the environment and relational (or subjective) aspects of the environment. For example, a stairway affords walking more than it does sleeping, and a bench with a backrest affords comfortable sitting more than a bench without a backrest. In this sense, affordances are functional and objective aspects of the environment. No distinction is made between different users or inhabitants, and a certain environment is seen to have the same effect on anybody and everybody. But what is afforded depends

both on the environment and the inhabitant (Gibson, 1979: 129), and what an environment affords is different for different users or inhabitants. For example, clinical research on affordances has found that perceived and attained boundaries in bipedal stair climbing are not only affected by body size and body proportions but even by hip joint flexibility and relative leg strength (Meeuwsen, 1991). In this sense, affordances are relational and subjective aspects of the environment. Knowledge about the relational and subjective aspects of affordances has been expanded by research in cognitive science, which argues that affordances are a result of people's past knowledge and experiences (Jordan et al., 1998; Lakoff, 1987; Norman, 1988), and, more recently, by research in the interface between sociology and science and technology studies, which argues that the use afforded by certain environments and artefacts is governed by social or technical rules that must be learned by inhabitants or users (Hutchby, 2001) [actor-network theory].

In management and organization studies, the importance of learning and knowledge is further emphasized through the concept of dynamic affordances (Cook and Brown, 1999). This concept is much informed by Gaver's (1991, 1996) work in ecological psychology, and in general terms it implies that what is afforded by an environment, an artefact, a technology or a discourse dynamically changes as one interacts with it. More specifically, Cook and Brown (1999) employ the concept of dynamic affordances to understand how learning, knowing and knowledge emerge through dynamic interaction with the world or with an artefact, a technology or a discourse in the world (see also McNulty, 2002). Although this research primarily deals with issues of organizational learning and knowledge management from a discursive perspective, the concept of dynamic affordances can be further applied to understand the affordances of a place or an environment [aesthetics; space]. As dynamic affordances 'emerge as part of the (dynamic) interaction with the world' (Cook and Brown, 1999: 390), learning, knowing and knowledge do not merely result from learning rules or from past experience and knowledge. People learn, know and develop new knowledge about an artefact or environment and how to use it by interacting with it – and what is afforded changes with the interaction. Changes in affordances create facilities or frustrations. Facilities result when more is afforded and frustrations result when less is afforded.

Prospects

While the concept of affordances makes it possible to analyze how a particular environment, artefact or discourse affords certain uses and users more than others, most research on affordances presumes a simplified notion of the human subject and bodily difference that implies a depoliticized understanding of social relations among humans. This may be the case because affordance research is rarely carried out in the social sciences and because it has primarily concerned itself with relations between humans and the natural or technical environment. It has largely ignored how affordances may affect social relations between humans. Arguing that the alteration of the natural environment by humans has made life easier for humans and acknowledging that humans thereby have 'made life harder for most of the other animals', Gibson (1979: 130) does not recognize that these alterations may profoundly alter relations between humans, frustrate rather than facilitate human relations, and make life harder for some humans. Moreover, research on affordances generally pays scarce attention to the socio-cultural and socio-political processes through which artefacts, objects, surfaces and environments are constructed and invested with dominant meanings that in turn affect human behaviour, social interaction and social life [*activity theory*]. Hutchby's (2001) attempt to reconcile social constructionism (q.v.) and technical essentialism in sociology through the concept of affordances complicates the otherwise 'asocial' flavour of research on affordances, emphasizing that affordances do not determine human behaviour, but constrain and enable human behaviour. Whereas a one-sided social constructionism would argue that what matters are the meanings attributed to artefacts, Hutchby argues that affordances constrain and enable the meanings and uses that are possible in the first place.

No matter how one sides in this debate, it draws attention to the symbolic and communicative aspects of affordances, which may constitute a new and complimentary trajectory for affordance research in general and for affordance research in management and organization studies. The social image and meanings associated with an artefact or an environment affect how and by whom it is being used. For example, a certain place or artefact may be associated with users of a certain social group or class which will tend to use it in a certain way. For instance, a certain park may be associated with middle-class family picnics while another may be viewed as a homeless hangout. Whereas symbolic affordances may be constituted materially – for instance through formal design and the use of pristine materials – this symbolism may be further communicated and maintained by social narratives and storytelling.

Organizational symbolism and storytelling have fairly long track records in management and organization studies, but research in these particular areas is primarily carried out from a social constructionist perspective wherein the material aspects of organizational environments and artefacts tend to be given a secondary role. In contrast, the concept of affordances is underpinned by a materialist realism (q.v.), and the concept itself draws attention to the specific ways in which particular artefacts and environments are materially constituted and how this may affect different users and inhabitants in both physical and social terms. Hence, it may, for example, help future research in management and organization studies to investigate in detail how a particular product design or office design is materially constituted and how this physically and socially affects users and consumers, employees and managers. Further on, research on dynamic affordances may be expanded beyond its current emphasis on the discursive aspects of organizational learning and knowledge management. For example, future research may explore the material aspects of dynamic affordances by investigating how the affordances of a particular product design or office design change as users and consumers, employees and managers interact with it. In conclusion, the concept of affordances may therefore play an important role in helping management and organization studies explore the material aspects of management, organizations and organizational life.

Torkild Thanem

ANTENARRATIVE

Definition

Antenarrative is not anti-narrative, it complements narrative (q.v.). Antenarrative is defined as 'the fragmented, non-linear, incoherent, collective, unplotted, and pre-narrative speculation, a bet, a proper narrative can be constituted' (Boje, 2001: 1). Antenarratives are 'in the middle' and 'in-between' (Boje, 2001: 293), refusing to attach linear beginning, middle and ending. Narratives must be coherent, developmental plots [*dramaturgy*] required by narrative theorists (Czarniawska, 1997: 79, 98; 1998: vii; 1999: 2; Gabriel, 2000: 20, 22). Narratives in narratology complement modernist conceptualizations of linear discourse, overlooking the fragmented and unformed antenarrative process that accomplishes intriguingly different communicative purposes. Antenarrative is rhizomatic flight continuing as long as there is context left to re-territorialize (Deleuze and Guattari, 1987) [*process philosophy; relativism*].

Critical antenarratology is defined as *in situ* interrogation or inquiry into relationships between narrative coherence and antenarrative non-linearity, between storyteller and expositor, and between researchers and researched. Storytelling (q.v.) is not just about linearity or non-linearity; it is both, and an interrelationship narrative and antenarrative. In 'antenarrative' (Boje, 2001), storytelling is no more than a bet, a scrawny pre-story that Latour (1996: 119) calls a 'whirlwind'. Latour (1996: 118) argues that there is a difference between the linear narrative *diffusion* model (narratives that erupt fully formed in the mind of Zeus) and the non-linear *whirlwind* model of what we call antenarrative. Looking at both models in the same story space of complex organization is a collaborative way to proceed. The result is a dance between linear narrative diffusion and antenarrative whirlwind; and in that dance are patterns we can interpret using complexity theory (q.v.). Strands of narrative *and* antenarrative are interwoven, ravelling *and* deravelling, weaving *and* unweaving in storytelling organizations. Critical antenarratology is a method to trace and deconstruct an ongoing interweaving antenarrating that is always composing and self-deconstructing [*deconstruction*].

The contribution of critical antenarratology is a focus on behaviour, on living storytelling practices that are fragmented, dialogical (between voices, styles, perspectives), prospective (not just retrospective), collectively co-produced (not solitary performance) and socially situated (in multiple contexts). Antenarrative derives its organizing force in emergent storytelling where plots are emergent, contested and speculative. Antenarratives have five dimensions (Boje, 2001: 3–5).

1. Antenarrative is about the *Tamara* of storytelling. *Tamara* is a play where ten characters unfold their stories before a walking, sometimes running, audience that fragments into small groups to chase characters and storylines from room to room.
2. Antenarrative is a collective memory before it becomes reified into the organization story, or consensual (official) narrative.
3. Antenarrative directs our analytic attention to the flow of storytelling, as lived experience, before the narrative requirements of beginnings, middles or endings.

4. Antenarrative gives attention to the speculative, the ambiguity of sensemaking and guessing as to what is happening in the flow of experience.
5. Antenarrating is both before story and a bet of transformation through supplements, dropping and picking up meaning in each successive context, and remaining unfinalized.

The crisis of narrative theory in modernity is what to do with the non-linear antenarrating, with polyphonic emergence in the *Tamara* of collective story production and simultaneous action. Telling stories that lack coherence and plot is contrary to modernity. Yet, people are always working and living in the middle of collectively mediate antenarrative processes, where few accounts attain narrative closure and fixity.

Discussion

There has been increasing interest in antenarrative theory and research (Barge, 2002; Boje, 2001, 2002; Boje and Rosile 2002, 2003; Boje et al., 2004a; Collins and Rainwater, 2005; Vickers, 2002). Vickers (2002: 2–3), for example, looks at how 'postmodern antenarratives encourage the possibility that there may be no story to tell, only fragments that may never come together coherently. She combines Heideggerian phenomenology (q.v.) [*existential phenomenology*] with an antenarrative exploration of multi-voiced ways of telling stories, of putting fragments together. Using in-depth interviews of people whose lives were shattered by chronic illness and suffering, Vickers presents what does not fit into coherence narratives.

Barge (2002), takes an antenarrative approach to organizational communication and managerial practice by focusing attention on ways people manage the multi-voiced non-linear character of organizational life. Antenarrative, for example, says Barge (2002: 7) 'requires managers to recognize the multiplicity of stories living and being told in organizations'. He gives examples of the managerial practice in the Kensington Consultation Centre

in London. Dalcher and Drevin (2003) are studying software failures in information systems using narrative and antenarrative methods. On the one hand, 'failure storytelling can be understood as a narrative recounting with the unlocking of patterns or a plot' (Dalcher and Drevin, 2003: 141); a more antenarrative process focuses on how 'the reality in failure stories is of multi-stranded stories of experiences and reactions that lack collective consensus'. During a lack of collective consensus, there are more disparate accounts and perspectives, where webs of narrative and antenarrative work things out. Gardner (2002) did a dissertation contrasting heroic, bureaucratic, chaos and postmodern narratives of expatriates. The relevant finding is that the quest and bureaucratic forms are cohesive and tidy narratives, while the chaos and postmodern forms are more akin to antenarratives. Gardner looked at the hybrids, how in the same conversation, the narrator switches between, say, bureaucratic and more chaotic forms. Boje et al. (2004a: 756, 769) looked at a set of eight antenarrative clusters, and their trajectory, that appeared to explain some of the dynamics of various types of Enron spectacle: 'Antenarratives are bets that a pre-story can be told and theatrically performed that will enroll stakeholders in "intertextual" ways transforming the world of action into theatrics', suggesting '[t]he antenarrative roots of Enron's collapse go back to its beginning in ways that are rhizomatic and intertextual'. Boje and Rosile (2003) studied the antenarrative bets made about Enron, sorting out their causal texture. Was it Fastow, Skilling or Lay, or do we put the blame on general greed and hubris, or say it was those Evil Corporations, something about Enrongate, or what we teach in the Business College? These are competing antenarratives still being sorted out. Boje and Rosile (2003) looked at the clash of Aristotle's epic and more tragic narrative poetics. Collins and Rainwater's (2005: 17) study is a 'sideways look' at storytelling, the local and fragmented understandings of Sears' transformation. Storytelling is not viewed as reflection of organizational reality, but as organic and vital constituents of organizing. Their significant finding is that at Sears there was an overlap of 'proper stories: and emergent "antenarratives"' (2005: 20).

Much of what passes for organizational story is sequential, single-voiced, linear narrative. There are several important implications of antenarrative theory for future projects. First, narrative methods can no longer ignore antenarrative dynamics. Second, analyses that refer to a unitary universal narrative miss the morphing of antenarratives and their changing intertextual relationships through complex rhizomatic practices. Third, it is important for future students to look at the emergence of networking of antenarratives in the unplotted soup of organizing. Antenarratives are self-organizing fragments that seem to cling to other fragments, and form interesting relationships.

David M. Boje

ANTI-DISCRIMINATORY RESEARCH

Definition

In discussing anti-discriminatory research it is important to consider whether this means researching anti-discriminatory management practices or researching in an anti-discriminatory way. It is also debateable whether it is legitimate to research anti-discriminatory practices in a discriminatory way. Anti-discriminatory research and practice are contested arenas that often lead to difficult and strained discussions in universities and workplaces with individual students, workers and managers seeking to avoid being labelled 'racist', 'homophobic', etc.

Discrimination refers to the identification of individuals and groups with identifiable characteristics and behaving less favourably towards this individual or group. These characteristics have often been associated with gender, race, disability, sexual orientation and age. At the level of employment opportunities it is clear that certain sections within the community are overrepresented at different levels of the organization. In the UK, for example, IDeA (2004) has shown that although social care is predominately a female occupation, there is still an overrepresentation of males in senior management positions while black and minority ethnic staff are proportionately less likely to achieve management or supervisory positions.

So qualitative management researchers who have a commitment to anti-discriminatory research will seek to challenge discrimination wherever they find it and in so doing will be reflective and reflexive (q.v.) concerning their own potential for discrimination as well as being discriminated against [*ethics*]. This is not to mean that they are eschewing academic standards:

> Are we abandoning the notion of objectivity if we espouse the principles of anti-discriminatory research? Are we allowing our prejudices, our biases, our preconceived notions to come in the way of 'proper academic research'? If we begin to answer these questions, we need to address the whole notion of objective research. Furthermore, if we accept that there is a dialectical relationship between theory and ethnography (q.v.), objectivity as a concept of purity begins to hold little meaning. (Barn, 1994: 37)

Discussion

Anti-discriminatory research is more than the need to avoid sexist, ageist, disablist, racist, homophobic and other types of discriminatory language in the use of questionnaires, interviews and the writing of reports. Anti-discriminatory research also implies the need to treat the research subjects as people and not as objects [*positivism and post-positivism*]. This may require a collaborative, participatory (q.v.) [*field research*] or emancipatory research approach. Everitt et al. (1992) identify three reasons why collaborative research may be beneficial to both the researched and the researcher alike. First, by giving credibility to the views of those less powerful, the researcher will gain access to the experiences of being discriminated against as well as to the behaviours and perspectives of those who oppress. Second, by having due regard for people in the research process, research subjects will become less suspicious of research and engage more honestly. It is also possible that by having one's views and experiences validated, research will be experienced as empowering, thus increasing the research subject's willingness to share. Third, those with the experiences the researcher wishes to explore are more likely to be aware of what questions matter and how answers should be interpreted.

Anti-discriminatory research requires the researcher to be aware of and make explicit who the research commissioner is and what the research question is. Is it a question that seeks to empower or one that will further discriminate particular groups? For example, researchers might wish to consider whether they should begin with what discriminated workers or communities see as a priority. So, instead of focusing on what managers or service providers see as important, they may wish to begin with what the research subjects consider to be important [*service user research*]. Failure to do this runs the risk of identifying only those priorities that are important to the researcher and research sponsor and so further oppressing research subjects. In a similar vein it is not enough to search for clues as to, for example, why are there are so few black managers without first asking what are the social processes which contribute to an underrepresentation of black people as managers [*structuration theory*]. Having undertaken the research, an anti-discriminatory research approach requires the researcher to ensure that research dissemination is accessible to all stakeholders, including those who have participated in the research as well as the research sponsor.

Prospects

There are a number of issues for anti-discriminatory research practices. The very nature of anti-discriminatory research is contested and there are those who see such an approach as inadequate and argue for an anti-oppressive research practice. Anti-oppressive practice is more proactive in that it is not only about treating individuals or groups equitably, it is also about conflict and change in relation to the power imbalance between 'superior' and 'inferior' individuals or groups (McLaughlin, 2006a).

Similarly, it is questionable whether our current listing of discriminated groups is sufficient; good arguments could also be made for the white Irish in the UK (Garrett, 2000, 2003), or for those who live in rural as opposed to urban areas (Pugh, 2003). More critically, concern might also be given to how, following conflicts or wars, conquered people's lives, practices and communities have become transformed into objects of knowledge for the 'superior' colonizers reinforcing dominant worldviews and marginalizing alternatives. Discussions about race, class, gender, disability and so on all have their location within the western world. They are, as Tuhiwai Smith (1999: 80) claims, framed in the colonizer's language [*post-colonial theory*]; associated research practices could best be summed up as: 'they came, they saw, they named, they claimed'. Finally, the 'list' approach encourages comparisons between groups and neglects that individuals can have multiple identities in that they maybe female, homosexual or disabled, or all three. It is then rather nonsensical to consider these cross-cutting features as arithmetical entities multiplying the original discrimination or suggesting that there is a hierarchy of discrimination. Anti-discriminatory research practice represents a challenge to qualitative management researchers wishing to adopt an ethical research approach that is both contested and contestable.

Hugh McLaughlin

APPRECIATIVE INQUIRY

Definition

Appreciative inquiry is a process that involves exploring the best of what is (or has been) and amplifying this best practice. Whereas action research (q.v.) promotes learning through attending to dysfunctional aspects of organizational functioning, appreciative inquiry seeks to accentuate the positive rather than eliminate the negative.

Discussion

Hayes (2006) examines appreciative inquiry from three perspectives: a philosophy of knowledge; an intervention theory; and a methodology for intervening in organizations to improve performance and the quality of life. This entry discusses these in turn. From the first perspective, appreciative inquiry assumes that how we behave and the consequences of our behaviour are critically dependent on the way we construct reality, on the way we see the world; and the way we see the world is determined by what we believe (Srivastva and Cooperrider, 1990) [constructivism; practice theory; practice-centred research]. Our beliefs govern what we look for, what we see and how we interpret what we see. 'The reality perceived ... is often a consequence of the reality believed, a situation that leads to self-fulfilling expectations within groups, organizations, or even whole societies' (Srivastva and Cooperrider, 1990: xvii). Cooperrider and Srivastva (1987) argue that to the extent that action is predicated on beliefs, ideas and meanings, people are free to seek a transformation in conventional conduct by modifying their beliefs and idea systems.

A widely held belief is that organizational life is problematic. This belief promotes a deficiency perspective that focuses attention on the dysfunctional aspects of organizations and has led to many interventions being designed on the assumption that organizations are 'problems to be solved'. An alternative belief about organizations, and one that underpins appreciative inquiry, is that rather than 'problems to be solved', they are 'possibilities to be embraced'.

Advocates of appreciative inquiry argue that not only are organizations' social constructions open to revision, but that this process of revision can be facilitated by a collective inquiry. They also argue that this collective inquiry should attend to the life-giving forces of the organization rather than to a set of problems that have to be resolved. It involves appreciating the best of 'what is' and using this to ignite a vision of the possible.

From the second perspective, appreciative inquiry involves the use of what Cooperrider (1990) refers to as the 'heliotropic hypothesis'. The assumption is that social systems have images of themselves that underpin self-organizing processes and that they have a natural tendency to evolve towards the most positive images held by their members. They are like plants, they evolve towards the 'light' that gives them life and energy. This leads to the proposition that interventions that promote a conscious evolution of positive imagery offer a viable option for changing social systems for the better [aesthetics].

The way organizational members construct and reconstruct the present and the past is a prelude to the way they imagine the future. Appreciative inquiry does not promote the imagination of unachievable fantasies. It promotes the imagination of a future that is based on an extrapolation of the best of what is or has been.

From the third perspective, appreciative inquiry involves the generation of a shared image of a better future through a collective process of inquiry into the best of what is. It is this imagined future that provides the powerful pull effect that guides the development of the group or the organization.

The critical part of the intervention is the inquiry [pragmatism]. The mere act of asking questions begins the process of change. Based on the assumption that the things we choose to focus on and the questions we ask determine what we find, it follows that the more positive the questions, the more positive the data. And the more positive the data, the more positive are the beliefs that people are likely to develop about what contributes to peak experiences. And the more positive these beliefs are, the more positive is the vision of the organization at its best; the more positive this image is, the more energy it generates for change.

Bushe (1999) describes the process of appreciative inquiry as consisting of three parts:

- **Discovering the best of ...** This involves discovering the best examples of organizing and organization within the experience of organizational members.
- **Understanding what creates the best of ...** This involves seeking insights into the forces that lead to superior performance and what it is about the people, the organization and the context that creates peak experiences at work.
- **Amplifying the people or processes that exemplify the best of ...** This involves reinforcing and amplifying those elements of the situation that contribute to superior performance.

Appreciative inquiry has been used in a wide range of different situations. Sorensen et al. (2003b), after reviewing 350 papers on appreciative inquiry, report that there is considerable evidence pointing to its successful application in many settings. Projects vary in terms of scale, organizational context and focus. Elliot (1999) presents a detailed account of an appreciative inquiry with a private healthcare provider in the UK and several accounts of the use of appreciative inquiry to develop communities in third-world settings. Zemke (1999) refers to a number of large-scale projects, Finegold et al. (2002) describe an appreciative inquiry in a Midwestern university and Bushe (1998) describes the use of appreciative inquiry in the context of team development.

Prospects

While appreciative inquiry provides the basis for a very attractive theory of intervention, Golembiewski (1999) sounds two notes of caution. The first concerns the outcome of appreciative inquiries. As predicted by the heliotropic hypothesis, social forms gravitate towards an imagined future that amplifies 'peak experiences' because people are motivated to move in that direction. However,

Golembiewski raises the question 'motivation for what purpose?' and notes that there are many examples where people have been motivated to level down human systems to the bestial (see, for example, Chang (1997) *The rape of Nanking*) as well as level them up to pursue some noble purpose. His second note of caution relates to appreciative inquiry's apparent aversion to 'negative' stories [*storytelling in management research*]. He suspects that this could encourage an incautious optimism about facts or beliefs.

John Hayes

AUTOPOIESIS

Definition

Autopoiesis is a Greek word and means literally 'self-production' (auto = self; poiesis = production). We observe self-production phenomena in all living systems. The cell, for example, produces and synthesizes macromolecules of proteins, lipids and enzymes, among others. In producing these myriad components the cell not only produces something else – *it produces itself*. The concept of autopoietic systems is meant to explain two basic phenomena in human intercourse: *life* and *knowledge*.

The word 'autopoiesis' was coined by the two Chilean cyberneticians and bio-epistemologists Humberto Maturana and Francisco Varela to describe how all living systems work. Autopoietic systems can be looked upon as networks of production of components that (1) recursively, through their interactions, generate and realize the network that produces them; and (2) constitute, in the space in which they exist, the boundaries of this network as components that participate in the realization of the network (Maturana, 1981).

In this way one could say that autopoiesis reinforces the processes of self-organization; systems not only produce and change their own *structures* (self-organization), but they also produce and organize the *components* of which they consist [*process philosophy*]. Consequently, autopoietic systems must be materially and energetically open, even though they are necessarily closed in their dynamics of states. The view that systems are either closed (autocratic, self-sufficient) or open (allopoietic) is rejected [*complexity theory; soft systems methodology*]. Rather, they are both open and closed at the same time. According to an autopoietic view, the organization is recursively generated through the interactions of its own products.

Discussion

The concept of autopoiesis has recently been applied to social systems, including organizations. It is, above all, the German sociologist Niklas Luhmann who has brought the concept further by translating it into a social context (Luhmann 1984/1995). With this, there is no direct analogy between social systems and organisms.

First of all, Luhmann's non-organistic concept of autopoiesis is much more *temporalized* than Maturana and Varela's biological concept. While the autopoiesis of organisms operates with relatively constant processes (e.g. operations of cells), the social autopoiesis and the autopoiesis of the consciousness are based on unities that have a character of 'events'. As events come into existence they soon disappear again. In organization and management one such type of event is that of decisions; once made, a decision becomes history. As a consequence, there will be a problem of 'connection' (between events), that is how can events connect if they disappear? This can be resolved by the notion of *meaning*, which serves to connect events to each other, and in organizations decisions are connected through meaning.

All social systems (organizations included) are based on meaning. Structures and processes which are based on meaning are distinguished from one another by the identification of external aspects (system boundaries and the environment). So as well as internal connections between decisions, boundaries and environments also provide

meaning for the system. Meaning makes it possible not only to interpret what is going on within the system but also what is going on in the system's environment. A further feature of the theory is that while social systems consist of decisional *communications*, the human beings engaging in such communication are not a part of the social system, but are part of its environment [*affordances*].

According to the concept of autopoiesis one can now define organizations as systems that consist of decisions that recursively reproduce the basis from which decisions are made (Luhmann, 2000). The different decisions are not connected by norms or values but by this recursivity of their reproduction. Every decision refers to previous decisions (decision programmes) and to future decisions, and is even itself referred to by other decisions; it has meaning in relation to other decisions. In this way a network of decisions is constituted which produces and reproduces decisions in an autopoietic (recursive) manner. And all kinds of organizations are operatively closed on this basis of decisions. Structures are produced through operations to be used in new operations, and then reproduced, changed or even forgotten. We also find this kind of recursive thinking in Anthony Giddens's (1984) theory of 'structuration' (q.v.), although he does not base it on autopoietic systems theory.

Although autopoiesis assumes autoproduction, it does not preclude change. There are always possibilities for change through connection to elements (events) outside the system, visible to the observer. Therefore, although the system operates from a basis of stability, this stability may be precarious. In this way the concept of autopoiesis opens up to view organizations in a 'constant state of insecurity' about themselves and their relation to the environment. Organizations control and produce this kind of 'insecurity' through their self-organization. The self-organization takes place through the recursive network of operations, which presents connections, as well as the ability to connect to other elements, with potentially different meaning. For instance, the ecological criteria of products can be interpreted as contributing to 'sustainable development'. However, they can also be connected elsewhere; for example, they can be interpreted as obstructions to free trade. This opens a paradoxical situation that the organization has to restrain in some way; something defined is always something different. Thus, the concept of autopoietic organizations is always open to the play of paradox [*postmodernism; relativism*].

The idea of organizations as autopoietic systems has been seen by researchers as potentially very interesting (Baecker, 1999; Bakken and Hernes, 2003; Hatch, 1997; G. Morgan, 1986/1997; Seidl and Becker, 2005). It is at present still at a somewhat early stage as far as organization and management theory is concerned. Yet a host of studies draw upon autopoietic theory. Examples of areas of study include: identity, decision-making processes, organizational learning, complexity, and organizational evolution. A common thread for most studies relates to issues of continuity versus change, where continuity and change are not seen as mutually exclusive. In much the same way as systems are both open and closed, they are also both reproductive of their basic features while being open to change. Perhaps a main contribution of autopoietic theory is that it avoids dualisms. Instead, a system, while reproducing itself around a relatively stable basis of meaning, is at the same time potentially unstable.

Prospects

Autopoietic theory, rather than point out that systems change, explores the internal dynamics of change, which makes it highly relevant to exploring organizational life in a complex world. Autopoietic theory is a highly abstract theory which applies well to complex problems. However, its high level of abstraction does pose some challenges to the study of micro-level problems, such as the level of actions and actors in management.

Tore Bakken, Tor Hernes

C

CAQDAS: COMPUTER-AIDED QUALITATIVE DATA ANALYSIS

Definition

By their nature, qualitative data tend to be rich and complex but also non-standardized. In addition to the usual interview transcripts, open-ended survey data and field notes, researchers are also handling summaries and abstracts, political or news discourses, bibliographies, film, paintings and photographs, diaries and tapes. Over the last decade, computer programs have been developed to assist in the management and integration of such data. Today, there are a number of software package available. All overlap, but they tend to concentrate on different aspects of qualitative data handling. The rather unwieldy term 'computer-aided qualitative data analysis software' has been coined when referring to such packages, although this is frequently abbreviated to CAQDAS.

When thinking about CAQDAS, try to imagine a sophisticated, relational database. This is all they really are. They come with many additional features and facilities to allow for sophisticated analyses, but at their heart they are nothing more than a database. These databases will not 'do' analysis. All they do is store data, in whatever form those data might take, and allow exploration of that data by showing various relationships within them. It remains for the researcher to decide what data to include, what analyses to undertake and the importance or otherwise of any relationships revealed. In this sense, CAQDAS is a useful *tool* for organizing, structuring and thinking about qualitative data.

Discussion

From a practical perspective, embarking on a qualitative research project which will utilize CAQDAS involves a number of issues:

- Reflecting on the methodological implications of the decision to use some form of CAQDAS in the study.
- Selecting a suitable software package.
- The data need to be converted into an appropriate electronic form. Transcripts and notes must be typed, interviews stored as MP3s, photographs and paintings scanned.
- Become familiar and comfortable with the notion of coding, writing memos, browsing and searching and hypothesizing.

General activities include:

- Transcription and creating of electronic formats or representation of data.
- Offline analysis, perhaps prior to transfer on to the computer.
- Creation of documents and other artefacts within the software.
- Developing attributes or some other basic representation of 'facts' about the data.
- Coding and the creation of nodes.
- Creation of links, memos, references, etc.
- Conducting quick, interim checks on relationships.

- Conducting 'analyses' and searches.
- Developing models.
- Producing displays and outputs that might be incorporated into a report.

Selecting the most appropriate or suitable CAQDAS program can be difficult. Although they overlap in what they can do, they tend to focus on different aspects of qualitative analysis. In broad terms, the available packages divide into one of four categories:

- Text retrievers.
- Textbase managers.
- Code-and-retrieve programs.
- Theory building software.

These categories are very blurred. However, nearly all CAQDAS packages will do the following:

- Some sort of cod`e and retrieve function.
- The facility for word (and even 'concept') searches.
- Data organization.
- Searches of positions of codes in the data (co-occurrence, proximity, etc.).
- Writing tools (memos, comments, etc.).
- Outputs (reports) of coded segments, memos, results of searches, etc.

Ultimately, the decision of which package to select will depend on a variety of factors, including the nature of the research being undertaken, accessibility, perhaps to existing software and support, an individual's preferred style of working and the nature and amount of data.

Some current well-known CAQDAS packages include: NVivo; N6; MAXqda; Hyper RESEARCH; ATLAS.ti; Qualrus; AnSWR.

Many advantages can be cited for using CAQDAS. Some are listed below. However, these are frequently refuted and, thus, are controversial. Suffice to say that there is nothing intrinsically wrong with using 'craft-based' methods, and this should always be considered as an option. Advantages include:

- Systematic data management and handling using self-generated (grounded) (q.v.) or imported (from established methodologies) classifications [*template analysis*].
- Dealing with 'data promiscuity', in that many forms of data can be stored and as data multiplies and broadens, the management of them is limited only by the computing power available [*process research*].
- Retaining context, in that coding and 'snippets' of information are usually linked back to the original document from which they were cut.
- Enabling continual reference to data – allowing researchers to investigate data from different perspectives and with varying degrees of refinement and depth.
- Facilitating testing and thinking processes in that different relationships can be explored without damaging the integrity of the original data. Moreover, each of these judgemental stages remains transparent [*systematic literature reviews*].
- Analyses can potentially be replicated in different contexts and by different researchers.
- Some packages allow collaborative working.

More controversial espoused advantages include:

- Improved rigour through detail of analysis, although some would argue about the definition of 'rigour' in a qualitative context.
- Transparency in analytical procedures, although it can be argued that the intervening technology of the computer and software in fact reduces transparency.
- Enhancing acceptability and credibility, especially by allowing for quantitatively framed 'summaries' (numerical proxies; tabular models) [*mixed methods in management research*]. This is a particularly controversial but apparent advantage. It is probably among the main reasons why CAQDAS is so popular. Very few qualitative projects are now reported having not being subjected to some form of analysis using a CAQDAS program.

Prospects

A major concern with CAQDAS, discussed at length in the literature, is that the use of the technology will influence the nature of the analyses undertaken. For one thing, it tends to distance researchers from their data. The intervening processes of electronic conversion followed by interaction through a computer create both a methodological and physical separation from the original data. Another danger is that researchers sometimes start to look for an 'answer' or 'solution' to research problems. Because the qualitative data become exposed to a technical process, it is sometimes easy for researchers to become seduced into a hypothetico-deductive approach – counting instances of phases or words or behaviours and imbuing these frequency and density counts with some kind of significance.

Another problem is becoming too reliant on the program. Researchers can look for it to 'generate' thinking and ideas. The sophisticated analysis and modelling tools can give the impression that the outputs in some way *represent* (q.v.) a product of thinking. They are better seen as the traces or residue of judgements by which further judgements might be made.

Finally, there is a debate over whether computer programs really lead to 'better' analysis. Certainly, they provide enormous scope in terms of functionality, depth and breadth, but in practice, much of the functionality remains redundant, and while closer and increasingly refined analyses might yield hitherto unforeseen relationships or themes, this is at the cost of significant time undertaking such analyses, possibly at the expense of time spent thinking about what the data really mean.

Mark Hall

CASE STUDY

Definition

Case studies embrace several approaches and purposes. First, case study research, in which the cases constitute the empirical evidence in a project, is the most relevant for researchers. Second, cases are used as illustrations, examples and anecdotes, not to prove anything but facilitate understanding of a concept or theory by making it more concrete. Third, practitioner cases are presentations of how an organization did this or that. Fourth, classroom cases are used for training purposes. In this entry, the focus is on case study research as an alternative to quantitative approaches such as surveys.

Efforts to define and classify cases for research purposes have been unsuccessful. Probably any real world management issue can be turned into a case. For example, an industry can be a case but so can a company within that industry, one of its departments, processes or individuals. A case should always be defined to suit a specific research purpose.

Case study research is especially effective in approaching phenomena that are little understood; phenomena that are ambiguous, fuzzy, even chaotic; dynamic processes rather than static and deterministic ones, and includes a large number of variables and relationships which are thus complex and difficult to overview and predict. Such phenomena are the rule rather than the exception in management disciplines (e.g. a merger between two companies, the factors that build long-term customer loyalty, or the introduction of new technology). To get an in-depth understanding of such phenomena, quantitative approaches are inadequate. These must reduce properties like complexity (q.v.) and ambiguity to make them manageable, whereas a case study can accommodate them. Even if a certain part of a phenomenon is singled out for case study, it is essential to establish its place in a systemic (holistic) context, making the concern one for complexity, context and change [*process research*].

Discussion

In practice, case study research is primarily qualitative although quantitative studies can be part of it (e.g. a time series analysis of financial indicators or a scale-based survey of employee perceptions of a re-organization) [*mixed methods in management research*]. Most qualitative research is concerned with cases and therefore any type of qualitative methodology might be appropriate. When elements from qualitative methodology are treated below, the purpose is to offer a case angle. Like other research, case studies can be primarily inductive (q.v.), deductive, exploratory, descriptive or explanatory; empirical or conceptual; and more or less objective, intersubjective or subjective.

An issue that creates discomfort among researchers is the number of cases necessary to generalize findings and conclusions. Cases primarily make possible understanding of mechanisms (analytical generalization: *what* is done and *how*) rather then counts (statistical generalization: how *many*, how *much*, how *often*). Note that statistical generalization does not offer guidelines for case study research. The number of cases needed in a study can stretch from one to any number, but is usually a few, sometimes 10 to 30. Often we are only interested in a single case ('How did Enron manage to deceive the financial market?') [*antenarrative*], although, within a scholarly spirit, there should always be a desire for generalization ('What deceptive practices are used in financial markets?'). The strategy is theoretical (purposeful) sampling, meaning that the type and number of cases are determined during the research process depending on what additional data are needed and the diminishing returns of additional information (saturation). By force of limitation in time and other resources there is always a trade-off between one or a few deep cases and many shallow cases.

The designation 'generate data' is more appropriate than 'collect data' as data of social process are rarely collectable objects but cues (words, numbers, actions, symbols, gestures) that can be perceived and organized in numerous ways. The pivotal guideline should be access: find a technique for adequate access to the studied phenomenon [*access*]. All traditional qualitative techniques – the study of archival data, formal and informal interviews, ethnographic observation – are candidates for data generation. Taking it a step further, management action research, a type of action science, offers superior access to complex cases, both to explicit and tacit knowledge [*action research*]. Here the researcher is both actor, decision-maker and scholarly researcher and through this close involvement gets superior access to the object of study.

A case can be primarily descriptive, although the researcher's paradigm and at least a light analysis are always underpinning every effort to make 'objective' and 'factual' descriptions. To fulfil the mission of scholarly research, however, raw substantive data should be brought forward to conceptualization and generalization. Cases can be used both for theory generation (including initial exploration of concepts and categories) and theory testing. If a theory is seen as tentative (the best we currently have), a modification of mainstream theory or the generation of a new theory under a different paradigm are never-ending processes, each new study making it possible to contribute improvements. These improvements offer a challenge to the state-of-the-art and a simultaneous, continuous test.

Analysing case data holds the same hurdles as any qualitative research. Constant comparison, interpretative (hermeneutic) approaches, grounded theory strategies, structured analysis (even software-based), intuitive analysis, and so on, can all be part of the researcher's arsenal.

In assessing the quality of case studies, various criteria can be used. Research should learn from efficient manufacturing, which essentially makes quality assessments in two ways. First, starting with the planning, try to do it right the first time. When the unexpected occurs, which is inevitable if new and complex areas are exploited, watch out for errors early and correct them. Second, evaluate the final product. Although inappropriate, too often criteria from quantitative research are applied to case study research, especially statistical estimates of reliability (q.v.), validity and generalizability. This is too simplistic; the evaluation can rarely be statistical but remains reflective and qualitative. Validity and generality – to assess if the cases mirror the phenomenon that is under scrutiny – are the most important. Other main criteria are: a reader being able to follow the research process; a statement of the researchers' paradigm and pre-understanding; indications of credibility; adequate access; contribution; a dynamic research process; and the satisfactory personal qualities of the researchers. Under each of these headings a series of sub-criteria can be applied.

Case study research can be reported in many ways. To make books, articles and oral presentations, a solution is to extract data and themes from the cases and merge them with theory, analyses, conclusions and narrative elements. Further, adapt to the audience, for example, academic researchers or managers. A complete documentation of each case is valuable but can be written up separately to avoid details obscuring the main message.

Prospects

The acceptance of cases for research purposes varies between management disciplines, countries and business schools. Common prejudices include that case study research is inferior to statistical research; lacks rigour; is only exploratory ('anecdotal evidence'); and cannot be used for generalization, explanation and testing. Cases seem to be common in organization theory but in marketing they are often considered second-rate by mainstream researchers. Whereas it is no problem to get PhD theses based on cases accepted in business schools in northern Europe and increasingly in the UK, it is difficult in the USA.

Evert Gummesson

CAUSAL COGNITIVE MAPPING

Definition

A causal cognitive map is a graphical representation where nodes represent concepts, and links (arcs or lines) represent the *perceived* causal relationships between concepts.

Discussion

Historically, cognitive mapping methods have been developed in order to investigate, and to depict, thinking in the form of information structures which are known variously as cognitive models, knowledge or belief structures, scripts and mental models (Walsh, 1995) and they are increasingly being employed as a powerful means of investigating and representing actors' beliefs. This is especially so in the context of strategic management research, where a wide range of techniques has been applied in an effort to map the mental representations of decision-makers (Huff, 1990) and, at times, to stimulate a thought or decision-making process (Eden et al., 1992).

The choice of mapping method depends largely upon whether the model of cognition is seen to be relatively simple, where, for example, simple counting and weighting of words in a text would be acceptable (making the assumption that concepts used often are more significant), or rather more complex and involving a considerable amount of researcher interpretation to get from the raw data to the finished map. Huff (1990) describes and summarizes the continuum of choices as maps that: (1) assess attention, association and the importance of concepts, (2) show dimensions of categories and cognitive taxonomies, (3) reveal understanding of influence, causality and system dynamics, (4) show the structure of argument, and (5) specify schemas, frames and perceptual codes.

Axelrod (1976) developed a causal cognitive mapping method that was used in political science and the cause map is now the most popular form of cognitive map (q.v.), used in many contexts, for example human resource management and technological innovation [*composite mapping; repertory grid technique*]. Investigators attempt to identify the salient constructs of a particular domain for an individual (or group) and the perceived causal relationships between these constructs.

The simplest forms are restricted to a consideration of positive (increases in one construct cause corresponding increases in one or more other constructs), negative (increases in one construct cause corresponding decreases in one or more other construct(s)), and neutral (no causality implied) relationships. More sophisticated variants of the technique enable these relationships to be differentially weighted. An emphasis on action, focusing on the perceived causal relationship between a given situation and its antecedents and likely consequences, renders these techniques particularly attractive not only for research purposes, but also as a basis for intervening in practical organizational decision processes.

Despite the growing popularity of causal cognitive mapping, there is currently no agreement concerning the most appropriate way to elicit actors' belief systems. As with all forms of cognitive mapping, fundamental epistemological beliefs, in particular the acceptable level of researcher intrusion, dominate issues of validity and reliability (q.v.). There needs to be some level of trade-off between fully capturing potentially complex data which are meaningful to individual participants and ensuring data are elicited in a manner which provides sufficient commonality to facilitate subsequent comparisons [process research].

Causal cognitive maps can be derived indirectly. This can be from secondary data sources such as documentary evidence [content analysis]. The major strength of this approach is that it is non-intrusive and unlikely to influence participants' thought processes. This material is, however, potentially problematic in terms of issues of authenticity and often only of tangential relevance to the investigator's purpose. Causal cognitive maps can be derived indirectly from primary sources, where data are elicited specifically for the research project but not in a manner that requires the participant to reflect on their beliefs in an explicit fashion. A major drawback of any indirect approach is the subsequent, cumbersome coding mechanism required for comparative analyses.

Direct elicitation methods require the active involvement of participants in the map construction process from the outset. Methods include structured questionnaires requiring participants to evaluate relationships among predefined sets of constructs, and the use of computerized systems (Eden et al., 1992), which enable maps to be constructed dynamically through an iterative interview process. Direct mapping procedures can be subdivided in terms of the extent to which the elicitation process permits participants to use their everyday language. Undoubtedly, ideographic techniques (whereby maps are captured in their natural language form) are inherently more meaningful to the individual participants. As with indirect methods, the major disadvantage with this technique relates to the laborious coding methods required for comparative analyses. Nomothetic elicitation, which entails the use of standardized lists of concepts, for example in the form of highly structured questionnaires, obviates the need for such procedures and facilitates systematic comparisons. They do, however, run the risk that the basic map construction task might prove meaningless for participants.

Prospects

Responding to the problems associated with both direct and indirect approaches, Markóczy and Goldberg (1995) developed a 'hybrid' form of causal cognitive mapping with considerable potential for the systematic collection and analysis of large-scale data, which recent developments in computer software have made technically feasible (Clarkson and Hodgkinson, 2005). Using this procedure, a common pool of constructs (developed via interview (q.v.) analysis or literature review) [systematic literature reviews] is presented to all participants, who select a fixed number to form the basic content of their map. Each participant then assesses the influence of each of her or his chosen constructs in a pair-wise manner (bypassing potentially problematic coding procedures). Some variants of this hybrid procedure then move on to present the map to participants in a graphical format for final edit and validation [*drawings and images*]. (Strengths and weaknesses are discussed in Hodgkinson and Clarkson, 2005.)

It is important to note that there is a wide spectrum of views concerning the ontological status of cognitive maps. For some, they are considered capable of representing an individual's literal beliefs concerning a particular domain at a given point in time. Others view cognitive mapping procedures as one method for accessing the thinking of individuals in applied settings, whereby the overall degree of literal correspondence between the data generated by such procedures and the human information processing system is of secondary importance, relative to the insights they yield into organizational life. At least they are viewed as a good methodological tool and a meaningful way of representing elements of the thoughts (rather than the thinking) of an individual (or group).

Gail P. Clarkson

COGNITIVE MAPPING

Definition

The earliest work on cognitive maps is generally believed to be Tolman's (1948). Since then the technique has captured the interest of many researchers from a range of disciplines, including management, psychology, sociology, etc. As a consequence there has emerged many different forms of cognitive mapping, each with their own theoretical, philosophical and practical bases [*repertory grid technique*]. Nevertheless, for the most part, each form works on the principle that we make use of maps or networks of statements/nodes to understand events around us and, to some extent, direct our behaviour and interactions within it. As such, maps aim to capture personal subjective data accessing memories, informed by values, and resulting in

particular perceptions – ultimately leading to determining whether action is required.

The different forms of mapping include the work of Ackoff (1974), Laukannen (1998), Bougon (1983), Langfield-Smith (1992) and Huff (1990) to name a few. The form of cognitive mapping discussed in the rest of this chapter is built on Kelly's Personal Constructs Theory (PCT) (Kelly, 1955a) and developed by Eden and colleagues (Eden, 1988).

Discussion

In essence, maps are a representation of how an individual (through a cognitive map) or group members (using a cause map) (q.v.) perceive a situation (which is the basis for action). Understanding this perception can be fundamental as it is this which influences action – a point emphasized by Thomas and Thomas's comment 'if men define situations as real, they are real in their consequences' (1928). Using a set of formalisms (Bryson et al., 2004), statements and their relationships are elicited, structured and reflected upon enabling further insight. They are thus rich in detail, providing in the case of cognitive maps detailed idiographic representations (group maps provide powerful negotiative devices). Through being able to tap into how an individual perceives the world (and thus make explicit some aspects of their cognition) it is thus possible to begin to get insights into understanding managerial behaviour.

Cognitive mapping initially was used in individual interviews as a means of eliciting representations of perceptions. By enabling both the capture and exploration of the maps, individuals are able to make sense of their thinking (addressing one of Kelly's PCT corollaries), explore alternatives in what is usually a messy, complex arena, and begin to consider how to move forward. From this position, it is natural to explore how individual representations (maps) can be woven together to support group working. By developing means for integrating cognitive maps into a group cause map (or directly mapping a group's shared contributions), it is possible to develop shared understanding (tapping into two further corollaries of Kelly's, PCT) as different group members are able to consider how their views relate to those of others and to begin to develop a common language. From this position it is more possible to begin to negotiate a way forward. This mode of modelling forms a significant part of the SODA (Strategic Options Development and Analysis) Problem Structuring Method (Eden and Ackermann, 2001), although its use has been far more widespread than just problem structuring [composite mapping].

Mapping has been used extensively within the field of management and organization research – both in an action research (q.v.) [action learning] paradigm, where working actively with organizations provides research insights, and as a data collection tool for research. For a good overview of different uses in managerial activity, see Ackermann and Eden (2004), whereas Jenkins (2002) provides useful insights regarding its use in data collection. Obviously the two purposes are not mutually exclusive. Through taking an interpretist philosophy [constructivism], the focus upon managerial research seeks to understand better the processes between stimulus (events) and action; by eliciting and examining the richness and complexity of managerial life, new understandings can be developed [inductive analysis]. In both cases content and structure are captured along with emotion (q.v.). When working with maps for data collection, rich, detailed and idiographic representations can be elicited and subsequently examined.

Regardless of the mode of working (individual or group) along with its structuring capabilities, there exists a wealth of analytical tools to manage the complexity inherent in maps (particularly group maps which can contain over 500 nodes/statements). These tools allow researchers to 'play' with the data, helping to identify emergent patterns through slicing the data in a range of different ways. These emergent patterns or properties subsequently can be compared – either over time, across individuals or organizations, etc. For example, on an individual basis a comparison of cognitive structures before and after a learning experience can be explored (Easterby-Smith, 1980) or particular structures in thinking (e.g. monolithic, segmented etc.) can be identified (Norris et al., 1970). On a group basis it is possible to compare value systems, central concerns, themes and dynamic properties.

Mapping through its inherent structure also increases the possibility of surfacing tacit knowledge, a key aspect in knowledge management research. The act of 'laddering' up and down the chains of argument (asking questions such as 'why is that important?' or 'how could that be achieved?') enables the interviewee to move away from simply providing superficial answers. As a consequence, not only does the interviewer gain more of an understanding of the theories in action (rather than the espoused theories [action science] or rhetoric) (q.v.), but the interviewee benefits as they begin to understand their own thinking (Weick, 1969/1979) [sensemaking].

Problems and prospects

However, as with many research techniques, gaining familiarity with mapping is not trivial. Remembering and applying the various formalisms while also maintaining a social interaction take practice. Moreover maps themselves do not give absolute answers. Their utility comes from being able to manage the complexity: capturing the richness, including dilemmas, contradictions and alternative points of view. While this enables groups to negotiate (through the implicit equivocality), it does not provide outright answers.

Fran Ackermann

COLLABORATIVE RESEARCH

Definition

The principle of collaborative research is simple: it involves conducting research with some other parties, either as a member of a team located in the same place, or working with people who are more distant in some respect. First, research can take place across disciplines, for example where geographers collaborate with people from marketing in order to understand the strategies of retail companies in locating new superstores. Second, research can take place between institutions in different parts of the same country, or between different countries. In each of these cases, there is an advantage in combining resources to increase the scale or the scope of the research to allow, for example, cross-national comparisons of human resource strategies or financial reporting standards.

The above examples all involve professional researchers working together. But it is also possible for collaborative research to take place with those who are either 'end users' [access], or the subjects of research. Some clients may choose to work closely with the professional researchers, either to control the process or to ensure that specific questions are answered. And this may be taken further by involving informants and those people in their research setting either in conducting some of the research and/or in making sense of the emergent results.

There are different degrees of engagement in any of the above cases. For example, collaboration can involve having an influence over the overall research questions and objectives, thinking through the design of the research, conducting parts of the research through carrying out interviews or helping with data collection, joining in the process of interpretation, and helping with the general exploitation and dissemination of the work.

Discussion

As I have indicated above, collaborative research and can cover quite a wide range of possibilities. Where it involves joint interpretation and exploitation of research alongside the informants and other research 'subjects', it may be very similar to participant (q.v.) action research (q.v.) [field research]. Proponents of collaborative research argue that it has a number of benefits: that it can

produce insights that are of higher quality than traditional research; that it can lead to a more balanced relationship between researchers and those on whom the research and has been conducted; that the results are likely to have greater credibility with potential users; and, of course, that it can lead to greater efficiencies, wider scope, and complementary use of resources.

On the other hand, it can be quite difficult to implement, and it is often difficult to work with others who have different objectives. People working together from different disciplinary bases are likely to use different specialist languages, and have different methodological preferences; people working across national boundaries will have both different institutional pressures and different cultural expectations (Easterby-Smith and Malina, 1999); and working together with people from other institutions in the same country may trigger competition with regard to who gets the most credit from the research.

More difficult issues arise when the research is attacked on the grounds of losing objectivity [phronetic organizational research; realism]. Of course, the criticism usually comes from those schooled in positivist (q.v.) methods, who believe that the quality of research can only be assured when the researchers maintain independence and objectivity from the subjects or the context that they are observing. To some extent, they are therefore missing the primary point of collaborative research, which is to increase the quality of insights, understanding, and applications arising from the research process. But researchers conducting this form of research still need to be careful to ensure that the results retain some credibility with other observers (e.g. when they are seeking to publish the results). In general, this credibility is ensured by the degree of rigour with which the research is conducted, and the extent to which all data, and the processes of interpretation, are recorded in a transparent manner. This means, for example, that if research results are being fed back to clients in order to get a reaction, then the discussion with those clients should be recorded so that it is possible to capture the process of (re)interpretation.

Prospects

So collaborative research is not necessarily that easy. It requires successful navigation between the philosophical critiques that suggest it is tainted by undue contact with the 'field', and the practical difficulties of working together in teams that may cross institutional and national boundaries. But it is likely that it will become more important in the future for two reasons. First, because there is continuing political pressure on management and social scientists, to demonstrate and to increase the relevance and value of academic research. Second, because many of those researchers who have dabbled with collaborative research have started to appreciate that it has great potential to generate major insights into social and organizational behaviour which could not be reached by more conventional means.

Mark Easterby-Smith

COMPARATIVE ANALYSIS

Definition

Social scientists are often in the business of making comparisons, even if they do not explicitly term their work 'comparative analysis' (May, 1997; Øyen, 1990). Particularly if working within a realist (q.v.) or critical realist (q.v.) epistemology, a key task for the researcher is to categorize phenomena and compare those categories over space and time, to develop an understanding of how social life is patterned and – perhaps, more importantly – to develop theory about *how* these patterns have come into being [*process research*].

In quantitative analysis, settings are compared by measuring variables using standardized conventions of categorization. These are

claimed to be both reliable (an accurate reflection of the material conditions) and replicable (a different researcher analysing the same data would have made the same measurements). Of course, these notions are controversial when applied to social research, particularly when attempts are made to quantify highly complex and context-specific phenomena such as meaning (Greenwood and Levin, 2005).

Comparative analysis conducted through qualitative research acknowledges that social relations are difficult to categorize and occur in local contexts that differ and are complex. It is much less concerned with making simplistic and standardized measurements of phenomena and more interested in comparing how social phenomena are understood, and how they occur, in different settings. However, many comparative analysts remain interested in broadly identifying patterns of phenomena (Seale, 2004) and making generalizations about the causal influences or powers that affect social life across settings (Øyen, 1990). The comparative analysis they present tends to be complex, subtle and cautious but, nonetheless, it rejects the postmodernist's view that every setting is unique and, so, incomparable.

Discussion

The types of comparison made in social research vary according to the level, scope and objectives of the study. Within-case comparisons are conducted to explore the interaction of factors within a single unit of analysis. Across-case analysis is conducted across units of analysis, comparing data between individuals, organizations or societies or, indeed, between the same setting at varying points in time. Through across-case analysis we begin to identify social patterns, become aware of factors that have influence across social settings *and* understand the particularity of local contexts [*composite mapping*].

Specific analytic techniques help us to ask interesting questions in our comparative analysis. For instance, we might analyze:

- Convergence and divergence between phenomena, to help identify factors that cause similarity and difference.
- How the manifestations of phenomena vary by social group and the processes causing this variance.
- Differences in the accounts given by different groups and factors that explain these differences.
- Negative instances – that is, identifying the absence of phenomena in some settings – to elucidate data that might otherwise be hidden and to moderate emerging theories.

Comparison can be built into data collection, as well as analysis, by selecting settings for comparison at the outset or doing so as the themes for comparison emerge inductively (Lewis, 2003). Through such theoretical sampling, sites and sources are selected to test or refine ideas as they emerge from the data; this is a different logic to constructing a sample to represent, and make generalizations to, a wider population (Dey, 2004). Similar, typical or average cases may be selected, but Flyvbjerg (2004) argues that atypical or extreme cases reveal more by activating the basic mechanisms in a situation [*critical incident technique*].

Seeking to identify social patterns can also be a legitimate pursuit in comparative analysis. This necessitates an understanding of how findings relate to the wider population. This must often be achieved by comparing a range of research findings in a meta-analysis. However, this depends on the adoption of comparable categories of analysis across research projects, a controversial issue within qualitative research.

If social patterns can be identified, then norms can be established and comparative research can be employed to study deviance or change. This approach is increasingly popular in evaluative studies, which may take an experimental approach by selecting a 'normal' group of the population under study to act as a control, and comparing this with a 'treatment group'. However, due to the effect of exogenous and local factors, it is dangerous

to interpret correlation between an intervention and an outcome as causal (q.v.) (Lewis, 2003), particularly when there is limited understanding of the 'normal' phenomena under study and/or how the intervention has affected change [*phronetic organizational research*].

Another function of comparison is validation. In qualitative research, this does not mean looking to multiple sources to support a single or simplistic account, but ensuring that differing or conflicting accounts are used to develop the subtlety of our analysis and to set appropriate limits to our generalizations.

Grounded theory (q.v.), with its method of 'constant comparison', offers more detailed mechanisms for conducting comparative research, including means of developing categories, engaging in theoretical sampling and integrating analysis (Charmaz, 2005). It has become most strongly related to the convention of data coding and, in contemporary times, to the use of software [*CAQDAS*]. Coding is particularly useful in comparative analysis because it helps to draw data together under themes, for internal and external comparison. If coding is conducted as an intensely analytic process – as recommended in grounded theory – it can also help to develop appropriate concepts or categories for comparison.

Another technique employed to manage comparative analysis is to summarize data in matrices (q.v.) (Charmaz, 2005). For instance, Miles and Huberman (1994b) present a Role-by-Time Matrix, in which the roles adopted by respondents at different points in time are summarized in cells. This provides a visual summary of each case, to aid within-case analysis. Columns or rows relating to a theme can then also be stacked into themed matrices to aid across-case analysis [*template analysis*].

Prospects

A major criticism of comparative analysis is that it privileges the study of commonalities over differences, and thereby loses a key advantage of qualitative investigation – understanding how phenomena occur in complex local contexts. In part, this objection can be managed by limiting the number of cases to be compared, relative to the analytic time available, so that each can be studied in-depth. Researchers should also ensure they adhere to the principles of appropriateness (ensuring that the methods and concepts or categories employed are appropriate to all settings) and equivalence (being certain that equivalent concepts are employed in all contexts, with particular concern for meaning-equivalence) (May, 1997). Validation panels, familiar with each context, can aid in monitoring this process.

Despite these safeguards, Teune (1990) argues that any set of comparative categories will be more appropriate to certain settings and, so, create biases in observations. This does not mean abandoning comparative analysis, but acknowledging that analysis and theory development occur in a context, of which the research design and analytic interpreters are an integral element (Dey, 2004). It may also mean limiting comparisons to more-alike settings (Øyen, 1990).

Julia Rouse

COMPLEXITY THEORIES

Definition

The term 'complexity theories' serves as an umbrella label for a number of theories, ideas and research programmes that are derived from scientific disciplines such as meteorology, biology, physics, chemistry and mathematics (Manson, 2001; Rescher, 1996a; Stacey, 2003; Styhre, 2002). As there is a diversity of viewpoints among complexity researchers, it is appropriate to use the term 'complexity theories' rather than theory (Black, 2000).

While there are a number of complexity theories, there is agreement over the nature of some key concepts, especially the following:

- **Chaos and order:** From the complexity perspective, chaos describes a complex, unpredictable and orderly disorder in which patterns of behaviour unfold in irregular but similar forms; snowflakes are all different but all have six sides (Tetenbaum, 1998).
- **Edge of chaos:** This is the condition where systems are constantly poised at the edge between order and chaos. It is argued that creativity, growth and useful self-organization are at their optimal when a complex system operates at the edge of chaos (Frederick, 1998; Jenner, 1998; Kauffman, 1993; Lewis, 1994).
- **Order-generating rules:** Systems are maintained at the edge of chaos through the operation of a limited number of simple order-generating rules, which permit limited chaos while providing relative order (Frederick, 1998; Lewis, 1994; MacIntosh and MacLean, 2001; Stacey et al., 2002; Wheatley, 1992).

Discussion

Complexity theories are increasingly being promoted as a way of understanding organizations and achieving organizational change (Bechtold, 1997; Black, 2000; Boje, 2000; Choi et al., 2001; Gilchrist, 2000; Lewis, 1994; Macbeth, 2002; Stacey et al., 2002; Tetenbaum, 1998). In the natural sciences, complexity theorists argue that disequilibrium (chaos) is a necessary condition for the growth of dynamic systems, but that such systems are prevented from tearing themselves apart by the presence of simple order-generating rules (Gell-Mann, 1994; Gould, 1989; Prigogine and Stengers, 1984). Management and organization theorists take a similar view, arguing that organizations are also dynamic non-linear systems, and that the outcomes of their actions are unpredictable but, like turbulence in gases and liquids, are governed by a set of simple order-generating rules (Brown and Eisenhardt, 1997; Lewis, 1994; Lorenz, 1993; MacIntosh and MacLean, 2001; Stacey et al., 2002; Styhre, 2002; Tetenbaum, 1998; Wheatley, 1992). For organizations, as for

47

natural systems, the key to survival is to develop rules which are capable of keeping an organization operating 'on the edge of chaos' (Stacey et al., 2002). If organizations are too stable, nothing changes and the system dies; if too chaotic, the system will be overwhelmed by change. In both situations, an organization can only survive and prosper if a new, more appropriate set of order-generating rules is established (MacIntosh and MacLean, 2001).

The key implications for organizations of adopting a complexity approach are shown in Table 2 (Burnes, 2005).

Prospects

Proponents of the complexity approach to organizations claim that the mathematics which has revealed the workings of the natural world can also reveal the workings of the social world. However, others take a more cautious view. Their key concerns are that:

- Some social scientists misuse chaos and complexity theories by espousing them even though they do not understand them, or by importing them into the humanities without the slightest conceptual justification (Goldberg and Markóczy, 2000; Sokal and Bricmont, 1998).
- Many organization theorists fail to recognize that complexity, as Lissack (1999:

112) notes, 'is less an organized, rigorous theory than a collection of ideas ...'. Also, once one moves beyond generalities, it becomes very difficult to grasp what is meant by complexity (Manson, 2001; Stickland, 1998). Furthermore, it is important to acknowledge that complexity-based prescriptions for managing and changing organizations are not, as yet, based on any hard evidence that they actually work (Rosenhead, 1998).

- In applying complexity theories to organizations, there appears to be a lack of clarity or explicitness in writers' attitudes towards them (Arndt and Bigelow, 2000; Brodbeck, 2002; Hayles, 2000; Morgan, 1997; Stacey, 2003; Stacey et al., 2002; Stickland, 1998). Are they:

- a metaphorical (q.v.) device which provides a means of gaining new insights into organizations? Many of the studies which have sought to explore and apply complexity theories to organizations, whether in nursing, teaching or manufacturing, do seem to use complexity as a metaphor (Boje, 2000; Hayles, 2000; Jenner, 1998; MacIntosh and MacLean, 1999, 2001; Styhre, 2002). This is perhaps why Allen (2001) suggests that complexity does not offer organizations a concrete picture of 'what is' or 'what will be',

Table 2   Applying complexity theories to organizations

Implication 1	There will be a need for much greater democracy and power equalization in all aspects of organizational life, instead of just narrow employee participation in change (Bechtold, 1997; Jenner, 1998; Kiel, 1994).
Implication 2	Small-scale incremental change and large-scale radical transformational change will need to be rejected in favour of 'a third kind' which lies between these two, and which is continuous and based on self-organization at the team/group level (Brodbeck, 2002; Brown and Eisenhardt, 1997).
Implication 3	In achieving effective change, order-generating rules have the potential to overcome the limitations of rational, linear, top-down, strategy-driven approaches to change (MacIntosh and MacLean, 1999, 2001; Stacey, 2003; Styhre, 2002).

but instead offers a picture of 'what might be'.

- a way of mathematically discovering how and why organizations operate as they do? Mathematical models based on complexity theories have been used to address scheduling problems in manufacturing operations (Tetenbaum, 1998), but not human behaviour in organizations (McKelvey, 2000). As Goldberg and Markóczy (2000: 94) observe: 'If the explicit [mathematical] modelling of complexity is removed, it is disturbing to imagine what will actually remain'.

Complexity theories are being used to bring about a fundamental re-evaluation of how we view the natural world. However, if organizations are to be reconceptualized as dynamic non-linear systems capable of continuous transformation through self-organization, advocates of this approach will need to show either that it is more than just a metaphorical device, or that even as such it is able to resolve the problems of managing and changing organizations more effectively than other approaches that are on offer.

Bernard Burnes

COMPLEXITY THEORY

Definition

The development of complexity theory, as it has been popularly titled, is regarded by some as signalling the arrival of a new scientific paradigm. Classical physics describes a universe where events are determined by a combination of initial conditions and mechanistic laws played out as the cogs of a huge machine roll forward. The focus is on systems establishing equilibrium, with every action met by an equal and opposite reaction. The second law of thermodynamics adds a

further twist to this image stating that, over time, mechanisms run down, losing both energy and internal organization.

Life in the more familiar sphere of human experience seems to contradict this classical view. Evolution points to a world where order emerges rather than is fixed. Nobel-prize winner Ilya Prigogine and colleagues, in the field of non-equilibrium thermodynamics and phase transitions, began to provide explanations for the generation and development of order in the world (Prigogine and Stengers, 1984). Essentially, their work indicates that change, development and transformation take place in *open systems* which exist in dynamic conditions that are far from equilibrium and where the potential for spontaneous emergence of radical novelty is ever-present [*process philosophy*].

Complexity theory, then, can be more accurately thought of as an umbrella term, covering Prigogine's work along with that of many others, conducted in a variety, of fields, including mathematics, biology, zoology, artificial intelligence and economics (Goodwin and Saunders, 1989; Haken, 1983; Lorenz, 1963; Mandelbrot, 1977; Thom, 1975). Coveney and Highfield (1996) provide a good historical account of much of this work.

Discussion

In the natural sciences, complexity theory can be described as being organized around a number of central concepts. A primary concern is with the *emergence of order* in so-called *complex adaptive systems* which exist *far-from-equilibrium* in an *irreversible medium*. Such order manifests itself through emergent *self-organization* as a *densely interconnected* network of interacting elements *selectively amplifies* certain random events. This propels the system away from its current state towards a *new order* in a way which is *largely unpredictable*. While the detailed form of such emergent structures cannot be predicted, the range of broad possibilities is to some extent contained within the configuration and structure of the system [*autopoiesis; soft systems methodology*].

Systems are of central importance in complexity theory in the natural sciences, and can be defined simply as a collection of interacting elements (Coveney and Highfield, 1996). Indeed, some writers claim that systems theory is the foundation of complexity theory (Capra, 1996; Levy, 1994). The term *'complex adaptive'* is usually applied to systems whose elements are so densely and variously interconnected, that simple, linear, cause-and-effect interactions are largely ruled out since an event in any given element could in principle travel through the system by an infinitude of routes, all of which will have different spatio-temporal dynamics. This multiplicity of potential *interconnections* is responsible for the flexibility or adaptiveness of such systems, in that any configuration of interconnections constitutes a possible system state. Thus any change in environmental or internal conditions can be addressed from within the system's vast range of possible configurations.

The idea of organizations as complex systems has been taken up by a variety of authors. Such work is typically concerned with strategic change and tends to style organizations or their constituent departments as having defined boundaries within which elements, usually people, interact at the micro-level to produce radical and often surprising global outcomes at the macro-level (MacIntosh et al., 2006 offer an overview).

However, some researchers, most notably Ralph Stacey and his colleagues, take the view that the application of systems thinking to organizations is problematic and are developing instead a view of organizations as complex responsive processes of interaction in which the emergence of meaning and configurations of power are central concepts (Stacey, 2001; MacIntosh et al., 2007) [*actor-network theory*].

The potential implications of complexity theory for research practice follow from turning the theory towards the conduct of research itself – an approach which many complexity theorists adopt. Management and organization research become a complex and unpredictable dynamic whose practices, processes and outcomes emerge from the conduct of the research as it proceeds, and which can neither be specified in advance nor controlled to any great degree.

Prospects

In methodological terms, the adoption or rejection of a systems theoretic approach has significant implications for research conduct. While both embrace the concepts of emergence and self-organization, and thus tend to steer away from research processes that are fully specified at the outset [*process research*], significant differences lie in the way the role of the researcher is conceptualized. In systems theoretic approaches, the notion of system boundaries introduces the possibility of the researcher as objective observer or intervening experimenter, who can step in and out of the organizational system at will. Examples here range from the use of computer simulations (Allen, 1998) at the 'hard' end of the spectrum to action research and various forms of 'mode 2' (q.v.) knowledge production at the other (MacLean et al., 2002). By contrast, the process perspective of Stacey and colleagues leads in methodological terms to a more subjective form of reflexive inquiry based on narrative ordering of the researcher's experience (Stacey and Griffin, 2005).

In conclusion, complexity theory casts management research itself as a complex dynamic phenomenon – an unpredictable and creative process of human interaction producing surprising results when and if they happen to emerge!

Donald MacLean, Robert MacIntosh

COMPOSITE MAPPING

Definition

Distinct from individual cognitive mapping (q.v.) [*causal cognitive mapping*], composite mapping is the process of integrating a collection of cognitive maps, each representing views held by an individual member of an organization regarding a common subject. The composite map provides a benchmark for – rather than a concurrent artefact of – group discourse and joint problem-solving, through which the scope and homogeneity/heterogeneity of its interwoven knowledge is visually elucidated [*visual data analysis*].

It is symbolic that the cognitive mapping technique has its genesis in Kelly's Theory of *Personal* Constructs (Kelly, 1955a) [*repertory grid technique*]. Issues immediately arise in the context of management research: could the technique be sensibly extended to study the *organizational* construction of the world? This question would evoke ontological issues, including whether an organization develops its own worldview just as individual human beings do, and what constitutes organizational knowledge. Associated with these issues is an epistemological inquiry into how we see such an organizational worldview and its knowledge. On one side of the debate are those who view organizational knowledge systems as distributed and decentred, but capable of turning unreflective individual practice into collective understandings (Becker, 2001; Tsoukas, 1996; Tsoukas and Vladimirou, 2001) [*practice theory*]. On the other side are those who believe the primary unit of organizational cognition is an intra-organizational social group with shared expertise and enterprises, or 'communities of practice' (Brown and Duguid, 2001; Fiol, 2002; Wenger, 1998).

Where an organization may be more diverse, more ambivalent and more inconsistent than any of its constituents, is there a better way to represent such cognitive complexity of an organization? The composite mapping methodology, an offspring of cognitive mapping, has been invented primarily for enabling this theoretical exploration.

Discussion

Among the earliest work is Bougon et al. (1977), who analyzed the distribution of knowledge across an organization by combining cognitive maps derived from individual members within one organization. The methodology has been used to investigate the level of the individual's perceived influence across the organization. Langfield-Smith and Wirth (1992) provided formalisms for measuring the difference between cognitive maps. Various group processes, such as strategizing, decision-making, negotiation and mediation, are reported to have benefited from the application of this methodology (Abernethy et al., 2005; Clarke and Mackaness, 2000; Eden, 1989; Langfield-Smith, 1992; Young, 1996).

The composite map can be technically defined as the 'union' of individual worldviews – that is, a map containing all the constructs in all the individual maps, with any duplication between them systematically removed. The rationale behind integrating individual cognitive maps is that it provides a medium with which one can examine the most exhaustive explanation for previous collective judgements made within the organization.

Practically, the integration of individual maps can be started by identifying those constructs which commonly exist among different maps. Such common constructs can be used as 'glue', through which the remaining segments of the maps are connected. It is rare that there is any individual cognitive map with no common constructs when they are produced by members of the same organization on the same subject. Hence this process usually results in a single large map with few disconnected cliques of constructs. In this process one may encounter those constructs that are worded differently, but effectively have the same meaning. It is also typical that a single concept in one map is represented by a set of more elaborated constructs in another. These are so judged in the process of coding, and reflected in the structure of the resulting composite map.

The process of composite mapping sometimes reveals conflicting worldviews within the organization. Some may consider that the construct A (say, 'presence of a competitor') positively affects the construct B ('group solidarity'), while another considers the relations between the two constructs are rather negative. Similarly, one may think that *A* causes *B*, while another may think that *B* actually causes *A*. Such variances provide a good measure of the complexity and diversity in organizational knowledge; hence many modellers take the strategy to include both – as opposed to choosing either – of the views by using multiple or bi-directional links between the constructs so that the multiplicity of the views is visually preserved.

As the entire process of composite mapping is inherently interpretative and exploratory, there is a methodological issue as to how a modeller can ensure analytical rigour. One strategy is to set out the mapping procedure explicitly and maintain the internal consistency throughout the mapping process. It also helps to check the consistency of interpretations between different modellers.

The composite mapping methodology can provide an expedient means for various types of organizational analysis. An example of applications can be found in Clarke et al. (2000), where unstructured interviews were carried out with corporate executives of the same companies. Their tacit knowledge has been represented first in the form of individual cognitive maps and then as an organizational composite map (see Figure 2).

Figure 2 exhibits a typically high degree of complexity and elaboration. As is shown in the example, a composite map can be used to visualize partitioned clusters of constructs that can be categorized under a common theme. It is also possible to highlight the 'owner' of each construct, representing who (or which part of an organization) is concerned with what domain of the organizational knowledge. By comparing the cognitive structure of a managing director and that of a specialist researcher, for example, their congruence, specialization and diversity in organizational knowledge can be visually or systematically examined. Though the composite map itself does not represent organizational decision-making schema, it can provide insight into how individual cognition interrelates among other individuals and groups.

Prospects

There are a number of topics in management research which may be tackled by employing the composite mapping methodology. While the illustration (Figure 2) is primarily concerned with the intra-organizational structure of knowledge distribution, the analysis could turn to another or multiple levels, such as inter-organizational comparison of composite maps by different organizations. In the context of action research, it would contribute to the current literature examining what impact the *process* of composite mapping has on the development of organizational competence and capability for problem-solving. There are also streams of research which have explored the synergy with positivist (q.v.) management research (Nadkarni and Shenoy, 2004; Wang, 1996). However, there is a debate about validation issues as the methodology's constructionist stand may conflict with the principle of empirical refutability that governs most positivist models [*phronetic research; social constructionism*].

Masahide Horita, William
Mackaness, Ian Clarke

CONFUCIANISM

Definition

Confucianism historically has been closely associated with the doctrine and traditions of Chinese literary scholars who have followed and developed the teachings of Confucius (c. 552 to c. 479 BC). In contemporary usage, the term refers to certain guiding principles for the social beliefs, attitudes, and behaviour of ethnic Chinese in mainland China and beyond. Such guiding principles are derived from Confucian literature and are mainly concerned with the enhancement of ethical social behaviour. It is believed that the reference point for ethical behaviour is in the efficient functioning of the traditional family of

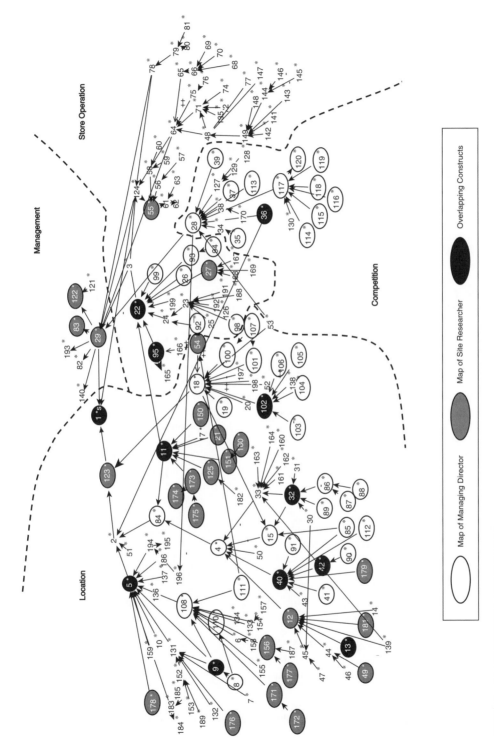

Figure 2 An organizational composite map

parents and their offspring, which is thought to embody a number of key, hierarchical relationships that are mirrored in human society.

Confucian teachings emphasize harmonious conduct and moral development in the family and describe how this is achieved and sustained by the faithful conduct of relationships between family members. In the constitution of 'good' family and social relationships, two central issues are discussed. First, the nature of differentiation between individuals, and second, the typology of relationships that are to be established between different individuals. The nature of differentiation between individuals depends on the type of relationships in which they are engaged. While there are many types of relationship, Confucian teachings focus on five cardinal relationships or virtues (*wu lun*) that are considered fundamental to the regulation of family and society. They are, in order of importance: affection (*chi'in*) between father and son; righteousness (*i*) between ruler and subject(s); distinction (*pieh*) between husband and wife; order (*hsu*) between older brothers and younger brothers; and sincerity (*hsin*) between friends [*feminism; post-colonialism*].

Building and sustaining cardinal relationships requires specific actions. In developing the father–son relationship, filial piety is emphasized in the son's obedience to his father's will and conformance with his opinions. Righteousness in the ruler–subject relationship requires considerate behaviour by the ruler in his subjects' interests. Distinction between husband and wife obliges each party to conduct complementary roles in sustaining the family unit. Order between brothers prescribes the loyal subordination of younger brothers to their older brothers, for instance in family succession, but also the lifelong support of male siblings in each other's endeavours. *Hsin* obliges integrity and truthfulness among friends. In performing these cardinal relationships, every individual in society is obliged to play a distinct role. The conduct of social roles is based on an established relational hierarchy. Social differentiation is important because parties in each type of relationship can then learn from Confucian teachings what specific 'stocks of knowledge' they are to apply relative to their social position in performing a particular relationship. All individuals should participate in social relationships as human beings are thought to exist only in relation to one another.

There are a number of sociological concepts that constitute the 'stocks of knowledge' that ethnic Chinese engage in relating with one another. Such concepts concern standards of behaviour that are expected in the public conduct of social relationships. Primary conceptual standards relate to propriety and etiquette (*li*), knowledgeable connections (*kuan hsi*), human sensibilities and obligations (*ren ching*), and personal social reputation, or 'face' (*mien tzu*). In daily life, these primary concepts constitute socially desirable standards against which the quality of individual relationships may be gauged and improved upon. Accordingly, the extent of *kuan hsi* would be determined by 'interpersonal feelings' (*kan ching*) and reciprocity of action (*shu*) between two individuals in a relationship as well as by an individual's public 'face' as he endeavours to maintain a high, socially-respected level of *kuan hsi*.

While the Confucian system of relationships builds on personal obligations, scholars suggest that there is considerable latitude for autonomy (*chi*), both in choosing certain relationships (for instance, the husband–wife relationship which parties voluntarily enter into, unlike the involuntary father–son relationship), and then in developing the dynamics of personal relationships which rely on individual will and skill.[1] In order, however, for free will in relationships to be exercised, the rules by which individuals conduct relationships need invariably to be overseen by a 'higher' governing authority. In a national context, this is represented by the state, which sets widely applicable rules, typically

---

[1] The Confucian conception of *Chi* – literally, 'self' – means both individual autonomy, and will and skill, although individual action is expected to promote social order (*hsu*) and harmonious relationships (*kuan hsi*).

through its education policy, in delineating the extent of 'good' relational behaviour. In tandem, therefore, with individual responsibility for building appropriate social relationships, the extent to which individuals may exercise free will depends on how effective governing rules for 'good' social behaviour are brought about. Hence, good government is a precondition of good social relationships.

Discussion

The conception and usage of Confucianism have developed since the demise of imperial China in the late nineteenth century. The scholastic influence of Confucianism that was symbolized by an imperial system of civil service examinations was held responsible for China's failure to modernize, and the direct influence of Confucianism through education and government was severed. In particular, the kinship system was singled out as a barrier to wealth creation because its fixed relationships were thought to bind individuals to persons and personal obligations while inhibiting the performance of impersonal, functional tasks for wealth creation.

Instead, the influence of Confucian teachings on managerial and organizational activity in the twentieth century has been of an indirect nature. Much of contemporary influence has been about the degree to which ethnic Chinese outside China (*hua qiao*) have been able to combine Confucian social beliefs based on the primacy of family relationships with non-Confucian economic goals that do not privilege family relationships. Particularly in jurisdictions such as Hong Kong and Singapore, where overseas Chinese form the majority, attempts by a number of local politicians, scholars and businessmen to combine Confucian beliefs within a capitalist business agenda have resulted in the contemporary appearance of 'Confucianism' as a set of guiding social and moral principles. The usage of Confucian principles as a cultural resource is seen to have succeeded spectacularly in East Asia. Here, the economic success of ethnic Chinese businesses has been attributed to the effectiveness of certain guiding

principles, including Confucian kinship relationships, which are said to be responsible for behavioural traits such as frugality, loyalty, dedication and industry, with which ethnic Chinese businesses are often identified. This perspective is consonant with the views of Confucian scholars who have long argued that there is considerable homogeneity in conception and practice among constituent elements of Confucianism. The perceived homogeneity has supported arguments in favour of a 'universal' particularity about Chinese behaviour in the way that social relationships have become motivating forces in shaping a 'special' co-operative system [*action science*]. It is suggested that this system has provided 'stocks of knowledge' that have been applied in improving the performance of ethnic Chinese firms.

What specifically has been applied by ethnic Chinese businessmen in China and beyond is a belief in the continuing applicability of 'harmonious', ordered relationships as the cornerstone of a cogent set of guiding principles for management and business conduct. Accordingly, business relationships among ethnic Chinese continue to be built and sustained through *kuan hsi* and other 'stocks of knowledge' that are still understood and drawn on by ethnic Chinese businessmen and managers across a wide social spectrum. In terms of management influence, a small number of large family groups continue to dominate business life in the ethnic Chinese constituencies of Hong Kong, Taiwan, and Singapore. In other East Asian constituencies, notably in Indonesia, Malaysia, and the Philippines, where ethnic Chinese have formed a tiny minority of the local population, the contribution of ethnic Chinese businesspeople and their organizations to wealth creation has been widely accepted although often not socially appreciated, as the poverty of indigenous populations relative to the wealth of ethnic Chinese is thought to have brought periodic violence on themselves and their property. Consequent upon the success of ethnic Chinese businesses in East Asia, some management scholars have suggested that Confucian principles on family and public life have become important constituents in a distinct system of governance in the publicly quoted but family-controlled firm.

Wilson Ng

CONSTRUCTIVISM

Definition

Schooled into some version of realism, most of us management scholars begin by presuming a Nature 'out there' that is the object of science's attention; that scientists observe that Nature and that there is no knowledge except about Nature (Kolakowski, 1972) [*positivism and post-positivism*]. Problems with this realist view go back to the Sceptics of Ancient Greece who showed we have no certain knowledge of reality. Sense-data are perceptions, not reality itself, and we cannot stand outside these to know for certain to what they refer. We might be dreaming the whole thing. Scientific evidence about reality is forever open to criticism that we are mistaken, for our proofs are tautologies that leverage our assumptions and perceptions, and we know these can be faulty. So in contrast to realism we have rival positions such as subjectivism or idealism [*critical realism; individualism*]. Their starting assumption is that we only find meaning in our sense-data by using ideas or 'frames of meaning' we have already imagined. These mediate and are logically prior to any sense-based knowledge of reality. Realists recoil from this position's relativism in epistemic horror. Sometimes dubbed 'anything goes' (Lakatos and Feyerabend, 1999), subjectivists can think whatever they like and it is true for them simply because they think it. Realists regard this universe of the imagination as utterly remote from reality.

Oceans of ink have been consumed by this contrast – much in the disciplinary wars between realist (q.v.)/objectivist (quantitative) and idealist/interpretist (qualitative) research methodologies. Dealing with this contrast, many present Society and Nature as fundamentally different, arguing that the social sciences differ from the physical sciences. Two strategies seem possible: (a) to establish the permanent predominance of either realism or idealism; or (b) to seek a middle way that reflects both without falling prey to either's fatal flaws. The first is demonstrably unsuccessful and has proved extremely destructive, especially to the social sciences of which management studies are probably a part (Delanty, 1997). There is much current interest in (b), especially in 'constructivist' approaches. These balance preferences towards Self, Nature and Human Society, arguing that what we take as reality is indeed constructed by our imaginative Selves, but it is constrained by Nature or Society. We are not free to create justifiable knowledge in whatever image we wish. Note Society often appears as language [*ordinary language philosophy*]. Wittgenstein (1972), preferring Society over both Nature and Self, argued that all knowledge is contained in language and the limits of language are thus also those of truth.

Discussion

Much current debate considers the different kinds of constructivism corresponding to what we choose to prefer as constraints to the imagination or 'warrants' for the meanings we use. Absent constraints and we have only anarchic relativism (q.v.). One variety of constructivism is social 'constructionism' (q.v.); while constructivism focuses on the internal mental processes, constructionism weights the processes external to individuals, such as language.

'Social constructivism' has achieved considerable popularity (Gergen, 1994a; Osborne, 1996). It argues all human knowledge is warranted by our social processes. In as much as culture is part of these, we can have 'cultural constructivism'. Institutional theory, too, can be regarded as a variety of social constructivism. To analyze social learning we must look at the processes that construct society, so balancing the members' imaginations against social processes that are presumed independent of them. Another variant, 'critical constructivism', looks at these social processes as barriers to the freer play of the Self's imagination.

'Personal or philosophical constructivism' is largely shaped by Piaget's ideas on the unfolding of our mental abilities, genetically determined (by Nature). His key concepts are assimilation and adaptation (Piaget, 1972). Truth is not a picture of reality; rather it is what we create to better negotiate the world of our experience. We assimilate the meaning of our experiences (learn) using the ideas we already have available (absorptive capacity) – except when we fail and adapt to some un-assimilable experience (evolve). Kelly's 'personal construct' theory is an operationalization of personal constructivism, again focused on negotiating the world of experience (Kelly, 1955b) [*cognitive mapping; repertory grid technique*].

Vygotsky's constructivism is predominantly social, denying the completely genetic shaping of human consciousness, preferring instead the impress of the developing individual's social interactions (Vygotsky, 1978/1979) [*activity theory*]. But the impact of the Social is balanced by the genetically given constructive processes of the individual Self. As a result, adaptation occurs in the individual's Zone of Proximal Development, as her/his prior knowledge evolves within the field of possibility dictated by the Social.

All constructivism stands on preferring the imaginative Self, rather than on realist notions of the Self as a passive but impressionable observer. It calls on ideas that go back to Descartes and Adam Smith that Man's defining characteristics are not only those of *homo sapiens* – our senses and logical thought – but include our imagination, so denying realism's dismissal of our creativity.

In addition to our knowing being constrained 'internally' by our genetics, a theme worked up by Kant and carried through philosophy to today's discussions about our neurological functioning (Penrose, 1989) or 'externally' by our social and cultural processes, 'radical constructivism' (RC) admits external constraints from Nature (Von Glasersfeld, 2002). While we can imagine and construct whatever ideas we

like, they inhabit the realm of our imagination. But our practice inhabits the world of the real and Nature is not passive towards that. She will often 'kick back' and remind us our ideas seem inappropriate as frames for knowing practice (Pickering, 1995). While there are some parallels to pragmatism, there are also crucial differences, especially in the assumptions about the Self.

Pragmatism (q.v.) looks to utility (cash value) as the warrant for truth while retaining the realist's images of a knowable 'out there'. The pragmatic notion of Truth is a use-based representation of the real. James (1946) argued the pragmatic method lies in valuing the practical consequences of different Truth-proposals, a notion extended into 'operationalism' (Bridgman, 1927). In contrast with pragmatism, which presumes the knowing Self, constructivism problematizes it, be it the individual of personal constructivism, the society of social constructivism, or the acting agent in RC.

So RC is more about our processes of attending to and ordering experience than about establishing rules for rigorously picturing the Nature we experience. As such, it is especially appropriate to the study of management in an incompletely known universe, where learning is more by doing than by hypothesizing and applying the scientific method. Instead of trying to develop theories of a fixed knowable world for rational decision-making, an RC approach focuses on helping managers attend better to their experience and develop improved learning practices [*action learning; social poetics*].

For researchers approaching the firm as an economic entity, RC converges importantly with 'radical subjectivism' and the work of economists who proceed from the Self's uncertainty about the future – 'Austrians' such as Hayek, von Mises, Shackle and Lachmann (Buchanan and Vanberg, 2002; Lachmann, 1977). Penrose's (1959) distinction between resources and services stands on similar subjectivism. For these economists, markets are not constraints that exist like some positivist reality. On the contrary, the market is perpetually being made over by those whose choices construct the future. Each choice is an act of entrepreneurial imagination about an as-yet uncreated future. Absent the realist's stable over-arching reality, equilibrium becomes an irrelevant concept.

Prospects

Radical subjectivism stands in opposition to today's 'positive' economics, just as subjectivism stands in opposition to realism (Shackle, 1972). But, by admitting constructive practice, it offers RC-like lessons for management researchers. We move on from a position that characterizes managers as sense-data and logic-equipped decision-making automata. Instead constructivism admits their humanity and imaginative responses to the fundamental uncertainties of a yet-to-be-constructed future, notions that lead us to new notions of profit, enterprise and the dynamic economy – and of management itself. The risk is that when nature and experience do 'kick back', a uselessness of ordering experiences using research is revealed, without any concomitant antidote. Consequently, contructivist perspectives, especially in radical frames, are backward-looking, having an atheoretical tendency to resist prediction or projection into the future. Realism, even critical realism (Bhaskar, 2002) presumes the constancy of the real, and sees knowing it as a way of predicting the future. RC rejects knowing Nature and, consequently, its constancy. RC remains open to surprise at unanticipated changes in context, but in doing so exposes us to the prospect of irrelevant experience [*existential phenomenology; phenomenology*].

J.-C. Spender

CONTENT ANALYSIS

Definition

Content analysis refers to the analysis of the content of both written and non-written documents. Within this technique, the contents of each document are quantified objectively in a systematic and replicable manner using predetermined categories, thereby allowing the data to be analyzed quantitatively. Krippendorff (2004) argues that the purpose of the technique is to make replicable and valid inferences regarding the relationship between the content of the document and its context. Context may include the purpose of the document as well as organizational, cultural and other aspects [*discourse analysis*].

Discussion

Content analysis has been used in a wide range of disciplines, including anthropology, education, history, management and psychology since its first use in the eighteenth century to analyze textual material (Harwood and Garry, 2003). Today, documents that have been subject to content analysis are extremely varied in type and scale, ranging from text through to images and from individual articles or photographs to entire newspapers or films [*visual data analysis*]. They include minutes of meetings, letters, e-mails, organizational policies, employment contracts, diaries, newspapers, newspaper articles, company reports, websites, advertisements, television programmes, films, photographs, and comic strips. The main uses of content analysis within business and management research have been the analysis of mass media items such as advertisements and newspaper reports, and of texts and documents produced by organizations such as annual reports and mission statements. Recent management research based upon content analysis has included the analysis of international advertising practices using advertisements placed by multinational companies (Harris and Attour, 2003), a comparison of European, Japanese and US firms' mission statements (Bartkus and McAfee, 2004), and an exploration of the dimensions of online service quality based upon customers' reviews (Zhilin and Xiang, 2004). However, although content analysis has been used as the sole or main technique in a research project, its most common use is as a secondary or supplementary technique in a multi-method study [*mixed methods in management research; triangulation*].

In overview, the process of content analysis starts with a research question. Where a large number of documents exists, the next stage is to select a sample using a clear rationale, both in terms of the nature of the documents and the time at which they were created. Subsequently, a coding scheme is developed to enable the data-relevant research question to be recorded. This consists of a coding schedule and a coding manual. The schedule comprises a form into which data relating to the document being coded are entered, the manual defines all the codes or categories that will be used and gives clear instructions regarding their precise interpretation. The coding schedule is then completed for each document using the definitions in the coding manual to record frequency of occurance. Computer-aided qualitative analysis software [*CAQDAS*] can facilitate such content analysis of both text-based and image-based documents. However, software to aid the analysis of images [*aesthetics; drawings and images; semiotics*] is less widespread and developed than that for analysing text-based documents.

Where documents being analyzed are already in existence, for example organizations' websites or minutes from meetings, content analysis is normally considered an indirect and unobtrusive technique. This is because each document that is being analyzed is not affected by the fact it is being used. In contrast, where the research necessitates the direct creation of documents, such as with diary (q.v.) studies, the involvement of research subjects within the project may result in a reactive effect such as altered behaviour. In such instances content analysis is considered an obtrusive technique.

Prospects

Content analysis therefore provides a technique for analysing documents by recording frequency of occurrence. Objectivity within content analysis is argued to come from the transparent nature of the procedures and processes used to select the sample and assign codes or categories to the document. This means that the person undertaking the analysis is merely applying rules and so their personal biases are minimized. Applying these rules systematically and consistently also helps minimize bias. In addition, a clear set of rules means that the analysis should be replicable. Despite this, it is unlikely to be possible to devise coding manuals that do not involve at least some interpretation by the coder, resulting in some bias [*reliability*]. The choice of categories considered relevant, and therefore to be coded, may result in large amounts of data being discarded that could have been helpful in answering the research question. If using historical (q.v.) documents, providing these are accessible, content analysis can facilitate longitudinal studies. However, like contemporary documents, these may be incomplete, worded for a particular audience or written for a different purpose from the research being undertaken. Any content analysis will therefore only be as good as the documents upon which it is based. Consequently, it is important that the authenticity and appropriateness of documents are assessed.

Mark N.K. Saunders

CONTINGENCY THEORY (STRUCTURAL)

Definition

Contingency theory states that the most effective organizational characteristics are those that fit the contingency variables. For instance, specialization in an organization produces highest performance when it fits the size of the organization, that is, the level of that contingency variable. Hence, highest performance results from low specialization in an organization of small size, whereas for an organization of large size, highest performance results from high specialization. There are contingency theories of a diverse range of organizational characteristics, such as leadership (Fiedler, 1967). Contingency theories of organizational structure are referred to as structural contingency theory, and it will be convenient to discuss it here because it has been extensively studied and it illustrates the general logic of contingency theory.

Previous theories of organizational structure were universalistic, holding that 'there was one best way' to organize, in that one structure produces the highest performance in all organizations, despite their varying attributes, such as size. Classical Management theory held that high formalization (rules and standard operating procedures) was the one best way that led to highest performance [*modernism and scientific management; Taylorism*]. Human Relations theory held that low formalization, relying instead on employee initiative, was the one best way that led to highest performance. Structural contingency theory rejects such universalism. Instead it holds that the effect of a structural variable on performance is contingent, so that a level of the structural variable only produces highest performance if it fits the level of some other variable, called the contingency variable. Thus the effect of the structural variable on performance varies widely depending upon whether structural variable fits or misfits the contingency variable and the degree of misfit.

Structural contingency theory provides a framework that synthesizes the Classical Management and Human Relations theories. Each theory is correct in its own place, while being incorrect in the other's place. The 'place' of each theory is defined by the contingency variable. The key is that the structure needs to fit the contingency. Classical Management theory works best in an organization facing a stable environment, so that the tasks facing its members are predictable and certain, allowing them to be efficiently conducted by following rules and procedures, that is, high formalization. Human Relations theory works best in an organization facing an unstable environment, so that the tasks facing its members are unpredictable and uncertain, and members need to solve novel problems by using their professional knowledge and initiative through mutual collaboration, so formalization is low. Thus, for highest performance, the level of the structural variable of formalization needs to fit the level of the task uncertainty contingency. High formalization fits low task uncertainty. Intermediate levels of formalization fit the corresponding intermediate level of task uncertainty. Low formalization fits high task uncertainty.

Discussion

Identifying task uncertainty as it is related to uncertainty arising from the environment of an organization has involved researchers looking to identify these environmental elements, from changing market demand and or new technologies. These more unstable environments are often found in industries that are experiencing high rates of innovation in new products or services. The need of the organization to innovate leads to task uncertainty inside the organization. Thus, the contingency of task uncertainty is related to environmental uncertainty and to innovation.

Another contingency is organizational size, that is, the number of organizational members. Small organizations are fitted by a structure that is low on specialization (because there are few members among whom work needs to be divided up) and low on formalization (because with few cases, sound personnel and operational rules cannot be developed), and that are high on centralization (because small organizational size makes it effective for top management to control operations directly through making many decisions personally). Conversely, large organizations are fitted by a structure that is high on specialization (because there are many members among whom work needs to be divided up) and high on formalization (because with many cases, sound personnel and operational rules can be developed), and that are low on centralization (because large organizational size means top management has to delegate many decisions down the hierarchy).

Another identified contingency is diversification, by product, service, customer, market or geography, which affects the structure that is required at the apex of the organization, that is, how responsibilities are divided up among managers reporting to the CEO and between them and the CEO. An undiversified organization is fitted by a functional structure in which heads of functions (e.g. Manufacturing, Marketing) report directly to the CEO. A diversified organization is fitted by a multidivisional structure in which heads of autonomous businesses (e.g. Industrial Products, Consumer Products) report directly to the CEO. Thus, diversification requires decentralization additional to that required by size. As seen here, structural contingency theory is used at the level of the whole organization, but it can also be used at lower organizational levels, such as sub-units and individual jobs.

Structural contingency theory is positivist (q.v.), in the sense that it offers a general theoretical explanation that applies to organizations across different industries and countries. It is also positivist in the sense that a consciously scientific style of methodology is often used to study it, featuring comparative methods [*realism*]. Moreover, many of the contingency factors are material factors: for example, size is the number of members, rather than ideational factors (see Donaldson, 1996).

Prospects

Some structural contingency theorists hold that there are few fits ('configurations' or 'gestalts'), while others dispute this and hold that there are many fits, in a continuous fit line.

Traditionally, a fit (between one level of the structural and contingency variables) and another fit (between some other level of the structural and contingency variables) have been held to produce the *same* (highest) performance; this view is called iso-performance. However, this provides no incentive for an organization to move from one fit at another, so it has been suggested that fits at higher levels of the contingency produce higher performance than fits at lower levels; this view is called hetero-performance.

There have been various criticisms of structural contingency theory, including that it is too complex, static and deterministic, but rebuttals have been offered. In particular, a contingency theory of structural change, termed Structural Adaptation to Regain Fit (SARFIT), has been articulated: change in the contingency leads to misfit, which lowers performance, leading to adoption of a better-fitting structure that improves performance.

Empirical support exists in the literature for structural contingency theory, but not all studies produce the expected results. Identifying fits and validating their effects on performance constitute part of the future research agenda.

Lex Donaldson

CONVERSATION ANALYSIS

Definition

Conversation analysis is grounded within an ethnomethodological (q.v.) tradition, which focuses on how people work together to order and make sense of their world. Garfinkel's *Studies in Ethnomethodology* (1967/1984) first drew attention to the notion that we rely on a range of shared basic conversational rules, expressions and practices, *ethnomethods*, to create coherence and understanding. We are implicitly knowledgeable about these linguistic practices, and use them in taken-for-granted, unconscious, routine and improvisational ways (i.e. *indexicality*) to make our actions rationally accountable to others. Conversation analysis draws on ethnomethodology to offer one way of studying how people make sense of their ongoing experiences in 'talk-in-interaction' [*field research; narrative research; storytelling in management research*].

Discussion

The work of Sacks (e.g. 1992; Sacks et al., 1974) has been particularly influential. Sacks differentiates between context-free and context-sensitive elements of conversation. The former suggests conversations can be carried out anywhere and by anyone because there are general understandings about how to speak and interact. We know, for example, that conversations involve taking turns speaking and that generally participants pay attention and respond to what has gone before. Yet conversations are also context-sensitive in that issues are understood within particular contexts. Within the field of management and organization studies, conversation analysis has been used to study how talk mediates organizational phenomena such as structure, authority and group relations, identity, managing change, emotion (q.v.) (e.g. Cooren, 2004; Ford and Ford, 1995; Samra-Fredericks, 2004; Tulin, 1997) [*ordinary language philosophy; rhetoric*].

Conversation analysis assumes everyday conversations carry expectations and 'rules' about how exchanges will occur and how one speaker orients their talk to another (Boden, 1994; Hutchby and Wooffitt, 1997; Silverman, 1993). Although participants may order their world in unconscious ways, meanings can be made visible to the researcher through an analysis of the exchanges and patterns occurring in talk [*interpretative phenomenological analysis; psychoanalytic approaches*]. The analysis does not incorporate the use of theoretical constructs, but rather 'common sense' or mundane reasoning. Data collection incorporates the recording of naturally occurring conversations in particular settings, such as meetings, interviews (e.g. performance evaluations), and work group or manager–employee discussions. The conversation is transcribed using transcription conventions and symbols, for example [represents, an interruption, (1) elapsed time of silence/overlap of utterances. An initial overview of the setting and normalized meanings may be given, followed by a fine-grained, detailed analysis of the ways in which participants achieve meaning, using a number of conversational cues and practices. These include:

- the sequential organization of talk – where words are placed,
- turn-taking – who speaks first, who speaks in response to whom,
- assessment – expressing an opinion,
- adjacency pairs – taking up the last comment (e.g. question and answer),
- whether statements are confirmed or challenged – interpreting and responding to the previous statement,
- pauses, gaps, and the choice of words (e.g. the use of pronouns).

The analyst will then examine the relationship between these practices and the issue under study.

Prospects

Conversation analsysis has come under critique, for example in relation to its micro-focus, the analyst's knowledge of the particular setting, and a lack of accounting for it's own reflexivity. See Lynch (1993) for a critique.

Ann L. Cunliffe

CRITICAL INCIDENT TECHNIQUE

Definition

Critical incident technique was devised by Flanagan (1954) for describing a set of procedures to collect evidence through direct observation of human behaviours with the purpose of facilitating their potential usefulness in solving practical problems [*action research; action science; pragmatism*]. Since Flanagan, the technique has been applied in various settings in social science and developed by a number of authors, notably Andersson and Nilsson (1964) and Ronan and Latham (1974). Classically understood, the method involved identifying: (a) a system of interest and its components (and related wider systems in which these are embedded); (b) the aim of the activity under investigation against which the efficacy of planned behaviours can be tested, along with the respective criticality of these aims; (c) the conditions, actions, people and places of which events are made up, concentrating on those events that make a difference to the aim (i.e. critical); (d) group incidents in categories of specific problem types (similar structures, magnitudes, and frequencies). The objective was to identify gaps in practical understanding. Chell (1998: 56) provides the following description:

> The critical incident technique is a qualitative interview procedure which facilitates the investigation of significant occurrences (events, incidents, processes, or issues) identified by the respondent, the way they are managed, and the outcomes in terms of perceived effects. The objective is to gain understanding of the incident from the perspective of the individual, taking into account cognitive, affective, and behavioural elements.

Discussion

Bitner et al. (1990), major catalysts for the use of the method in management research, defined an incident as an observable human activity that is complete enough to allow inferences and predictions to be made about the person performing the act. A critical incident is described as one that makes a significant contribution, either positively or negatively, to an activity or phenomenon (Bitner et al., 1990). Its most prominent use in management research is within the service research literature (Edvardsson and Roos, 2001; Gremler, 2004). It has also been used in entrepreneurial marketing (Stokes, 2000) and the wider learning domain (Burgoyne and Hodgson, 1983; Curran et al., 1993). In a more broad sense, much of the literature on organizational learning and knowledge management makes explicit or implicit reference to the technique as a means of recognizing the significance of critical events in shaping organizational activities such as strategy

(Chia and Holt, 2006) or learning (Gherardi, 2000).

Critical incidents can be accounted for using a variety of methods: (a) traditional interviews, (b) focus-group interviews (q.v.), (c) direct or participant observation (q.v.), and (d) questionnaires. Edvardsson (1992), for instance, used a model as an interview guide to investigate critical incidents in a study of customer relationships in an airline. Stokes (2000) and Wong and Sohal (2003) used focus groups, interviewing with a view to understanding entrepreneurial marketing and customers' perceptions respectively. Johnston (1995) used questionnaires to collect data followed up by focus-group interviews so to better understand the reported incidents [focus groups; interviews].

Within the field of entrepreneurship, Chell (1998), echoing Flanagan's approach, has described a fairly structured process for identifying critical incidents where the participants are asked to select three incidents at the beginning of the interview – two 'positive' incidents and one 'negative'. Chell's aim is to capture the thoughts, processes, feelings and frames of reference that are both 'memorable' and 'meaningful' to the participants. Cope and Watts (2000) focus on the learning and personal development experienced by entrepreneurs. Within a case study (q.v.) research strategy, they use relatively unstructured interviews to find out 'the best and worst' times that the participants experienced during their time in the business. The emphasis is on self-criticality because not only are the events under discussion distinct (the sequence of happenings, purposive frames, rules and objects encountered are organized within an acceptable narrative), but they are also personally authored (they have been experienced by the participants). Here Flanagan's detached observer looking to define behavioural laws gives way to a more involved researcher who, in attempting to elicit the definitive elements of the participants' thought and action, accepts an active role in encouraging conscious and consistent efforts to view the subject matter from different angles.

Prospects

There are a number of benefits associated with the use of the technique. First, data are collected from the respondents' perspective based entirely on his/her own words. The method therefore offers a rich source of information by allowing respondents to identify incidents that are most relevant or meaningful to them. Second, the technique is an inductive method which can provide the researcher with rich data upon which hypotheses may be formulated, patterns may emerge, and concepts and theories may be generated. Third, mainly due to the technique's flexibility – a lack of a rigid set of rules to follow – the researcher can modify or alter its structure in order to meet the requirements of the topic being studied. Furthermore, the technique has relevance since it provides unambiguous and concrete information for management teams that could suggest practical areas for improvement (Davis, 2006).

There are also a number of disadvantages associated with its use. First, it has been criticized on issues of reliability and validity (Chell, 1998). More specifically, respondent stories reported in incidents can be misinterpreted or even misunderstood by the researcher. Second, participants' memory may play an important role in determining which incidents are worth reporting and which ones should be left out. The researcher is solely relying on reconstructions of events that took place some time in the past and therefore may not be representative of the feelings and thoughts prevalent at the time. Third, data collection relies on respondents providing detailed descriptions of what they consider to be critical. One implication of this is that respondents may not be accustomed to, or willing, to tell (or write) a complete story when describing a critical event [diaries; storytelling in management research]. Particularly in questionnaire-based research, instances of low response rate and/or insufficient data are likely to occur chiefly because the respondents did not dedicate the necessary time and effort to describe their experiences fully.

Panagiotis Kokkalis

CRITICAL REALISM

Definition

Much of the history of management research, and debates about its methodology, can be described as 'positivism versus the rest' (Burrell and Morgan, 1979; Easterby-Smith et al., 1991/2002) [contingency theory; phronetic organizational research; positivism and post-positivism; structuration theory]. This debate is often, and unhelpfully, subsumed as the quantitative versus qualitative research methods argument.

Positivism (Popper, 1968) is taken to be the pursuit of understanding of the principles governing the behaviour of a real world, based on forming theories (induction) from data and testing them against it (deduction).

'The rest' is some form of social constructionism (q.v.) (preferred term from sociology, Berger and Luckmann, 1966) or constructivism (q.v.) (preferred term from psychology, Kelly, 1955a, 1955b). These positions take at least some of reality to be created from the meaning we attribute to it. You cannot dissect me and find any evidence that I am a professor – that is a construction of my identity created in a certain social and institution context. Not all reality is out there to be observed. Berger and Luckman, Kelly and people like Freud, who emphasize the meaning-making and subjective side of life, are modest in their claims for subjective reality – there is likely to be a reality out there as well. However some, for example Latour and Woolgar (1979), would want to go the whole way and say that the whole world is nothing but a social construction [actor-network theory].

There are two things that a research approach needs to take a position on – what there is to know (what the world is) and how we can know about it (how the world can be known). Never using short words when longer ones will do, we call these ontology and epistemology. Positivism and construction/iv/ism both take their positions from epistemology – the world can be understood on the basis of the observation of factual data, the world can be understood via the meanings attributed to it and generated within it. The debate appears irresolvable, and certainly seems sterile.

Critical realism (CR, origins in Bhaskar, 1975, 1979a, 1979b; perhaps most accessibly articulated by Sayer,1999) offers a 'third way', which is neither positivist nor construction/iv/ist, but which may be synthesis to the thesis and antithesis of each.

The critical realist position begins by suggesting that it is a mistake to start with an epistemological assertion. We do know that there are certain stabilities in our world (event regularity in CR speak), but these do not always occur (the milk did not get delivered today). If there are event regularities, albeit unstable ones, there is likely to be something behind this. Equally, whatever it is cannot be relied on to be there or to 'work' all the time – it varies with situation and context.

The ontological proposition of CR is that the world is an *open system* with *emergent properties* [*autopoiesis; complexity theory*]. This contrasts with the positivist assumption that the world is a *closed system* – a determinist machine with stable properties – and the (extreme) construction/iv/ist position that the world is nothing but the meaning that we individually and collectively give to it.

Discussion

There are two things about *management* research to which CR is relevant. First, management research is arguably a *design science* rather than an *analytical science* (Van Aken, 2004), and, to a significant extent, a 'mode 2' (q.v.) one (Gibbons et al., 1994 – serving a broader community than just the researchers themselves). Design sciences are like engineering and medicine rather than physics and biology – oriented to producing knowledge relevant to improving the world by some criterion, not just understanding it, and those involved in producing and consuming this 'improvement' are the broader, mode 2, stakeholders in the research in the Collaboration discussion section.

Second, management research is not (just) a social science (a common and very expensive mistake). Management is concerned with the organization (and disorganization) of all that exists – phenomena traditionally mapped by the physical, natural, biological, psychological, social, economic and political sciences. Management is genuinely a post- and multi-disciplinary area.

In practice, CR tells us that the world is not mechanically predictable (and if it was it would not be susceptible to management – the machine would just run on), but what we see and observe (the empirical) is part of the actual (what actually happens) which is a manifestation of the real (what could happen given the underlying powers and mechanisms that exist, and can be activated and have different effects in different contexts).

Management research, on the CR approach, is best seen as understanding what *stimuli* (including specially management actions) have triggered what *processes* and how these are affected by the *context* leading to what *outcomes* (see Pawson and Tilley, 1997, for an elaboration of this in the context of evaluating deliberate programmes of action). The knowledge generated in this way will not enable researchers to give definitive advice to managers, but it will enable helpful advice (like you cannot make an omelette without breaking eggs, and if you want to make an omelette a hot frying pan is useful). According to CR, this is as good as it gets, and CR also explains why – managerial actions always take place in contexts that have not occurred before in exactly the same way, and interact in their influence with other managerial actions being taken at the same time. A growing understanding of the *real* – mechanisms that can work – and how these may *actually* manifest, and with what *effects* in the *context*, is what managers can achieve: a mixture of the 'P' (programmed knowledge) and 'Q' (questioning knowledge) in terms of action learning – the pedagogical approach specifically developed for the challenge on management (Revans, 1983/1998).

What is critical about CR? First, it is critical of knowledge production or use that does not do its best to understand the basic realities of situations. Second, it asserts that there may be both moral and technical truths and that one can be critical of actions that are not taken on the basis of the best possible understanding of these, and evaluated to increase these understandings.

In practice, for management and organization research, this offers us an approach that gets beyond the tired debates between quantitative and qualitative research, and will allow us to use many of our old tools, in terms of methodology, in new ways.

John Burgoyne

CRITICAL THEORY

Definition

Critical theory (CT) refers to an intellectual movement – also known as the Frankfurt School – whose central figures include Max Horkheimer, Theodore Adorno, Herbert Marcuse, Erich Fromm and, of greatest contemporary importance, Jürgen Habermas. It forms a central part of a wider, radical tradition of politically engaged analysis that stands in direct opposition to various forms of leftist and rightist dogma and tyranny. The diversity of CT – in terms of its members' indebtedness to a wide range of critical thinking (e.g. Marx, Freud, Nietzsche) – is connected by a concern to apply elements of sociology, philosophy, psychoanalysis, economics and psychology to critique the necessity, and challenge the basis, of contemporary forms of alienation and oppression.

At the core of CT is a concern to develop more rational, enlightened social relations – from the interpersonal to the international – through a process of critical reflection upon, and transformation of, existing institutions. CT has had a deep and extensive impact upon the development of social science, including the study of management, where it has been a significant contributory influence in the formation of Critical Management Studies (Alvesson and Willmott, 1992). However,

CT's impact upon social science has occurred as a consequence of being imbibed as a deep and refreshing reservoir of ideas rather than as an approach that has been seized upon as a blueprint, or unified standpoint, for conducting research. There are, for this reason, rather few students of management who are devoted advocates or followers of CT but many who have been touched by its far-reaching influence.

Discussion

At least since the Enlightenment, the powers of critical reasoning have been applied to challenge and overturn oppressive institutions, including witchcraft, slavery and, more recently, the patriarchal denial of universal suffrage. In common with other contemporary strands of critical thinking (e.g. Foucauldianism, poststructuralism), CT draws upon this legacy to scrutinize the rationality of contemporary practices, such as the rationality of relentless economic expansion that it feeds upon and magnifies acquisitiveness, divisiveness and destruction. Since management theory and practice are centrally implicated in advancing and legitimizing such developments, they become relevant targets of CT-informed analysis.

In terms of methods, CT is pluralist. It can accommodate almost any method of data collection and analysis, whether quantitative or qualitative, so long as it is self-critically applied with respect to its claims to objectivity [reflexivity] and is mindful of the human purpose of knowledge production with respect to its emancipatory and/or enslaving conditions and consequences. The orientation of CT to methodology is therefore fundamentally critical and political. Among key and interrelated themes of CT are (i) the critique of positivist science; (ii) the critique of technocracy; (iii) an emphasis upon communicative action; and (iv) the critique of one-dimensionality and consumerism.

The critique of positivist science
A rosy view of science, pictured as the benevolent agent of enlightenment, was forcefully

challenged by Horkheimer and Adorno (1947) in *The Dialectics of Enlightenment*, where they argued that modern civilization has become progressively mesmerized by a one-sided, means–ends (instrumental) conception of reason. Whenever the connection of scientific knowledge to an interest in emancipation is lost or taken for granted, science becomes an ideology that operates as a force of domination – for example, in the ruthless exploitation of scarce natural resources and in the pursuit of scientific knowledge for dehumanizing and destructive purposes. It is not difficult to see how a positivist conception of 'objective knowledge' has filtered into the field of management through processes of quantification and the development of seemingly impartial means of legitimizing instrumental rationalizations – from scientific management [*modernism and scientific management; Taylorism*] through human relations to business process reengineering.

The critique of technocracy

Technocracy is distinguished by its denial of the role of moral–practical concerns in processes of social development such that the ends of human existence are assumed to be self-evident or to be beyond rational debate. In the (technocratic) selection of means, decision-making is deemed to be the province of experts (technocrats) who, because they are considered to be most knowledgeable or best informed, are assigned responsibility for identifying the most efficient and/or effective way of achieving given ends. The absence of industrial democracy and the associated formation of managerial elites unaccountable to subordinates are symptomatic of technocracy – whether capitalist or socialist in inspiration. Technocratic consciousness is criticized because it fails to acknowledge that, far from being value-free or neutral, it is constitutive of a particular kind of social order, in which non-experts are effectively disenfranchised, there is no debate about ends, and experts determine the means. To counter the tendency for (bourgeois) democracy to degenerate and drift towards technocracy, Habermas stresses the importance of distinguishing *communicative* rationality, which exposes and removes restrictions upon communication (see next section), from *instrumental* rationality which serves solely to develop and strengthen (technocratic) systems of purposive-rational action.

An e]mphasis upon communicative action

Habermas contends that all communication, including that which facilitates instrumental rationality, depends upon a structure of understandings (e.g. the understanding that utterances will be truthful which can nonetheless be doubted in the process of communication) that enables processes of dialogue through which it is possible to reach a rational consensus. Habermas understands this 'universal pragmatics' to be a condition of communication; and that its practical realization is anticipated by its embeddedness in the very structure of language [*ordinary language philosophy*]. In so far as it is only imperfectly fulfilled, the frustrations and sufferings, manifest as communicative distortions which accompany its partial realization, are conceived to operate as recurrent and potent sources of motivation for emancipatory change. The contemporary emergence of social movements (e.g. anti-globalization, ecology, peace, animal rights, etc.) outside of formally democratic institutions is illustrative of the questioning of received wisdom and standardized patterns of behaviour. Such movements are celebrated as manifestations of a vibrant lifeworld of face-to-face interaction where, despite the pacifying effects of the mass media and pressures to accept received wisdoms, individuals advance and articulate a capacity for critical reflection and self-determination. Conversely, if the spurs to emancipatory transformation are unheeded, domesticated or suppressed, the prospect is for ethics and democracy to be progressively weakened and eventually to 'disappear behind the interest in the expansion of our power of technical control' (Habermas, 1971: 113).

The critique of one-dimensionality and consumerism

The term 'one-dimensional man' was coined by Marcuse (1964) to highlight how the organization of advanced capitalist societies frustrates or deflects the emancipatory impulses of oppositional movements – for example, through forms of 'repressive tolerance'. In affluent societies, Marcuse argues, people are enjoined to become passive, unreflective consumers who, even as we are encouraged to pursue/consume our 'careers', to buy premium 'green' products from WalMart and Tesco and to watch the melting of the icecaps on TV, struggle to imagine forms of life that differ from the present. Instead of being applied to facilitate radical, qualitative improvements in the lives of people across the planet, human development is seen to be driven primarily by the logic – or illogic – of consumer capitalism that, in the name of increased satisfaction, spreads waste, destructiveness and avoidable misery.

Prospects

CT comprises a weighty and exceptionally broad set of intellectual resources for critiquing received wisdom and inspiring emancipatory action. It is not, however, without its limitations. Notably, radical feminism (q.v.) draws attention to a major blind spot in CT: the key importance of patriarchy as a source of domination. Another related limitation is an emphasis upon cognitive (q.v.) processes to the neglect of embodiment. Both criticisms connect to a widely rehearsed complaint that CT is excessively 'intellectual', making inadequate connections with local and mundane processes of emancipatory praxis. A person may become well versed in the theory of communicative action, for example, but this may exert little influence upon his or her day-to-day conduct. A further criticism is that CT's advocacy of reflexivity does not extend to radical critical reflection upon the basis of its own (foundationalist) assumption of universal pragmatics. Finally, CT's neglect of management in its key texts and studies – despite the centrality of management for 'modernization' and the

contemporary efforts to extend and contain 'globalization' – is perhaps symptomatic of the potent, yet limited, nature of CT's engagement with day-to-day, practical processes of collective self-(trans)formation.

Hugh Willmott

CROSS-CULTURAL RESEARCH

Definition

Cross-cultural (sometimes called cross-national) research occurs when researchers set out to examine phenomena in two or more countries (or regions) with the intention of comparing their manifestations in different socio-cultural settings, whatever they might be. They could include institutions, customs, traditions, value systems, lifestyles or language. When conducting cross-cultural research, Usunier (1998) distinguishes between those comparing national and local customs from those focusing on the interaction of such cultures.

One important difficulty that lies at the heart of any cross-cultural study is the definition of culture itself. In the first instance, it should be made clear that though they can coincide, culture and nationality are not the same thing; all nations comprise subcultures and pan-national identities associated with geography or religion also complicate any simple ascription of nation with culture. While there is no single, all-embracing definition, Margaret Mead (1951: 12); suggested a culture to be 'a body of learned behaviour, a collection of beliefs, habits and traditions, shared by a group of people and successively learned by people who enter the society'. From a business and management perspective, perhaps the most widely quoted definition is Hofstede's (1984: 21): 'the collective programming of the mind that distinguishes the members of one human group from another'.

From these definitions it follows that culture (Mead, 2005: 8): includes systems of values; is particular to one group and not others; is learnt and is not innate – it is passed down from one generation to the next; and influences the behaviour of group members in uniform and predictable ways.

Culture, it can be argued, is more than just a mental programme. It also includes behavioural aspects of people and the artefacts they produce. Thus, activities that people are not programmed to do, do nevertheless occur, such as waiting in traffic jams (Harris, 1993).

Discussion

From a management perspective, the research interest normally focuses on the appropriateness or adaptability of a managerial theory or model, developed in one cultural setting, to another cultural setting (e.g. transferring the lean production techniques of Japanese automotive manufacturers to American and European settings). More critically, cross-cultural studies investigate how the conjunction of different cultures can create exploitative conditions as one set of interests prevails over others [*critical theory; post-colonial theory*].

To date, understanding cultural influences in organizational life has been presented in the form of models. Those of significance include: Hofstede's model, Hall's model and the Kluckhohn–Strodtbeck model.

Hofstede's model

Despite its flaws, perhaps the most influential model used in management and business cross-cultural research is that of the sociologist, Geert Hofstede (2001). The major benefits of Hofstede's (and Bond's, 1988) work are that it is based on quantitative data (providing the suggestion, at least, of scientific rigour) and that it compares a wide range of countries using a series of five dimensions. The dimensions are:

1. Power distance: the distance between individuals at different levels of a hierarchy.
2. Uncertainty avoidance: more or less the need to avoid uncertainty about the future.

3. Individualism versus collectivism: the relations between individuals and their fellows.
4. Masculinity versus femininity: the division of roles and values in society.
5. Long-term versus short-term orientation: temporal orientation towards life.

Bearing in mind the influential nature of Hofstede's model, it is worth noting that its validity is questionable. The findings were based on a large data set of the value orientations of IBM staff in different countries. There are several concerns with the Hofstede model that should be borne in mind if it is being used:

- The model assumes national territories and national cultures correspond.
- Some of the dimensions overlap and, even, paraphrase one another.
- The research itself is 'culture bound'. Thus the results reflect the methodology employed, and hence the cultural biases of the researchers.
- The research is out of date (e.g. Yugoslavia no longer exists).
- Hofstede's sample worked in one industry for one multinational. IBM employees are unlikely to be typical of their countries and certain social classes (unskilled manual, for instance) will have been excluded altogether.

Hall's model

Edward Hall was an anthropologist whose main contributions to intercultural research were the concepts of proxemics (1959) and contexts (1976). His main concern was communication between people of differing cultures. In particular, the notion that cultures can be high-context or low-context in character has been particularly influential.

For Hall, high-context cultures depend on heavily shared experiences and the interpretation of cultural environments. Communication in these cultures is through covert clues, and the ability to interpret non-verbal signals and indirect allusions is valued. Meanwhile, low-context cultures are less concerned with the environment and more concerned with direct, verbal communication and explicit information.

Hall's model was built on qualitative insights. Its main value lies in seeking to provide an understanding as to why people from different cultures behave and communicate in the way they do.

The Kluckhohn–Strodtbeck model

Kluckhohn and Strodtbeck (1961) were also anthropologists who designed a highly influential comparative model. Their model was predicated on the notion that members of cultural groups exhibited constant 'orientations' towards the world and other people. It followed that, on the basis of these different orientations, one culture could be compared with another. The orientations were:

- What is the nature of people?
- What is the person's relationship to nature?
- What is the person's relationship to other people?
- What is the modality of human activity?
- What is the temporal focus of human activity?
- What is the conception of space?

The main problem with the model was that it was based only on anecdotal evidence and therefore is only very subjective. Perhaps its most important influence was to view culture as a series of dimensions that could, in some way, be measured.

Prospects

Cross-cultural research is not without a number of problems, both practical and methodological in nature. From a practical perspective, such studies usually involve considerable funding which can be difficult to secure. An alternative is to use secondary data (such as that employed by Hofstede). However, this leads to problems in ensuring that the data are comparable in terms of categories and data collection methods.

Where new data are being collected, a chief concern lies in the translation of the data collection instrument (e.g. questionnaire or interview schedule) so as not to undermine genuine comparability [*reliability*]. In international circumstances, the many problems of question design become even more problematic due to both the translation of the words used and also the meaning invoked by those words. This is because the instrument itself may be insensitive to specific national and cultural contexts.

Cross-cultural research creates particular issues in achieving equivalence between the samples, variables and methods to be used. For example, nationality is frequently used as a proxy for culture. Differences are thus attributed to culture where they could, more readily, be attributed to the national situation. Equally, people inhabiting a country under the same government may belong to quite different cultures that reflect historical or religious affiliations [*social constructionism*]. Further issues are raised by language differences.

Finally, there is a danger of falling into the trap of undertaking what Osland and Bird (2000) call 'sophisticated stereotyping' – using the comparative models to stereotype entire cultures and allow easy analysis, despite the numerous paradoxes that arise.

Mark Hall

D

DECONSTRUCTION

Definition

The notion of deconstruction was developed by French poststructuralist philosopher Jacques Derrida during the 1970s in a series of books (Derrida 1976, 1978/2001, among others) that explore how we understand written text. Deconstruction begins from the premise that language has no fixed meaning [*ordinary language philosophy; phenomenology*]. This means that we cannot assume we know what words mean, either to ourselves or anyone else. Instead, Derrida argues, we should acknowledge written language (and therefore attempts to communicate through it) as continuous processes or struggles that are never finally closed or clear in their meaning. If we accept this argument, then we must see texts as unstable and open to infinite interpretation [*metaphor; semiotics*]. Derrida goes on to argue that the meaning of words is always constructed with reference to what they do not mean – so we understand what 'day' means by referring to what it does not mean and in particular what any opposed terms (such as 'night') imply. Meaning can only be deferred through the process of establishing temporary *différance*, a term Derrida created to emphasize that meaning is produced by the difference between words and by deferring to other unstable meanings [*relativism*]. Further implications of a deconstructive approach to texts are: that context is central to meaning, therefore if the context of a word is changed, then its meaning is also changed; and that deconstructive readings will inevitably expose what a text excludes as much as what it includes. Derrida's work is generally acknowledged as exceptionally difficult, dense and resistant to authoritative interpretation (Cooper, 1989). This is perhaps appropriate, given the ideas that he developed in his work.

Discussion

Scholars have taken two approaches to deconstruction in management research. The first involves reading texts produced within organizations to establish what they emphasize and therefore also seek to exclude. Learmonth (1999) takes a short segment of text (134 words) from a paper written by a chief executive on the subject of structural change. Learmonth's analysis explores the unintended messages the text carries and questions our taken-for-granted ways of making sense of descriptions of management. The analysis suggests that the chief executive intended to prioritize reason in the change process, but in so doing he also acknowledges the emotion that will pervade the restructuring [*emotion research*]. Deconstruction is most often practised on literary texts; however, it can also be practised on the many symbols and artefacts found in organizations. Bell et al. (2002) take the symbols that are awarded to organizations that conform to quality management systems as their organizational text. They suggest that deconstruction is inevitable with organizational badges such as ISO certification, as employees' readings of symbols or texts will often challenge the dominant meaning promoted by managers [*aesthetics*]. This form of deconstructive analysis also emphasizes that apparently banal texts that have superficially obvious meanings can be analyzed in depth and provide useful insights into the concepts that lie behind managerial activity (Learmonth, 1999).

The second approach to deconstruction in management research builds on Cooper's (1989) suggestion that the method provides the means to open up our understanding of how we write organizational analysis [*representations*]. For example, Kilduff (1993) provides a deconstructive reading of a classic management theory text to support his argument that employees continue to be portrayed as machine-like, even in analyses that claim to challenge such a depiction. Readings such as this are intended to challenge and change how management research texts are presented to students and emphasize the potential within deconstruction for practical action, by directing attention to 'the importance of texts in constituting reality' (Kilduff and Kelemen, 2001: S57).

Whether organizational texts or management research texts are taken as the object of analysis, it is important to 'keep in mind, however, that in deconstructing these texts, the goal is not to destroy or demolish them but to (a) explore how certain themes and notions are at the centre of the text, and (b) how these themes are employed to systematically exclude or inhibit other themes or categories' (Prasad, P., 2005: 241).

Prospects

Analysis through deconstruction has not been adopted very often in management research; it has certainly proved less popular than other poststructuralist approaches, such as Foucauldian analysis (Prasad, P., 2005). Cooper (1989) suggests that this lack of engagement is because of the challenge that deconstruction presents to the producers of management research. If deconstruction is pursued to its logical end and applied to the analytical texts generated within business schools then the authority of academics and the reality of the knowledge they produce must both be questioned. As deconstruction involves the recognition that managers should not be seen as 'authoritative interpreters' of organizational activities or texts (Bittner, 1965), so it also implies that academic analysis cannot provide authoritative interpretations either. Clegg et al. (2005) argue that this loss of authority should be embraced rather than feared, and that deconstruction can be a political act that opens up space for new meanings and engagement with management instead of authoritative critique of managerial practice [*relativism*]. Echoing Kilduff (1993), these authors also note that education is an ideal context in which to attempt to do this, bringing the perhaps esoteric notion of deconstruction into close contact with current and future managerial practice.

Scott Taylor

DELPHI METHOD

Definition

We owe the existence of the Delphi method to Cold War confrontations that provoked a need to forecast future technological capabilities that might be of military relevance. At the end of the 1940s the United States Air Force launched what became the RAND Corporation to foresee technology trends in order to develop its military capabilities. What emerged was a systematic and interactive forecasting approach known as Delphi because of its consulting independent selected experts.

The initial problem for RAND researchers was the sheer complexity of what might evolve, when and how. It offered no grip for standard probabilistic forecasting based on mathematical modelling and random statistical sampling. The alternative was to consult a limited group of known experts, but this encountered problems of personal bias and undue influence from dominant personalities. The answer was to spread the involvement of experts, canvassing opinions of different kinds, with different perspectives on technology and technology uses.

Discussion

Linstone and Turoff (1975) define Delphi as a method for structuring group communication processes in order to deal with complex problems. Through this perspective, the Delphi method acts as a formal intervention to integrate knowledge through structured communications that utilize the diverse and subjective judgements, opinions, experiences and intuitions of participants. In the context of forecasting exercises, the Delphi method provides a means for collecting and synthesizing expert conjectures about the future without foreclosing alternate views.

Although the implementation of the Delphi method varies in different research projects, they share some basic principles:

- It is a repetitive process. The same experts are asked the same questions at least two times. Feedback on the previous round is provided in order to enable experts to change their estimations.
- It is a structured process. The information flow is co-ordinated by researchers. There is no direct information flow among experts.
- The experts give estimations, judgements or opinions.
- The anonymity of experts is maintained throughout the process.
- The survey is designed to enable the statistical presentation of final results.

Although these principles link the Delphi method to quantitative research, its process involves many qualitative aspects, especially the so-called unstructured 'zero round' of the survey (Tichy, 2004) [*mixed methods in management research*]. In this case an open-ended questionnaire is sent to experts in order to develop statements or hypotheses using a bottom-up approach, meaning the selected experts actively participate in the statement or hypothesis development. Workshops can also be involved. In the Pan-European Delphi study concerning the future of European manufacturing (Manufacturing Visions, 2005), 22 such workshops were organized around Europe. In these workshops smaller groups of experts discussed the proposed statements, suggested modifications and the exclusion of statements, and developed new ones. This shows how participating experts are actively involved in the codification of knowledge in order to develop shared cognitive structures that facilitate the structured process of knowledge flows [*cognitive mapping; composite mapping*].

The next stage in which qualitative data complement the Delphi survey is in the second round. At this stage experts receive the same questionnaire, but this time accompanied with the statistical results of the previous round. The statistical results inform experts about the mean value of what other experts think, but do not say anything about *why* they think that way. The second Delphi round, therefore, benefits from additional qualitative information, that better explains the mean value of the results in the previous round. This is especially true if the first round leads to dispute and contradictions. For example, in the already mentioned Manufacturing Visions Delphi forecast, the second round was exclusively designed around contradictions that emerged in the first round. The experts were informed about the contradictions that resulted from different assessments of particular statements. In the second round these statements were juxtaposed and short explanations of why current assessments had led to contradictions were provided. Experts could than change their initial estimation, resolve the contradiction and develop a consensus, retain their existing opinions, or even come up with still contradictory alternatives. Advances in information technology also offer promise for the better capture of such qualitative data. Gordon and Pease (2006), for example, report the use of real time data capture and exchange using web-based IT systems that enabled participating experts to consult one anothers' views without researchers having to translate back and forth.

Prospects

Typically, in social science Delphi methods have been for technological forecasting which in turn is used to support national research policy. The increasing complexity of the relations between technological progress and competitive, social and environmental consequences implies that governments are forced to make choices under uncertainty and in this context experts are increasingly requested to bring knowledge and legitimacy to policy decisions (for example, Blind et al., 2001; Kameoka et al., 2004; Munier and Ronde, 2001; Shin, 1998). In the field of management, the Delphi method has been rarely used. The fall of strategic planning instigated a demise in the in-house use of the Delphi method for strategy formulation. It is also not surprising that as a method unfitted to theory testing, it has not found its way into mainstream management research. Some research attempts, however, hint at interesting applications. Scott (2000) used a Delphi method to identify important technology management issues in new product development, Harland et al. (1999) adopted it to identify enablers and barriers to supply chain management, and MacCarthy and Atthirawong (2003) used it to focus on factors influencing international locations decisions. All these researchers shared a common interest, realizing findings of practical relevance, and adopted the Delphi method because of its explicit use of industry experts able to identify problems, solutions and challenges that were of a 'live' and economically relevant nature.

Krsto Pandza

DIALECTIC

Definition

Dialectic is often defined as the *triad (or triplicity) of thesis, antithesis and synthesis*, and then attributed to Hegel or Marx. Actually, Friedrich von Schelling came up with the cycle, where each synthesis begins a thesis, which repeats the cycle until some absolute change is reached. Hegel and Marx were not as mechanistic about it. Still, the Schelling model is a place to start. A thesis (idea or historical movement) inevitably generates its opposite, and antithesis, and as they interact, a new synthesis (idea or movement) emerges. Thesis is an idea or historical movement that contains inherent contradictions in its structure, and there creates the opposite, an antithesis (an opposed idea or movement).[1] This conflict of thesis with antithesis results in a period of conflict between the two until a synthesis emerges out of the conflict. The triad is called *progressive* because each subsequent cycle of thesis, antithesis and synthesis is seen as an advance over the prior one. The cycle continues as the synthesis discovers its internal contradictions.

Discussion

Carr (2000a: 214–216) gives four reasons why thesis–antithesis–synthesis (triad) is a gross oversimplification of dialectic [*activity theory*].

First, every presentation of two sides of the story is not a dialectical argument. Rather, the point of dialectic logic and thinking is to break out of the coercive and hegemonic aspects of the logic itself. Neither is juxtaposing point and counterpoint (reality and myth) dialectic, which is just another form of dualism.

Second, synthesis is not the same thing as compromise or taking the middle road. For a dialectic argument one has to go beyond thesis and antithesis to look at the important connection (interplay between) that constructs

---

[1] In Sartre, it is the paradox of the thesis 'is what it is not' (its 'other') and 'is not what it is.'

the new working reality, synthesis. 'The frame of references which made the poles opposites in the first case is transcended' (Carr, 2000a: 215).

Third, thesis and antithesis as a contradiction are not dialectic if they do not move beyond the oppositional (dualistic) thinking of most western thought. Carr notes the reversal of oppositions, and then the look to the hierarchical relationship of two arguments. This, I would add is precisely the step taken in deconstructing binary oppositions (Boje, 2001: 18–34). Reversal serves to unlock hidden logics [*process philosophy*].

Fourth, dialectics is often called a form of negative thinking or negative discourse that does not result in real change. Yet the very purpose is liberatory, to go beyond hegemonic logics that have people stuck in a rut; and the point is changing the rules of the game.

How dialectical approaches might be used depends very much on the vein in which they are taken. As already suggested, there are different concepts of dialectic to which different potential appends. By way of introduction, the figurative versions include the following.

Before Hegel

Before Hegel, Socrates used dialogue as a method of question and answer in cross-examination, to surface another's assertions. Nigel Laurie contemporalizes:

> Today Socratic Dialogue is practised by non-philosophers in many parts of the world, especially in Europe, Australia and the United States. It has been employed in education and by public and private sector managers and staff to solve problems, create shared knowledge, develop ethical understanding and reach robust decisions. Individuals take part in public dialogues out of a desire to philosophize, to enhance their thinking skills or to develop their ability to communicate with others.[2]

The Financial Times (6 June 1998) says that Socratic Dialogue 'is for the managers to learn what they really believe, not by shouting or pulling rank, but by slowly and rigorously arguing the thing through. Only thus can they reach a durable agreement'. Plato developed dialectic into a logical method to reduce multiple experiences of phenomena to arrive at greater unity of systematic ideas. Aristotle's dialectic is the art of logical discussion.[3] Immanuel Kant developed 'Transcendental Dialectic' (*Critique of Pure Reason*) to expose the illusion of judgements that transcend the limits of experience.

Hegelian dialectic

George Fredrick Hegel (1770–1831) disagreed, rejecting Kant's limits on reason, and asserting the existence of a Spirit that determined the dialectical *progress* of history: 'world history exhibits nothing other than the plan of providence' (Hegel, 1807/1910). Marx (q.v.) and Engels rejected Hegel's romantic thesis that Spirit shapes the universe. Yet, there is much they appreciated. In the Hegelian system, according to Engels:

> for the first time the whole world, natural, historical, intellectual, is represented as a process – i.e., as in constant motion, change, transformation, development; and the attempt is made to trace out the internal connection that makes a continuous whole of all this movement and development. From this point of view, the history of mankind [*sic*] no longer appeared as a wild whirl of senseless deeds of violence, all equally condemnable at the judgment seat of mature philosophic reason and which are best forgotten as quickly as possible, but as the process of evolution of man himself. It was now the task of the intellect to follow the gradual march of this process through all its devious ways, and to trace out the inner law running through all its apparently accidental phenomena. (1880/1970: Ch 2)

Marxian Dialectic

For Marx and Engels, dialect focused on how one consciousness (idea system) was transformed and replaced by another in 'dialectic materialism'. Marx argues that labour is not

---

[2]Message from Nigel Laurie, 12 May 2005; used by permission.
[3]See Aristotle's *Rhetoric*, Book 1, section 1354a, 1; 1355a; 1355b, 20 (Aristotle, 1991).

paid by 'use value' but according to 'exchange value' (or commodity price); labour becomes a commodity. Profit is the difference between what the capitalist pays the worker (other costs) and the products/ services' selling price. This difference is called surplus value. By applying technology (machines), supervision (hierarchy) and the division of labour (specialization), skilled labour becomes deskilled; this can expand surplus value. When more than one machine is run by one man (multi-tasking), downsizing of the labour force occurs. Overproduction is a result which also leads to more downsizing of labour. This deskilling and downsizing demoralizes labour. Technical staff and much of management are also outsourced, in further applications of deskilling (via technology and globalization). As capitalism expands globally, Marx believed people would begin to question the irrationality of producing more than we need (over-consumption) and the deskilling of labour.

Hence while Marx and Engels rejected Hegel's Spirit, they kept the principle of negativity as the motor of human progress in their theory of dialectical materialism. Negativity is an energy (or force) that opposes something to its *other* and self-develops by deposing the character of a movement into its other. Hegel saw the positive aspect of negativity: negativity serves to individuate and determinate by actualizing content (potentiality) by disrupting certainty; negativity transforms the hypothetical into content.

Dialectic Materialism contends that during the Middle Ages an aristocracy of landowners ruled in feudalism (thesis). The aristocracy was eventually opposed by a city-dwelling bourgeoisie merchant class (antithesis). In the conflict, the bourgeoisie became stronger than the aristocrats. Out of the conflict emerged capitalism (synthesis), that becomes a new thesis in the Industrial Revolution; one of the contradictions is the alienation of the working class from ownership of the tools of production. The new thesis (capitalism) becomes opposed by the proletariat workers who are still oppressed by the bourgeoisie. During the ensuing conflict the proletariat rise up and seize the tools of production.

Praxis

Dialectic is also a type of *praxis* (a combination of theory and practice) that would transform institutions (corporations, governments and non-governmental organizational behaviour and management) with a logic that is both synchronic and diachronic [*practice theory*]. 'Synchronic' looks at interrelationships of parts and the whole at one point of time, while a 'diachronic' approach looks at the historical transformations of society and its social concepts.

Frankfurt School

Marxist dialectic was revised by the Frankfurt School of Critical Theory (q.v.) that includes Theodor Adorno, Leo Lowenthal, Walter Benjamin, Max Horkheimer, Franz Newmann, Otto Kirchheimer, Fredrich Pollock, Eric Fromm and Herbert Marcuse. Most had different versions of dialectics. Adorno, for example, in *Negative Dialectics* held that synthesis be ignored. And recently, Habermas and Analytic Marxism (Mayer, 1994) have gone in other directions. The Frankfurt School builds on Hegel's dialectic which 'is transition (in both thought and being) brought about by negativity' (Berthold-Bond, 1993: 81–91). For Marcuse (1993: 445 in), dialectic logic 'invalidates the a priori opposition of value and fact by understanding all facts as stages of a single process – a process in which subject and object are so joined that truth can be determined only within the subject–object totality' [*structuration theory*].

In sum, Socratic, Hegelian, Marxist and Frankfurt School dialectics are quite different from Schelling's thesis–antithesis–synthesis model'.

David M. Boje

DIALOGIC

Definition

It is unfortunate that management research has not proceeded beyond basic approaches to polyphonic dialogism. This is because management studies have taken a narrow view of dialogic as just dialogue: the immediate here-and-now communication between stakeholders. Dialogic is not dialogue (interaction among stakeholders in one time and place). Dialogic is defined as modes of expression (verbal, written, architectural, etc.) that are intertextual answers anticipated across times and places. Dialogic, for example, can be intertextual answers (anticipatory or respondent) to societal (Fairclough, 1992) or environmental discourse (Christensen, 1995) [*discourse analysis; hermeneutics*].

Discussion

The main concern with dialogic in management and organization studies is with Bakhtin's (1929/1973) polyphonic construct, which is a derivative of an orchestration of voices that are fully embodied, with often quite disparate points of view. Monologic denies consciousness outside the narrator's version (Bakhtin, 1929/1973: 292). The challenge to management is to move from monophonic and monologic to polyphonic (many voices) and polylogic (many logics) communicating and organizing. For Bakhtin, this is not about finding/imposing consensus; polyphonic dialogism is letting the disparate logics inform and shape each other.

Hazen (1993, 1994) called for polyphonic organization. Mumby (1994) accused management research texts of being monophonic; he stresses that in polyphonic text each voice is equally valid. Barry and Elmes (1997) challenge management strategy to move from monologic (single-authored) to polyphonic (multiple authorship) strategies where stakeholders meet as equals to craft strategy that is dialogically unfinalized. Barry and Elmes (1997: 442) add: 'strategists adopting this

method would be less focused on promoting their own strategy and more concerned with surfacing, legitimizing, and juxtaposing differing organizational stories'. They give Semler (1993), Boje (1995), and Smircich, Calás, and Morgan (1992a, 1992b) ways to juxtapose dialogically linked views/stories [*social poetics; storytelling in management research*]. Despite these calls, moving from polyphonic to more complex forms of dialogic has been a challenge to management studies. Polyphony becomes used as a metaphor in order to colonize domionant discourse. Palmer and Dunford (1996), for example, focus on ways that authorities stylize dialog by reframing context in order to sustain managerialist influence over business practices. Along this vein, Phillips (1995: 628–629) explores examples of how a dominant character in a text can bring in another point of view without the sense of closure of an omnipotent author [*deconstruction*]. Payne and Carlton (2002) apply dialogic to stakeholder theory using a polyphonic approach. The challenge in dialogic research is to move from theories of one (stakeholder) consciousness (be it omniscient narrator or research) reading to direct enactment of various other consciousnesses.

Bate (1997, 2000) picks up Hazen's call for 'polyphonic organization' in a study of change in a hospital, from hierarchy to networked community. Methodologically, he does not study the way the voices (heard) are dialogically dynamically intertextual *in situ* to one another. Instead, Bate collects a plurality of subculture voices, and culls out *emotion* (q.v.) *schemas* within the narratives/stories he collects. Barry and Elmes (1997) argue that strategic narratives are moving from monophonic to polyphonic. Just how this is done remains a management research challenge. For example, Ng and de Cock (2002) argue that they do not want to give a polyphonic interpretation to collected boardroom (strategic) narratives, since it would compromise the story they (as researchers) prefer to tell. This seems to replace one hegemony with another. One possibility is suggested by Roth and Kleiner (1998), who view Van Maanen's 'jointly-told tale' as polyphonic fieldwork, 'sharing authorship' and giving 'equal validity' to two (or more) meaning systems [*rhetoric*].

Oswick et al. (2000) looked at how a team player developed consensus around a univocal narrative in a hegemonic exercise of power. More accurately, it was not only monologic but homologic. A homophonic text is one where 'all aspects of plot, dialogue and characterization are subordinated to the monologic will of the author' (Gardiner, 1992: 27).

In sum, polyphonic studies are finding that stakeholder dialogues are hegemonic, and polyphony is applied metaphorically without attention to equal rights of participation.

Prospects

Besides polyphony, Bakhtin imagined several other types which have yet to be researched in management.

Stylistic dialogic

Defined as when different stylistic modes are juxtaposed in ways that are dialogically intertextual. Bakhtin (1981: 262) provides five stylistic modes:

1. Artistic style – that comes from the voice of a narrator (examples: storied bits from a CEO letter to shareholders).
2. Skaz – taking a fragment of someone else's everyday narration, and narrating another narrator's intention (e.g. a corporate one) through it (examples: Coca-Cola's 'I'm lovin' it', or Nike's 'Just Do It!).
3. Everyday narration (example: a letter, a diary, a report) [*content analysis; diaries*].
4. Scientific, non-artistic narration (examples: a scientific statement, a chart of numbers from an account, an ethnographic description, or a philosophical treatise).
5. Characters and speech acts of individuals or organizations coupled to official narrations.

Here is the challenge: if one can read the five styles and step back to see how the modes interact.

Chronotopic dialogic

Chronos means 'time', and a chronotope is defined as the interaction of time and space. As the definition implies, it is Bakhtin's (1981) way of paying homage to Einstein's theory of relativity. Chronotopicity is the study of the hierarchy of narrative over event, how events are constructed, and how they are temporally and spatially relativized in various chronotopic choices. Barry and Elmes incorporate two of Bakhtin's chronotopes (Greek romance adventure and chivalric romance adventure) into their typology. There are ten ways to conceptualize time/space in Bakhtin (1929/1973, 1981): four adventure chronotopes (romantic, chivalric, everyday and autobiographical) and five folkloric types of chronotopes (clown–rogue–fool, reversal of here-and-now time/space, Rabelaisian, grotesque and idyllic); plus a tenth chronotope called 'Castle', a special living room where dialogues become important because the character's passionate ideas are revealed, and a key idea is the omnipresent power of a new owner of life: 'money'.

Discursive dialogic

A discursive type of dialogic is defined as multiple discourses that interanimate one another. Bakhtin (1990) began to study this problem, which he called 'architectonics', in his earliest published writings. There are four adventure chronotopes and five folkloric types of chronotope. A tenth chronotope is called the Castle. There are few discursing dialogic studies. Boje (1995) developed a language-based discursive model of organization where Disney people are treated as 'discursing beings' in Tamara-land. Disney, for example, is analyzed as a managerialist group wielding its power by reading context as if it were one story with one perspective (management's). In a dialogic Disney, there is a diversity of counter-official stories and perspective, negotiating a *Tamara* of stories in ongoing dialogues among various subcultures. Disney is replete with dissensus, not consensus. Christensen (1995: 600–661) emphasizes that 'any utterance is in dialog with prior dialogue' so that, as Bakhtin's work suggests, the discourse of the general culture is intertextual related to the dialogue within a organization.

Kenneth Boulding (1956) saw that an open system with its information processing (input–sender–feedback loop) was not very high up on the scale of system complexity (he gave it a 4). Each time you move higher up, you get into Bakhtin's territory, into languages, symbols, and into multi-brained systems. As management research moves from polyphonic studies of people or subcultures in dialogue to stylistic, chronotopic and discursive dialogics, we approach Boulding's higher orders of system complexity. The highest level is to look at the dialogism of these four types of dialogic. Management studies can begin to attend to stylistic modes of dialogic communication, to the polytemporality and polyspatiality of chronotopoic dialogism, and to the discursive dialogism of architectonics.

David M. Boje

DIARIES

Definition

In diary studies people provide temporally ordered reports on the events and experiences of their daily life, offering management researchers the opportunity to investigate social and psychological processes within everyday organizational situations.

Discussion

'The breadth of subject matter is as large as the imagination of the researcher' (Breakwell and Wood, 2000: 295) and a variety of diary techniques have been employed to study change processes during major events and transitions, various forms of social interaction, and many areas of occupational health research. Illustrative research contexts concern explorations of company directors at work (Carlson, 1951), studies of occupational stress and well-being (Harris et al., 2003), and investigations into work events and associated emotions (q.v.) (Basch and Fisher, 2000). Researchers have also used their own work diaries as a research guide and a source of insight through reflection on the data (Dalton, 1959). Diary techniques can also be utilized as a precursor to other methods, for example as a means of generating questions to be used in an interview (q.v.), or to fulfil many of the purposes of direct observation [*field research; non-participant observation; participant observation*] in situations when the latter is precluded by access or resource considerations. Diary methods are, however, relatively unexploited in management research. This may be a consequence of several common misconceptions regarding the flexibility of this data collection strategy.

Diary reports are not always collected on a daily basis and the frequency and overall duration of the assessments are determined by the phenomenon under investigation, which may require respondents to detail their experiences at specific times, over hours, days, weeks or even months. Neither is data always captured on an interval-contingent basis and information may instead be recorded at every instance that meets the researcher's pre-established definition. Diary reports are not always self-reports, and individuals can be required to produce a diary on themselves and/or others. Nor are they always individual, and researchers have used dyadic and group diary methods to study interpersonal processes [*focus group; interviews – groups*].

Diaries can differ substantially in terms of the amount of structure imposed by the researcher. In line with generic qualitative versus quantitative debates, there are inevitable tradeoffs to be made in terms of the degree to which the diary method allows participants to record their responses in a free-flowing format, as opposed to a predetermined structure provided by the researcher, which must be determined by the study questions, context and analytical concerns. Gains in rigour also equate to losses in terms of the depth of insight that is arguably the fundamental promise of the diary method, with qualitative techniques rendering deeper insights than might be gained through conventional quantitatively oriented longitudinal report procedures.

While paper and pencil diaries were the earliest and are still the most commonly used approach in diary research, researchers have employed various media of report, including photographic or video (q.v.) techniques [*visual data analysis*]. Particularly over the past decade, technological developments have enabled the use of electronic forms of data collection [*interviews – electronic; postcards*], the most popular to date being hand-held computers but others include web-based questionnaires and phone-in protocols, interactive contact with participants and voice recording and recognition. The diary method allows the medium of the record to be chosen to best suit the topic and type of respondent studied.

All diary designs possess their own particular associated costs and benefits. However, there are some general strengths and weaknesses of the diary approach and key strategies to help ameliorate the latter. Clearly, the major strength of diary collection strategies is that the data gathered are temporally ordered. While there are other methods by which data can be gathered over time, diary methods can permit data to be gathered in a less intrusive and labour-intensive manner, this being particularly notable when compared with qualitative methods for the gathering of data, such as interviews and observation. This means, in turn, they can be a very cost-effective measure of data collection, particularly in situations where data are gathered from the same person over a considerable period or repeatedly over relatively short-time periods. Diary methods have the potential to capture data at points closer in time to the moment events occur, thereby minimizing problems associated with retrospective recall. There is little known about the effect of diary completion on participants' experiences or responses, but little evidence to suggest that reactance poses a threat to diaries' validity. However, self-reflective recollection processes and repeated exposure may change a participant's understanding and behaviour over time and only in a study context can this be considered beneficial or otherwise.

Prospects

One potentially significant disadvantage of diary research is that they demand a level of commitment from the participant that is rarely required in other data collection strategies. Especially over long time periods, completing a diary may be a daunting task, resulting in people being unwilling to participate in the study, low compliance in providing full information throughout the study period, and a high level of drop out. This means that the sample may be highly biased by the end of the study. Researchers have utilized various mechanisms in order to control data elicitation. For example, one variant of the diary method entails the recording of self-identified critical incidents (q.v.) (Flanagan, 1954), which attempts to get people to notice specific happenings that may be important. Thus, in a managerial context, these might be whatever is crucial for achieving a satisfactory outcome in a particular task. Good piloting is particularly important in all forms of diary research to ensure that all reporting instructions are comprehensive and comprehensible. The specific diary design needs to be made on the dual-basis of analytical concerns (how close was the recording of events to the actual event) and operational circumstances (there is a likelihood that diaries become intrusive when participants are asked to complete their diaries in a manner which interferes with their normal work patterns). Maintaining ongoing contact with participants, in a personal but unobtrusive manner, permits insight into compliance and has been shown to enhance retention. Bolger et al. (2003) and Breakwell and Wood (2000) provide clear and informative reading for anyone contemplating the use of diaries in their research, the former giving in-depth detail regarding analytical techniques.

Gail P. Clarkson

DISCOURSE ANALYSIS

Definition

Discourse analysis (DA) is a term covering a number of approaches to research that analyze language use. These approaches range from a focus on language itself, to a broader examination of the relationship between language use, social action, and social theory. Although its rationale is often traced back to Austin's (1962) idea that talk is performative (i.e. we accomplish or *do* things with words), discourse analysts draw from a number of theoretical sources, including speech act theory (Austin, 1962), linguistics and discursive psychology (e.g. Bakhtin, 1984; Potter, 1996) and poststructuralism (e.g. Derrida, 1978/2001; Foucault, 1972). Similarly, discourse is viewed in various ways as talk, written text, social practice, and/or physical and symbolic artifacts [*semiotics*].

Discussion

A number of authors have offered ways of categorizing the various approaches (Alvesson and Kärreman, 2000; Phillips and Hardy, 2002). Gergen (1999), for example, proposes three different discursive lenses: discourse as structure, discourse as rhetoric, and discourse as process. Discourse as structure treats discourse as a set of recurring conventions (e.g. metaphors (q.v.) and narratives (q.v.)) woven throughout our speech and ways of living. Discourse as rhetoric (q.v.) is not just about the art of persuasion but also about power; this lens emphasizes how particular linguistic constructions structure social realities that favour some groups over others. Discourse as process (q.v.) is concerned with how our lives and selves are constituted in the ongoing, back and forth flow of conversation. Discourse analysis not only explores how we construct social and organizational realities, it 'prioritizes subjectivity, acknowledges instrumentalism, explores rhetoric, values multiplicity and celebrates uncertainty' (Grant et al., 1998: 12–13). Early influential work includes that by Potter and Wetherall (1987), Billig (1987/1996), Fairclough (1989), and Tannen (1988) [*dialogic*].

Two broad approaches exist within organization studies: critical discourse analysis (CDA), which draws on postmodern (q.v.) and poststructuralist thought (broadly equated with discourse as rhetoric) [*deconstruction*], and discourse analysis (DA), which draws on social constructionist (q.v.) notions [*constructivism; conversation analysis*]. While both approaches agree that language is constitutive and that we are born into a number of ongoing discourses influencing the way we view and experience the world, they differ on the question of human agency. CDA often denies human agency and relegates human identities to the products of discursive structures and processes. CDA focuses on the broader context, seeing discourse as systems of thought, social, economic, political, institutional, or cultural discourse [*cross-cultural research*]. A number of authors have taken a Foucauldian perspective to examine how discursive practices, power, and ideology combine to perpetuate and maintain systems of domination and oppression. These analyses explore how discursive practices constitute both objectivities (social institutions, knowledge) and subjectivities (identities and actions). A number of organizational and critical communication theorists have used discourse analysis to assess the relationship between discourse and broader societal processes of colonization, struggle, and fragmentation (Ashcraft and Mumby, 2004; Deetz, 1998; Fairclough, 1992; Harrison and Young, 2005) or individual examples of oppression and resistance (Clair, 1994) [*critical theory; individualism*].

Discourse analysts study the structures of meaning, expressions, themes, routine ways of talking, and rhetorical devices used in constructing reality. They use a range of research methods, including quantitative methods such as coding and content analysis, and qualitative methods focusing on the subjective meaning and interpretations of utterances. Discourse analysts assume social structures and social organization are produced in naturally occurring talk. Such talk may include conversations, e-mails, and/or a variety of written documents exchanged between organizational members. Some discourse analysts do use interviews, but these are generally seen to be more contrived forms of talk initiated by the researcher and therefore subject to researcher assumptions. See Coupland et al. (2005); De Graaf (2001); Doolin (2003); Grant et al., (1998); and Heracleous and Marshak (2004) for examples of various approaches to discourse analysis.

Problems and prospects

While discourse analysis covers a wide range of approaches to studying language use (written, oral, symbolic), it is inductive (i.e. based on an interpretation of talk) and hence always exposed to the riposte that there is much more to the world and meaning than what is spoken about. Discourse, in short, is not all there is; nor, perhaps, is it as structurally determining as some analysts make out. Care has to be taken when asserting the primacy of discourse above those using it, as though language users were mere conduits of socially constructed meanings and interests [ordinary language philosophy].

Ann L. Cunliffe

DRAMATURGY

Definition

All the world's a stage,
And all the men and women merely players:
They have their exits and their entrances;
And one man in his time plays many parts,

(Shakespeare, As You Like It.
Jacques: 2.7 139)

These famous words of Shakespeare literally set the stage for a scene (or perhaps this should be an Act) in the history of organization studies which draws on theatre to make sense of organizational life. This approach to analysis of behaviour in organizational contexts gathered strength during a particular time in the evolution of organization studies when symbolic interactionism and social constructionism (q.v.) [constructivism; semiotics] were burgeoning, in stark contrast to classic positivistic (q.v.) research theorizing and its assumptions of 'rational, economic man'. Drawing from pragmatic (q.v.) philosophy, sociology and communication studies, dramatism and dramaturgy effectively recognized the importance of social being and drew attention to the processes by which human beings establish meaning in their lives.

There is a distinction to be made between research based on the ontological assumption that social and organizational life *is* theatre, which lies at the heart of dramatism, and that which holds the position that social and organizational life can be seen *as if* it were theatre, which lies at the heart of dramaturgy: a fine but important distinction in the relationship between theatre and organization studies.

Discussion

Early influences on the field include the work of Kenneth Burke, Berger and Luckmann, Strauss, McCall and Simmons, and Erving Goffman. Of these, Burke provided the most literal exposition of the assumption that life *is* theatre through his *Dramatism Theory*. Burke's Pentad identified five key elements of human drama/communications:

> The act ... ie. what has been done by the communicator.
> The scene ... which gives context or background to the act.
> The agent ... who is the person who performed the act.
> Agency ... which is the means to get the job done.
> The purpose ... which is the stated or implied goal of the communication.

Together with his complex concept of ratios, described as 'an array of heuristic strategies for grasping the intelligibility of social action' (Clark and Mangham, 2004: 39), the Pentad provided an important, integrated (i.e. you must have all five parts of the Pentad present) framework for analysing language and social action. Methodologically, attention thus turns to interaction which provides the linkage between two or more people and more importantly, to how people create meaning during interaction [*dialogic*]. In so doing, of course, the role of the self and perception of identity cannot be ignored hence methods and measurement become significantly more challenging.

Goffman was a key inspiration to this field, in particular through his text, *The Presentation of Self in Everyday Life* (1956/1959). He elaborated at length how human action is dependent on time, place and audience in the drama of life, which takes place on a stage, in settings, as individuals play roles assigned to them in part, through the socialization of norms and values. This way, we learn of social and self-expectations for behaviour, of altercasting[1] and of scripts which may be used to perform roles, and where front and back-stage arenas encourage different interactions and meanings, leading to different performances for different audiences and the notion of acting out of character [*rhetoric*]. Thus Goffman's ideas provide the link between dramatist and dramaturgical perspectives and have inspired and provided foundations for a wealth of classic organization concepts and studies: for example, on symbolic meaning and meaning-making (Smircich et al., 1992a, 1992b), on culture and symbolic action (e.g. Frost et al., 1991), as well as more contemporary conceptualizations of identity work, face work and emotional labour [*emotion research*].

The best in-depth, comprehensive, intellectual exploration of the dramaturgical perspective and analogic model is Mangham and Overington's *Organizations As Theatre: A Social Psychology of Dramatic Appearances* (1987). While acknowledging Goffman's significant influence on the field, in their view, there was

'little evidence that he ever went near a theatre; his understanding of actors, rehearsals, performance and the like does not appear to be informed by actual contact with plays and players' (1987: 201). However, Iain Mangham had taught theatre, produced, directed and acted in amateur theatre, and had researched professional theatre in the UK as well as working over many years with senior management teams in organizational development situations. As well as tracing its historical and contemporary roots, the text is peppered with illustrations of the dramaturgical perspective on organizations being used to make sense of and analyze senior executive decision-making in different organizational settings. Skilfully weaving together both theatre and organizational life, they draw our attention to the micro-details of sets and properties (props), of costumes and characters, as well as plots and scripts, rehearsals and performances, and, most importantly, the characterization of action that comprise the lived experience of everyday organizational life. They also challenge readers to answer some of the criticisms which were often levied against the dramaturgical perspective: for example, that if people are only actors playing parts or roles, what place is there for self and identity, or unity of actor and performance, and what of authenticity and ethics (Mangham and Overington, 1987: 152) [*existential phenomenology*]?

Whether one assumes it as a way of life or a metaphor (q.v.), theatre offers a very powerful and enduring influence on analysing and making sense of behaviour in organizational settings. More recent developments include the use of theatrical texts as a model for leadership and organizational development. For example, Richard Olivier has developed on his father's acting legacy to use Shakespeare's plays as a means for inspirational leadership development and developing authentic leaders 'based in theatre, rooted in psychology and focused on organizational

---

[1]Which at that time, was taken to mean the way in which our performance not only expresses 'an image of who *we* are but also simultaneously expresses an image of who we take *alter* to be' (McCall and Simmons, 1978/1966: 136, emphasis in original).

development' to facilitate 'transformational learning' (see www.oliviermythodrama.com).

Another development is corporate or organizational theatre, where an organization specifically employs dramatists, actors, directors, set designers, and so on to create a unique play to deal with a specific issue for its employees. Clark and Mangham (2004) describe this as an example of theatre as technology. There are also links between dramaturgical approaches to analysing social action and the field of discourse and narrative studies, seen particularly through the metaphor of storytelling.

Prospects

In the last ten years, there has been a growing interest in improvization as a metaphor for organizing (e.g. *Organization Science*, Special Issue, 1998). Improvisation is not a case of 'anything goes', and elsewhere, Mangham (1987: 13–16) gives fascinating insight into its origins in the sixteenth century troupe of improvisers, Commedia dell' Arte, who arrived at order through improvisation, working within the broad constraints of character and headings. As Mangham (1987: 13–16) concludes, '[t]he essence of improvisation is that one discovers what one is about by doing something hence reflecting a classic assumption of the dramaturgical model: 'that meaning is a guide to action and that meaning arises in interaction'.

There are certainly many echoes of Weick's work in the dramaturgical perspective and vice versa [*sensemaking*]. So it is perhaps not surprising that he concluded:

> My bet is that improvizing is close to the root process in organizing and that organizing itself consists largely of the embellishment of small structures. Improvising may be a tacit, taken--for-granted quality in all organizing that we fail to see because we are distracted by more conspicuous artefacts such as structure, control, authority, planning, charters and standard operating procedures. ... In organizing as in jazz, artefacts and fragments cohere because improvised storylines impose modest order

among them in ways that accommodate their peculiarities. (Weick, 1998: 553)

Annie Pye

DRAWINGS AND IMAGES

Definition

Organizations are often seen as rational places, where careful thought and planning produce effective decisions and strategies. Almost anyone who has experienced life in organizations knows that they are also complex and contradictory environments, where decisions and strategies are just as likely to be the result of barely acknowledged emotions, complicated relations and organizational politics and power relations. This raises questions about the qualitative methods that might be used to research emotions (q.v.) and power relations in organizations [*actor-network theory; critical theory; dialogic*]. One method that is useful for capturing the emotional and political dynamics of organizing is visual data (q.v.) – and particularly the use of drawings and images in addition to interviews and questionnaires [*postcards; projective techniques*].

The history of this approach in management and organization studies can be traced back to the late 1980s. One of the key early examples is Shoshana Zuboff's book *In the Age of the Smart Machine: The Future of Work and Power* (1988). Professor Zuboff asked clerical workers to draw pictures showing how they felt about their jobs before and after the installation of a new computer system. These drawings helped staff to articulate feelings that had been implicit and were hard to define [*aesthetics*]. In terms of understanding and developing the method, a key paper was published in *Organization Science* in 1991 by Alan Meyer called 'Visual data in organizational research'. Meyer acknowledges that 'visual instruments seem uniquely suited to ... efforts to build theory and research focusing on human awareness, interpretation and consciousness' (Meyer, 1991: 232). There are a number of published papers that will provide the researcher with discussions and/or examples of this method (Holliday, 2000; Kearney and Hyle, 2004; Stiles, 2004; Strangleman, 2004; Vince, 1995; Vince and Broussine, 1996).

Discussion

The generation of drawings or imagery is a particularly good research method when the researcher is interested in capturing emotional and/or unconscious dynamics, processes and experiences (Vince and Broussine, 1996) [*inductive analysis; psychoanalytic approaches*]. Drawings tend to portray individual emotions effortlessly, since there are often unexpected and enigmatic aspects to an image. However, their real value in research is in the way that they can reveal aspects of *collective* emotional experience and knowledge about a specific work context. Asking a group of respondents to draw their team or organization is an invitation to generate multiple interpretations and to promote dialogue over the collective meaning of individuals' images. This inevitably raises questions about the power relations that shape both experience and interpretation.

This method has particularly been used by researchers interested in revealing the links between individuals' real and imagined idea of 'the organization' they work in (Hutton et al., 1997) and the organizing dynamics and forces that shape and are shaped by their interpretations and actions. Therefore:

Everyone who is aware of an organization, whether a member of it or not, has a mental *image* [my emphasis] of how it works. Though these diverse ideas are not often consciously negotiated or agreed upon among participants, they exist. In this sense, all institutions exist in the mind, and it is in interaction with these in-the-mind entities that we live. Of course, all organizations also consist of certain real factors, such as other people, profits, buildings, resources and products. But the meaning of these factors derives from the context established by the institution-in-the-mind. These mental images are not static; they are the products of dynamic interchanges, chiefly projections and transferences. (Shapiro and Carr, 1991: 69–70)

There are a number of potential developments in the method. A recent example involved university students in a collective inquiry. They took, viewed and discussed digital photos and used their reflections and associations to reveal what seemed to be 'unseen, unnoticed and unthought' in the organization (Sievers, 2007).

Prospects

There is an evolving interest in drawings and imagery, although it is an underused method. One of the reasons for reluctance may be because there have been no systematic attempts to undertake in-depth research in order to explore and to begin to theorize its appropriateness and value as a research method. A second reason is that researchers feel that the method is risky, either in terms of the fears and anxieties that are generated for the researcher and/or for respondents. Where this method has been used, researchers often find that images reveal feelings and emotions; they provide 'a succinct presentation of participant experiences'; they offer opportunities to engage overtly with researcher bias; and the approach triangulates well with other qualitative data generation methods (Kearney and Hyle, 2004). While there is little doubt that the use of drawings is not an easy method, it would also be true to say that this is an approach that is well worth the risks.

Russ Vince

E

EMOTION RESEARCH

Definition

Researching emotion presents considerable challenges, not least because emotion is considered elusive, even 'unknowable'. Feelings are real (the increasing concern with developing 'emotional intelligence' is testimony to this (Fineman, 2000)), but cannot always be observed, identified, controlled or labelled with sufficient surety [*drawings and images; visual analysis data*]. Burkitt (1997: 37), for example, argues that emotions are not simply expressions of inner processes, but multi dimensional (thinking, feeling, moving) 'complexes' or 'modes of communication' which are both cultural *and* corporeal/embodied and arise in social relationships of power and interdependence. Indeed, for others, rational academic discourse can itself preclude, suppress or exacerbate the 'knowability' of emotion and its experiential or even mystical qualities (Albrow, 1997). Furthermore, and perhaps more so than other organizational phenomena, emotion is readily recognized as being multidimensional. It has yet to be fully colonized by a discipline (e.g. biology, psychology and sociology) and therefore is not considered knowable through a single frame. For example, love can be seen as having *interconnected* visceral, discursive, social interactional, ideological/structural and other (e.g. subconscious) qualities (Jackson, 1993). Discourses, chemicals or structures, *on their own*, are insufficient.

Discussion

Concerns about unknowability, however, have not prevented attempts to know emotion (Sturdy, 2003). Electrical impulses, chemical changes, psychoanalysis, observation, written tests, interviews or texts have all been used to identify or indicate emotion. There are numerous approaches, associated with a range of disciplines (e.g. psychology, sociology, philosophy, history, linguistics, biology, etc.) and covered by Kemper (1990). For example, one might focus on one or more particular *dimensions* of emotion – feeling, behavioural, physiological, linguistic, cultural, cognitive, social structural. These may be explored in relation to specific emotions or particular perspectives – emotion as judgement, communication, sense and control, for example – though this can obscure the multi-dimensional nature of emotion. Some degree of focus is inevitable, however, such as exploring emotion as display, disguise, experience, discourse, embodied or socially structured.

What remains common to many approaches is awareness of the social nature of feelings and emotion [*actor-network theory; practice theory; social constructionism*]. They are scripted and others' immediate interpretation(s) may influence what a person feels, especially if it is initially inchoate. Accordingly, given some cultural understanding of the immediate social context, we can necessarily offer a valid or plausible interpretation of sentiments through observation, where there is a long and continuing tradition (e.g. Darwin, 1872/1955). However, observation alone may reveal little about the actor's perceptions, physical condition (e.g. tiredness) and immediate and biographical/cultural history – feelings have been defined in terms of perceptions in relation to context (e.g. Laird and Apostoleris, 1996) [*non-participant observation*].

These issues, combined with cultural sensitivities, prompt many to probe more deeply 'under the surface' in an attempt to know others' 'real' (cf. hidden) feelings and/or their underlying (e.g. subconscious) causes [*action science*]. Duncombe and Marsden (1996), for example, review traditional and contested views on the best methodological tactics to get respondents to reveal sensitive issues 'faithfully' in interviews (q.v.). Aside from methodological (and ethical) issues, such approaches mistrust actors' accounts in seeking to uncover 'truth' in terms of authentic feelings and/or the subconscious [*inductive analysis; psychoanalytic approaches*]. Both are, of course, central issues in research on emotion and subjectivity and there is not the scope here to explore them fully (e.g. Gabriel, 1999).

In contrast to positivist approaches to emotion which seek out underlying variables and causal factors, interpretivist accounts are more descriptive and processual, to be judged partly on whether they 'bring emotional experiences alive' (Denzin, 1990: 86). For example, worker and executive autobiographies, narratives and memoirs typically often reveal rich and explicitly emotional pictures of organizational life (Sandelands and Boudens, 2000; Terkel, 1975), as does research of 'emotion in process' using shadowing and 'narratives based on live dialogue, stories [q.v.], observations [q.v], diary accounts [q.v.], taped personal musings...' (Fineman, 1993: 222) [*narrative research*].

Prospects

Critiques of such discursive approaches come from different quarters, pointing to alternative, if connected, biological, subconscious (e.g. Gabriel, 1999) and/or social structural

realities (e.g. Craib, 1995). Even among sociologists, few discount some biological component in feelings, although positions vary in the emphasis given to it and what is meant by biological and the body (Barbalet, 1998; Elias, 1987; Harré and Parrott, 1996; Kemper, 1990: 20). So for many studies, confining explanation to the biological ignores the intimate links between emotion and social structures, particularly of power and inequality (Barbalet, 1998; Kemper, 1990). This link and its consequences have been explored in a long history of sociological and critical psychological literature, even if emotion was not an explicit focus – alienation, suicide, 'fear of freedom', anxiety, racism, etc. (Weiss and Brief, 2001). As Williams and Bendelow (1998), after Wright Mills, point out, the study of emotion links personal troubles and public policy issues. Furthermore, probably the greatest contribution to 'structuring' emotion has come from feminist and gender studies (e.g. Duncombe and Marsden, 1993), in which the traditional congruence of rational–emotional, masculine–feminine, mind–body, public-private and powerful-powerless dualisms is typically challenged (see Fineman, 1993; Hochschild, 1983).

What does this all mean for particular research methods? Clearly, there are general methodological issues and choices to make. However, Table 3 (see page 88) summarizes the ways in which particular methods can provide insight and privilege and silence different aspects of emotion.

Andrew Sturdy

ETHICS

Definition

Research ethics concerns issues related to what is appropriate and acceptable in the conduct of management research. This involves consideration of how researchers should treat the people who form the subjects

Table 3   Selected approaches to emotion research – a summary

Approach	Possible insight	Privileges	Silences
Observation	short-term emotion dynamics	emotion (cf. feeling)	history
Interview	construction of authenticity	individualism	real-time emotion
Autobiography/ Participation	rational–emotional interplay	subjectivity	objectivity
Discourse	diversity of meanings/emotions	dominant texts	Non/partially-discursive
Social structures	power and emotional tension	history and cultures	interaction and transience
Non-traditional data	non-rational knowing	humanism/romanticism	objectivity/closure

of their investigation and whether there are certain actions that should not, or indeed should, be taken in relation to them [*access; anti-discriminatory research*]. Research ethics are pertinent to all research, whether quantitative or quantitative, particularly if the study involves human subjects. Some writers see ethics as predominantly a consideration in research that deals with sensitive topics, or involves the use of controversial methods like covert observation or deception in experiments. However, others have argued that research ethics should be seen as integral to all management research, rather than a consideration that only needs to be taken into account in exceptional circumstances (Bell and Bryman, 2007).

The issues that are covered under this remit include: avoiding harm or risk of harm, whether physical or psychological; maintaining the privacy of research participants and ensuring the confidentiality and anonymity of data where appropriate; making sure that participants are fully informed about the nature of the research and gaining their consent to being involved with it; and minimizing the possibility for deception at all stages of the research process, from data collection to dissemination. In each case it is the researcher's responsibility to demonstrate that these issues have been considered and that steps have been taken to address them. There is also an obligation to declare sources of funding and support that

may affect the affiliations of the researcher, thereby causing a potential conflict of interest. In addition there is a developing interest in the ethical issue of reciprocity, which entails a positive commitment to undertaking research that is of mutual benefit to researcher and participants through seeking to involve them more fully in the research process [*collaboration*].

Discussion

Discussions of research ethics are complicated by the fact that there is limited consensus regarding what is and is not ethically acceptable. Some writers adopt a universalist stance, which assumes that ethical principles should never be transgressed as to do so would be morally wrong, others take a more situationist stance, in which it is argued that in certain cases the transgression of ethical principles may be justified, arguing, for example, that covert observation might be the only way to access a particular research setting (Bulmer, 1982a) [*participant observation*].

In discussing research ethics there is a tendency to focus on certain notorious examples of social science research which are widely considered to be unethical, even if at the time the studies were carried out the research designs were not so clearly seen this way. Milgram's (1963) obedience experiments and Zimbardo's prison studies (Haney et al., 1973) are two often-cited examples where research subjects were deceived to a certain extent about the purpose of the experiments and their role in them, and were unknowingly exposed to the possibility of psychological harm as a consequence of this. These examples highlight the changing nature of research ethics, as such ethical decisions would be much more difficult to justify today than forty years ago [*social constructionism*].

Recommendations concerning research ethics tend to be made by professional associations that represent the management research community or other related social science disciplines, such as the Social Research Association or the American Psychological Association, agencies that fund management research, and institutions (usually universities) that employ management researchers, through the operation of Research Ethics Committees or Institutional Review Boards. These recommendations often take the form of ethics codes which set out the main ethical issues that researchers tend to face and provide guidance on how they should respond to them. The Academy of Management has played a role in fostering the development of ethical awareness among management researchers through its ethics code (see www.aomonline.org). It is good practice to consider potential ethical issues at the design stage of the research rather than when a particular issue is confronted. Some funding bodies make grant awards conditional on the researcher having demonstrated that ethical issues have been considered prior to the study. The consequences of conducting research that is considered to be unethical can involve a loss of integrity for the researcher and a lessening of the credibility accorded to research findings. In extreme cases, the validity of published work based on research that is judged to be unethical has been publicly discredited and the reputation of the individuals concerned has suffered. However, it has been argued that ethics codes leave too much to the discretion of the individual researcher and can be interpreted instrumentally, generating minimal compliance but doing little to develop ethical research practice (Lincoln and Guba, 1989).

Prospects

The main debates surrounding research ethics have remained relatively static in the period from the 1960s to the 1990s (Bryman and Bell, 2003) and the issues covered by social science ethics codes have remained very similar (Bell and Bryman, 2007). However, research ethics are currently in a state of some flux due to the introduction of new regulatory mechanisms at disciplinary, university and state levels which are likely to give rise to ethical governance regimes that will be less 'light touch' in orientation than current structures (Kent et al., 2002). For example, in the UK the Economic and Social Research Council (ESRC), the major funding body for social science research, recently commissioned the development of a Research Ethics Framework for Social Scientists. From 2006, the ESRC will only provide funding to institutions which satisfy this framework. Management researchers may also be affected by changes announced in 2005 by the Academy of Management which seek to make its code of ethics more readily enforceable through a process of adjudication.

Emma Bell

ETHNOGRAPHY

Definition

Ethnography, as a research methodology, had its origins in social anthropology, with particular reference to the study of the culture of social groups and societies. The great social anthropologist, Clifford Geertz (1973), who has been very influential in the development of ethnographic approaches in organizations, suggests that human beings live in complex networks in which we give the natural and human world meaning and significance [*cross-cultural research*]. The culture of a social group is made up of these complex networks of meaning and the key task of ethnography is to develop an interpretation and understanding of culture. When Geertz reflected in 2000 on the purpose of ethnography, he suggested that one of its jobs is to provide us, alongside the arts and the study of history, with an understanding of ourselves (and others) as members of societies or groups or organizations that are by their very nature 'strange' and diverse and that it is this very 'strangeness' that we should celebrate. To do this requires what Geertz called 'thick descriptions' of culture [*field research*]. This means that as a first step the ethnographer undertakes close observation (q.v.) of the group by such means as establishing a rapport with people, carefully selecting the people with whom the ethnographer talks, keeping diaries, exploring documents and so on. Then as a second step the ethnographer undertakes processes of *interpretation* and *analysis* [*inductive analysis*]. The aim of this process is to reveal the underlying structures by which behaviour or ways of communicating with each other are produced, perceived and interpreted by members of the social group and indeed the ways in which these same behaviours and communications can be misunderstood by other social groups (or even within the same social group) [*dialogics; hermeneutics*]. Geertz suggests that doing ethnography is like trying to interpret a document that is in a 'strange' language, which is faded, with many aspects which seem like contradictions, and in which other authors have made mysterious notes and additions.

Discussion

When ethnography is undertaken in organizations it involves a number of choices: the extent to which it is participant (q.v.) or non-participant (q.v.), covert or non-covert, unstructured or structured [*ethics*]. In the study of organizations there has been a tradition of participant observation where the researcher is a member of the organization. This can give particular richness in that the researcher can penetrate into areas and meanings that are not open to the outsider. For the participant observer it means that the researcher needs to be able to be an 'insider' at one moment and an 'outsider' at another as the researcher explores the significance of the events in which he/she has just participated. Alternatively, the researcher can adopt a non-participant stance so that he/she takes a more explicitly 'distant' view of events, behaviours and communications in the organization. A second area of choice in methods is to take a covert or non-covert approach to the ethnography. In the former the ethnographer deliberately avoids announcing his/her research intent and in this way can penetrate into highly informal – and even discrediting – aspects of the organization; in the latter the ethnographer is clear about his/her intent in undertaking the research and although this approach may not reach the deeper areas of the organizational life, its ethical implications are often considered to be less onerous than covert research. The third key choice made by ethnographers is around the issue of unstructured or structured processes of observation (q.v.). In the former the ethnographer follows the action and will often use his/her intuition in order to develop an understanding of behaviours, processes and actions. In the latter the researcher establishes a clear schedule of observation and interview and will follow that process rigorously so that his/her research is more amenable to triangulation (q.v.) and replication. The ways in which the ethnographer makes choices among these three key areas – participant or non-participant, covert or overt, unstructured or structure – indicates a preference for subjectivist, hermeneutic (q.v.) approaches to the social sciences or approaches that are more akin to a 'natural sciences' model.

In the study of organizations, perhaps one of the most enduring ethnographies that was participant, covert and unstructured was that of Melvin Dalton, whose study of the relationships between 'line' and 'staff' managers in a chemical factory developed a new understanding – rich description – of relationships in organizations. In an article written in 1964 he discusses the processes that led him to his study (by the way, he does not use the expression 'ethnography' to describe his research approach) and he gives useful insight into the ethnographic process. He begins his account with a number of 'confusions and irritations' and the ways in which there was 'name calling' and 'insults' exchanged between members. As he witnessed and participated in the weft and warp of daily life, he began to develop what he called 'hunches' about what was going on. He began to develop these hunches through his research. His core subjects for the research were a group of what he called his intimates – a group of people who trusted him and who gave him really useful information that could have endangered their careers. These intimates knew that he was undertaking research of some sort but not in detail. Beyond this he also undertook a few formal interviews, maintained detailed 'work diaries' and undertook participant observation. Although he was aware of the limitations of all these approaches, he saw the merits as flexibility in research design, he was able to avoid asking 'pointless questions', he was able to get closer to the motives of people, and the development of the feelings of rapport and empathy enabled him to get to more difficult issues.

By way of contrast, in an article written in 2004, Brewer discusses ethnographic research that he (and a colleague) undertook in the late 1980s that was non-participant, overt and structured with the Royal Ulster Constabulary – research that was closer in spirit to the traditions of social anthropology. He suggests that key issues of having to undertake the research in a covert manner raised some interesting issues. The researchers had to obtain 'permission' from the Chief Constable and in this process had to make some difficult compromises in the research and, when they started the research with people lower down in the organization, they found that some regarded the researchers with suspicion – the researchers were seen as 'agents' of the Chief Constable. They found, however, that a key to the success of the research was the development of trust and that reassurances had constantly to

be given. One of the issues they encountered was in their constant inquisitiveness and sometimes the presence of tape or video recorders caused a degree of irritation [*interviews – electronic; video*].

Prospects

Perhaps the most persistent problem of ethnography is that of closeness. This can manifest itself both as being too proximate to those being understood and too introspective with oneself. Dalton and Brewer's research uses trust as a conduit for gaining access to data that otherwise remain hidden, but with trust comes obligations surrounding issues of disclosure, anonymity and legal compliance. Moreover, both cases also show the dangers to researchers themselves. One interesting issue from Brewer's research was that they were not able to retain their sense of detached researcher; in particular the female Catholic researcher was met by a number of quite difficult situations that had quite profound effects on her own identity as an ethnographer working in that situation [*reflexivity*]. In this sense, as with Dalton, there was the need for constant self-reflection and self-awareness in undertaking not only the research itself, but in the processes of interpretation and understanding.

John McAuley

ETHNOMETHODOLOGY

Definition

Ethnomethodological studies look closely at and explicate work practices. By 'explicate' we mean something slightly different from 'explain'. The idea of 'explaining' is often understood in terms of causality: what factors cause what phenomena? But 'explicate' means to show by unfolding something, making it visible in a more detailed way. Another phrase might be to 'render' something in a fresh way. Rather than pure representation, in which one term is transparently and instantaneously equated with another (e.g. X = Y, e = mc²), the terms 'explicate' and 'render' suggest a temporally structured practice. Rendering and explicating are processes of unfolding or opening out, in order to make visible details so far missed.

Another phrase, which captures the sense of explicating or rendering is 'respecifying', a term to which Garfinkel has devoted much discussion (Garfinkel, 1991). The studies in Garfinkel (1986) illustrate the practices of explicating, rendering and respecifying, as do several studies by Michael Lynch (such as Lynch, 1990; Lynch et al., 1983). Of all these studies, perhaps the one by Bjelic and Lynch (1992) is the most lucid. In order for the reader to follow their argument, she or he must have a prism to hand and be able to look at certain figures in the text of the chapter through it in order to 'see' Newton's and Goethe's alternate theories of 'prismatic colour'. To read this chapter becomes, in itself, a practice demonstrating both ordinary and scientific ways of seeing *theoretically*. In this way, ethnomethodology draws our attention to ways of seeing in which the very act of seeing (made strange by the practical necessity of using a prism) becomes the point of the chapter.

Discussion

'Seeing' is of course an action, an ordinary everyday action, which we who are sighted people perform without thinking very much about it. Ethnomethodological studies set out to show how such ordinary practices of 'looking and telling' (Garfinkel, 1967: 1) are done. Ordinary practices are shown to be methodical in ways which are surprising. If 'methodology' generally means the study of scientific methods of knowledge production, 'ethnomethodology' generally means the study of ordinary methods of knowing, such as looking at something and knowing what it is. Whereas most management and organizational research simply assumes that we know what we see, ethnomethodology shows that

how we look at things comprises, in itself, a range of phenomena in its own right and one which can itself be looked at [*existential phenomenology; ordinary language philosophy; postmodernism; practice theory*]. Practices of looking become an object of observation. They are shown to involve work, effort, training, and skill, and are shown to be done in ways that embody method and technique.

According to Karl Weick (1995: 24), what is significant about ethnomethodology is its emphasis upon retrospective sensemaking (q.v.); pointing out that Alfred Schutz's (one of the 'fathers' of ethnomethodological approaches) emphasis on *lived* experience, that is, 'lived' in the past tense, captures 'the reality that people can know what they are doing only after they have done it'. Whereas Weick (1995) emphasizes the role that ethnomethodology has played in his concept of sensemaking as something one can *only* do in retrospect, it is fairer to ethnomethodology to emphasize that it has actually focused on 'retrospective-prospective' modes of looking and telling (Garfinkel, 1967: 89). Here, the order or organization of the world appears as human agents' practical attempts to make sense of their experience – these practical attempts themselves possess orderly properties which ethnomethodology discovers and examines and are amongst the methodical or orderly ways in which members socially construct the scenes and settings of everyday affairs [*process philosophy; relativism*]. But for Garfinkel this practical construction is not entirely backward-looking.

To make sense of this sensemaking Garfinkel's proposed the use of the 'documentary method', in which the researcher reads off any social setting features which 'document' an 'underlying pattern' (Garfinkel, 1967: 95):

> The documentary method is used whenever the investigator constructs a life history or a 'natural history.' The task of historicizing the person's biography consists of using the documentary method to select and order past occurrences so as to furnish the present state of affairs its *relevant past and prospects*. (Garfinkel, 1967: 95, my emphasis)

In other words, when we look at the social world, we do not simply make sense of it in retrospect, but, *prospectively*, we search its horizon for a sense that will unfold. How do we do this searching, this looking? Through everyday and ordinary processes of investigating, inquiring, searching and looking for what will follow on from what went before.

Ethnomethodological studies of work, some of which are referenced above, explicate the methods whereby members do such looking and finding: they demonstrate their looking practices. Apart from showing the method involved in seeing through the theoretical lenses of, say, Goethe's or Newton's colour theory, the methods through which we see other more prosaic things are shown. Baccus (1986), for example, shows how mechanics see 'what happened' in multipiece truckwheel accidents by consulting the remains of the wheels. Girton (1986) shows how exponents of kung fu see in old manuals the secrets of their practices. Thus, as Garfinkel (1967: 32) argues, '... inquiries of every imaginable kind, from divination to theoretical physics, claim our interest as socially organized artful practices'.

Prospects

Inquiries [*pragmatism*] of all sorts are what ethnomethodology studies. The practices of merely looking at the world and seeing it for 'what it is' are shown to be organized and methodical in ways we can study as organized phenomena. The effect of seeing the world this way is to see it being organized in the ways we look at it. The ways we look are not simply understood as, say, theoretical or other 'interested' or 'motivated' perspectives, but as temporally structured ways, the features of which can themselves be rendered or explicated. In recent years, Garfinkel has published several new books which substantially add to *Studies in Ethnomethodology* which he published in 1967. The later books do much to clarify ethnomethodology's position in relation to wider social theory and in terms of its own core principles (Garfinkel, 2002, 2006). A special issue of *Culture and Organization*, edited by David Richards in 2004 and a special issue of the *Sociological*

Review, edited by Steve Linstead in 2006, brought ethnomethodology and management studies into coversation with each other.

Steve Fox

EXISTENTIAL PHENOMENOLOGY

Definition

Existential phenomenology describes subjective human experience as it reflects people's values, purposes, ideals, intentions, emotions, and relationships. Existential phenomenology concerns itself with the experiences and actions of the individual, rather than conformity or behaviour. The individual is seen as an active and creative subject, rather than an object in nature: in other words, the existential person is not merely passive or reactive, subject to environmental influences, but also a purposeful being who has inner experiences and can interpret the meaning of his or her existence and relationships with others in a social world. As US existentialist Rollo May (1973) points out existential phenomenology looks at the individual – a 'living, acting, feeling, thinking phenomenon' – in organic relationships with others.

Existential phenomenology blends two philosophical traditions: the existentialist thoughts of Søren Kierkegaard, Friedrich Nietzsche, Martin Heidegger, and Jean-Paul Sartre, and the phenomenological (q.v.) concepts and methods of Edmund Husserl, Maurice Merleau-Ponty, and Alfred Schutz. To a large extent, the influence of existential phenomenology is its theoretical and methodological contribution. Existentialism questions the ability of positivistic, natural scientific thinking to deal with various existential issues. It seeks to understand the human condition in everyday situations. For example, when the existential-phenomenological approach is applied to management studies, we attempt to understand what is unobservable about people in organizations: that is, their thoughts, their emotions, their values, their consciousness, their sense of freedom, their existence in a dehumanizing environment, and the meaning of their actions that reflect their private world of experience [*interpretative phenomenological analysis*].

Existential phenomenology assumes an inseparable interrelationship between the individual and the social world. The person has no existence apart from the social world, and that world has no existence apart from persons; in the organizational world, the employees and the organization are interdependent, needing each other to maintain the status quo or to change the status quo. In organization, it would be inconceivable to think that an individual could exist without interacting with the social world in which he or she works. It is the everyday life of the social world that gives an individual's existence meaning. For example, the organizational world in which a person works would not exist if the organizational members did not find meaning and purpose in their involvement. According to the existential-phenomenological thought of Heidegger (1962), human existence implies that 'being' is actually 'being-in-the world'.

Discussion

In existential phenomenology, people and the social world are always in a dialogue (q.v.) with each other. People develop a sense of commonly shared reality through interaction, including face-to-face dialogue, interviews, commentaries, and the formal expression of ideas in speech, conversation and writing. Edmund Husserl (1859–1938) is concerned with the constitution of an individual's inter-subjective life as the transcendental ego connects with the experience of other egos, with alter egos, and with the other in general. His main focus is how the experience of the other person helps an individual to find his or her own transcendental experience, the transcendental subjectivity (Husserl, 1931/1962). Husserl sees the intersubjective nature of people's experience, but always grounds this experience in the subjective; his interest lies

in how the other enters into an individual's consciousness. An individual's 'life-world' is always an important part of his or her consciousness.

Dialogue leads to another important concept of existential phenomenology: the construction of an intersubjective reality [*constructivism*], in which individuals share their ideas and experiences by mutually tuning into one another's consciousness (Zaner, 1970) [*antenarrative; dialectic*]. By reflecting upon one another's biases and experiences, individuals can, together, produce a socially meaningful project. Alfred Schutz (1889–1959), a student of Husserl, emphasizes intersubjectivity in the interactive and reciprocal process. According to Schutz (1967), in face-to-face-situations, people can produce socially (mutually) shared phenomena, that is, an intersubjective reality in which, through a face-to-face encounter, its members share a sense of 'we-relation' [*ethnomethodology*].

Existential phenomenology seeks to understand the everyday world of the individual. Thus the vital role of phenomenology in particular is to describe meanings of social actions (or organizational actions) and the experiences of everyday life from the individual's point of view. Phenomenological inquiry aims not only to illuminate the multifaceted and qualitative nature of people's experiences, but also to understand the meanings that people assign to unique experiences [*individualism*]. Since the late 1950s, phenomenological methods have become the foundation of qualitative research grounded in a human science perspective, which provides descriptions and insights regarding the dynamic meanings of human experience.

Scientific and positivistic research produces empirical knowledge by the direct and neutral observation of reality and by establishing a cause and effect relationship [*positivism and post-positivism; realism*]. 'Human science', on the other hand, employs a wide range of diverse approaches to understanding social phenomena; these approaches have little in common, other than a tendency to interpret the real meaning of a human situation from the subject's points of view [*constructivism; phronetic organizational research*]. One assumption of human science is that social reality is grounded in the meaning of a person's actions, as interpreted by the subject. To understand an organizational situation, you must study it from the subject's (or employee's) point of view so that you can describe the lived experiences of individuals in a social situation. Phenomenological (or qualitative) [*critical realism*] researchers argue that positivistic research methods stress objective measurements of phenomena, and therefore they are inherently unqualified to deal with human values.

Investigating the existential and phenomenological dimensions of human experiences requires methods of inquiry such as: narrative (q.v.), storytelling (q.v.), and open-ended interviews (q.v.); the focus is on observing the social and relational context, understanding people's linguistic expressions, and a reflexive analysis of research assumptions, suspending any preconceptions. Thus it shares with these methods the problems associated with verifiability, repeatability and generalizability [*reliability*]. Immersing oneself into the lifeworld of those with whom one is working does not lend itself to producing objective, dispassionate and scientific knowledge. But these standards of research, though important, are not themselves generalizable to all scientific endeavour.

In conclusion, the concepts and methods used by scholars of existential phenomenology differ from those used by scholars with an objective view of organization and management; the latter emphasize overt behaviour. Behaviourally and scientifically oriented modern management theories, which largely dominate the mainstream business and public administration schools, objectify people in organizations, treating them as reactive and malleable beings conforming to organizational demands. They underestimate people's faculty for subjectivity, for inner experience, and for consciousness. Because of the amazing quality of people's subjectivity, however, people have intentions (consciousness), reinterpret experience, bring newness into being, and discover alternative ways of doing things. People who are part of the organizational world create meaning and alternatives, reflecting upon their experiences in relation to other people and organizational demands, and it is this activity that existential phenomenology accentuates as both significant and often overlooked.

Jong S. Jun

F

FEMINISM

Definition

Theoretical and/or socio-political movement addressing the systematic unequal treatment of women *vis-à-vis* men. The movement originated in the eighteenth century and was first predominantly concerned with women's political rights, such as voting, etc. The most recent phase started in the 1960s and focuses, among other issues, on the unequal treatment of women in the workplace and in organizations in general.

Discussion

A description of feminist theory and research within management and organization studies is, by needs, multifaceted and at times contradictory as there is no single theoretical paradigm or 'history' to hold the strands together. The field is united by its common issues, which take on two characteristic forms. The first is the issue of male domination in the workplace, in organizations, and/or in institutional and societal structures. It focuses on themes like harassment, oppression and job inequality, and mostly draws on various kinds of empirical research from quantitative statistics to in-depth case studies. The second issue is more concerned with theory and seeks to uncover the hidden postulates of 'malestream' thinking. The argument here is that the apparent normalcy and objectivity of academic and non-academic

reasoning is, in truth, already gendered and establishes male norms and preferences without reference to their gendered nature [*emotion research*]. Once these constructions are in place, women are automatically viewed as 'not normal', or in the case of organizations, 'organizations supposedly adjust to the appearance of women [...] who are presumed not really to belong there' (Hearn and Parkin, 1993: 150). Many authors in this sub-domain employ Derridaen deconstruction (q.v.) as a method, for example of such central concepts as 'bounded rationality' (Mumby and Putnam, 1992) or 'charismatic leadership' (Calás, 1993), or of organizational taboos (Martin, 1990).

The theoretical sources of feminist approaches, as mentioned above, are diverse, and in each case the label 'feminism' takes on a somewhat different reasoning and political agenda. Calás and Smircich (1996) have identified six theoretical perspectives to inform feminist theorizing in management and organization studies: liberalism, radical theory of women's liberation, psychoanalysis (q.v.), Marxism (q.v.)/socialism, poststructuralism, and post-colonialism (q.v.) [*critical theory; postmodernism*]. Each provides different conceptions of human nature in general and gender in particular, as well as different views of what makes a 'good society' and what should be done to achieve it. The latter basically clusters around the question of whether women should be promoted into the same positions as men in existing (western) societies, or if gender equality calls for a more radical break with existing societal and economic structures [*Confucianism*]. Despite these differences in theoretical provenance, it is probably fair to say that the majority of feminist authors embrace, in the widest sense, a constructivist approach, which distinguishes the biological category of 'sex' from the social(ly constructed) (q.v.) category of 'gender'.

Prospects

Due to the cross-theoretical nature of feminism, a general critique has been rare as most critics concentrate on a specific perspective or argument. One of the few is brought forward by Foucault. He argues that viewing women as different from men, and even emphasizing the differences, already marks or even stigmatizes women as different and is the first step to exclusion. Quite poignantly, Calás and Smircich (1992: 229) have summarized this by the equation 'gender = sex = women = problem'. From this point of view, every feminist agenda relying on 'women' as an identifiable collective suffers from an inherent contradiction between its assumptions and its political aims. Foucault's critique has itself been criticized by some feminist authors (e.g. McLaren, 1997), but has been adopted by other theorists deploring the under-theorization of men and masculinity (Collinson and Hearn, 1996) with the aim to show that all concepts, and to an extent all reality, are gendered, not just the part that is concerned with women's rights or equality in the workplace. Finally, a far more worrying development in political terms might be the fact that many non-academic women avoid or explicitly refuse to be regarded as feminists, even though they confirm the persistence of gender inequality and/or actively seek to remedy it and/or have at least personally managed to 'get to the top'. This threatens to break the traditional phalanx of 'women against men' and may (have to) lead to new or at least modified feminist agendas.

Elke Weik

FIELD NOTES

Definition

Field notes are contemporaneous notes of observations or conversation taken during the conduct of qualitative research. Depending on the circumstances, the notes taken can be full (e.g. verbatim transcripts of conversations taken by hand or recorded by a tape recorder) or brief notations that can be elaborated on later. Bryman and Bell (2003) identify three classifications of field notes based on suggestions by Lofland and Lofland (1995) and Sanjek (1990). These are: mental notes when it may be inappropriate to take notes; jotted or scratch notes, taken at the time of observation [*non-participant observation; participant observation*] or discussion and consisting of highlights that can be remembered for later development; and full field notes written up as promptly and as fully as possible.

Discussion

Keeping good systematic field notes is an essential part of undertaking qualitative research as observations and interviews are only useful to the extent that they can be remembered and recorded. Researchers should not make the mistake and believe that notes only relate to when the researcher is in direct contact with their respondent(s). As is advocated by many (Bogdan and Taylor, 1975; Burgess, 1984), field notes can be kept at all stages of the research process, from gaining access to a setting, when bargains are struck with the more powerful gate keepers; at the stage where the researchers might be handed around to others in the organization on their way to an interview; and after the interview or observation has taken place. Many researchers talk of the importance of spending time sitting in their car/train in order to capture important last-minute reflections. For many there is a feeling that some of the most important insights come when an interview (q.v.) has come to a close, the tape recorder has been switched off and the paper and pens have been put away and the respondent is walking you to the door – probably thinking they will never see you again. Also included under the heading of field notes is the use of a research diary (q.v.). Diaries can be an extremely useful ways for researchers to record the perspectives and even the feelings they had at the time and an important source of data if the research is to contain a reflective component.

Bogdan and Taylor (1975) indicate that systematic and analytical participatory research, for the most part, depends on recording accurate and detailed field notes. They recommend that notes be taken at each *and every* stage of the fieldwork process as well as after all meetings, casual as well as formal, including phone calls. They suggest also that researchers need to guard against spending all their time in 'the field' [*field research*] as they will have too little time left to write up their notes. They offer the following good field note practice to help recall conversations and other details (Bogdan and Taylor, 1995: 62–64):

1. Look for keywords in your subjects remarks.
2. Concentrate on the first and last remarks of each conversation.
3. Leave the setting as soon as you have observed as much as you can accurately remember.
4. Record your notes as soon after the observation session as possible.
5. Don't talk to anyone about your observation until you have recorded your field notes.
6. Draw a diagram of the physical layout and setting and if you walk about trace your movement through it.
7. On the diagram indicate where specific parts of the conversation occurred before the detailed field notes are written and ensure you attempt to pick up missing data at a later date.

Using a tape recorder to collect data should not be seen as a substitute for keeping good field notes. Recorders can fail, and fail to collect important additional information such as your views and the respondent's non-verbals. Tapes are useful though for the fact that when replaying tapes of conversations one often has the impression that you are back in the interview. The intonations in the voice that you hear serve to transport you back into the room, allowing you even to recall certain other clues such as body language.

Field notes become very detailed and very complicated. If, for example, the researcher is undertaking conversational analysis (q.v.) (see Silverman, 2000), then the amount of information that needs to be collected will be of an order of magnitude more than for general observation of interviewing. Silverman (1993: 118) has a good example of a basic transcription. Another detailed approach is discourse analysis (q.v.). This takes into account a much broader social context, is less concerned with the detail of the actual conversations and requires a much wider range of information to be collected (e.g. other texts such as newspapers and company reports). Finally, critical discourse analysis takes this even further by placing emphasis on things such as the power within relations and the ideologies that are represented within language (e.g. Fairclough, 1995; Fairclough and Hardy, 1997).

Prospects

The writing of field notes can often have a considerable effect on respondents and this provides real problems for researchers who may wish to record details of what they have observed but are not able to find the time or space to make the recording. This problem is most acute if the researcher is conducting a covert participant observation study where leaving the workplace would arouse suspicion or upset the flow of work. Another related issue is individuals seeing you take field notes. As with all research notes, they are often written in a style and in a form that make sense to the researcher. They might also contain sensitive or personal information that is not intended for others to read. The issue is a serious one as divulging personal or sensitive information to third parties would break a researcher's ethical (q.v.) code and, moreover, jeopardize the prospects of others should sensitive information be released. Concerns along these lines might suggest completion of field notes is best done away from the workplace and kept private.

Richard Thorpe

FIELD RESEARCH

Definition

An important tradition which emerged in twentieth-century social science was one of researchers getting themselves deeply involved or immersed in whichever part of the social world they wanted to investigate. The impulse was to get away from the desk or the academic library and go out into the field to do something more than simply conduct interviews. That impulse was realized in two ways: first, in the anthropological work in economically non-developed settings by such figures as Malinowski, Boas, Evans-Pritchard and Mead and, second, in the sociological studies of aspects of modern, mainly urban, social life by sociologists inspired and led by Park and Burgess of the Chicago School of sociology.

Discussion

Such studies can be bracketed together as *field research*, and included within this category are both *participant observation* (q.v.) and *ethnography* (q.v.) These two terms are sometimes used interchangeably and sometimes to distinguish between different things. We find each of the terms sometimes being used in a 'weak sense' and sometimes in a 'strong sense'. To clarify matters in a way that is helpful to researchers, I shall differentiate here between participant observation and ethnography, and, in the course of doing this, suggest that we restrict the use of each of the terms to its 'strong' sense. This is done in the hope of checking an unfortunate trend for researchers to seek the legitimacy that is felt to come from 'getting close to one's research subjects' by too cavalierly grabbing at the ethnographic or participant observation label.

The very expression 'participant observation' invites its application to a very wide range of research practices. Almost any observational (q.v.) work involves a degree of 'participation', even if that participation involves little more than entering the same room as the research subjects and watching and listening to them. To avoid the 'participant observation' label losing any real distinctiveness, it would therefore be helpful to restrict its application to the strong sense of the term and, indeed, to what I would claim to be the original Chicago impulse: one of getting closely involved with the people being studied in their 'natural' setting (as opposed to a laboratory or interview room) and actively interacting and sharing experiences with them in a manner which goes way beyond simple 'observation'. In this spirit we can take participant observation to be a research practice in which the investigator *joins* the group, community or organization being studied – as either a full or partial member – and both participates in and observes activities, asks questions, takes part in conversations (q.v.) and reads relevant documents [*content analysis*]. This happens over a period of time which is sufficient for the researcher to come to understand the significance to the people being studied of the range of norms, practices and values – of both a formal/official and informal/unofficial kind – which pertain in the research setting. In the field of work organization and management studies, we can see this approach exemplified in the *Boys in White* study of the medical school (Becker et al., 1961), the *Men who Manage* study of managerial work (Dalton, 1959), the 'Banana time' study of work group behaviour (Roy, 1958) and the *On the Shopfloor* study of factory life (Lupton, 1963). This selection of significant studies illustrates the above recognition that the participant observer may be 'either a full or a partial member' of the group, community or organization being studied; although they got very close indeed to the experiences of their research subjects, none of the *Boys in White* research team actually became students or doctors. Roy did, however, become a shop-floor worker.

Ethnography, in what I am calling the strong sense of the term, requires a participation observation style of fieldwork. Participant observation can thus most usefully be seen as a *means* of producing ethnographies rather than as something synonymous with ethnography. One could carry out a fully worthwhile participant observation study without producing an ethnography. What is it that makes research ethnographic, then? It is where sequences of observation are related 'to a cultural whole', where there is a 'global reference which encompasses these observations and within which the different data throw light on each other' (Baszanger and Dodier, 2004: 13) [*dialogic; structuration theory*]. An ethnography is a written account of the cultural [*cross-cultural research*] life of a social group, organization or community. Within that, there can be a focus on a particular aspect of life in that setting, but the written ethnography 'wraps up' any specific concerns within broader attention to 'the construction of cultural norms, expressions of organizational values, and patterns of workplace behaviour', as Bryman and Bell (2003: 317) put it, giving examples of Kunda's study of an American high-technology company, Watson's (2001, originally 1994b) account of managerial work in a UK telecommunications manufacturing company, Casey's (1995) exploration of change in a US-based multinational, and Delbridge's (1998) study of new manufacturing techniques and worker experience in two factories.

Prospects

My own contribution to this work (Watson, 1994b/2001) required a whole 12 months of working as a senior manager within the selected business. And, in the light of that experience, I would advise those considering working as a participant observer, especially if they have an interest in producing a full ethnography, that it is an immensely challenging undertaking. Every day 'in the field' requires a sophisticated level of *identity work* (both 'inward-looking' and 'outward-looking') to handle the tensions of switching back and forth between being a 'native' and a 'stranger' (Watson, 2007). And after leaving the field there is not just the challenge of making sense of an inevitably enormous mass of research material. There is an equally enormous writing challenge [*representations*]. The ethnographer must produce a social-scientifically credible account of the investigation, yet, at the same time, they need to apply the skills and techniques of the creative writer (Humphreys et al., 2003; Van Maanen, 1988; Watson, 1995a). All of this is vital if full justice is to be done to the richness and complexity of the analyses and the stories that participant observation and ethnography make possible.

Tony Watson

FOCUS GROUP

Definition

Using focus groups involves gathering data using an extended, moderated discussion among a small number of selected individuals. The discussion concerns a topic or topics introduced by the moderator. The moderator steers the participants' discussion using a pre-determined, pre-sequenced list of question areas (and/or other stimulus materials). The distinguishing features of focus groups are five-fold. First, they are discussions – interaction between participants is a key part of the approach [*dialogic*]. Second, the participants are small in number – authorities suggest between five (Robson, 1989) and 12 (Stewart et al., 1990) participants. Third, the participants are relatively homogeneous, as far as their characteristics germane to the topic under investigation are concerned. Fourth, the moderator stimulates and 'steers' the conversation (q.v.), soliciting or limiting participation appropriately. Finally, they are research tools. The terminology remains unsettled, with 'focus group', 'focus group interview' and 'group interview' being used by some to designate the same thing, while others seek to differentiate (subtly) using these and related names (Boddy, 2005; Kitzinger and Barbour, 1999) [*interviews – group*].

What are today known as focus groups had their origins in the 'focused interviews' and 'group interviews' that came to be widely used during the Second World War. These wartime interviews were conducted in both social science and market research settings – and this duality of use remains true today (see Krueger and Casey, 2000; Merton et al., 1956; Morgan D.L., 1997). Group interviews fell somewhat out of favour in the social sciences, particularly in the USA, but the market research community has remained steadfast in their use. Schlackman (1989) provided a comment on their usage in marketing research in the USA and the UK. Focus groups have had a renaissance in the social science community, and now are a widely used tool in their own right and, particularly, in combination with other methods [*mixed methods in management research*].

Focus groups are today widely used because they result (in appropriate conditions) in the generation of insightful, useful research data in reasonable time and cost. Unfortunately, because of their apparent simplicity, many groups may be conducted that result in the generation of little useful data. To be successful, focus group research needs to be well planned and carefully conducted. Planning for focus groups must consider what is to be asked (and/or what stimulus materials are to be presented); of whom, in what setting; how and by whom the group is to be assembled, built, moderated and recorded; the period over which the group will extend; and how gathered data are to be analyzed. Issues of the number of groups, the nature of any quotas to be used in selecting participants and more general 'sampling' questions are also relevant.

Discussion

Krueger and Casey (2000) identify eight non-exhaustive areas of use for focus groups: decision-making, product/programme development, customer satisfaction, planning and goal setting, needs assessment, quality movements, employee concerns, policy-making and testing. Each one of the areas has its place in management research. The 'classic' application in management research of focus groups is as a precursor to larger-scale sample survey work. Focus groups are used to generate insight for the development of questionnaire items. A widely cited study of this type is the SERVQUAL work of Parasuraman et al. (1988). This type of application continues to be used: Douglas and Craig (2006) report an extensive use of this approach. Others have used focus groups as the primary vehicle: Becket et al. (2000) report making this choice because of previous research success and its appropriateness in developing understanding.

Developments in the use of focus groups continue to be recorded: Imrie et al. (2002) used focus groups to both (in part) generate a model and then critique it, because of their particular usefulness in this context. They then analyzed data using computer-aided methods – and the use of computers and communication technologies is a growing trend, both in the conduct and analysis of groups. For example, in 1997 Catterall and Maclaran called for programs capable of dealing with video (q.v.) and interaction data, not simply the word-based data conventionally selected for analysis (though even here, traditions and approaches differ from those seeking a 'gestalt' perspective on focus group contributions to those like Imrie et al. using QSR Nud*ist) [*CAQDAS; interviewing*]. Easton et al. (2003) present and experiment in using a Group Support System (GSS) and cite other authors calling for 'electronic' support for focus groups [*interviews – electronic*].

Prospects

The use of focus groups is widespread; searching management literature databases identifies thousands of papers using the method. However, there remains wide variability in what authors regard as a focus group, with points of difference concerning size, composition and operation. There are further differences concerning the most appropriate methods to analyze data, and indeed what constitutes the data to be analyzed. Some of these divergences may be attributed to different cultural traditions (for example, the widespread use of quasi-domestic settings for groups in British research, and their almost complete absence in America) and to different disciplinary traditions (those emerging from consumer behaviour/psychology and those from management decision support). Boddy's (2005) paper is testimony to the continuance of these debates. Some of the differences may also be attributed to a failure by researchers to engage with the wider body of management research beyond their own tradition.

Barry Davies

G

GROUNDED THEORY

Definition

Grounded theory appeared on the sociological scene in 1967 as a polemic against the formal deductive theorizing and dedicated quantitative empiricism that then characterized the discipline. Its authors, Glaser and Strauss (1967), were among a group of sociologists interested in reviving sociology's Chicago School tradition of participant observation (q.v.) [*field research*] of focused social situations to theorize action in context. Grounded theories were developed through intensive and direct engagement with the social situation studied and reflected an initial rejection of a priori theory – the abstract theorizing of the time. Its informing meta-theoretical perspective on social life is symbolic interactionism (Blumer, 1954) [*individualism*].

Consistent with their interest in reasserting the primacy of intensive first-hand engagement with a social scene as the basis for theorizing [*ethnography*], grounded theory's research procedures follow a concept-indicator model of theory development (Glaser, 1978). Theorizing proceeds by developing conceptual categories that are indicated by sets of similarly patterned empirical observations. These observations are generated through various naturalistically oriented data-gathering modes, including participant observation (q.v.), semi-structured interviewing, and sourcing archives [*content analysis; historical analysis; interviews*].

The constant comparative method in which data observations are closely read, compared and conceptualized, and theoretically driven sampling, provide the foundation for analysis and category development [*matrices analysis*]. This process begins nominally with the 'naming' of observations. By comparing data observations with each other and to provisional names assigned to them, researchers attempt to develop common and distinct conceptualizations for multiple observations across a data set. As conceptualization progresses, in addition to comparing data observations to each other, observations are compared with the drafted conceptual categories to refine and elaborate them, and conceptual categories are examined and compared with each other as a stimulus to thinking about how they might be arranged in relation to each other to form a theoretical framework [*comparative analysis; inductive analysis*]. Various coding paradigms (e.g. Glaser's '6 Cs' (1978)) are available as heuristics to help researchers think about the types of theoretical element implied in their categories.

Sampling in the grounded theory approach always proceeds on theoretical grounds, to find information-rich sources on a particular phenomenon. This commitment drives sampling decisions throughout the study as researchers are always actively thinking about and searching for observations that will provide additional information on and help them better to understand their in-process conceptualizations. This means that data collection is an iterative and flexible process as the materializing theory drives it. Furthermore, in-process conceptual categories are in an ongoing state of flux as additional data and comparisons result in their being revised, refined or discarded. Theoretical development comes to a close (temporarily at least) when the theoretical implications of the categories stabilize – that is when additional data and comparisons result in no new information or understanding. This is the point of theoretical saturation.

Discussion

By the early 1970s, grounded theorizing was informing studies appearing in prominent management journals (Locke, 2000/2001) and it is the canonical citation for theory-building studies. In many respects, Barry Turner's work modelled the approach; his disaster studies that theorize the contributing informational conditions for failures of organizational foresight are exemplary (e.g. Turner, 1976). In another classic study, Burgelman (1983) adopted the approach to develop a stage model of the internal corporate venturing process.

That the grounded theory approach should have been so readily taken up in management is not surprising as much of the discipline's theoretical concern is with situated social processes. Further, the approach's intensive naturalist data collection strategies and attendant logic for an open-ended approach to theorizing enable it to capitalize on new substantive areas as they arrive on the managerial scene as well as to refresh established ones. For example, as technology increasingly became a feature of organizational life, researchers drew on grounded theory to understand how organizations adopt technological tools. Orlikowski (1993) used a grounded theory approach to produce a multifaced conceptualization of how organizations adopted and used computed-aided software engineering tools. More recently, Gopal and Prasad (2000) drew on grounded theory's analytic processes to examine the interactional milieu in which Group Decision Support Systems are used. Parry (1998) has been pursuing a grounded theory approach to refresh the well-worn area of leadership.

While grounded theory is a clear fixture in management research discourse, the approach has evolved as researchers selectively integrate into it the logics and practices of other qualitative research styles and other theoretical traditions. For example, Ailon-Souday and Kunda (2003) integrate grounded theory's analytic procedures with an ethnographic approach to theorize how national identity serves as a symbolic resource in social struggles engendered by globalization. Eisenhardt and her colleagues have integrated grounded theory's analytic procedures with Yin's (1994) rendering of case study (q.v.) research to create a hybrid approach exemplified in a study of how dynamic capabilities reconfigure division resources in multi-business firms (Galunic and Eisenhardt, 2001). And, Coopey et al. (1998) integrated grounded theory's procedures for developing conceptual categories with structuration theory (q.v.) to understand innovation.

Problems and prospects

Grounded theory has enjoyed almost forty years of elaboration and debate. As with any cultural artifact, research 'methodologies' change over time. The originators went separate and somewhat contentious ways (cf. Glaser, 1992) as Glaser insisted on its being executed as 'pure' induction, letting concepts 'emerge' from the data, while Strauss increasingly acknowledged, and encouraged, researcher agency in the interpretative process and elaborated various ways in which extant literature might be integrated into grounded theory's analytic processes (Strauss and Corbin, 1990/1998). Challenges have also been made to the practice of fracturing data to assign meaning, arguing that the researcher loses sight of the 'whole' in the process. Yet it persists and evolves.

While the grounded theory approach appeared at a time when methods discourse was decidedly modernist, forty years of development reflect the paradigmatic plurality of current qualitative research. Reflecting this, management researchers have selectively drawn from the canonical texts to resource a paradigmatically varied array of studies, including those that are more modernist (e.g. Rafaeli and Sutton, 1991), interpretative (e.g. Gopal and Prasad, 2000) and postmodern (q.v.) (e.g. Covaleski et al., 1998) in their orientation. Interestingly, variations of the approach developed by the originators' students have yet to be drawn on. Charmaz (2000) develops a constructionist [*constructivism*] extension of the approach well suited to studies of identity processes. Recently, Clarke (2005) draws on a 'social worlds' theoretical framework to create a provocative extension of the grounded theory approach that includes consideration of more postmodern (q.v.) elements such as voice, discourse (q.v.), texts, the non-human, and power.

Karen Locke

HERMENEUTICS

Definition

The quest for understanding motivates most qualitative research methodologies. In turn, how we come to *understand* depends on how we interpret, and give meaning to, language and action. Hermeneutics is central to this process, defined by Ricœur (1981) as the 'theory of the operations of understanding in their relation to the interpretation of texts'. But, before moving on to equate action with language, or analysing 'action as text' [*discourse analysis; narrative research; social poetics*], it is useful to plot the development of hermeneutics from its origins in biblical exegesis, to its role in contemporary social science and philosophy.

The root of the term lies in the Greek *hermêneia*, generally translated as 'interpretation', and *hermêneuein*, 'to interpret'. The origin of these words probably rests with the messenger to the gods, Hermes, whose function was to bring to human understanding messages from the gods which would have normally been beyond the ability of human intelligence to decipher. In ancient times, *hermêneuein* had three strands of meaning: to say, to explain, and to translate; each of which may be expressed as 'to interpret', yet each which has its own distinct meaning within the act of interpretation, and each distinguishing itself from the other. To *say* means to proclaim, or announce, and in terms of the messages of the gods, this would

have been seen as the first act of interpretation. *Explanation* adds the interpretation of meaning to the proclamation; and *translation* gives meaning when the original language may not be one's own, but may also be appropriate if the style of language used is unfamiliar to the audience. All three might have been part of Hermes' task as he delivered messages from the gods.

Thereafter, hermeneutics developed as a means of interpreting biblical texts (exegesis), and although the first reference to this activity is probably in 1654 (Palmer, 1969), it is likely that such interpretation dates from biblical times, when scriptures were written on tablets in ancient languages. Biblical exegesis achieved a fresh momentum at the time of the Reformation as Protestant ministers sought new interpretations to complement their movement away from the teachings of Rome.

Discussion

The emergence of hermeneutics in philosophy and the social sciences can be traced to a development from a general philological methodology in which the techniques employed in interpreting biblical works were applied to other texts. The first writer to identify and explore this 'science of linguistic understanding' was Schleiermacher (1768–1834), followed by Dilthey (1833–1911), for whom interpreting human action required both a historical understanding and a recognition of the distinction between understanding events and expressions (*verstehen*), and obtaining explanatory knowledge (*erkennen*).

It was Heidegger (1880–1976), however, who developed hermeneutics to the position of importance it now occupies, by using the phenomenological (q.v.) approach of his mentor Husserl (1859–1938) [*existential phenomenology*] towards the question of one's everyday 'being in the world' (*in-der-Weldsein*). In doing so, he moved from an epistemological imperative to an ontological approach which grounds hermeneutics in the social sciences as a means of relating phenomena to one's underlying notions of being.

This approach was further developed by Heidegger's pupil, Gadamer (1900–2002), and by Ricœur (1913–2005), whose combined works inform, either intentionally or not, much of what is written on interpretative methodology today. It was Heidegger who first engaged with the problems he saw in common with positivism, traditional hermeneutics, and phenomenology: the subject – object dichotomy. Heidegger rejected this as problematic and instead advocated a position of 'situatedness' and 'belonging' (Sköldberg, 1998), and focused on the place of humans in the world. From this position he felt it would be impossible for any human to approach any investigation without bringing to it their already felt experiences and knowledge of the world, a *pre-understanding*. This gives rise to the notion of the hermeneutic circle, between pre-understanding and understanding, where one's understanding of a phenomena depends on how one's previous experiences impact on the experience of that phenomena: 'interpretation is never a presuppositionless apprehending of something' (Heidegger, 1926/1962). More bluntly expressed, '[r]eality is always already interpreted' (Alvesson and Sköldberg, 2000).

These notions stand in stark contrast to the Anglo-Saxon sociological tradition of the early to mid-twentieth century, and may represent one response to the 'toppling of the orthodox consensus' (Giddens, 1984) [*structuration theory*]. That it did not become more influential earlier might be explained in the tardy translation to English of many of the core texts, and reluctance by some to engage with the works of Heidegger, mostly to do with his political associations with German facism.

Notwithstanding this, if, as qualitative researchers, we set out to try to understand why human beings behave as they do, then we need to grasp the meaning behind the activities in which they engage. In turn, to give meaning to these activities we need to interpret behaviour with reference to the rules and norms which govern these activities and behaviour. It is in this sense that Ricœur commends us to view action as text, and interpret it in the same way, applying our historical *pre-understanding* to the current phenomena. How we make sense of metaphors in text, elucidating 'similarity in difference' (Gadamer, 1989), can be applied to our interpretation of action. No better example of this can there be than Morgan's (1980, 1986/1997) analysis of organizations, where they are likened to machines, theatres, political systems, etc., and where within each scenario the actors fulfil the behaviour patters relevant to the particular metaphor (q.v.).

The contemporary relevance of hermeneutics in social science is that it sits with critical theory (q.v.) as a method of analysis of actual social realities. Indeed, both offer related approaches which Kelly (1990) suggests are important for three reasons: that each has a history of critique dating since the mid-twentieth century; that in each there is an awareness of historicity; and that each already inspires ethical and political critique in our present climate. Notwithstanding this association, exponents of critical theory, such as Marcuse, remain steadfastly critical of what they see as the mythologizing tendencies of Heidegger's hermeneutics; the idealist desire to identify a bedrock of human pre-understanding to which all meaning ultimately must recur and of which the human subject partakes in a state of mute awe or wonder [*method; process philosophy*].

Alan Murray

HISTORICAL ANALYSIS

Definition

Historical analysis is a method of the examination of evidence in coming to an understanding of the past. It is particularly applied to evidence contained in documents, although it can be applied to all artefacts. The historian is, first, seeking to gain some certainty as to the facts of the past. Establishing the facts also gives the researcher a chronology [*dialogic*]. The second task is to seek to establish cause and effect between those facts in order to understand why things happened. It is important to remember that while the past is the immensity of everything that has happened, history is what we know of the past [*hermeneutics*].

Historical analysis is not only applicable to archive-based research. Any management research where the researcher is using documentary evidence, however recent, should bear in mind the principles of historical analysis [*oral history*].

The modern concept of historical analysis stems from the move to a scientific approach to history advocated by Ranke and the German school of historians in the mid-nineteenth century. The focus was moved to the rigorous analysis of documents as the material for the re-creation of the past, the perceived historical patterns and an explanation of them. In addition, the emphasis was placed on understanding the context of the past. This understanding should be informed, but not overwhelmed, by the preoccupations of the present, either of society as a whole or of the specific historian (Jeremy, 2002). Classic studies using historical analysis are Chandler (1990) and North (1990).

Discussion

In a business context, there is a wealth of documentary evidence retained as a matter of routine in archives or current files, which is a prime source of research material [*content analysis; narrative research*]. However, its interpretation is subject to the same rules of analysis as any other form of historical document. The key rules, adapted for the business context, are as follows.

1. When was the document written? Was it contemporary with the event being described, some time after the event or in anticipation of it? The closer the document is to the past event, both temporally and physically, the more reliable it should be.
2. Where was it produced? Was it in that part of the organization closely connected with the events under review? A divisional report may have an immediacy of detail, but where the division is seeking to protect or enhance its own reputation, a report may differ significantly from a more dispassionate account prepared by a central function with a wider perspective.
3. By whom was it produced? What was his/her position in the organization; what was her/his expertise and motive? A senior manager may produce a more wide-ranging account than a junior manager whose preoccupation and expertise run only to the immediate involvement. Equally, a senior manager may use more diffuse, diplomatic language than a junior professional.
4. For whom was it produced and for what purpose? A report issued to a superior may differ from an action memo to a subordinate in its account of events. Is the document seeking to make a case for a specific course of action, or excusing a mistake, or in anticipation of a performance review, either the author's own or that of the document's recipient? In each case the same author is liable to select a very different series of facts involved in a single event, the selection dependant on the story he/she is wishing to tell.
5. What is the form of the document? A formal report to the Board is more likely to be the product of careful thought, structured in such a way that it is defensible by the author when reviewed by experienced critics. An informal memo

108

between peers is less likely to be carefully drafted, but for that very reason may be a more accurate reflection of reality than a politically sensitive report.

6. What is not said in the document? The author may consider certain things as so obvious that they do not need to be said, she/he may merely have overlooked them as she/he did not think them significant or she/he may be ignorant of them. The reason for the absence may influence the reliability of the author or reflect some more fundamental fact. For example, the absence of any mention of the impact of a strategy on employees may be significant in understanding industrial relations at that time. In each case an understanding of the wider context of the document is essential to make an assessment of its contribution.

These questions are specifically addressed to text, but they can, with modification, be applied to maps, statistical tables and other records, or even artefacts, in order to determine their evidential value (Marwick, 2001).

Prospects

In the latter part of the twentieth century the poststructuralist [*postmodernism; semiotics*] concern with the problems of language put a new emphasis on discourse analysis (q.v.). In particular, the role of power and politics in the selection of language by an author has come to the fore in the interpretation of discourse. There is an emphasis on the location of the author in the hierarchy of the organization if the influence of power on the author's language is to be understood. It has been argued that this is simply a sociologist's belated recognition of what has been understood by historians for centuries (Alvesson and Sköldberg, 2000: 206).

At a more extreme level, there is a postmodernist view that each reading of a discourse could produce a new interpretation; deconstruction (q.v.) (or interpretation) of the text did not lead to understanding meaning, only to an endless deferral of meaning (Munslow, 1997). There is an implication that no history, in the sense of a truthful account of the past, can therefore be written and some postmodernists claimed that therefore any account of the past can be valid. In the light of the reaction to controversial histories, and in particular to those denying the Holocaust, there has been a withdrawal from this extreme view and a return to an assessment of the evidential value of the discourse. However imaginative an interpretation of the past, it must be constrained by the undeniable empirical evidence (Jordanova, 2000).

Theoretical concerns with the validity of positivist research and the inevitably subjective interpretation of documents have raised the question whether truthful history could ever be written. The prevailing view among historians currently is that while we cannot achieve a wholly accurate picture of the past [*realism*], nevertheless with scrupulous care in relation to the analysis of sources, the account, even if it is partial and provisional, can be claimed to be the historical truth. 'The stories we tell will be true stories, even if the truth they tell is our own, and even if other people can and will tell them differently' (Evans, 1997: 249).

David Bricknell

INDIVIDUALISM

Definition

Assumptions about the nature and relationship of individuals and society are central to how we research social phenomena because they determine our understanding of how individual action is related to structural features of the society and how action is structured in everyday contexts. Economists, for instance, tend to treat their *homo oeconomicus* as if it were a completely autonomous decision-maker and therefore propose that all accounts of economic interaction are to be *explained* by reference to the aggregated doings of individuals. This 'methodological individualism' also forms the basis for the 'rational actor models' which have invaded management studies in such guises as 'game theory' or 'agency theory' (Arrow, 1994).

Max Weber (1972) is most commonly associated with the origins of methodological individualism in sociology, arguing for interpretative explanations that get at subjective understandings of the actions of component individuals (Schatzki, 2002). The implication is that '... social phenomena must be explained in terms of individuals, their physical and psychic states, actions, interactions, social situation and physical environment' (Udehn, 2001: 354).

Discussion

The concept of the self-contained, 'entitative' individual that is endowed with a 'knowing mind' is also prevalent in organization and management studies. This view derives from the Cartesian depiction of the individual acting autonomously from and hence upon their social world through the mediation of such personal properties as 'expert knowledge', 'mind maps' or 'personality traits'. 'Possessive' and 'knowing' individuals are thus seen to be the architects and controllers of the internal and external order, with their individual possessions and intentions 'causing' human action (Dachler and Hosking, 1995; Eberle, 1995). Management and organizational research within such subjectivist and cognitivist frameworks consequently focuses on the inner dynamics, or human psyche, of individuals (Shotter, 1993).

In opposition to the view that social phenomena are to be explained by individuals' make-ups and their interaction are scholars who view human action as fundamentally shaped by broader social and cultural processes. Structuralists, for instance, argue that social phenomena can be studied objectively and scientifically on a collective dimension without a concern for individual-level properties (Mayhew, 1980). From this position, social phenomena can only be explained by reference to the behaviour or the properties of 'social entities' such as organizations or cultures, not that of individuals or groups of individuals. In such accounts, social phenomena such as economies or political parties are made up of, or governed by, 'abstract' structures. These structures are termed 'abstract' because they are irreducible in an individualist sense. Collectivist views thus prioritize the whole over the part by proposing the thing-like existence of a collective consciousness and collective bonds of solidarity that precede and have determinate powers over individual actions and beliefs. Contemporary collectivist paradigms in sociology and management research include versions of network theory, structural sociology, sociological realism and neo-functionalism (Sawyer, 2002).

However, the unresolved debate between individualists and collectivists is riven by terminological and conceptual inconsistencies, in particular as many claims address not only epistemological but also ontological issues (Udehn, 2001) [*actor-network theory*]. Ontological individualism refers to the nature of social life. It maintains that any social phenomenon, whether a family, a government, an economic system, a religion, or an interaction on the street, is a constellation of interrelated individuals (Schatzki, 2002). Culture [*cross-cultural research*] and society are thus just one feature or variable of the environment of which the individual's inner self is capable of making a representation (McHoul and Rapley, 2005). Alternatively, ontological 'collectivists' maintain that not all aspects of sociality can be reduced to individuals and their relations. For instance, Durkheim's (1893/1964) *conscience collective* represents an ontologically *sui generis* realm that is *different in being* from individualist matters and exists outside individual consciousness. Society thus holds a set of values and beliefs and the individual's personality is subjugated to the moral authority of the community. Any deviation from the collective consensus results in sanctions and punishment by the community. From such 'functionalist' positions individual agents are conceived to be the play-balls of the external forces of large-scale cultural or social facts (Stueber, 2006).

Prospects

Increasingly, however, both individualist and collectivist understandings and explanations of social phenomena are regarded as inadequately explaining the complexity and ambiguity of organizational life (Hosking et al., 1995). Individualist approaches often fall short of recognizing the influence of broader contexts on individual actions. As a result, they struggle to establish theories of cognitive collectivity (Spender, 1998) and thus tend to dismiss the implicit, tacit or unconscious layer of knowledge which enables both the habitual and symbolic organization of reality (Reckwitz, 2002). This criticism is further fuelled by many contemporary philosophers who find the empiricist assumptions concerning the existence of individual minds no longer credible (Hosking et al., 1995). Collectivist concepts, on the other hand, are only limitedly suited to explaining organizational behaviour, and thus relating to the questions posed in the organizational literature because they focus on social phenomena in human societies and thus propose an entirely different set of questions from those of organizational researchers (Mayhew, 1980). Furthermore, collectivist approaches fall short because of a conspicuous failure to agree upon what features, in addition to individual actions, are to count in providing scientific explanations [*positivism and post-positivism; realism*]. Are they those of a deep collective unconscious, modes of production, social structures, or discourse (q.v.)? The result tends to be a dogmatic assertion of divisions as to which of these features are simply effects, and which have originary power.

In the case of management and organizational research the question is, furthermore, whether collectivist researchers claim that sociological concepts and structures actually exist or whether they make the weaker claim that they are convenient means of describing and explaining organizational behaviour. However, if one makes only methodological claims and thus views the realm of the social as a useful rather than real concept, then this realm cannot exert determinate powers. If collective phenomena can have causal power over individuals, they must be real. To accept that social structures are real raises the question of the ontological status of the individual. Assuming the existence of both, structures and individuals, represents a problematic 'dualist ontology' of two distinct social orders (Sawyer, 2002). Alternatively, simply erasing human agency from the picture gives rise to methodological difficulties in determining what it is that makes up the social realm if not individuals, or groups of individuals and their relations (Eberle, 1995). The response has been to suggest third ways in which neither individuals nor collective structures are primary, but each remains complicit with the other. This has been referred to as the 'practice (q.v.) turn' in the social sciences and organization theory. One influential work in this movement is Mead's classic (1934) book *Mind, Self and Society*. While from an individualist view social relationships are not natural, but optional to the self-sufficient individual, Mead's idea of 'symbolic interactionism' emphasizes human interdependency. In this view, mind is inseparable from social processes and thinking has its origins in social interchange. This stream has developed into particular forms of social constructionism (q.v.) (Gergen, 1999) and *relationally responsive* versions of our understandings of everyday doings in managerial and organizational life (Shotter, 1993).

While relational concepts make an essentially epistemological claim, practice-theoretical concepts suggest an ontological shift. For instance, Giddens's (1984) 'structuration theory' (q.v.) and Bourdieu's (1990) 'structuralist constructivism' place 'social practices' at the core of our theoretical understandings of social nature. They thus attempt to reconcile the individual and the social *qua* social practices which provide a background understanding of what counts as things, what counts as human beings and what it makes sense to do, on the basis of which we can direct our actions towards particular things and people (Dreyfus, 2006). Social structures are therefore no longer viewed as merely constraining individual agency but instead enable it. Agents reproduce and transform existing structures and practices while at the same time being influenced by them (Stueber, 2006).

Mike Zundel

INDUCTIVE ANALYSIS

Definition

Inductive analysis aims to systematically generate theory grounded in specific instances of empirical observation. As such it sharply contrasts with hypothetico-deductive methodology in which a conceptual and theoretical structure is constructed prior to, and is tested through, observation. Inductive analysis has a long history in anglophone philosophy (e.g. Bacon, 1620/1960; Locke, 1690/1988; Mill, 1874) which pre-dates deductive approaches. However, it is the latter which has become the established mainstream methodology, especially in management research, under the aegis of Popper's (1968) falsificationism, which disputed the possibility of the inductive verification of theories [*critical realism*]. Although debate between rival exponents of induction and deduction in the social sciences is complex (Johnson and Duberley, 2000), a key contemporary justification for induction centres upon the view that, with deductive analyses, the testing of theoretical predictions entails the researcher's *a priori* conceptualization and operationalization of dimensions of actors' behaviour in which the subjective basis of that behaviour is often necessarily lost, or at best distorted rather than captured (Guba and Lincoln, 1994). In order to access the subjective or cultural dimension, it is argued, explanations must be generated through *verstehen* [*hermeneutics*] which necessarily entails the inductive description and analysis of the subjective interpretations deployed by the actors who are being investigated (Giddens, 1976; Shotter, 1975) [*phenomenology*]. Hence induction is closely related to what Denzin (1971: 166) calls the logic of naturalistic inquiry where the researcher actively enters 'the worlds of native people ... to render those worlds understandable from the standpoint of a theory that is grounded in the behaviours, languages, definitions, attitudes, and feelings of those studied' and tries to theoretically explain what shapes and influences their behaviour.

As noted above, inductive analysis usually entails developing descriptions of actors' subjective cultural experiences, which await discovery (Glaser, 1992: 16), in order to explain their behaviour. However, a fuller analysis will also entail the development of explanations of any observed variation in those cultural elements (Lofland, 1970). Although there are different forms of inductive analysis, including different types of grounded theory (q.v.) (e.g. Glaser, 1992; Strauss and Corbin, 1990/1998) and analytic induction (Cressey, 1953; Denzin, 1978), below a composite overview of inductive analysis is presented which outlines and integrates key aspects of these different approaches. Although at risk of some over simplification, inductive analysis can be broken down into five key interrelated elements, some of which are synchronic.

First, at the outset of induction, many researchers would follow Blumer's (1954: 7) advice that they should use what he calls 'sensitizing concepts' which give 'the user a general sense of reference and guidelines in approaching empirical instances ... [and] ... merely suggest directions in which to look'. This idea is of particular importance because it clarifies the relationship between prior conceptualization and subsequent data collection during induction. For Blumer, concepts must be used in a way that only gives a sense of direction in which to look. They must act merely as guides for uncovering empirical variation in the phenomenon of interest, rather than imposing conceptualized prescriptions of what to see and how to record, as is the case of what he calls 'definitive' concepts. Once the latter are developed, and operationalized into sets of indicators, they become fixed benchmarks which guide data collection in deductive research so as to enable testing whereas sensitizing concepts enable researchers to uncover variation in the phenomenon of interest because they are not fixed.

Second, armed with sensitizing concepts, the next element entails gaining access (q.v.) to and defining the phenomenon whose variation is to be explained. The aim here is to look for patterns in the phenomenon and create a taxonomy of categories which embraces all observed variations in terms of shared characteristics and differences. Here it is important to review data for any deviant instances of the phenomenon that do not fit into the emergent observer-identified categorization of those variations. The aim here is to adjust those categories appropriately so that any deviant cases are then included in the taxonomy so as to create an exhaustive categorization of all variance in the phenomenon of interest.

Third, this element involves the creation of a provisional list of case features, common to each identified category, whose variation between categories might explain variation in the phenomenon of interest. As with the second element, various forms of coding [*matrices analysis; reliability; template analysis*] can aid these processes in order to elaborate the properties of categories and their interrelationships (Strauss and Corbin, 1990/1998). This is a key aspect of what Glaser and Strauss have called the constant comparative method (q.v.) (1967: 106) and entails data collection and analysis occurring together and recursively informing one another so as to generate theory.

Fourth, in principle, the second and third-elements, with their constant revision and iterations between data collection and analysis, continue simultaneously until what Glaser and Strauss (1967: 61) call 'theoretical saturation', where no additional data are being found which can either develop the taxonomy of categories, or their relationships to one another, or their properties in terms of case features. This might entail the theoretical sampling (Glaser and Strauss, 1967: 184) of new settings of the phenomena that will provide good contrasts and comparisons and thereby confront the emergent theory with the patterning of social events under different circumstances. Once no new variation in the phenomenon in terms of its categorization and attendant case features is evident, data collection is completed. Throughout it is necessary to compare across all the established categories and identify case features shared by more than one category and those unique to a particular category.

Finally, according to Bloor (1976, 1978), who seems to draw upon Mill's original inductive (1874) methods, shared case features are necessary but not sufficient for generating a category whereas unique case features are sufficient for generating a category. By analysing these patterns in the case features of established categories, the aim is to present theoretical explanations of observed variance in the phenomenon of interest. Once this process of theorization is accomplished by presenting explanations that fit the data, it is possible to then attempt what Morse (1994) calls recontextualization by abstracting the emergent theory to new settings and relating it to established knowledge.

Discussion

In sum, inductive analysis seeks to capture aspects of the social world from the perspective of actors and allows the revision of hypotheses and conceptual structures through the analysis and elimination of negative cases. Often the outcome is theory grounded in empirical data gathered from a relatively small number of cases of the phenomenon of interest. A significant issue is that the researcher must provide a processual (q.v.) account, or audit trail, of how inductive analysis of the social settings under investigation was accomplished by demonstrating how categories were derived and applied as well as showing how alternative theoretical explanations have been considered but rejected (Adler and Adler, 1994; Locke, 1996). In this manner a grounded theory, which is applicable to a number of cases of the phenomenon of interest and is taken to constitute a theoretical generalization because it is exhaustive, is slowly developed. This aspect has lead to the criticism that due to the small samples used, the method can rarely make claims about the representativeness of its samples and therefore any attempt at generalizing is tenuous. However, for Mitchell (1983; see also Stake, 2000), such a conception of generalizability entails a confusion about the

procedures appropriate to making probabilistic inferences from survey research. He argues that generalizability in survey research is based upon both statistical and logical (i.e. causal) inference and that there is a tendency to elide the former with the latter in that 'the postulated causal connection among features in a sample may be assumed to exist in some parent population simply because the features may be inferred to co-exist in that population' (Mitchell, 1983: 200). He proceeds to argue that, in contrast, inference in inductive research can only be logical and derives its generalizability from unassailable logical inference based upon the demonstrated all-inclusive power of the inductively generated and tested theory (1983: 190).

While there may be a growing recognition that inductive analysis is particularly appropriate for research into management and organizational issues, examples of the overt use of all aspects of the inductive analysis outlined above are relatively sparse. However, much of what is available has been nicely covered in books by Goulding (2002) and Locke (2000). In particular, there are interesting recent examples of the use of grounded theory's constant comparative (q.v.) method in various forms that derive from the disagreements that arose between Glaser and Strauss (Locke, 1996) and has resulted in Straussian (e.g. Browning et al., 1995) as opposed to Glaserian (e.g. Parry, 1999) forms of grounded theory. Meanwhile, a helpful example of the use of analytic induction is provided by Bansal and Roth's (2000) account of the motives underlying corporations' engagements in ecologically responsible initiatives and how contextual factors affected those motives and the kinds of initiative they engaged in.

Prospects

Usually researchers who use inductive analysis tend to deploy neo-empiricist (Alvesson and Sköldberg, 2000; Lincoln and Denzin, 1994) assumptions regarding the possibility of the unbiased and objective collection of qualitative empirical data while simultaneously rejecting falsificationism in favour of induction primarily because of their commitment to *verstehen*. However, the increasing influence of various forms of social constructionism (q.v.) has recently begun to impact upon inductive analysis. Social constructionist approaches in part arise out of a critique of neo-empiricism by questioning the possibility of a neutral observational language because it allows researchers to present themselves as neutral vessels of cultural experience. Social constructionists are thereby united by their dismissal of any claim to scientific objectivity as naïve. For instance, Charmaz (2000/2003) explores the implications for grounded theory of this philosophical development by arguing that categories etc. do not inhere in the data assembled independently of the researcher's discovery but emerge from the researcher's 'interaction within the field and questions about the data' (Charmaz, 2000/2003: 222). In many respects, what Charmaz appears to be developing is a more reflexive and epistemological subjectivist form of grounded theory (which she calls constructivist (q.v.)) that puts the impact of the researcher and his/her theoretical and philosophical baggage at centre-stage in the development of inductive analysis.

Phil Johnson

INTERPRETATIVE PHENOMENOLOGICAL ANALYSIS

Definition

Developed over the last fifteen years interpretative phenomenological analysis (IPA) has established itself as an increasingly popular qualitative research method for psychologists, particularly in the fields of clinical and health psychology. An accessible and flexible approach, the clarity and rigour of IPA's analytic procedure, along with its inclusion in the curricula of courses in organizational psychology, leave it poised to make a significant contribution to the field of management research.

IPA takes its place in the broad and diverse tradition of phenomenological (q.v.) approaches to inquiry which has its roots in the transcendental phenomenology of Husserl. Such approaches tend to be concerned with the ways particular individuals experience the world in their particular contexts rather than with abstract generalizations about the objective nature of the world (Giorgi and Giorgi, 2003) [*existential phenomenology*].

IPA is phenomenological in this sense, dealing as it does with individuals' personal perceptions or accounts of phenomena rather than striving to arrive at objective statements regarding these phenomena. IPA is also an interpretative endeavour, the researcher attempting to get close to the participants personal world, to take an 'insider perspective', while acknowledging the necessary role played by the researcher's own perceptions and concepts in making sense of other peoples' accounts of their experience [*field studies*].

The idiographic character of IPA should also be noted [*individualism*]. Individual cases provide the starting point and general categorizations are only gradually developed from these. The individual voices of participants are privileged even in those IPA studies which present their findings in more general terms.

Theory development is not a necessary aim of IPA, which values richness and depth of description of focal phenomena over explanation. Such a description may of course lead to the development of explanatory or theoretical constructs.

A further distinctive aspect of IPA is its acceptance of a connective chain between the accounts individuals give and those individuals' underlying cognitions [*causal cognitive mapping; cognitive mapping*]. The recognition of cognitive entities such as beliefs and attitudes provides a bridge between IPA and the social cognitive approach in psychology.

Discussion

A typical IPA project might proceed along the following lines. Participants are selected purposively to provide a sample homogeneous with regard to their experience of a particular phenomenon (e.g. becoming a mother, being promoted, undergoing training). They are then asked to describe this experience. Semi-structured interviews employing open-ended and non-directive questions are the most usual way of eliciting the description and the interviews are recorded and transcribed. Accounts using diaries, journals or other means may also be considered. IPA is a way of engaging with and making sense of such participant-generated texts. These texts are analyzed one at a time. To begin with the researcher will read through the transcript a number of times, noting the initial responses and interpretations prompted by the account. The researcher will then attempt to methodically identify and record themes which seem to capture the gist of what is being said by the participant [*conversation analysis*]. The next stage involves looking for connections and similarities between themes and grouping them into a more manageable number of superordinate themes [*matrices analysis*]. This may occur in a number of stages. Eventually, a summary table of overarching themes is produced. This aims to encapsulate the essence of the researcher's reading of the participant's account.

Analysis of the other participants' data usually proceeds in one of two ways. Each participant's account may be treated in the same manner as the first so that a collection of individual master themes is gradually accumulated which can then be integrated into a set of overarching group themes. Alternatively, the table of themes from the first participant may be used as a template (q.v) to code the material from further participants, the template developing and undergoing revision as each participant's account is analyzed. The final integrated list of group themes should aim to capture the quality of the participants' shared experience of the focal phenomenon and to reveal something about the nature of that phenomenon.

IPA projects are often written up in a fairly conventional manner, with introduction, method, results and discussion sections. The most distinctive aspect of IPA reports is the analysis/results section, organized as it is around the themes that emerge from the analysis, aiming to provide a coherent account of the participants' experience, using quotation to illustrate that account and distinguishing between participant report and researcher interpretation. A detailed description of an IPA project, with illustrative examples of each stage in the research process, may be found in Smith and Dunworth (2003).

Prospects

IPA has only recently begun to receive critical attention. For example, Willig (2001) highlights IPA's reliance on the representational validity of language [*representations; semiotics*], notes the possible constraints on the applicability of an approach which requires participants to be able to reflect upon their experience in interesting ways, and suggests that IPA's concern with the how rather than the why of experience may constitute a further limitation.

IPA is a particularly useful approach when examining process (q.v) and change. It provides an accessible, flexible, researcher- and participant-friendly method for exploring the experiences of individuals and groups. As with all phenomenological approaches, however, the emphasis on subjective accounts exposes the method and subsequent findings to concerns of generalizability, reliability (q.v.) and replicability. Moreover, theory development is only ever an incidental outcome rather than a defining purpose, making this a practically mannered, rather than overtly explanatory, technique.

Frazer Dunworth

INTERVIEWING

Definition

An interview consists of one person, the interviewer, asking questions and directing conversation with one or more other persons, the interviewee(s). Some interviewers expect their interviewees to be passive, and simply to answer questions to the best of their ability. Other interviewers expect more interaction and more of a collaborative production of knowledge on the part of all those present. In either case, the interviewees are active human beings who are likely to have their own agenda for the conversation, to have points that they wish to make and an impression that they wish to create; they are not simply a repository of ideas that can be tapped [*anti-discriminatory research; ethics; phenomenology*]. Some interviewers are afraid of losing control of the interview. They feel that they should know clearly where they are trying to go and what they are trying to find out, and they should not allow the interviewee to take over. This may be reasonable, depending on what they want to know – for example, if the interviewer is certain they have already understood the issues satisfactorily, and only need the details filled in. On the other hand, in many research projects the interviewer may need to know what is on the interviewee's mind, and this will only be achieved by leaving the agenda reasonably open. The interviewer may want to know the interviewee's definition of what is relevant to the question, and therefore to allow them a fair degree of control over the agenda. It is quite possible for the interviewer to divert someone from what they are saying because it is not relevant to the interviewer's definition of the subject, but in so doing the interviewer can easily fail to hear excellent data about what the interviewee defines as relevant.

Discussion

The interview can be thought of as a more or less theatrical performance. Many who have been interviewed for research have said how much they enjoy the experience; it is a rare chance for them to talk about themselves and their situations to an attentive listener. However, this also means that the data produced have to be seen as a performance (Goffman, 1956/1959), as a piece of discourse (q.v.) work (Potter and Wetherell, 1987) on the part of the interviewee. The interviewee will be led to think about something they may not have thought about before, to form views on it, and to give those views in a way which will always pay attention to the relationship they wish to create with the interviewer as well as the content of what they wish to say (Wortham, 1999) [*rhetoric*]. Because the interviewee is active and may talk about things they have not considered before, an interview is often not so much a matter of data *collection* as data *creation* [*case study*]. The data collected do not exist before the interview [*oral history; stimulated recall*].

There has been considerable concern about how to minimize the 'contamination' of interview data by the influence of the interviewer. For example, several approaches to 'non-directive' interviewing have emerged. We have to ask, however, whether any interview is non-directive; is it not likely that an interview may give the most learning when it resembles a normal conversation (q.v.), because we all have more experience of normal conversations than of carefully controlled interviews, and are therefore better placed to interpret what we hear in those conversations. If an interviewer attempts to be 'non-directive' the interviewee may simply guess what the interviewer wants from the conversation, and respond accordingly. So the interviewer is still being directive, but they do not know in what way. As Harré and Secord (1972: 101) put it, if you want to know something from an interviewee, 'why not ask them?' Interview data come from the relationship between the two parties, and the data should be seen as the product of this relationship, not as having emanated solely from the interviewee.

Some researchers use a very structured interview guideline, which is the opposite of the non-directive approach. This may constrain the freedom of the interviewee to influence the agenda, but may also help the researcher to focus; having a guideline in case the interviewee is uncommunicative may help the interviewer to relax and perform better, so paradoxically it may be that when you have created an interview guide you are less likely to need one.

Interviews are often recorded for later analysis, and transcribed for the same purpose. Data are lost in these processes. A transcript, even if heavily annotated, will lose the non-verbal aspects of the performance [*aesthetics; representations*]. It is difficult to pick up the interviewee's emotions (q.v.) from the transcript alone, and even if the interviewer was present in the original interview, it is difficult to remember. An audio recording will give you more information than a transcript on such matters as voice tone and inflexion, but it will still give you less information than a video (q.v.) recording on facial expression, the way the interviewee is carrying themselves and other non-verbal cues. However, some interviewees find any recording, and especially video recording, invasive, and are unwilling to talk freely when recorded. In most cases this anxiety is forgotten early in the interview. This forgetting is less likely with the constraints of video recording. Having a record of the interview is often very important for the interviewer; re-reading the transcript and listening again to the recording often produce flashes of insight, new ways of looking at what is being said, rather like when a kaleidoscope image suddenly shifts, and these may be the best and most insightful moments in research analysis.

Prospects

The interview has become the default means of collecting qualitative data. In the same way as some quantitative researchers assume that all data are collected by questionnaires, qualitative researchers may assume that all data are collected by interview. Others, such as Watson (1994a), feel this needs challenge and criticism. Because they have had widespread use, they are in danger of being used by default, without considering whether they are the best way of collecting what the researcher needs on the topic that they want to find out about.

David Sims

INTERVIEWS

Definition

The qualitative interview can be seen as a conversation with a purpose, where the interviewer's aim is to obtain knowledge about the respondent's world. It is probably the most popular method of data collection in organization studies, either as the main method or as a part in a broader research design (such as an ethnographic (q.v.) study). In a society that Atkinson and Silverman in 1997 labelled an 'interview society', the qualitative interview has moreover become the most pervasive mode of generating knowledge of other human beings, be it in job interviews, news interviews, celebrity interviews, or within social science research.

Discussion

The use of qualitative interviews in organization studies is far from a uniform practice. Interview research is conducted in an array of modes and can be based upon a variety of epistemological and ontological premises. Standard overviews of different types of interview often stress the degree of structuring (structured, semi-structured, unstructured), the number of people involved (individual or group) and the media of communication (face-to-face conversation, telephone, e-mail). However, on a more overriding level, three broad approaches to qualitative interviews in organizations can be identified: neo-positivism, romanticism and localism (Alvesson, 2003). To some extent, the three approaches – in this order of appearance – also represent the historical development of interview-based research in the social sciences in general and in organization studies in particular.

The neo-positivist (q.v.) interviewer aims to establish a context-free truth about reality 'out there' by means of following a research protocol and getting responses relevant to it. The idea is that the researcher's influence and other sources of 'bias' hereby are minimized. Rooted in a representational conception of the language/reality relation – that is, the view that language can mirror reality [*critical realism*] – the interview is here understood as a pipeline through which information regarding events, behaviour and state of affairs can be transported. Kelly et al's (2005) study of the production of advertisements is an example of a neo-positivist treatment of interview material. Although the authors adhere explicitly to discourse analytical ideas, the object of study (i.e. the production of advertisements in advertising agencies) is, *in effect,* explored by means of interviews with eight advertisers (copywriters and art directors). The interview accounts are hence used here as indicators of the creative everyday work at the advertising agency.

An interviewer taking the stance of romanticism advocates what is considered a more genuine human interaction. The romanticist stance towards interviews is based upon a belief in establishing report, trust and commitment between interviewer and respondent in the interview situation, which is regarded as a prerequisite to be able to explore the inner world (meanings, experiences, ideas, feelings, intentions, etc.) of the respondent. The romanticist interviewer is thus, like the neo-positivist one, guided by a representational understanding of how language works, but interview accounts are here seen as potential representations of inner states of mind, that is cognitive (q.v.) and emotional (q.v.) phenomena. This approach is prevalent in the post-positivist (q.v.), interpretative tradition of organization studies, where the primordial ambition is to explore the meanings and experiences of organizational phenomena. One example of an interview study of this ilk is Sandberg's (2000) study of competence. Competence is here studied from a phenomenological perspective and seen as a matter of the ways in which individuals define and relate to their work task. Through a number of interviews and careful interpretations of deeper meanings and the respondents' modes of relating to their work, the researcher suggests a phenomenologically (q.v.) derived understanding of what competence is about.

The localist position on interviewing is still a relatively small, yet growing, approach to interviewing that breaks with the assumptions and ambitions of neo-positivists and romantics. It is a position informed by the linguistic turn that has come to characterize much of contemporary social sciences and management research [*ordinary language philosophy; practice theory*], a turn that has fostered a sceptical attitude towards a view of language as a medium of meaning as well as a raised awareness of language use as a productive practice that constructs social reality [*individualism; social constructionism*]. Consequently, localists do not ascribe to the interview an ontological status different from that of other social situations, but hold that interview statements must be interpreted in their specific, local context. In contrast to the neo-positivist and romantic approaches to the qualitative interview, the latter is here not conceived as a pipeline to something existing outside the interview situation, but as a local interaction in which morally adequate accounts are produced. Thus, the interview should, from the point of view of a localist, be seen as an empirical situation that is potentially interesting in its own right. Alvesson's (1994) study of advertising professionals is an example of work with a localist orientation. Here the advertisers described themselves as emotional, creative, interpersonally sensitive and intuitive, but instead of seeing these descriptions as reflections of inner meanings and convictions, the interview accounts were interpreted as situated constructions of temporary images which contributed to ongoing identity construction work [*dialogic*]. The interview was thus interpreted as a site for identity production, rather than as one where identity was being expressed and mirrored.

Prospects

Critique of conventional views of interviews (e.g. neo-positivism and romanticism) has been addressed from a variety of perspectives, and has been concerned in particular with the relation and interaction between the interviewer and the respondent. This critique, some of which has been adopted by the localist approach, is grounded in an unwillingness to treat the interview as an experiment-like situation, isolated and situated beyond society, norms and culture.

Ethnomethodologist (q.v.) critics have emphasized the importance of treating the interview situation as a social situation *per se*, in which things are accomplished, identities are produced, morality is enacted, competence is displayed, and so on. The empirical material generated in the interview should, according to this stance, be understood as a co-production by the interviewer and the respondent.

Feminist (q.v.) research has recognized that conventional approaches to interviewing have neglected the gendered features of the interview situation. The interview interaction is not immunized from the patriarchal society as a whole, but involves and reproduces asymmetries, gender stereotypes and gender relations. In so far as these topics are of interest for the researcher, the interview situation must, to some extent, be understood *in terms of them*, not only as a pipeline *leading to them*.

The notion of the interview as a neutral tool for information obtainment is, moreover, challenged by postmodernist tenets. According to these, the interview cannot be separated from the rest of society, but should be understood as one of many institutionalized practices of knowledge generation. As such, the interview practice brings with it certain relations of power and subject positions (e.g. expert/novice, active questioner/re-active respondent). Whereas conventional approaches to interviews would assume the presence of two pre-defined subjects (the interviewer and the respondent), who meet and exchange information in the interview situation, a researcher informed by postmodernist (q.v.) ideas would see the interview as a normative and discursive context that constitutes (or defines) its participants. The 'interviewer' and the 'respondent' are here understood as a *product of*, rather than the *premise for*, the interview situation.

The use of interviews in organization studies – in particular those belonging to critical management studies – would benefit from an acknowledgement of this sort of critique of conventional interview approaches. Taking into account such scepticism is germane for the development of a more reflexive

methodological agenda in critical research on organizations, one that does not only study power, ideology and discursive closure *by means of* interviews, but also seeks to explore these issues *within* interviews themselves.

Mats Alvesson and Peter Svensson

INTERVIEWS – ELECTRONIC

Definition

Electronic interviews are a method of data collection using electronic communication facilities to access and communicate with participants. Interviews can be held online, in real time, or using e-mail to communicate asynchronously. The emphasis is on developing a series of communication events, encouraging a flow of discussion to substitute for or complement face-to-face interviews. The method offers the potential to carry out research without concern for spatial and temporal differences. It is therefore particularly suitable for broad geographical, including international, studies. It has the advantage of low administration costs and speed, and the data are available for immediate processing, with no need for transcription.

The term is used specifically to apply to personal interviewing, and does not include the use of the computer alone to interview participants (such as CASI (Computer Assisted Self Administration); see Moon, 1998), nor observation of internet groups (sometimes termed 'netnography'; see Kozinets, 2002). The focus is on the use of the researcher-participant relationship and qualitative research. Similarly, the use of e-mail for quantitative surveys is not covered by the method (Schaefer and Dillman, 1998; Simsek and Veiga, 2000).

Discussion

The method is still in the early stages of use in management and organization studies, although has been used in educational settings, market and consumer research (Montoya-Weiss et al., 1998; Oliviero and Lunt, 2004) and the social sciences (especially on sensitive issues or hard-to-access participants; see Mann and Stewart, 2000). Although research in management has considered how managers and staff use e-mail (e.g. Romm and Pliskin, 1997), and the impact of communication technology on communications, decision-making and teamworking (Whitty and Carr, 2006; Zhuge and Shi, 2001), there has been little research specifically using electronic interviews for data collection in management [postcards].

An example of one-to-one electronic interviewing in management research is discussed in Morgan and Symon (2004). Here, staff from a number of European countries experiencing an outsourcing transfer were asked a series of questions regarding their feelings about the process and relationships with the organizations involved. Ongoing research includes consideration of the effects of cultural differences on the management of offshore outsourcing contracts [cross-cultural research; ethnography].

Focus groups (q.v.) can also be held using the internet and world wide web (www), although there are different issues surrounding their use (Clapper and Massey, 1996). Similar issues arise with electronic focus groups as with face-to-face groups [interviews – groups], in that individuals may be less inclined to open up and talk about sensitive ideas. Online interviews can include the use of internet forums, discussion groups, and chat rooms. Chen and Hinton (1999) suggest these may be more spontaneous than e-mail, although there are issues with authenticity, and there is debate regarding the impact of a researcher on the group. There are also specific technical issues involved with creating online interviews, or indeed standard surveys, on the web. Further information concerning these can be found in Batinic (1997).

Many of the debates related to the use of electronic interviews will be similar to the issues around qualitative interviews (q.v.) and have some similarities to diary studies

(q.v.). The dilemmas of most will depend on the epistemological stance of the researcher (see Morgan (2001) and Morgan and Symon (2004) for discussions specific to this method). Positivists (q.v.) will be more likely to use the method as exploratory research, before developing a questionnaire, and will be concerned with issues of validity. Those of a more constructivist (q.v.) [social constructionism] leaning will be more concerned about changes in the joint construction of knowledge created by the method.

Prospects

Kvale (1996) highlights that interviewing (q.v.) is above all about the relationship between the researcher and participant. However, in electronic interviewing the relationship is in many ways 'disembodied' – distanced by time and space – and decontextualized. The extent to which a relationship can be developed must be considered, and there is a danger of minimal interaction. However, time and self-disclosure have been shown to positively influence relationship formation (Walther, 1996). Therefore a more in-depth research relationship may be possible than with one-off interviews. Certainly there are issues around the differences in social cues, possible changes in power relationships, and the effect of time and distance on communications. In particular, the time delay may increase levels of reflexivity (q.v.), which can be viewed as a strength or a weakness. Those who believe spontaneity is important may be concerned if the participant takes time to reply; others may welcome the increase in reflection allowed. This issue can be partially resolved with the use of real-time online interviewing (O'Connor and Madge, 2001), although this then loses the advantage of asynchronous communications, in that agreements must be made regarding specific interview times. With either method, there are both advantages and disadvantages in terms of lack of socio-demographic information (although this can be built-in and if shared can help build rapport) and power relationships. Participants may feel the medium allows them more control over the presentation of self, and over the communication. However, potential power imbalances may still occur, as the researcher is often viewed as a particularly well-educated expert.

At a practical level, it is vital to ensure your sample is not skewed by internet-savvy respondents (Cheyne and Ritter, 2001). An example of this problem in organizational settings may be research on nurses – those based in the community are less likely to access their e-mails regularly. Once a sample has been selected, it is vital to brief the participants fully, ensuring they understand the nature of the research and the need to respond within certain time-frames. 'Advance Organizers' can be useful here (Mann and Stewart, 2000). In one-to-one electronic interviews, a series of e-mails is exchanged over an extended time period focusing on specific topics or questions. If focus group versions are held, exchanges are made between a group of people on a list, again over a period of time. Whichever version is used, it is vital that the researcher remains responsive, sensitive, and works at maintaining interest. Analysis can, in principle, be carried out as with any interview data, although there may be differences in response due to the written form that need to be taken into account.

Technological advances, such as the increasing use of broadband, web-cams, and voice-based internet communications, may change the nature of electronic interviews. Given the extensive use of communications media in organizations, the method is likely to gain increasing acceptance in management research.

Stephanie J. Morgan

INTERVIEWS – GROUPS

Definition

Group interviews involve a method of data collection based on the questioning of several individuals simultaneously using an unstructured, semi-structured or structured interview format. The configuration and size of the group will vary according to the topic and researcher preferences. Some textbooks are more prescriptive than others in terms of numbers but, beyond ten people, managing a group would become unwieldy. Group interviewing has a long history (e.g. Bogardus, 1926), but this has gained popularity in the form of focus groups (Morgan, D.L., 1988, 1996; Morgan and Krueger, 1997; Stewart et al., 1990/2006).

Focus groups (q.v.) may be distinguished by three essential features (Morgan, D.L.,1996: 130). First, they are a *research method* for collecting data. Hence, they are different from group discussions that are not research, such as therapy sessions, job interviews or discussions of political issues. Focus groups are held to address a particular topic in which participants may impart views, experiences, motivations, meanings and values in relation to this topic. Second, focus groups allow *interaction* between participants. It is this interaction which produces data, insights and issues that would not be easily collected by other methods. Thus, focus groups are different, for example, from 'nominal group' interviews or 'Delphi' (q.v.) groups (Boddy, 2005; Stewart et al., 1990/2006). Third, focus groups are *planned* and hence different from spontaneous or naturally occurring groups where there is no research objective or moderation. Within this, the researcher's role is recognized as important in the data collection and discussion. Hence, focus groups fit within the broad toolkit of qualitative research methods that is often referred to as social constructionist (q.v.) or interpretivist [*constructivism; individualism*].

The academic origins of focus groups rest in sociology. Merton and colleagues are often accredited with the earliest publications using focus groups as a method of data collection for studying the effectiveness of the Second World War training and propaganda films (Merton and Kendall, 1946; Merton et al., 1956). Since the 1960s, focus groups have often become associated with consumer and marketing research as a means of sensitizing and testing products for consumers. However, the social sciences have adopted the method more recently, and they have been increasingly used in management research to address a range of issues. They are especially appropriate where the researcher seeks to gain an understanding of the 'worldviews' of participants often in their own language. Although focus groups have continued to be used in marketing research (e.g. McQuarrie and McIntyre, 1988), other management fields of study have used them, including ethical issues (Carter, 2000; Vyakarnam et al., 1997); the motivations of migrants (Aggergaard et al., 2005); innovation (O'Regan et al., 2006); organizational research (Lee, 1999); organizational culture (Hartman, 2004); small business behaviour (Blackburn and Stokes, 2000; Fallon and Brown, 2002); health care management (Steinhauser et al., 2000) and human resource management (Truss et al., 1997).

Discussion

The diversity of application of the focus group method makes it difficult to be prescriptive regarding its use. Focus groups have been used at any point in a research programme, from generating ideas through to interpreting results. They can be used as a stand-alone technique or part of a wider mixed-method approach. Focus groups have often been used to help sensitize a research project that is in the early stages. This approach is frequently used in marketing and consumer research where the researcher seeks to become closer to the object of study or issue under scrutiny. From this the researcher may then generate more relevant research questions or hypotheses for subsequent investigation (Krueger, 1997a, 1997b). Conversely, they have been used after a large-scale survey, to allow participants to help researchers explain patterns in the data. Focus groups have also been used in the evaluation of initiatives, asking participants to report their experiences of engagement in a scheme or event. One interesting theme is that they have been shown to be popular by researchers where there is a difference in perspective or social position between the researcher and the researched [cross-cultural research].

In practice, the focus-group method tends to go through a number of stages:

1. Clarifying appropriateness and purpose.
2. Identifying and recruiting participants.
3. The selection and training of moderators.
4. Selecting a location.
5. Running the focus group.
6. Recording the focus group.
7. Analysing and writing up the results.
8. Integration with a broader research programme (where appropriate).

There have been a number of texts explaining the setting up of focus groups (Krueger, 1977a, 1977b; Morgan and Krueger, 1997; Stewart et al., 1990/2006). Practical examples discussing these stages can be gleaned from Blackburn and Stokes (2000) and MacDougall and Fudge (2001).

Prospects

There are a number of *advantages* and *disadvantages* of focus groups as a research method. Focus groups generate data specific to the method. The 'synergistic group effect', in which ideas are stimulated through interaction with others, is one of the main claimed advantages of this approach. Depending on the extent of group synergy, participants may be more prepared to 'open up' to researchers if there is sufficient psychological security from them to do so. This has the advantage over one-to-one interviews where the interviewee may be less forthcoming because of differing socio-economic positions, worldviews and perspectives between the researcher and the researched.

As a result, group discussions may generate more critical comments on a topic than individual interviews where the interviewee may be more conscious of the 'world position' or response of the interviewer. If a semi-structured or unstructured approach is adopted, the focus-group method can allow sufficient scope for adaptation to the main topic. The focus group, therefore, may be regarded as sharing an agenda whereby the moderator has to strike a balance between allowing the free-flow of discussion and sticking to the agenda. Finally, the focus group also allows the opportunity for a diversity of opinion and experience. Thus, it may be useful for generating a variety of different perspectives on an issue and the reasons for these differences [*dialogic*]. The overarching advantage, however, is that the focus group generates data that cannot be captured by conventional interviewing (q.v.) techniques.

There are, however, disadvantages of focus groups and, as with all methodologies, care should be taken to ensure that it is the appropriate method. The success of the focus-group method depends on detailed preparation and the management skills of the researcher. A great deal of data can be generated in a group discussion but without good facilities, the engagement of participants, appropriate moderation and proper recording it can be a waste of time and effort. However, it is important that the research team is well prepared for an event that will happen relatively quickly. It is advisable to have an assistant to help with room settings, refreshments and so on, as well as to take notes to help with the subsequent analysis. Choosing the appropriate group membership is also important. In some cases it may be necessary to choose members who have similar particular characteristics (e.g. age, gender, occupational status), while for others a diversity of characteristics may be appropriate. The group moderator needs to be particularly skilled in ensuring that all participants are able to express their views and experiences in the group. Again, much will depend on the researchers' abilities in ensuring that participants are comfortable with the research setting and other members of the group. Dominant personalities or sub-groups may require some control, while others may need drawing into the discussion. The moderator needs to be able to allow the free-flow of discussion while also knowing when to move on. These skills may be summed up as being 'flexible, objective, empathic, persuasive, a good listener' (Fontana and Frey, 1994: 365).

Focus groups are also not without their critics. A common criticism is that they produce results that are not generalizable or reliable [*phronetic organizational research; positivism and post-positivism*]. Thus, while they are good for generating ideas or testing preconceptions regarding a particular subject, the data produced cannot be related to a wider population and hence their *external validity* and *reliability* are weak. Fern (2001) provides a robust response to these criticisms. Without doubt, focus groups generate a great amount of material which is probably more difficult to transcribe or analyze than individual interviews. Although some researchers have argued that the costs of focus groups are relatively cheaper than face-to-face interviews, this is debatable, particularly when the set-up and interpretation costs are taken into account. The analysis of focus groups is also challenging, particularly when the interventions of various contributors shape the discussion and the role of the moderator can be influential in this process of data generation.

In sum, group interviews are a member of the broader family of interview methods and interpretative accounts of human behaviour. There is some discussion on the differences between focus groups and other types of group interview (Boddy, 2005; Morgan, D.L.,1996: 131), but broadly, focus groups are a type of group interview (Bryman and Bell, 2003: 368; Fontana and Frey, 1994). If used in appropriate situations group interviews, and focus group methods in particular, can be fruitful methods of qualitative data collection.

Robert Blackburn

M

MARXISM

Definition

Fundamentally, Marxism is based on a concern with the practical activity associated with human nature and basic human needs (Ollman, 1976), and how these needs are provided for by economic systems (Marx, 1857/1973, 1867/1976). In contemporary societies the capitalist economic system is predominant, and as a result Marx's analysis explores the dynamics of capitalism by explaining the production and distribution of commodities.

Marxist analysis is methodologically based on the belief that it is necessary to go beyond the way things present themselves to identify the underlying reality [*critical theory; discourse analysis*]. For example, capitalism appears to be based on free labour, but for Marx it is actually based upon exploitation and control of the ability to produce; so in 'A contribution to a critique of political economy' (Marx, 1859/1970) he draws our attention to the organization of production through focusing on the relations we have with each other, believing these to be historically determined, specific to the economic mode of production, and class-based as a result of the division of labour required to organize production [*activity theory*].

The development of the economy of a particular society, over time, is viewed as a process of conflict and change. The assumption is that the relations of production develop less slowly than the technological ability to produce (the forces of production) and so become fetters to these forces; social change is materially (technologically) driven. Consequently, the attempts to accommodate changes in production lead to a breakdown of the existing relations within a given society and the rise of alternate ones bound by differently configured classes (Marx, 1973, 1976) [*dialectic*].

Capitalism is thus one such phase of relations and forces among other phases in human history, each of which represent stages in a cumulative dialectic that reaches a full and final stage: communism. Capitalism is communism's precursor. Its instability characterized by cycles of growth and depression results from a lack of co-ordination between demand and production leading to over-production or under-consumption. The result is unsold commodities, unrealized values, bankruptcies and crises. Individual capitalists are forced by competition and the fear of going out of business to increasingly exploit workers and to introduce more productive machinery to realize economies of scale. In crises, firms go out of business and others grow, leading to concentration and centralization where firms consolidate through mergers and acquisitions. The result is an increase in concentration both of capital and labour, and labour-saving technology.

Discussion

When reading Marx we have to remember the historical context at the time of writing. Capitalism was relatively new and undeveloped, and consequently, although Marx predicted many developments, it would be obtuse to expect Marx to foresee our current situation in all of its complexity. For example, the growth of international economic relations, the role of the state in late capitalism, and the analysis of the labour process are all beyond Marx's initial analysis.

Subsequent Marxists, in particular Lenin (1970), took the economic aspects of Marxism to develop a theory of Imperialism [*postcolonial theory*] which explains why capitalism expands into less developed areas in the pursuit of markets and profits. The impact of this international expansion can be seen as perpetuating the underdevelopment of the less developed countries (Amin, 1974, 1976; Emmanuel, 1972), and perpetuating economic divisions on a global scale. In this global context, Marxism has been used to consider the role and development of the state in capitalism (Jessop, 2002). Since Marx wrote, the state has grown and its involvement in production and society has increased. It has both helped capitalism to survive through overcoming its contradictions and preventing excesses but it has also reformed aspects of the capitalism system.

Marx's work was very much concerned with manufacturing production and the changes taking place in industrializing Britain, as was that of his collaborator Engels (Jenkins and Engels, 1964; Marcus and Engels, 1974). Capitalists exploited workers by controlling/managing their labour. Machines increased this control by reducing workers' autonomy and skill, a theme further developed by Harry Braverman, in his analysis of postwar capitalism. Braverman (1974) analyzed how the capitalist labour process separated conception from execution in work and used machinery and organizational methods, such as assembly lines and scientific management, to increase control over the nature and pace of work [*Taylorism*]. This led to deskilling and the development of Fordist systems of mass production with their assembly lines and large factories. More recently, and undoubtedly influenced by poststructuralist understandings (Willmott, 1993a, 2000) [*critical theory; postmodernism*], labour process theorists have explored the changing

nature of production based on more flexible methods of production, smaller runs and workers undertaking a number of tasks.

Prospects

One of the most consistent criticisms of Marxist approaches is that Marxism promotes Economism through technological determinism (also called 'vulgar Marxism'). This vulgar Marxism views all social phenomena in society, including social, political and intellectual consciousness, as determined by the economic base [*individualism*]. Critics regard this as reductionism which fails to account for diversity. However, Althusserian Marxists have developed a stance which argues for a 'relative autonomy of the superstructure with respect to the base' (Althusser, 1971), where ideological practices such as the mass media are relatively autonomous from economic determination. In response to these developments, some critics argue that Marxism is just another ideology, a 'grand theory' that eschews empirical research.

Although recent developments within the Marxist tradition have sought to avoid and overcome these pitfalls, it would be naïve to believe that all challenges have been dealt with. While Althusserian Marxism (Althusser, 1971) helps to undermine the myth of the autonomous individual, other neo-Marxist stances see the mass media as a 'site of struggle' for ideological meaning, opening up the possibility of oppositional readings.

Jason Ferdinand

MATRICES ANALYSIS

Definition

Data matrices can be used as a tool for making qualitative data analysis more manageable. Taking case study (q.v.) analysis as an example, a researcher may have a sophisticated design which includes data from a number of different research methods *[mixed methods in management research; triangulation]* such as interviews (q.v.), observations (q.v.) and documents [*content analysis; historical analysis*], across a range of different case study sites, and potentially at different points in time. The question of how to manage that data so that appropriate interpretation is possible is an important one. The use of data matrices is one way of addressing this. Data matrices are a way of displaying qualitative data in a format where it is readily accessible for the process of analysis and interpretation. Additionally, although the main purpose of matrices is as a way of illustrating various types of data, they can also be used as part of the qualitative data analysis process.

Matrices derive from the work of Miles and Huberman (1994a) and their uses are outlined in detail in their book *Qualitative Data Analysis: An Expanded Sourcebook* (1994b). They outline that 'a matrix is essentially the "crossing" of two lists, set up as rows and columns' (Miles and Huberman, 1994b: 3). It typically takes the format of a table, although it may also take the form of 'networks' – a series of nodes with links between them. Each row and column is labelled, with rows usually representing the unit of analysis. The columns typically represent concepts, issues or characteristics pertinent to the research questions. For instance, in a study of psychological contracts in smaller firms, Nadin and Cassell (2004) outline how the different case companies were represented in the rows of a matrix, while key research issues, such as the type of contract and the expectations of employers and employees, formed the basis of each of the columns within the matrix.

Discussion

In making decisions about how to present the data within a matrix, the researcher is already starting along his/her analytical path. Deciding upon what the columns and rows represent is an integral part of data analysis and interpretation, informed by the research questions and decisions about what is important and what

isn't in relation to those questions. Another factor influencing the content of the matrix is the function of the matrix. In some cases this may be to provide a general description of cases along particular factors, whereas in others it may be to provide for in-depth comparative (q.v.) analysis [*inductive analysis*]. Examples include, towards the start of the analytic process, getting an overview of the data in an exploratory way, or later in the project to carry out a more detailed analysis. Matrices also have the advantage of being able to be used at different levels of analysis. As part of a case study research design, for example, a matrix may be used to depict each individual case. For this kind of 'within site analysis' the matrix enables parallel data from a range of different research methods to be displayed. The individual matrices can then be compared to allow 'cross-site' analyses, or a new matrix [can be] created which combines data from several cases (e.g. Cassell et al., 1988) [*composite mapping*].

Although matrices have been used to display data in published work within the business and management field, in by far the majority of cases the term 'data matrix' has not been used. For example, in Kathleen Eisenhardt's classic (1989a) *Academy of Management Review* paper about how to develop theories from organizational case studies, she describes how 'tabulated evidence' is useful as a way of enabling theory to develop from a range of cases. This tabulated evidence is part of a 'roadmap of building theories'. The tabulated evidence that Eisenhardt refers to here is similar to a data matrix. Here again the indication is that having the data displayed in an accessible manner will aid the analytic and interpretative process. Other examples where matrices have been used, but have not been referred to with that terminology, are Wright et al. (2005), who use a matrix to highlight the questions that various theoretical approaches infer regarding strategy in emerging economies; and Edwards et al. (2005), who consider the various characteristics of reverse diffusion of employment practices in five multinational case studies.

Prospects

Being able to display data in an accessible manner is the key selling point in the use of matrices. A key advantage of matrices is that they can be used flexibly. Data entry can take a variety of forms, such as blocks of text, quotes, phrases, ratings, or symbolic figures. This is useful when one considers that qualitative data can take a range of different formats. However, for some qualitative researchers this approach may be too reductionist, in that a key tension in the creation of a data matrix is achieving the appropriate balance between retaining the richness of the qualitative data generated, while attaining the advantages that any summary technique provides [*process research*]. Nadin and Cassell (2004) argue that the charges of reductionism can be avoided if matrix analysis is dovetailed with template analysis (q.v.), thus establishing a clear audit trail and enabling issues to be followed up in greater detail. Additionally, although, as highlighted earlier, the simple design of the matrix itself may require that initial analytic decisions are made, the majority of analysis and interpretation of the data needs to come after the matrix has been constructed. When the data are more easily accessed, then the more challenging analytic work begins.

Catherine Cassell and Sara Nadin

METAPHOR

Definition

Metaphors are forms of language use by which we talk about and hence understand one subject (e.g. an organization) in terms of another (e.g. a machine). Metaphors are pervasive in the language of management and organization theory and provide particular understandings and inferences about organizations and organizational life. Metaphors allow us to redescribe reality by, at one and the same time, alluding to what something is like using phrases that associate it with what it is not. It is the incompleteness of, and hence potential in, definition that lends power to metaphor [*projective techniques; relativism*]. Using metaphors is not simply using one word to replace another in order to reframe an 'external' referent, but to influence in some way the manner in which the world is experienced by language users [*dialogic; ordinary language philosophy*].

Discussion

In the last two decades, metaphor has achieved a remarkable prominence in philosophy and psychology, as well as in management and organization theory. This trend stands in sharp contrast to an earlier view of metaphor as a derivative issue of only secondary importance. That is, metaphor was thought to be either a deviant form of expression or a non-essential literary figure of speech. In either case, it was generally not regarded as fundamental in a cognitive or epistemological sense. This denial of any serious cognitive role for metaphor is principally the result of the long-standing popularity of strict 'objectivist' assumptions about language and meaning [*constructivism; realism*]. The objectivist view suggests that the world has its structure, and that our concepts and propositions, to be correct, must correspond to that structure. Only literal concepts and propositions can do that since metaphors, as a figurative and playful combination of concepts, assert cross-categorical identities that do not exist objectively in reality. Metaphors may exist as cognitive processes of our understanding, but their meaning must be reducible to some set of literal concepts and propositions.

Pinder and Bourgeois (1982), proponents of this objectivist view in organization theory, critiqued metaphors for being inherently imprecise, ambiguous and lacking an exact theoretical definition of whatever it is that is being studied. Because of this imprecision and ambiguity, which Pinder and Bourgeois (1982: 643) contrasted with 'literal' language that in their view would enable connections between observable phenomena and theoretical constructs to be made, they argued that metaphors cannot be tested and falsified as they 'are stated in terms that do not have enough clear content to be falsifiable'. There is quite a large body of work in management and organization theory supporting the view that metaphors are indeed cognitively reducible to literal propositions (Oswick et al., 2002; Tsoukas, 1991). In these works, metaphor is generally considered as a deviation from, or a derivative function on, proper literal meaning. More specifically, metaphor is seen as a comparison in which the first term A (i.e. the target) is asserted to bear a partial resemblance (i.e. the ground) to the second term B (i.e. the source); and our ability to process the metaphor depends upon our seeing that the A-domain shares certain literal properties and relations with the B-domain (Tsoukas, 1991, 1993).

Gareth Morgan's (1980, 1983, 1986/1997, 1996) well-known contributions provide a rather different reading of metaphor. In his view, metaphors provide a cognitively fundamental way of structuring our understanding of organizations that cannot be reduced to more literal concepts and propositional comparison statements. This happens, Morgan suggests, as with a metaphor an entirely new meaning is created through the creative juxtaposition of concepts (e.g. seeing 'organization' as a 'machine') that previously were not interrelated. Cornelissen (2004, 2005) has recently followed in Morgan's footsteps by showing that rather than just retrieving and instantiating frames or lexicalized relationships between terms, metaphorical language sets up a creative and novel correlation of two terms which evokes our imagination and leads to the production of a new, emergent meaning that was not readily available before. Both Morgan and Cornelissen argue that metaphors are therefore cognitively fundamental in their own right and that most if not all of our knowledge and understanding of management and organizations, theoretically and practically, is constituted through metaphors [*rhetoric*]. Consider, for example, the dominant theoretical perspectives upon organizations: that is, organizations are seen as 'rational systems' or 'machines', as 'natural systems' or 'organisms', or as 'open systems' [*autopoiesis; complexity theory; soft systems theory*] (Baum and Rowley, 2002). Each and every one of these perspectives is clearly based upon metaphorical reasoning.

Prospects

Taking this point a bit further, Weick (1989) has argued that management and organizational researchers need to recognize the pervasive role of metaphor in theory construction, and to use the logic of metaphor in their theorizing and research in a much more deliberate and informed way. Researchers need to recognize, Weick argued, that in theory construction they use the logic of *metaphor* to provide them with vocabularies and images to represent and express managerial and organizational phenomena that are often complex and abstract [*sensemaking*]. In Weick's (1989: 529) own words: 'theorists depend on pictures, maps, and metaphors to grasp the object of study', and 'have no choice [in this], but can be more deliberate in the formation of these images and more respectful of representations and efforts to improve them'. In other words, management and organizational researchers should be mindful and reflective of their own theoretical assumptions and the metaphorical images that lie at the root of their work, and ideally should spell these out together with the thought trials in which they engage. Such a reflective (q.v.) use of metaphor, it can be anticipated, will not only be beneficial to the individual theorist who becomes more mindful of his/her own theorizing and of ways of improving it (Weick, 1989, 1999), but also to the field of management and organization theory as a whole as it enables a more wholesome discussion and comparison of different theoretical positions and knowledge claims.

Joep P. Cornelissen

METHOD

Definition

The Greek word *hodos* gives us our modern-day word *method*. *Hodos* means 'way' or 'path' or 'journey'. It can also mean 'a manner, a course of action or speech'. Combined with the prefix *meta-*, we get *methodos*, a 'following after, pursuit, especially pursuit of knowledge, a plan or system of pursuing an inquiry' (Liddell et al., 1940).

Discussion

Our modern-day understanding of method, especially the scientific method, strongly resonates with *methodos*, which emphasizes the methodical system of generating and legitimizing knowledge. The importance of the right *methodos* is well established in management research. Contributions to management knowledge are scrutinized through the methodology and methods adopted for research. As Popper (1945, 1963) argues, we need to scrutinize what we accept as knowledge in order to guard against dogmatism, irrationalism and fanaticism. *Methodos* provides the research with legitimacy, if not finality, and is central to the modern epistemological project (Rorty, 1980; Taylor, 1995) which aims to base legitimate knowledge on secure foundations. The right method addresses the 'Cartesian anxiety' (Bernstein, 1983) of finding firm legitimizing grounds for making knowledge claims and ensuring scientific progress [*constructivism; individualism; positivism and post-positivism*].

Although our understanding of method is dominated by *methodos*, *hodos* also implies a more subtle and paradoxical understanding of method. This is illustrated by Heraclitus, who states: 'The path [*hodos*] ... is straight and crooked ... The way up and the way down are one and the same' (Kahn, 1979: 63, 75). *Hodos* is a way that is both straight and crooked at the same time. *Hodos*, as a paradoxical method, works by inverting our everyday understanding of 'way' or 'path'. 'We commonly view [the usage of way or path] as metaphorical rather than literal; in rhetorical terms, the path is a picturesque *topos* (commonplace) and a vivid trope (figure), turning our attention toward something other than a real road' (Schur, 1998: 17). By inverting this common-sense understanding of 'way' and 'path', Heraclitus exposes us to a paradoxical method in three different

ways. First, he inverts the 'way' of verbal expression, which is a *topos*, an expression of conventionality, something that is customary, captured by our everyday phrases 'of course' or 'that's the way of the world' [*ordinary language philosophy; phronetic organizational research*]. Hence, the way describes something that is familiar and methodical. By referring to the way as both straight and crooked, Heraclitus juxtaposes *topos* with *a-topos*, which means out of place or strange or paradoxical. Second, he inverts the 'way' as a trope. *Tropos* means 'turn' and is related to the verbal 'way'. *Tropos* can mean 'turn' as in 'direction' or 'manner'. By juxtaposing straight and crooked, up and down, Heraclitus raises questions about the status of tropes. The Greek word *poros* (way) suggests the third paradoxical movement. The *topos* of the *poros* becomes an *atopos* (paradoxical) declaration of the *aporia* (waylessness) [*relativism*]. The three inversions of 'way' by Heraclitus serve as an intimation to question our taken-for-granted 'way'. Heraclitus's inversions of *hodos* are aimed at being evocative and provocative, and challenge our dominant understanding of method and the notions of direction and correctness that it entails.

Ajit Nayak

MIDDLE RANGE THINKING

Definition

While the descriptor of 'middle range thinking' can be traced to Robert Merton (cf. Merton, 1968) it is important to distance our conceptualization (Broadbent and Laughlin, 1997; Laughlin, 1995, 2004) from his. Merton was of the view that prior to the production of grand general theories there was a need for more modest 'middle range' theoretical and empirical studies but only on the assumption that 'our little systems have their day; they have their day and cease to be' (Merton, 1968: 53). Our view of middle range thinking is something uniquely different from this convenient stopping point on the route to a grand theory. It relies on what we call 'skeletal' theories, which can never get to the point where all key elements are captured in the theoretical terms. Middle range thinking, to us, requires specific empirical 'flesh' to develop a complete understanding of any situation. Merton would not acknowledge 'skeletal' theories as theories at all – theories only exist when everything of importance is encapsulated in the theoretical terms (such as in the theory of gravity in which the relationship between weight and volume expresses everything of significance, such that it is immaterial what specific empirical phenomenon is being measured). Such theories leave the empirical data having no importance in their own right apart from forming a basis to 'test' these all encompassing general theories.

Our understanding of middle range thinking is a distinct research approach with assumptions on ontology, theory use, methodology and method. Its major characteristics in terms of how to generate understanding are encapsulated in Figure 3, taken from Laughlin (2004). The characteristics of middle range thinking are depicted in the middle column of Figure 3 and can be understood by contrasting its nature with a positivist (q.v.)/realist (q.v.) research approach (the far left column) and interpretative, ethnographic (q.v.) thinking (the far right column). In Laughlin (1995), the positivist line is aligned to the thinking of Auguste Comte (the 'father of positivism') – the Comtean line as we call it – and the interpretative to the thinking of Immanuel Kant and his student Johann Fichte (the Kantian/Fichtean line as we call it). Middle range thinking is also traceable to Immanuel Kant but, in this case, in combination with his other notable student Georg Wilhelm Friedrich Hegel [dialectic] (the Kantian/Hegelian line as we refer to it). In Broadbent and Laughlin (1997) we make clear that middle range thinking shares a common (Kantian) ancestry, and rapport, with interpretative thinking. It does not share similar sympathies with Comtean thinking, which is why it is so distant from Merton's

understanding of theories of the middle range.

What Figure 3 makes plain is that all three research approaches are trying to make sense of the empirical world (the base of the diagram) and rely on a range of key theoretical and methodological characteristics. At the top of the figure is the key ontological belief giving overall direction for the view on the relevance of prior theories underlying the three research approaches. Comtean thinking assumes that there are complete empirical patterns that exist and therefore any prior theories that have exposed these patterns are both highly relevant as well as assumed to be all-defining. At the other extreme, Kantian/ Fichteans assume there are no general empirical patterns and as a result any prior theories are seen to be irrelevant since they apply to different unique empirical situations. Middle range thinking, on the other hand, is of the view that 'skeletal' general empirical patterns exist [*inductive analysis; pragmatism; process research*]. Prior theories that have discovered these skeletal patterns therefore provide a language to enable a discussion and analysis of empirical situations but not to the exclusion of the richness and diversity of any specific situation.

These different ontological and theoretical assumptions are aligned to and require different methodological approaches and data collection methods to enable empirical investigations to occur. These are represented in the bottom four levels of Figure 3. The Comteans are at pains to ensure that the role of the observer's subjectivity is minimal, involving a highly formalistic, mathematical and statistical methodological approach using data drawn from highly formalized documentary analysis, structured questionnaires and formal, structured interviews leading to a quantitative data narrative. The Kantian/ Fichteans encompass and accept observer subjectivity. They rely on a rigorous interpretative and subjective methodological approach using data drawn from interviews (q.v.), participatory observation (q.v.) and a less structured, more impressionistic analysis of documents leading to a qualitative data

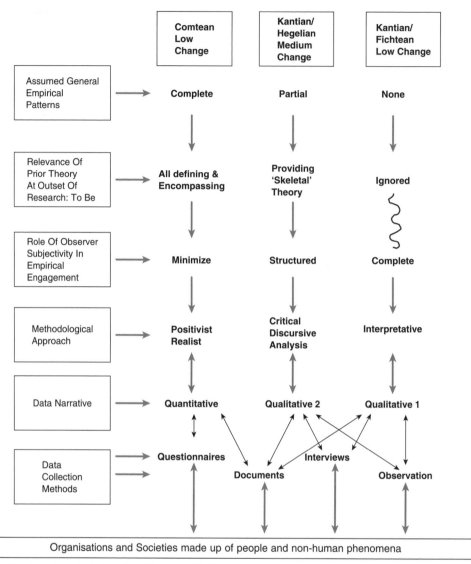

Figure 3 *The characteristics of middle range thinking*

narrative. Middle range thinking accepts the involvement of the subjective observer, but sets some structure and transparency around this involvement. Its methodological approach is based on formal discursive analysis, the design of which, for us, comes from an adaptation of Jürgen Habermas's Critical Theory (see Habermas, 1987; also Broadbent, 1998; Broadbent and Laughlin, 1997; Laughlin, 1987). It is reliant on a

qualitative, skeletal theory that informs the nature of the data narrative which, in turn, is drawn from similar data collection methods to the Kantian/Fichteans.

Discussion

The distinctive theoretical and methodological underpinnings of middle range thinking are accompanied by a similar attitude to change in the phenomena understood. Both the Comtean and Kantian/Fichtean approaches preclude change from the discovery process for different reasons – for the former because change is a value-laden activity and for the latter since, if all understanding is subjective, it is difficult to find substantive grounds for agreement on whether change should occur [*process philosophy*]. For middle range thinking, change is not excluded nor is it a necessity. What is a necessity is a consideration of whether change should occur in the phenomena under investigation and which we seek to understand. Middle range thinking also develops a mechanism for deciding when this should be the case.

An example of a middle range theoretical approach is a framework for analysing organizational change processes developed by Laughlin (1991). This framework provides a model of four possible 'pathways' by which organizational disturbances can track their way through an organization, resulting in different (first-order and second-order) levels of changes in the key elements constituting an organization. The theory is only 'skeletal' and not predictive but provides a language for analysing specific organizational change processes. The empirical detail provides the 'flesh' to the 'bones' to one of the theoretical pathways pursued as well as possible refinements in the tracks and framework used (see Broadbent, 1992; Broadbent and Laughlin, 1998).

Prospects

Problems in applying middle range thinking can arise in analysing which empirical insights are of a skeletal theoretical nature, having some level of generality, and which are unique to the situation being analyzed. This is, in many ways, inevitable given the interactive nature of the research approach. Yet it also is the strength of the approach, allowing and encouraging theoretical and empirical 'surprises'. The process of discourse used provides the arena in which these understandings are clarified.

The prospects for middle range thinking are considerable on two counts. First, it provides a basis for the development of a meaningful theory of management. Management theory is not like a theory of gravity with the same outcome each time an action is embarked upon. Equally, not every management problem and concern is unique to each situation. Middle range thinking provides meaningful theories of management, while recognizing the unique aspects of actual situations. Second, it has provided a powerful and significant research approach that has informed not only our research over many years, but others as well, notably a number of doctoral students who will be the research leaders of tomorrow.

Jane Broadbent and Richard Laughlin

MIXED METHODS IN MANAGEMENT RESEARCH

Definition

The term 'mixed methods' has developed currency as an umbrella term applying to almost any situation where more than one methodological approach is used in combination with another, usually, but not essentially, involving a combination of at least some elements drawn from each of qualitative and quantitative approaches to research. In so doing, it covers multi-method research and triangulation (q.v.), each of which has a somewhat more restricted meaning.

Most authors trace recent interest in and debates about mixed methods research to the multi-trait–multi-method measurement strategies of Campbell and Fiske (1959), which were designed to ensure that differences in the measurement of psychological variables reflected true differences rather than measurement error; the application of the surveyors' concept of triangulation to methods of social investigation by Webb, et al. (1966); Denzin's (1978) development and popularization of that concept; and the distinction drawn between qualitative (naturalistic) and quantitative (rationalistic) approaches to research by Lincoln and Guba (1985). Anthropologists and sociologists (particularly those from the Chicago School) had, however, been actively employing multi-method strategies in community settings throughout the last century, often more implicitly than explicitly. The combination of multiple methods 'has a long-standing history' also in evaluation research where both formative and summative aspects of a programme are considered (Rallis and Rossman, 2003). In contrast, management researchers have remained strongly oriented to employing quantitative data with statistical analyses for the purpose of theory testing, with few adopting qualitative or mixed methods approaches (Currall and Towler, 2003).

There have been many attempts to classify mixed methods designs according to a combination of the purpose of the study, whether a study is single or multi-stage, the sequence and priority given to various components within or across stages, and the point at which integration occurs. Maxwell and Loomis (2003:263) proposed an alternative 'interactive' model which recognised that, regardless of the stated design, 'different components tend to grow "tendrils" backward and forward, integrating both qualitative and quantitative elements into all components of the research'.Choices in design are dependent primarily on the purpose of the research and must be guided by the demands of the research question.

Multiple or mixed methods might be used when:

- complementary data are sought, either qualitative data to enhance understanding of quantitative findings, or quantitative data to help generalize or test qualitative insights;
- different methods are appropriate for different elements of the project, with each contributing to an overall picture;
- data are sought from multiple independent sources, to offset or counteract biases from each method, in order to confirm,

validate or corroborate the results and conclusions of the study (triangulation).
- the goal of an evaluative study is to understand both process (q.v.) and outcome;
- One method provides data that are useful in preparation for the other, for example, when interviews (q.v.) or focus groups (q.v.) provide the basis for the design of survey or scale items, or when a quantitative survey is used to design a sample for qualitative interviewing.

Studies for these purposes are designed to have complementary strengths and non-overlapping weaknesses. Design issues include the staging and sequencing of the components and the relative dominance of the qualitative or quantitative elements. Integration of the different components in these designs typically occurs only at the stage of interpretation or discussion of the results. Mixed methods might alternatively involve the combination of different data sources in a unified analysis, the conversion of one form of data to another, or the application of both text and statistical analysis techniques to the same data sources (Bazeley, 2006). These studies involve much earlier integration of approaches.

Discussion

Because management and organization research asks a large variety of questions, draws on numerous theoretical paradigms from a range of disciplines, and is characterized by investigations involving multiple levels of analysis, there is benefit in combining the complementary strengths of quantitative and qualitative approaches (Currall and Towler, 2003). '[T]he careful measurement, generalizable samples, experimental control, and statistical tools of good quantitative studies are precious assets. When they are combined with the up-close, deep, credible understanding of complex real-world contexts that characterize good qualitative studies, we have a very powerful mix' (Miles and Huberman, 1994b: 42).

Of the seven 'exemplary' studies in organization science from the 1980s reviewed by Frost and Stablein (1992), four involved the use of mixed data and/or analysis methods, including statistical hypothesis testing based on coded linguistic features of text; detailed case studies drawing on data from observations, anecdotes, surveys, documents and archives, combined with regression analyses on a larger sample; regression analysis of coded non-participant observational data followed by participant observation; and secondary analysis of archival survey data combined with review of historical sources.

A review of the 16 most recent research articles in *Administrative Science Quarterly* (*ASQ*, June 2005–March 2006) and 19 from the *Academy of Management Journal* (*AMJ*, February and April, 2006) confirmed the continuing predominance of quantitatively-based, statistical, hypothesis-testing approaches in management studies (N=21; see Table 4). Six purely qualitative studies employed, primarily, grounded theory techniques within a case study framework. These, at most, made an occasional reference to frequencies. Eight of the 35 might be classified as using mixed methods, although the most common approach in these was to quantify qualitative data for statistical analysis according to an a priori coding scheme (including two where themes were generated from the qualitative data), with little or no

further reference to the qualitative material. In others, a significant amount of interview data was gathered for use in designing or to supplement quantitative measures, but was referred to minimally (if at all) in elaborating the results or for discussion of the statistical analyses.

Prospects

Paradigmatic positioning

Mixed methods are typically employed in applied settings where it is necessary to draw on multiple data sources to understand complex phenomena, and where there is little opportunity for experimentation. The majority of those using mixed methods have consequently adopted a pragmatic (q.v.) position, looking for 'what works' in any particular situation (Tashakkori and Teddlie, 2003: 680). The social issues or questions to be investigated are seen as more important than ideological arguments which ultimately cannot be resolved (Caracelli and Greene, 1997).

Analysis and interpretation

Fielding and Fielding (1986: 12) have argued that:

...ultimately all methods of data collection are analysed 'qualitatively,' in so far as the act of analysis is an interpretation, and therefore of necessity a selective rendering, of the 'sense' of the available data. Whether the data

Table 4   Methodological approaches in a sample of recent management research articles

Method	Source		Total	
	AMJ	*ASQ*	N	%
Statistical analysis of archival/database, experimental or survey data	12	9	21	60.0
Qualitative data and analysis	3	3	6	17.1
Quantitative analysis of qualitative data	2	2	4	11.4
Preliminary qualitative data but primarily quantitative data and analyses	2	2	4	11.4
Total	19	16	35	100.0

collected are quantifiable or qualitative, the issue of the warrant for their inferences must be confronted.

For the mixed methods researcher to arrive at an interpretation, issues to be addressed include those relating to sampling methods and numbers; the adequacy with which particular methods have been applied including adherence to assumptions; the appropriate use of data, particularly where conversion from one form to another is involved; procedures for confirmation or validation of results; and appropriate generalization.

The kind of conflicting results which are potentially generated through a mixed methods approach are often welcomed as 'it is in the tension that the boundaries of what is known are most generatively challenged and stretched' (Greene and Caracelli, 1997: 12). Jick's oft-quoted (1979) study of the effect of a merger on employee anxiety, early in the history of triangulation, provided a case in point, as does that by Meyer (1982) on unpredicted, organizational responses to environmental jolts. Erzberger and Kelle (2003) offer eight rules of integration for such situations, arguing that they require not only additional analyses, but potentially also the gathering of additional data to test conclusions from abductive reasoning.

The most obvious practical issues to impact on mixed methods research are that the use of multiple methods potentially increases the amount of time required to complete a study and the cost of conducting the study. A more critical practical problem relates to the breadth and level of researcher skills and knowledge available, and/or the ability of those with different perspectives to work together in a team.

Management and organization research has a distinctively applied focus. Practitioners need to understand the results of research being presented to them. Industry partners, granting bodies, thesis examiners, journal editors and readers each may struggle with particular (but different) elements of a presentation each bringing their own biases and methodological preferences to colour

their understanding of what is being presented. Nevertheless, multiple methods may be employed specifically so that data are available to meet the expectations or 'lenses' of particular or multiple stakeholders.

In order to become interesting to an academic audience, management research needs to be 'counter-intuitive', to challenge established theory (Bartunik et al., 2006). Skilful employment of mixed methods can significantly contribute to creating such a challenge. Clearly there is considerable scope for the wider adoption of a greater variety of mixed method techniques within management research studies.

Pat Bazeley

MODE 2

Definition

From time to time, those researching in the field of management have a panic attack. What is this subject area really about? Is there anybody out there in the world of managerial practice who wants to hear what we have been discovering in our research, or are we simply talking to ourselves? The most recent of these panic attacks was prompted by the work of Michael Gibbons and his colleagues (1994) on something they called *The new production of knowledge*, in which they identified a distinct shift in terms of the way knowledge was both produced and consumed in contemporary society. In the introduction to the book, they draw attention towards a new form of knowledge production (mode 2), which, although originally an outgrowth from its traditional counterpart (mode 1), is becoming increasingly distinctive (Gibbons et al., 1994: vii):

... our view is that while Mode 2 may not be replacing Mode 1, Mode 2 is different from Mode 1 – in nearly every respect ... it is not being institutionalised primarily within university structures ... [it] involves the close interaction of many actors throughout the process of knowledge production ... [it] makes use of a wider range of criteria in judging quality control. Overall, the process of knowledge production is becoming more reflexive and affects at the deepest levels what shall count as 'good science'.

They elaborate further by contrasting such new, mode 2 approaches to knowledge production with the more traditional and established scientific traditions of mode 1.

Mode 1 problems are set and solved in a context governed by the, largely academic, interests of a specific community. By contrast, Mode 2 is carried out in the context of application. Mode 1 is disciplinary while Mode 2 is transdisciplinary. Mode 1 is characterised by homogeneity, Mode 2 by heterogeneity. Organisationally, Mode 1 is hierarchical and tends to preserve its form, while Mode 2 is more heterarchical and transient. In comparison with Mode 1, Mode 2 is socially accountable and reflexive. (Gibbons et al., 1994: 3)

Discussion

The implications of adopting what Gibbons et al. recognize as the five salient elements of a mode 2 approach can be summarized as follows:

Mode 2 is not, however, a new research method. Rather, mode 1 and mode 2 are broad labels that allow us to classify and contrast different research methods. Given the five features of mode 2 set out above, an obvious question is the extent to which each, or any, of these five features need to be present for research to legitimately be described as being done 'in mode 2'. Existing research methods such as action research (q.v.) and grounded theory (q.v.) have been examined to assess precisely how 'mode 2' they are (MacLean et al., 2002). What is interesting is that each of the five features of mode 2 set out by Gibbons et al. are interrelated, meaning that when all five features are co-present, a new and distinct form of management research emerges called mode 2 (MacLean and MacIntosh, 2002; MacLean et al., 2002; Tranfield and Starkey, 1998).

The Features of Mode 2

Knowledge produced in the context of application	i.e. where the real-world problem and the theoretical development are co-negotiated
Transdisciplinarity	i.e. research which pulls together a diverse range of disciplinary perspectives in response to the specifics of the problem at hand
Heterogeneity and organizational diversity	i.e. research involving a transient team of researchers, drawn from a range of different organizational settings
Social accountability and reflexivity	i.e. processes of research which involve reflection on the real-time production and consumption of knowledge, and the wider societal impacts of that knowledge
Diverse range of quality controls	i.e. where the 'quality' of the knowledge is judged in more than purely academic terms. Peer-reviewed academic journal articles are one form of quality control, whether the research is usable, actionable and appropriate opens us up to a far wider set of debates

Prospects

Since being introduced to the vocabulary of the management research community, mode 2 has become an important theme. A special issue of the *British Journal of Management* (December, 2001) explored the implications and some pointed counter-arguments, notably the implications of closer practitioner engagement for ideas of academic independence and scientific rigour. Somewhat more critically, Wood (2002) notes how mode 2 approaches, while recognizing the closeness and transdisciplinary nature of those producing and using knowledge, still operates with a correspondence view of knowledge in which spatially discrete communities (academics and practitioners) are urged to accurately embody the demands of social orthodoxy. [*process philosophy*]

Robert MacIntosh and Donald MacLean

MODERNISM AND SCIENTIFIC MANAGEMENT

Definition

Modernism and scientific management are two separate intellectual traditions, originating in diametrically different domains, which nonetheless came together during the early twentieth century. Organizational and management scholars are well versed in the origins of scientific management [*Taylorism*] and in its main postulates. Modernism, however, continues to be a foreign term in the field, although its impact on industry and organizations is large. In essence, modernism is the attempt to bring art into line with the new realities and opportunities offered by industrialization and mechanization. Modernism became an important artistic movement in Europe and the USA, first in literature and the visual arts, and later in architecture.

Discussion

Historically, modernism comprised several discontinuous movements not always fully compatible with each other (Banham, 1980 [1960]). An important early influence was the English Arts and Crafts movement, which contributed to modernism ideas about the well-crafted object, art for the people (as opposed to for the elite), coherence and simplicity in design, and architecture's moral role in setting the tone of the entire modern town [*affordances*]. Art Nouveau, in spite of its conspicuous (though disciplined) use of naturalistic decoration, incorporated iron columns and frames into architecture. Cubism pioneered new conceptions of light and space, turning the picture and the building into autonomous artifacts that depicted the psychic or the social rather than the physical, representing three dimensions on the flat canvas without the illusion of perspective, a principle entrenched in art since the Renaissance [*process philosophy*]. Abstractionism also made a huge impact on artistic production with its conception of 'art as "research", art as an end in itself, art as an expression of "modernity", art as "avant-gardisme", art as a means of creating "surprise", art as "not-art", and art as "pure art"' (Collins, 1998: 274) [*representations*].

Research in a variety of fields has demonstrated that scientific management became a source of inspiration to modernist artists and architects, especially during the interwar period. In turn, the modernists found in scientific management a series of aesthetic (q.v.) ideas and notions that lay hidden in the highly detached, calculative, and draconian methods of scientific management (Guillén, 2006).

It is easier to appreciate the parallels between modernism and scientific management in the specific case of architecture. The institutionalized concept of modernist architecture included first and foremost the trinity of 'unity, order, purity' as the guiding principles of any design, from the building itself to the furniture and paintings inside it. Clean shapes and clarity of form became paramount; 'less is more', declared one leading architect of the period (Mies van der Rohe), invoking a sort of economy of taste. The aesthetic order that emerged from European modernism in architecture has been defined by its three main principles:

> Emphasis upon volume – space enclosed by thin planes or surfaces as opposed to the suggestion of mass and solidity; regularity as opposed to symmetry or other kinds of obvious balance; and, lastly, dependence on the intrinsic elegance of materials, technical perfection, and fine proportions, as opposed to applied ornament. (Barr, 1995: 29)

Modernism was a reaction against the imitation of the classical canons and approaches rescued from oblivion during the Renaissance, an attack on classicism's arbitrariness, an emphasis on perspective and proportion, an insistence on symmetry, and a pervasive use of ornament. The endless repetition – or 'mass production' – of architectural elements became the modernists' technique for achieving an effect similar to symmetry.

However, just like scientific management, modernism in architecture was more than an aesthetic proposal. It included ideological and technical elements as well. European modernism sought to achieve order through the systematic application of method (q.v.), standardization and planning. Ideologically, modernism was anti-traditional, anti-romantic [*interviews*], futurist (i.e. forward-looking), and somewhat utopian. It was rational in the sense that 'architectural forms not only required rational justification, but could only be so justified if they derived their laws from science' (Collins, 1998: 198). It was functional in the dual sense of using modern technology and approaching planning from a scientific perspective. Moreover, modernism aspired to revolutionize the process of artistic creation itself by applying method and science to both the design and construction of buildings and other artifacts. Traditional building practices – performed by a small number of craftsmen – were to be replaced by modern construction methods involving dozens of specialized subcontractors working independently, as in automobile manufacturing.

European machine-age modernism embraced scientific management in part because cost and efficiency were socially and politically constructed as important concerns. However, the romance of modernism with scientific organizational ideas went well beyond immediate economic considerations, leading to the formulation of an aesthetic based on the idea of order, on the promise of efficiency, and on technical virtuosity. The modernists 'sought to merge aesthetic innovation with economic rationality' (Larson, 1993: 50). By applying a mechanical metaphor (q.v.) to the design of houses, public buildings, schools, factories, and everyday objects, modernism magnified the impact of scientific management, extending it into new realms. If scientific management argued that organizations and people in organizations worked, or were supposed to work, like machines (Perrow 1986), modernism insisted on the aesthetic potential of efficiency, precision, simplicity, regularity, and functionality; on producing useful and beautiful objects; on designing buildings and artifacts that would look like machines and be used like machines; on infusing design and social life with order.

Prospects

The formulation by modernist architects of an aesthetic based on the beauty of the machine and on the new scientific management methods of the turn of the century provides an excellent laboratory for exploring the aesthetic content of organizational theories (Guillén, 2006). Traditionally, scientific management has been seen as a highly constraining, overtly exploitative, and ideologically conservative model of organization [*critical theory*]. It has been portrayed as a paradigm of reckless deskilling, impersonal production, and mediocre quality (Perrow, 1986). Modernist artists and architects found an aesthetic message in scientific management, producing an unlikely synthesis between art and the rationalized world of machines. Thus, the view held by many social scientists and organizational researchers that scientific management intrinsically leads to seamy, unpleasant, or stultifying outcomes needs to be reconsidered or at least qualified. It is important to realize that scientific management is much richer and more complex an organizational theory than either the cold proponents of its technical postulates or its unwavering critics are willing to admit. To be sure, scientific management has served as an implacable instrument of domination and condemned many people to dreadful working conditions. The point is that scientific management has had a much larger impact on the society and the culture than previously assumed by organizational researchers. The historical link between modernism and scientific management offers an opportunity for scholars to explore the aesthetic context of organizational and managerial behaviour. Are job performance and satisfaction influenced by aesthetic factors? Are different authority structures consistent with specific aesthetic orders? Is decision-making in organizations affected by aesthetic considerations in addition to ideological and instrumental ones? Do organizational cultures and occupational communities contain aesthetic elements? Research on organizational design, decision-making, occupations, conflict, and leadership can benefit from an explicit consideration of the aesthetic dimension as a cultural variable.

Mauro F. Guillén

N

NARRATIVE RESEARCH

Definition

Narratives are an inevitable and unavoidable aspect of social life and, as such, are integral to the processes of managing and organizing. They are discursive constructions where 'events and happenings are configured into temporal unity by means of a plot' (Polkinghorne, 1995: 5). That said, it is important to emphasize that narrative events do not need to be 'real' (e.g. past occurrences) and the temporality of a plot does not necessarily have to be linear. As Jaworski and Coupland (1999: 29–30) explain:

> Stories or narratives are discursive accounts of factual or fictitious events which take, or have taken or will take place at a particular time. We construct narratives as structured representations of events in a particular temporal order. Sometimes, the ordering of events is chronological (e.g. most fairy stories) although some plays, novels or news stories … may move backwards and forwards in time, for particular reasons and effects.

Discussion

Narrative research has its origins in literary theory. In particular, the use of narrative methods in management inquiry has been informed by Vladimir Propp's (1928/1968) classification of narratological attributes (e.g. characters, motives, and so on) derived from his analysis of the structure of Russian fairy tales and Northrop Frye's (1957) identification of dominant narrative plots (i.e. comedic, tragic, romantic and satirical). For a comprehensive general treatment of narrative approaches, Reissman's *Narrative Analysis* (1993) should be consulted, whereas its general application to organizations and management is outlined by both Czarniawska (1997) and Gabriel (2000). Beyond this, Boje (2001) offers a more radical and provocative rendition of the application of narrative methods to organizations and organizing processes. As regards specific applications to a range of phenomena in the management field, these include corporate strategy (Barry and Elmes, 1997), organizational change (Dunford and Jones, 2000), sensemaking (Brown, 2004), and management style (Beech, 2000).

Edwards (1997: 271) has suggested that there are three basic foci for narrative analysis: '(1) The nature of the *events* narrated; (2) people's perception or *understanding* of events; and (3) the *discourse* of such understandings and events.' A concern with the 'nature of events' treats the narrative under scrutiny as the *means* to other topic-specific *ends*. The consideration of 'perceptions or understandings' of agents is oriented towards individual predispositions, preferences and motives. Finally, the foregrounding of 'discourse' (q.v.) privileges a wider perspective on the narrative and, in doing so, addresses the implicative and performative dimensions of events and understandings as a form of social action [*social constructionism*].

There are also different forms of narrative analysis. Boje (2001) highlights several narrative methods, including 'causality analysis' (i.e. analysis of the assignment of attribution and agency), 'plot analysis' (i.e. analysis of the 'within-narrative' emplotment of events), and 'theme analysis' (i.e. analysis of the broader, overarching aspects beyond just the focal narrative) [*storytelling in management research*].

There are two significant debates regarding the application of narrative approaches to management. First, there is what is referred to as 'antenarrative' (q.v.) (Boje, 2001) where the use of 'ante' is intended to draw attention to that which precedes narrative. For Boje (2001), insufficient attention is paid to questioning what informs, prefigures and predisposes the formation of a coherent narrative from fragments of events [*hermeneutics*]. In short, how, and why, do particular narratives emerge?

Second, there is considerable contestation surrounding the extent to which management narratives have traditionally offered univocal, positivist accounts of organizational events. More recently, critical and poststructural interpretations have sought to reveal hegemonic struggles between dominant and marginalized narratives and the plurivocal reading of events (Boje, Oswick et al., 2004). A particularly influential example of work which explores the existence of multiple and intersecting stories and narratives is provided in Boje's (1995) analysis of the Disney corporation [*dialogic*].

Cliff Oswick

NON-PARTICIPANT OBSERVATION

Definition

Observation methods have a long tradition in organizational research, and offer the promise of 'thick descriptions' (Geertz, 1973) of what people 'really' do as opposed to what they say they do [*action science*]. Although very few researchers subscribe to an a-theoretical assumption that observation allows them to 'see (and tell) it how it is', there is still

a temptation to believe that observational research provides an unproblematic window on to real-world behaviours, events and settings [*constructivism; phronetic organizational research*]. Having said that, thoughtful and judicious use of observational methods provides one of the most effective ways to begin to understand what goes on in naturalistic settings.

Observation methods come in several forms, of which participant observation (q.v.) [*field research*] is probably the most widely known. Participant observation is traditionally associated with anthropology and particularly the Chicago school of sociology. Non-participant observation which, although sharing many of the operational issues of participant methods, is also quite distinctive in many ways.

In non-participant observation the researcher-as-observer makes no claim to be a participant, and rarely claims to develop an intersubjective understanding of the setting he or she observes. In this sense, the observer is and remains an outsider whose research involvement is either known to participants (e.g. if watching a project meeting) or unknown though passively accepted (e.g. a member of the audience at a political rally). To some extent, of course, this involvement also constitutes 'participation' with the result that the observer unavoidably influences the way activities unfold. However, it is not complete in the sense meant by the phrase 'participant observation'.

Discussion

Non-participant observation may be unstructured and grounded (q.v.) in the data, or structured and systematic. Given that the former is typically associated with participant methods, this section will focus on the use, operationalization and limitations of structured methods. First, though, it is worth pointing out an important area of convergence; namely that both approaches carry an ontological orientation which recognizes the significance of social interactions, behaviours, ritual, artefacts and symbolism [*semiotics*].

The assumption is that this type of data reflects the nature of 'social reality' in a way which is ontologically more relevant than, for example, interviewees' *post-hoc* accounts and rationalizations of these same events. The point of departure (taking a stereotypical position) revolves around the degree of reliance on theoretically-derived or empirically-informed frameworks to guide what one looks *for* [*inductive analysis*]. Structured observation, almost by definition, tends to rely on prior theory or research to develop observation schedules even before going into the field, although of course experience may lead to adjustments through processes of analytic induction (e.g. see Robinson, 1951).

Structured observation has a strong tradition in the fields of organization and education studies (e.g. Delamont, 1976; Martinko and Gardner, 1984; Mintzberg, 1970), though perhaps less so in sociology, which has tended to favour participant methods. Mintzberg's (1973) highly influential study of managerial work provides a useful example. In this research, Mintzberg followed five CEOs as they went about their daily work for a period of five days each. Data were collected using a *chronology record* (times and activities of the CEO's day), *mail record* (nature of mail received and generated by the CEO, its purpose, level of attention and action taken), and *contact record* (details of meetings, tours, formal and informal interactions, participants and so on). By recording this data, Mintzberg was able to record the amount and proportion of time spent on different activities and, as a result, generated his influential categorization of ten managerial roles.

In another early example of structured observation, Delamont (1976) used the Flanders Interaction Analysis Categories (FIAC) scheme to provide quantitative indicators of interaction patterns in school classrooms. The FIAC scheme enabled her to count incidents although, as Delamont found, the reasons behind the observed differences could not be easily explained from the data. Here we see one of the classic constraints of structured observational methods – the self-imposed inability of observers to 'go behind'

the behaviours to ask individuals about the intentions, rationalizations and frames of reference which influenced their actions. In this particular example, and in common with much observational research, the data where supplemented with data collected through informal/unstructured observation as well as self-disclosure methods such as interviews to facilitate the interpretation of observational data.

These examples illustrate some of the advantages and limitations of structured observation, and give an indication of key operational issues. The first is the perennial difficulty of gaining access (q.v.). The negotiation of research access is often time-consuming and challenging, and the resultant permission may be full, partial, intermittent or conditional. Access constraints will of course have a bearing on the potential claims one can make from the research, and also on research design and implementation strategies. For example, while Mintzberg was able to shadow CEO's for complete days at a time, with minimal apparent limitations, many organizational researchers find themselves confined to observing only large-scale (and relatively formal) interactions such as group meetings. Second, the particular point-of-access will give researchers a selective perspective on the phenomena under observation, but never a full perspective. Researchers cannot be omnipresent, just as they cannot be a-theoretical. Key informants who open doors to some interactions will inevitably (and perhaps intentionally for political or other reasons) close doors to others. Third, researchers have to consider the extent to which their involvement (albeit not as a fully participant observer) changes the setting being observed. Such issues require sensitivity and reflexivity.

In addition to issues of access and influence, researchers have to consider what they are looking *for*, even if their methodological standpoint allows them to be open to unexpected phenomena and conceptual insights. This is particularly important in structured observation methods where a key component of the research design is the observation schedule used to identify, categorize, count, time-stamp and/or comment on the phenomena of interest. Clearly, the possible units of analysis are many and varied. Selectivity, informed by one's theoretical and empirical interests, is essential. Possible points-of-focus include spatial layouts (e.g. who sits next to whom); people (present or invoked); objects and artefacts; specific acts; events; sequences of action; linguistic behaviours and so on (e.g. Smith, 1975: 203; Weick, 1968). Each point-of-focus will have implications for recording methods. Sequences of behaviour, for example, may be recorded using event, state, time-sampling or interval coding (Robson, 1993/2002: 214–220). The operationalization of phenomena requires careful thought and clear justification. If two or more observers are involved, they may aim for convergence on how to categorize instances of the phenomena, aided by statistics measuring inter-observer reliability (q.v.) such as Cronbach's Alpha.

Prospects

Robson (1993/2002: 213) recommends that when developing a structured observation schedule, researchers should ensure that it is focused, objective, explicitly defined, exhaustive, mutually exclusive, easy to record, and non-context dependent. This is an ideal which may be difficult to achieve in practice. Furthermore, the excessive emphasis on overt behaviour means that insufficient attention is given to underlying intentions and rationalizations, although, as with Delamont's research discussed above, this may be overcome through the use of complementary ethnographic (q.v.) methods. Perhaps a more serious critique is that the ideal of structured observation may be ontologically and epistemologically problematic for researchers sensitized to the influence of context and situation. Are interactions ever context-independent? Or do they – at least to some extent – reflect and enact the relational structures implicit in the socio-cultural communities in which those interactions are embedded [*reflexivity*]? These are important questions which will influence the scope and claims for structured observation, and may go some way to explaining why this method is not as popular as it was a few decades ago. Nevertheless, if used judiciously, it can provide important data to supplement and inform other research activity.

Karen Handley

0

ORAL HISTORY

Definition

Hoffman (1996: 88) describes oral history as '... collecting, usually by means of a tape-recorded interview, reminiscences, accounts and interpretations of events from the recent past which are of historical significance'. Oral histories have been described as conversational narratives and collaborative, negotiated products (Roberts, 2002: 99). Oral histories might be utilized singly or as one of a number of primary sources acting as archival material for subsequent analysis. This latter function, argues Thompson, ignores the flexibility offered by oral history to interrogate evidence as it emerges (Thompson, 1998), whether from active interviews (q.v.) or from sound archives such as found at the British Library (www.bl.uk/collections/sound-archive/ nsa.html).

Discussion

Following the 1920s Chicago School life history studies, in the late 1940s Allan Nevin and his colleagues at Columbia University developed oral history as a coherent methodological perspective. After a decline in interest, Chamberlayne et al. (2000) identify a 'turn' to biographical methodologies once more. These include folklore, gerontology, legal studies, literary history, media studies, sociology and community studies, business history, gender studies (Dunaway and Baum, 1996). There has also been an increasing association with genre and narrative analysis (Heikkinen, 2002; Miller, 2000; Portelli, 1998). Of particular interest in these fields, is, as Thompson suggests, that through life history '... the dimension of time is reintroduced to sociological enquiry...' (2000: 288). With this introduction of time, researchers can provide voices for ordinarily unheard people and complement these with analysis of historical records.

Much of the debate in using oral histories centres on whether they reflect an empirical reality or are life stories inevitably 'prejudiced' by personal, cultural, societal factors and 'narrative (q.v.) conventions [*interviewing*]'. These questions raise important ontological matters, for example that between realism (q.v.) and [*interviewing*] social constructionism (q.v.) [*constructivism; structuration theory*] (Roberts, 2002: 7) and in turn the validity and reliability (q.v.) of oral histories themselves. Here, validity is described as the verification of a history by other sources; reliability as the similarity between the same story when repeated (Hoffman, 1996). How, for example, is the accuracy of recall to be assessed? Is memory reliable (Thompson, 2000)? Although the validity of oral data might be improved by triangulation (q.v.) and aggregate recollection, Portelli (1998: 68) proposes that the subjectivity of oral sources is a strength, and that the conception of credibility employed by the natural sciences is inappropriate [*phronetic organizational research*]. Correspondingly, for Grele (1998), whose text lists key publications, handbooks, contacts and international oral history societies, interviewees represent historical processes not statistical randomness. Indeed, 'samples' of interviewees are 'representative at a sociological level' (Bertaux, 1981: 37).

The literature on management and organization studies reflects an ongoing but uneven interest in oral history. Oral history can provide insights into past management mistakes and complex organizational processes such as leadership, understanding organizational socialization, career development, diversity, employability, restructuring and the management of change (Bryman and Bell, 2003; Chamberlayne et al., 2000). Summerfield (1998), for example, utilizes oral history to understand changing patterns of women's employment. Only through oral history, not quantitative methodology, Summerfield argues, is it possible to gain in-depth access to individual work histories, something Thompson (2000: 86) picks up on in an investigation of the lives of industrial managers and entrepreneurs. Niece and Trompeter (2004), relying upon oral history alongside financial and documentary evidence, have analyzed organizational change within Aurther Andersen. Relatedly, Mitchell (1997: 122) conducted in-depth interviews with US entrepreneurs and concluded that 'because oral history illuminates insider meanings' it offers the opportunity to understand the factors relating to success and failure. In the management of tourism and leisure activities, Trapp-Fallon (2002), relates oral history to the future viability of the tourist and leisure industries. From a more critical perspective, oral history has been utilized to assess the accuracy of 'official' accounting history, particularly in the absence of documentary evidence (Hammond and Sikka, 1996; Matthews, 2000). Van de Rijt and Santema (2001) conclude that documentary information about, for example, corporate strategy provides only limited, inadequate information.

Prospects

The transcription of oral histories is contested terrain. Debate centres on the accurate capture of oral nuance versus that of 'verifiable' text (Starr, 1996) [*content analysis*]. This reflects the wider debate as to the 'truth' of documentary data and whether documentary evidence represents 'facts' or the social, tendentious, perception of facts [*constructivism*]. For Bertaux (1981: 31), qualitative social research offers direct access to social relations and hence forms the bedrock of sociological knowledge. Oral histories are one way of probing these relations, offering insight into the 'why' and 'how' of important organizational events and relationships, providing fertile ground for a deeper understanding of processes such as industrial restructuring and change (Carson and Carson, 1998).

Ian Greenwood

ORDINARY LANGUAGE PHILOSOPHY

Definition

Ordinary language philosophy is the inquiry after the use of language as a method of dealing with problems of meaning. Concerns with truth, fact and proof are threaded in our grammar as to what counts as such, so to investigate human activity well is to investigate the manner in which people say and do things as part of their everyday, or ordinary, linguistic activity. The approach is often associated with the analytic school of mid-twentieth century Oxford philosophers such as Austin and Ryle, but its influence in social science in its 'ordinary' guise is more specifically associated with the later work of the Austrian and Cambridge philosopher Ludwig Wittgenstein (d. 1952), in which linguistic investigations took the form of recognizing the myriad of practices, or games, in which language use was played out [*practice theory*].

Discussion

Identifying meanings through research is a process of appeal, first to what we do in fact say in our everyday lives, and second, pointing out where what we say can confuse us. The focus is on ordinary concepts (as opposed to abstract concepts as used in mathematics or logic). Here exactness and clarity are still concerns, but not in the same way as the provision of proof. The assumption is that typically people mean what they say and so to understand what they say is to understand this meaning. Yet definitions (such as in this dictionary), when examined, invite further inquiry; the meaning is never fixed, and so the researcher looks to instances of use. Moreover, sometimes people do not know what they mean, do not fully realize what they mean, or can't say what they mean. Here the use of words is vague, or wrong, or reified even, requiring a form of reminder, or recovery, whereby the manner of entanglement becomes apparent. This entanglement is, for Wittgenstein (1953: §123), a philosophical problem; it has the form 'I don't know my way about'; it is where grammar 'takes a wrong turn'. Ordinary language philosophy's job is to put things before us to remind us how it is we go about life. This can be done by recognizing 'language games', ostensibly simplified exchanges of word, deed and things that demonstrate how meaning arises from use, and how it collapses from lack of use, or ill-use, or radical use. Philosophy's role is to make clear how we experience the ensuing confusions under which we can labour; confusions that are inherently *civic* in nature (Wittgenstein, 1953: §125).

The 'game' metaphor (q.v.) used by Wittgenstein is both illuminating and itself potentially confusing. Language games refer to the entire gamut of distinct but connected activities – meetings, sacking people, purchasing and forecasting are examples from a business perspective.

Undertaking these activities requires language users to acknowledge the conditions of 'play', to submit themselves to the actions by which the language game has become established and is experienced by others. So in the language game of a business meeting, for example, ranting monologues are treated with suspicion; similarly, forecasting cannot

be accepted as simply hunch-work. Within and between each game meanings are held in place through what Wittgenstein calls 'family resemblance' – common patterns of proximate use for whose form and themes we develop a kind of musical sensibility (1953: 206e). Thus, we come to appreciate how the game is played. Wittgenstein (1953: §67–68) likens this appreciation to spinning a thread; as we use a word we twist fibre on fibre, use on use: 'And the strength of the thread does not reside in the fact that some one fibre runs through its whole length, but in the overlapping of many fibres.' It is the identification of these fibres that makes for better understanding. For example, in using the word 'quality', managers and management researchers twist uses together, typically referring to concerns such as: the elimination of waste; continual improvement or integrated processes. Some threads are frayed, some more commonly used than others, and there is nothing outside their continued use to prevent them being unravelled. Over time, with familiarity, we become adroit, and either confirm the viability of the game by continuing to adhere to typical uses, or rub up against the limits of what the game permits – and as a result, introduce alternate ways of acting, or even new language games. Threads are re-woven or snap completely.

So undertaking research from an ordinary language perspective involves researchers asking '[i]n what ways can confusions arise and how can we overcome them?', which in turn requires an empirical investigation of word use coupled to a recognition of the normalizing pressures whereby word use is kept within appropriate limits; pressures to which the researcher is party. Because, as has been elaborated on, word use is never fixed, the researcher is not in a position of revealing established or formal definitions, but of noticing typical and provocative use, and even provoking such use, in order to comment on the range and malleability of standard use (Hänfling, 2002: 57). Taking the use of the metaphor 'organizational knowledge' as an example, there are two related modes of response in which meaning can be recovered

(Mulhall, 2001: 150–153). First, we can as researchers remind ourselves of what we and others mean when we use the word 'know'. From analysis of statements, we might conclude that 'know' is used either as a means of inquiring after something or someone ('Do you know where …?'), or as a means of commenting on a state of affairs ('Did you know that …?', or 'I know that ..?') (Hänfling, 2002: 96–97). On further reflection, we may then realize how our uses of the word 'know' can confuse us – for example, referring to 'knowledge' in the same way as we talk of material objects such as 'soil'. Appending prepositions or articles to both 'knowledge' and 'soil' may lead us to think both words represent an existing, external entity – an asset. This confusion can be compounded when we link such words with verbs; so both knowledge and soil, for example, are 'entities' that can be 'mined', or 'stored', or 'managed'. Yet while we can, for example, ask how much soil fits into a skip, can we sensibly ask how much knowledge does (though perhaps we can imagine a skip being full of data)?

Second, and more arrestingly, we can recover meaning through the use of aphorism. The aphorism invigorates ordinary language approaches because it reveals the potential or possibilities in meanings that are only ordinarily fixed. The aphorism exemplifies the creativity of grammatical definitions, most ably exhibited by the most famous of aphorists, Georg Lichtenberg. Take his following aphorism on knowledge:

> The desire to know a lot in a short time often hinders us from precise examination, but even the man who knows this finds it hard to test anything with precision, even though he knows that if he does not test he will fail to attend to his goal of learning more. (Lichtenberg, 1990: 1800/6).

The intimate link between knowing more and learning less is succinctly and provocatively put – its value is not in representing something in words that exists in reality, but in provoking us into thinking about the nature of what it is we know when we say 'we know'.

Here the use of 'know' has an alluring, mobile quality. Wittgenstein (1953: §99)

conveys the sense of looseness by equating a language game to an enclosure with a hole. By and large, we can identify the boundaries of a game, but there is always the possibility of moving outside. This is where the metaphor of 'game' can itself confuse. By 'game' Wittgenstein did not mean all actions can be reduced to 'rules', as if explaining the rules (such as those of the legal or accountancy professions, for example) explains the actions and practices undertaken (Cavell, 1969: 51). The purpose of, and sense of involvement with, language games are not conveyed by rules (Hänfling, 2000: 34) and disputes of meaning are not about the violation of rules but a lack of integration between a practice and an individual's identity, group interests or wider environmental conditions (Mulhall, 2001: 85) [*constructivism*].

So as a mode of research, ordinary language approaches resist the tendency to theorize consequent upon the identification of regularities that can be generalized as rules. Meaning is not something applied to, or distilled from, activities, but insists within them; theories are working rather than wholly abstracting [*pragmatism*]. Researching those activities involves close attendance to: the ways in which people use words; the similarities and distinctions between these uses; the modes of agreement by which these uses are deemed more or less permissible; and the ways our language can sometimes force itself upon us in potentially confusing ways. It is this closeness that betokens its own problems; not least that of any observer for whom observing is and remains distinct from participating. The words are akin to empirical data, but are understood more through participation than observation, so that rather than create additional knowledge, what is required of researchers is an organization of what is already known in patterns that others can recognize (Hänfling, 2000: Ch. 4). Instead of definitive solutions, questions are answered with yet more questions, or at least 'open' answers. The emphasis is upon getting a 'grip' on the meanings that already exist, and in reflecting on their function in everyday activities: 'we want to walk: so we need *friction*. Back to the rough ground!' (Wittgenstein,

1953: §107). Some may find this approach too apologetic or passive. It is a method for the terminally curious and ruminative rather than those wanting to 'move forward' with definitive statements about the world and our place within it. It might be likened to the 'go slow' movement, but for research rather than food production. As Wittgenstein suggested: 'It is a happy co-incidence that fast rhymes with last.'

Robin Holt

P

PARTICIPANT OBSERVATION

Definition

There are two major elements of an ethnography (q.v.): the process of fieldwork and the writing of a text (Van Maanen, 1995). Participant observation is an essential element of fieldwork and often the only method of data collection deployed by an ethnographic researcher. The purpose of the researcher working in the field (q.v.) (working alongside research informants) is to uncover accounts which may not have been accessed by more formal methods like interviews (q.v.).

The term 'participant observation' is quite misleading; it is a general heading for four types of researcher engagement:

- The *complete participant*, who operates covertly, concealing any intention to observe the setting.
- The *participant-as-observer*, who forms relationships and participates in activities but makes no secret of an intention to observe events.
- The *observer-as-participant*, who maintains only superficial contacts with the people being studied (for example, by asking them occasional questions).
- The *complete observer*, who merely stands back and 'eavesdrops' on the proceedings (Burgess, 1984).

The first two categories are properly participative, whereas the final two methods are included in the above list for completeness but barely constitute participation as the researcher's role is not embedded within the setting [*non-participant observation*].

Discussion

Covert observation carries substantial ethical (q.v.) considerations. Indeed, in organizations where codes of research ethics exist (most notably, the National Health Service (NHS) in the UK) covert observation would be impossible due to the need for researchers to declare their intentions to an ethics committee and seek approval for their activities – their cover would be 'blown' from the outset. There may be a fine line between covert observation and muck-raking – newspapers are experts at 'infiltrating' groups and exposing their darkest practices – so researchers should take care that acting as a complete participant is fully justified. There is also a danger in that research subjects may discover that the researcher is working covertly; a decision should be made between being able to collect accurate information and sustaining good relationships with those under scrutiny [*access*]. Rosenhan's (1973) work 'On being sane in insane places' describes the experience of 'normal' people admitted to psychiatric hospital in order to gain data about their treatment in, and experience of, such institutions. It could be argued that this piece of work would not have the same credibility and impact were it not for the covert nature of the fieldwork. However, ethical (q.v.) questions arise around the impact on the researchers, the subjects (mainly the staff in the psychiatric hospital who could legitimately feel duped by Rosenhan and his colleagues) and the 'real' psychiatric patients in these hospitals.

There are many other celebrated cases of covert research: 'Tearoom Trade' (Humphreys, 1970) is a sociological study of male homosexual activities in public restrooms; and Fielding's (1981) research on the National Front, in which he presented himself both as a researcher and as a 'potential convert' in order to gain access.

There are three major demerits of covert research (Bulmer, 1982b): violation of the principle of informed consent, invasion of privacy and deception, all of which are exemplified by Humphreys' (1970) study of homosexual men which involved significant acts of deception. He collected car registration numbers of men and then obtained, (by deception) from the police, their names and addresses in order to interview them for a 'social health survey'.

The participant-as-observer is the most common model of fieldwork in management studies. Here, the researcher openly declares herself as such and seeks to embed herself in the organization, learning about the particular aspect of work which she is interested in and developing relationships with informants. Some accounts of participant observation carried out in this way report that the researcher label is often forgotten about by informants who are generally more concerned about getting on with their jobs rather than being observed.

Lupton's (1963) study of two Manchester factories is an absorbing and detailed account of shop-floor workers' lives. His description of the social process by which levels of output are determined and maintained and their links with earnings could not have been achieved by interviews and questionnaires. Lupton's view was that there was no alternative to first-hand observation if such rich data were to be collected and understood. In effect, he felt he had to personally experience the working life of a shop-floor employee in order to explain 'restriction of output' or, seen from an employee's perspective,

'controls on behaviour'. His work builds on the Bank Wiring Observation Room (Hawthorne) studies but analyses the social process through the lens of the worker rather than the researcher working on management-defined problems.

Watson's (1994b/2001) study of the fictional ZTC Ryland provides a modern example of in-depth participant observation of and with managers in a telecommunications company. The account is interspersed with dialogue, designed to illustrate how managers make sense of their roles in their struggle to achieve objectives in a difficult business environment. This verbatim reporting of 'real' conversations (q.v.) as opposed to research conversations is typical of participant observation studies and allows Watson to describe managers' roles in a way which takes us beyond the normative models traditionally offered to students of management, portraying it, instead, as 'human social craft' (Watson, 1994b/2001: 223).

Prospects

Participant observation allows the researcher access to people's working lives and, as such, researchers owe a debt of respect and care to informants; it is the researcher's privilege to enter and be part of their lives, not theirs to admit us. It is in preserving this intimate balance that participant research often struggles. Particular groups may feel that they have been singled out as being especially interesting and worthy of being researched and therefore welcome the researcher; others may feel threatened by her presence. Naturally, the researcher's ability to build relationships and develop rapport with subjects is crucial. The danger here is that the researcher may 'go native', that is, feel so embedded and sympathetic to the group being studied that interpreting events objectively becomes difficult. The associated difficulty is the time-consuming and open-ended nature of this kind of research, which means it often doesn't get done. In a cost-conscious research climate in which specific and often short-term, definitive objectives are required to secure funding, sustained participation is a risky strategy.

Lisa Anderson

PHENOMENOLOGY

Definition

Phenomenology is a method of explaining meaning that strips out reference to abstracting, historical or structural influences, and instead looks to the experiencing subjects' direct and unmediated awareness of phenomena.

Discussion

Any adequate theory of meaning, including that of science itself, has to account for the nature of consciousness; it is only by a conscious, intentional act that a world is brought into life from amidst the hurly-burly of experience. It is this acknowledgement that transcribes the edges of the phenomenological worldview. The use of objectifying criteria, such as exactness, generalized explicability and validity, takes researchers away from this intimate configuration of meaning because as accounts of meaning they tend to privilege the observer above the observed [*individualism; phronetic organizational research; positivism and post-positivism; structuration theory*]. One of the originators of phenomenological approaches, Edmund Husserl (d. 1938), argued that to fully understand meaning we have to restore the originating influence of persons who experience it. What is being restored in the researcher's analysis is a condition of the intentionality of what is being researched; hence the primary concern of the phenomenologist is not whether things or objects actually exist, but whether these are intended in consciousness. This levelling of objects dissolves the implicit hierarchies of meaning – the symbols of epic stories are as 'real' as tables and chairs and equally as valid as a source of data for researchers [*aesthetics;*

semiotics]. Meaning is the meaning given to objects by those in whose intentional states the objects are known in what Hussurl calls 'meaning acts'. So to understand an object such as 'a firm' the researcher looks to the specific episodes of thinking, perceiving, believing, etc. (Smith and Smith, 1995: 21) by which a firm is experienced. From the perspective of employees, or regulators, or shareholders, an object such as a 'firm' may differ according to the different ways their meaning acts 'bracket-off' (époche) their experience. Hence a firm can be understood as an opponent, as opportunistic or as an opportunity (or a blend thereof) without contradiction.

At its transcendental extreme the loneliness of this sense-giving consciousness can provoke an almost existential (q.v.) indifference; why, if reality is nothing more than what we as individuals impute to it, should we care about the everyday meanings of others [*relativism*]? But if consciousness and intentionality (as meaning acts) are taken not to refer to private mental states informing agency, but to the ways our conscious life is *embodied* in things and relations and symbols *through* action, and if objects are seen as having a presence that somehow invites, or elicits conscious focus, then what has meaning arises from the complicity of subjects and objects [*practice theory*]. This 'prosthetic' development of Hussurlean phenomenology stems from Merleau-Ponty's (1988: 194–199) 'philosophy of nature', requiring what he calls an awareness of the 'encroaching' field of subject and object in which the subject is understood as both an object (an object amidst a world of objects) and a subject that sees and touches objects. This phenomenological approach involves getting behind our observer conventions to invoke a raw or more basic appreciation of what can be meaningfully felt, or intuited; to trace the rhythms of how the world opens itself out on to subjects and of how subjects open out on to the world.

A basic example would be our human intentional interest in the object 'warmth', which prompts inquiry into identifying and controlling sources of heat, and thence adequate generalizations concerning the properties and classification of these sources. While subject awareness is rooted with intentional acts of interest, these acts involve active orientations around already established modes of understanding. So the associated 'need' for power to provide warmth might, if experienced by a consumer in a western market economy, might be configured using the object of a commodity (rather than, say, an emblem of divine power). This market economy background then elicits specific actions in relation to the object 'warmth', such as purchasing, expending, storing and so on [*hermeneutics*]. As subjects, we are both temporally and spatially configured; experience from which we cannot wrest ourselves as separate, phenomenologically distinct beings (Derrida, 1973). Yet despite market economy upbringings, the need for heat need not be commodified *in toto*; the subject flows back on to the world; and so, for example, silent vents are passed over for fireside aesthetics which in turn may restore a more direct, less commodified relationship with the object warmth.

Robin Holt

PHRONETIC ORGANIZATIONAL RESEARCH

Definition

Phronetic organizational research is an approach to the study of management and organizations focusing on ethics and power. It is based on a contemporary interpretation of the Aristotelian concept *phronesis*, usually translated as 'practical wisdom', sometimes as 'prudence'. *Phronesis* is the ability to think and act in relation to values, to deliberate about 'things that are good or bad for humans' in the words of Aristotle (1976: 1140a24–b12). Phronetic organizational research effectively provides answers to the following four value-rational questions, for specific problematics in management and organization studies:

1. Where are we going with this specific management problematic?
2. Who gains and who loses, and by which mechanisms of power?
3. Is this development desirable?
4. What, if anything, should we do about it?

Phronetic organizational research concerns deliberation, judgement, and praxis in relation to the four questions. Praxis is the process by which *phronesis* as a concept becomes lived reality [*practice theory*]. Answers to the questions are used as input to ongoing dialogues (q.v.) about the possibilities and risks that management and organizations face and how things may be done differently. The 'we' in the questions consists of those researchers asking the questions and those who share the concerns of the researchers, including people in the organization under study. Phronetic researchers see no general and unified 'we' in relation to which the questions can be given a final, objective answer. What is a 'gain' and a 'loss' often depends on the perspective taken, and one person's gain may be another's loss. Phronetic researchers are highly aware of the importance of perspective, and see no neutral ground, no 'view from nowhere', for their work.

The focus of phronetic organizational research is on practical activity and practical knowledge in everyday situations in organizations [*action research; mode 2; pragmatism*]. It *may* mean, but is not limited to, a focus on known sociological, ethnographic (q.v.), and historical phenomena such as 'everyday life' and 'everyday people', with their focus on the so-called 'common'. What it *always* means, however, is a focus on the actual daily practices [*practise-centred research*] – common or highly specialized or rarefied – which constitute a given organizational field of interest, regardless of whether these practices constitute a stock exchange, a grassroots organization, a neighbourhood, a multinational corporation, a government office, an emergency ward, or a local school board.

The result of phronetic organizational research are concrete examples and detailed narratives (q.v.) of the ways in which power and values work in organizations and with what consequences, and to suggest how power and values could be changed to work with other consequences. Phronetic research holds that in so far as organizational situations become clear, they are clarified by detailed study of who is doing what to whom. Such clarification is therefore a principal concern for phronetic organizational research and provides the main link to praxis.

The methodological implications of following a phronetic approach may be briefly described by the following methodological guidelines, which should be seen not as imperatives but as indicators of direction:

1. Focus on values (what's 'good or bad for humans in organizations').
2. Place power at the core of analysis [*actor-network theory; critical theory*] (because, as Bertrand Russell observed, the fundamental concept in social science is power, in the same sense in which energy is the fundamental concept in physics; power is productive).
3. Get close to reality (to improve understanding and ensure practical relevance).
4. Emphasize 'little things' (God is in the detail – and so is the Devil) [*ethnomethodology*].
5. Look at practices before discourse (what is done is more important than what is said, and understanding the difference between the two is an effective means for learning about management and organization).
6. Study cases (q.v.) and context (because the practical judgement central to *phronesis*, and to good management, is case-based and context-dependent).
7. Ask 'How?', do narrative (to understand the process and what to do).
8. Move beyond agency and structure (to internalize externality in organizations and externalize internality).
9. Do dialogue with a polyphony of voices (phronetic organizational research is dialogical (q.v.) with no one voice, including that of the researcher, claiming final authority).

Discussion

Because *phronesis* concerns values it goes beyond analytical, scientific knowledge (*episteme*) [*realism*] and technical knowledge or know how (*techne*) and it involves judgements and decisions made in the manner of a virtuoso social actor. Aristotle was explicit in his regard of *phronesis* as the most important of the three intellectual virtues: *episteme*, *techne*, and *phronesis*. *Phronesis* is most important because it is that activity by which scientific and instrumental rationality is balanced by value-rationality; and because, according to Aristotle, such balancing is crucial to the viability of any organization – from the family to a business to the state. To ignore value-rationality in human organizations is to ask for trouble, according to Aristotle. The many recent scandals of corporate governance may be seen as cases in point. They result from executives not understanding the importance of and not being proficient in *phronesis*.

In terms of the history and theory of science, Aristotle and Machiavelli are the classic thinkers of *phronesis*. More contemporary scholars within this tradition are Pierre Bourdieu, Michel Foucault, Clifford Geertz, Alasdair MacIntyre, Martha Nussbaum, and Richard Rorty, who emphasize phronetic before epistemic knowledge in the study of social organization, despite important differences in other domains.

A curious fact can be observed, however. Whereas *episteme* is found in the modern words 'epistemology' and 'epistemic', and *techne* in 'technology' and 'technical', it is indicative of the degree to which scientific and instrumental rationality dominate modern thinking and language that we no longer have a word for the one intellectual virtue, *phronesis*, which Aristotle and other founders of the western tradition saw as the most important condition of successful social organization [*positivism and post-positivism*].

Epistemic science, modelled after the natural sciences, has gained dominance to a degree, where even intellectual activities like organizational research and social science, which are not and probably never can be scientific in the epistemic, natural science sense, have found themselves compelled to strive for and legitimate themselves in terms of the epistemic model. According to Czarniawska and Sevón (2003: 9–13), epistemic organizational research is the mainstream of organizational research and it claims universality based on a search for generic truths about management and organizations.

Prospects

It is a problem that management scholars generally do not recognize the distinctions between *episteme*, *techne*, and *phronesis*, because they are very different intellectual activities with very different implications for practical research. It is often the case that these activities are rationalized as *episteme*, even though they are actually *techne* or *phronesis*. However, it is not in their role as *episteme* that one can argue for the value of organizational research and other social sciences. In the domain in which the natural sciences have been strongest – the production of theories that can explain and accurately predict – the social sciences, including organizational research, have been weakest. Nevertheless, by emphasizing the three roles, and especially by reintroducing *phronesis*, we see there are other and more satisfying possibilities for organizational research than vainly emulating natural science.

The theoretical and methodological implications of *phronesis* for organizational and management research were first explained in Flyvbjerg (2001, 2003). The following may serve as examples in an emerging body of organizational research that contains elements of *phronesis*. In the study of power and organizations, the work of Clegg (1997) and Clegg and Kornberger (2003) stands out. In the organization of the firm and of accounting, the work of Miller (2003) must be mentioned. In the organization of science and technology there is the work of Latour (1999b) and Rabinow (1999). And in the organization of government there is Schram and Caterino (2006), Flyvbjerg (1998), and Dean (1999). Examples exist as well from more specialized fields of research, such as the

organization of consumption (Miller and Rose, 1997), policing (Harcourt, 2001), and space (q.v.) and architecture (Crush, 1994) [*modernism and scientific management*]. More examples of phronetic organizational research may be found in Flyvbjerg (2001: 162–165) and Dean (1999: 3–5).

Bent Flyvbjerg

POSITIVISM AND POST-POSITIVISM

Definition

Within the social sciences, advocates of positivism argue that the only legitimate source of knowledge are sense data, through which reality is experienced. In order to guard against the personal and subjective basis of this sensory experience, findings are claimed to be reliable when they can be repeatedly verified. Positivism's roots lie within empiricist philosophy in which wider metaphysical and ethical questions of meaning and value were 'cut away' from the rational pursuit of factual truth based upon an unalloyed experience of nature using the method, or logic, of verification. By letting metaphysics go as a kind of archaic outlier, positivism brings the material world into confined, codified and tidy structures. Its acknowledged founder in social science – Auguste Comte – used the approach as a counter-blast to clerical dominance; it had a democratising tone. The rise of post-positivism is, similarly, a counter-blast, but this time against the dominance that the empirical, scientistic worldview that Comte championed itself came to occupy. Verification became its own metaphysics, open to challenge from those who felt there was more than one – empirical – way of understanding the world.

Discussion

As early modern management sought to transfer the traditions of applied engineering in the natural sciences to the social sciences

(Shenhav, 1999), it was quickly established in a positivist vein. The subsequent influence of economics, sociology, and psychology on the development of management education as university-based hardened this vein, and led to the idea of management and its research being positivist. In other words, it attempted to explain knowledge according to the standards and methods of natural 'science'. By definition, it was able to lay claim to modern assumptions of rationality, universality, objectivity, and value freedom, coupled to a belief in the possibility of the progressive rationalization of action – a ready embrace of the modernist (q.v.) assumption of the progressive and cumulative character of knowledge (Roberts, 1996: 55).

The founders of business schools in institutions of higher education were attracted to claims of value freedom, objectivity, universality, and the possibility of generating law-like predictions in knowledge. The invention of science-based management (Locke, 1989) was essential if business education was to be removed from its vocational origins and given the status necessary for recognition as an academic discipline. Its proponents strove for scientific knowledge that was equivalent to the natural sciences. However, there are significantly different conditions of knowledge between the realm of a science of nature and a science of practice [constructivism; phronetic organizational research; realism].

Practice-based (q.v.) knowledge is bounded by its contextual nature, as can be illustrated by the following simple contrast between the 'laws' of natural science and the 'science' of management. Iron filings, a staple of school physics, always display the same dispositional behaviour when introduced to the poles of a magnet, irrespective of whether the experiment occurs in Japan or the USA or the identity of the experimentalist. These variables simply are not important to the 'sense' that the filings make of their patterning around the magnetic poles, which is to say, as phenomena from the object realm, rather than the subject realm, they can make no sense whatsoever. Nor is it relevant to the sense that the experimentalist makes.

Experimentalists do not, typically, refer to the particulars of their own identity in making the sense that they make.

In contrast, however, had we been thinking about how managers might respond to the twin poles of a strategic threat, rather than iron filings responding to a magnet, the situation would be very different. The patterns that emerge are not the result of laws that inexorably create a certain pattern. There is far more indeterminateness. Patterns in practice are established by rules that are applied locally, in situ, by the actors themselves. These rules are not external – even though they may exist as such, as material traces, in manuals or procedures. They are, instead, the result of a complex mastery of skills that enable the actors to cope with new situations according to some categories for making sense that involve the application of members' implicit rules. That is what constitutes skill. But, once such skills are well learned they become reflexively automatic. That is, they cannot be analyzed simply in terms of those rules that might be thought to constitute them [ordinary language philosophy]. Such rules become themselves the unspoken and tacit ground of any action, action that is capable of improvising in unpredictable ways around and between any sense that the rules might make. Rules cannot account for their own interpretation in situ by actors. The proficient manager's response to a strategic threat is thus made not just according to some externally learned rule about 'how to deal with a strategic threat' taught to them in a business school, although this may form part of their implicit rules. On the contrary, it is governed by skills that have in time become reflexively automatic (Flyvbjerg, 2001: 20) in ways that resist precise correspondence in propositional structure or detailed description.

Those who create and disseminate management knowledge often aspire to be neutral observers of what just happens to be. They take no stance towards the nature of being. In other words, they simply register that which is without reflection – which could only be speculative and prescriptive – or why it might be that way [hermeneutics]. Their ethic of value freedom places them beyond ethics – it is a kind of ethics that you have when you don't presume any other ethics. Of course, these articles of faith are designed to protect 'management science' from contamination by other, 'lesser' forms of knowledge. Against this view of the world, a post-positivist view would argue that while the nature of reality is unequivocally real – it is 'out there' – our ways of knowing it as such are somewhat more contestable. While we have highly elaborated codes for making sense of phenomena – such as the methods of empirical science – we should recognize these for the codes they are. Reality cannot be represented in some propositionally pure form that is untouched by the context of meaning in which it is embedded. Experience ordered though our sense data may cause us to hold certain views of the matter in question but it cannot tell us which views we should be considering in the first place (Rorty, 1989). That certain causal regularities may be empirically observed of a phenomena does not enable one to ask why these regularities and not some others? For instance, authority is achieved as a set of patterned preferences whose prevalence demonstrates its facticity.

Prospects

Future management and organization research might more vigorously engage matters of ethics (q.v.) and take stances on political matters in a way that positivist work shuns. In as much as positivism seeks either to translate other concerns into its domain or ignores them (Donaldson, 1996), an argument basically in favour of methodological and other forms of pluralism, as well as being against positivism, could only be considered as philosophically healthy. In addition, such a practice might better articulate the range of normative diversity on power, fairness, efficiency, and the other contested domains of organizational life, that are routinely found in the broader social sciences but seem so often to be filtered out of management.

Stewart R. Clegg

POSTCARDS

Definition

Postcards first appeared in the UK in 1870 when they were introduced by the Post Office as a single card with the address on one side and a message on the other. Until 1894, there were no private cards and all cards carried a pre-paid stamp. Elsewhere, pictures were more in evidence, initially as envelopes and then as single postcards. For example, in the USA, cards were printed with advertising while the construction of the Eiffel Tower in 1890 resulted in early souvenir postcards. By 1902, the Post Office in the UK had adjusted its rules to allow pictures on a front and message and address on a back, which became divided by a line and this became the standard for postcards.

Discussion

Postcards as a method of data-gathering in organizations provide one means of overcoming some of the recognized difficulties of research. Such difficulties include, first, the viewing of outside interference from researchers by managers and others with suspicion allied to competitive pressures and work intensification which limit the time available for research [access]. Second, the tendency to disperse organization activities from the centre in time and location with the consequence of multiple localities, each with their own cultural and historical interpretation of events [ethnography]. Third, each organization and each locality can no longer be viewed as a single, unified or fixed entity; there is always a plurality of voices and those voices work in interaction with others [antenarrative; dialogic; hermeneutics]. Researchers of management and organization need to feature the voices of the variety of social actors and this is often seen as the strength of qualitative research through such devices as narratives (q.v.), diaries (q.v.), life-histories [oral history], etc. (Atkinson et al., 2001) and to this list, I would propose adding postcards.

Postcards are such an easy means of collecting information, it is surprising there are not many examples in the research literature. Betts and Holden (2003) provide one example, using 'hard' postcards in their evaluation of an employee-led development initiative in a local authority in the north of England, in combination with focus group interviews. The initiative was open to all 7,000 employees, although restructuring and low morale reduced participation to fewer than 14 per cent. The cards, entitled 'Postcards from the Learning Zone', were used to collect data as part of the evaluation and to 'facilitate a degree of reflection' (Betts and Holden, 2003: 281).

Recently, the arrival of e-postcards has provided new possibilities. The internet increases the stretch of research methods. In many parts of the world, fears about poor access to electronic media, leading to an exclusion of the voices of some research subjects and biased samples, have subsided. Consequently, there are new opportunities to access subjects who are usually hard to get in touch with or where the issues being researched are contentious and/or sensitive. Coomber (1997), for example, used the internet to research illicit 'drug dealers', including an attempt to contact German and French subjects via electronic newsgroups. E-mail probably provides the main extension of the postcard for the researcher. In contrast to some approaches to electronic research using software tools of growing sophistication, the e-postcard essentially retains the simplicity of the traditional paper-based version. The key principles of postcard design can be maintained so long as the malleability of the electronic medium is not used to turn what is meant to be quick and easy research tool into a questionnaire. For example, Thorpe et al. (2004) used e-postcards (shown as Figure 4), in an interpretative study of entrepreneurial 'maturity'.

The method sought access to language and images to understand multiple frames of reference and entrepreneurial sensemaking. The card asked for responses to three questions relating to business goals and how these could be realized: 102 cards were 'sent' and 44 'returned'. An interesting finding was that the process enabled a degree of self-understanding by entrepreneurs, allowing a degree of reflection on their ideas, goals and overall reasons for adopting this form of business/life [*interviewing*].

While no method can ensure certainty, postcards are recognized by potential respondents as quick and easy to complete; they have a structure which is familiar and comprehensible. They offer the researcher spatial and temporal flexibility that does not require proximity to research locations, so long as the addresses of the sample or some other means of distribution are available. The option of providing pre-paid postage can increase response rates and an e-postcard sent as an attachment via e-mail can be opened, completed online and returned within minutes. Of course, both traditional and e-postcards can be ignored, the latter particularly can be deleted, confused with Spam or fall foul of a growing tendency towards information overload. Postcards can be completed asynchronically. Respondents have the discretion of when to write their cards and this allows consideration rather than immediacy, if they wish. As Horschild (1998) has shown, writing may be better for the expression of emotional and imaginative aspects of understanding. Further, the completion of a postcard could provide for interaction between researcher and subjects which, as suggested by Boshier (1990), is free from coercion and hierarchical influence. While traditional postcards contain less text than, for example, interview data or questionnaires, they still need transcribing. E-postcards, on the other hand, pass the transcribing process to the subject so the data can come 'ready-transcribed' (Selwyn and Robson, 1998: 1).

Prospects

It may be argued that the commitment to writing postcards reduces its connection with the richness and immediacy of a spoken process, including access to the intentions of meaning and avoidance of misunderstanding and reducing interaction to restrictive digital

Images of Britain: Stonehenge

Just a bunch of old stones, or a significant human achievement in astronomy, engineering and spiritual insight?

Please answer the three questions below by clicking on and typing in the spaces and return as an email attachment to .... Many thanks.

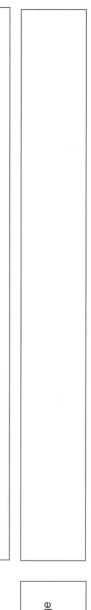

What is your ultimate goal in business?

Why is this your goal?

If you could picture your goal – what image or object would best symbolize it?

Figure 4 *Postcard*

communication [*interviews – electronic*]. However, there is compensation in the opportunity for voices to be heard, often for the first time, without the inhibiting presence of a bodily other. Crucially, such understanding is usually expressed in language with the production of a text, which according to Bleicher (1980: 230), drawing on Ricœur's paradigm of a text, provides for a 'fixation of meaning'. As a consequence, there is a detachment of what is said from speaking where what is written has a meaning in abstraction just for itself. The value of this for researchers is the combination of what is present with its past which Gadamer (1989: 390) saw as 'unique', often revealing features of the writer's situation and context which are not immediately obvious in spoken interactions. As such, the data become available for further analysis within text-based approaches such as discourse (q.v.) and narrative analysis.

Jeff Gold

POST-COLONIAL THEORY

Definition

Post-colonial theory is a broad term of relevance for a range of disciplines in the humanities and the social sciences, such as literature theory, sociology, anthropology, and organization studies (for an overview and introduction, see P. Prasad, 2005: Ch. 14; A. Prasad, 2005). Rather than being an integrated and unified theory or perspective, post-colonial theory denotes a loosely coupled theoretical framework capturing how colonialist, imperialist, neo-colonialist, and post-colonial practices and ideologies are influencing contemporary culture, society, and the economy. Post-colonial theory is complex and syncretic rather than monolithic and unitary. In addition, post-colonial theory does not have a distinct origin but must, as Young (2001) argues, be as old as colonialism itself; with expansion comes the critique of expansion.

The emergence of post-colonial theory is entangled with both political activism (embodied by political leaders such as Ho Chi Minh and Mahatma Gandhi) aimed at decolonializing parts of the world under western governance, and more intellectual endeavours, for instance the literature accounting for the human, social, and cultural costs caused by colonialist projects. In 1950, Aimé Césaire published *Discourse on Colonialism*, a critical account of the effects of the colonialist projects. Following this, the Martinique-French author and psychoanalyst Franz Fanon (1925–1961) published two major works, *Black Skins, White Masks* (1952/1986) and *The Wretched of the Earth* (1963), wherein he examined the psychological effects of the colonialist project. After Césaire, Fanon, and others' foundational works, post-colonial theory gradually became increasingly institutionalized. In 1978, the Palestinian-American literature professor Edward Said (1935–2003) published the seminal work *Orientalism,* wherein Said, influenced by Michel Foucault's genealogical method, sketched how images of the Orient as a mystical, elusive, but also backward part of the world were being fabricated in western culture. More recently, the Indian-American literature professor Gayatri Chakraborty Spivak (b. 1942), testifying to a deconstructive (q.v.), feminist (q.v.) and Marxist (q.v.) [*dialectic*] epistemology, has become one of the most important writers in the post-colonial tradition. Although Spivak's thinking is too complicated to locate to one single perspective and is not presented in one single work, her analysis of the colonial subaltern – a concept borrowed from the Italian Marxist Antonio Gramsci – has been influential in post-colonial discourses. Other important contributors to post-colonial theory include Homi K. Bhabha, Arjun Appadurai, and Robert Young. Ryszard Kapuściński and V.S. Naipaul have published more journalistic and literary accounts of a post-colonial world.

Discussion

In management and organization theory, post-colonial theory plays a complementary but increasingly important role. While Marxism and class-oriented thinking have been somewhat unfashionable since the 1970s, and feminist theory has established itself as an influential and important analytical perspective on managing and organizational life, post-colonial theory (and to some extent queer theory examining the 'heteronormativity' in western societies) is emerging as an alternative view. Researchers such as Pushkala Prasad, Anshuman Prasad, Stella Nkomo, Subhabrata Bobby Banerjee, Stephen Linstead, and Bill Cooke have advocated and employed post-colonial theory in analyses of business activity (e.g. Banerjee and Linstead, 2001, 2004; Cooke, 2003; Nkomo, 1992). In addition to organization and management studies explicitly drawing on a post-colonial theory framework, there is a number of studies presented by anthropologists, sociologists, and other social scientists examining post-colonialist aspects of organizations. Two examples of this literature are Ong's (1987) ethnography (q.v.) of female factory workers in a Japanese company in Malaysia, and Drori's (2000) study of the relationship between Jewish managers and Arab and Druse workers in the Israeli textile industry. The anthology edited by Prasad (2003) offers a number of examples of how post-colonial theory can be of relevance in the analysis of managerial practices as diverse as accounting, management control, and cross-cultural (q.v.) management studies. Elsewhere, Prasad and Prasad (2002) point to a number of fields where post-colonial theory may make a fruitful contribution, for instance studies of the growing museum and exhibition industry where colonialist, neo-colonialist and post-colonialist ideologies are manifested (Harrison, 1997), or research on the tourism industry, essentially relying on the representation of 'the Other' as exotic, intriguing, and above all different.

Diversity management, today a major industry in its own right in terms of providing a range of consultancy services, courses, and a management guru literature, is another field of interest where post-colonial theory is applicable [*anti-discriminatory research*]. The bulk of the mainstream and normative diversity literature does not address the topic in terms of a post-colonial agenda but favours presentations of 'show cases' (Prasad and Mills, 1997), pointing at the short-term financial performances derived from the employment of a more diverse workforce. In general, the relationship between post-colonial theory, in essence critical of the predominant colonialist heritage in organizations, and the normative diversity management literature, is a complicated one (Mir et al., 2006).

Prospects

Critics of post-colonial theory argue that the literature is abstract, overtly theoretical, poorly integrated, and incapable of synthesizing any comprehensive and unified theory or theoretical framework examining social systems in terms of its colonialist or post-colonialist practices. Seen in this view, the critique is similar to that of post-structuralist and post-modernist (q.v.) thinking, queer theory, or any other post-positivist (q.v.) theoretical framework recognizing hybridity, assemblages, and intersectionality. Proponents of post-colonial theory would respond that the very critique of Eurocentric thinking must be formulated in a non-Eurocentric vocabulary and recognize alternative ontologies and epistemologies. Therefore the critique on the lack of unity is inadequate. However, from a practical point of view, it is complicated to treat post-colonial theory as more than a loosely-coupled framework of concepts, studies, arguments, and narratives, sharing the objective to critically evaluate past, present, and future social practices that in a variety of ways draw on colonialist, imperialist and neo-colonialist ideologies and practices. The recent interest in globalization, diversity, and a general critique of Eurocentric thinking suggests that post-colonial theory is becoming increasingly important for the analysis of organizations. Similar to other critical orientations in the social sciences and humanities, such as feminist theory, post-structuralism and queer theory, post-colonial theory partially represents a new regime of thinking wherein hybridity, fluidity and movement are the norm rather than the exception.

Alexander Styhre

POSTMODERNISM

Definition

The term 'postmodernism' made its first appearance in the title of a book, *Postmodernism and Other Essays,* written by Bernard Iddings Bell as early as 1926. In the latter half of the 1960s a number of social commentators and literary critics, including Ihab Hassan, Leslie Fiedler, and Daniel Bell, began actively promoting usage of the terms 'postmodern' and 'postmodernism' in their work. Despite these developments in literary-critical circles, however, it was not until Lyotard's (1984, but originally published in 1979) publication of a report entitled *The Postmodern Condition* that wider public attention was drawn to the debate between modernism and postmodernism. Increasingly loosely employed in much of the academic literature in art, science, literary criticism, philosophy, sociology, politics and now even in management and organization studies, its use nonetheless evokes vastly contrasting reactions. On the one hand, postmodernism is frequently equated with relativism (q.v.) and dismissed as an extremely cynical tendency towards nihilism within contemporary culture, and on the other, it is regarded as an extremely subtle and complex philosophical attempt at reworking the metaphysical bases of modern knowledge. Within the context of this discussion, postmodernism is best understood as an *experimental and reactionary movement* against the perceived excesses of modernism (q.v.). It is an attempt to 'restore to the world what modernity, presumptuously, had taken away; as a *re-enchantment* of the world that modernity had tried hard to *dis-enchant'* (Bauman, 1992: x) [*positivism and post-positivism*]. Postmodernism seeks to show that what underpins modern rationality is a damaging reductionistic 'logic of representation', in which fluid, living experiences are forcibly subjected to mental dissection and symbolic representation in order to render the latter more amenable to instrumental manipulation and control. Modern rationality, and hence representation, is thus fundamentally a method of ordering which radically distorts our experiences of reality. The postmodern argument is that through representation the subjective and ephemeral aspect of human experiences is inadvertently overlooked and denied epistemological legitimacy in the modernist scheme of things since it privileges the explicit over the tacit, qualitative aspects of human experience. *The postmodern critique, then, is centrally concerned with giving voice and legitimacy to those tacit and oftentimes unpresentable forms of knowledge that modern epistemology inevitably depends upon yet conveniently overlooks or glosses over.*

Discussion

Much has been written about postmodernity as a cultural condition resonating with the collective mood and orientations of late capitalism; postmodernism as an experimental movement or reaction to the perceived excesses of modernism in architecture, the arts and the sciences; and 'the postmodern' as reflective of an immanent ontological tension created by the modernist obsession with order, systematization, control, and predictability, in virtually every aspect of human endeavour. These three moments and movements provide a loosely-clustered but recurrent theme reverberating within the contemporary western consciousness. They help us grasp, amidst the unquestioned achievements of modern science and technology, the accompanying sense of alienation, loss, disillusionment, fragmentation of identities, and apathy precipitated by the mechanisms of modernity over the past two hundred years. Yet, the postmodern is not to be associated with all that is negative. The idea of a progressive postmodern science superseding Newtonian rationality and subscribing to a vastly different worldview has been proffered as an alternative set of metaphysical principles for comprehending post-quantum reality (Bohm, 1988; Prigogine, 1996) [*complexity theories*].

Three intellectual axioms and imperatives are detectable in the postmodern approach to analysis that could be insightful when used in management and organization studies. First, postmodern analyses seek to emphasize the Heraclitean primacy accorded to process (q.v.) [*method*], indeterminacy, flux and incessant change in place of the modernist emphasis on the ontological primacy of form, substance, stability and order. It privileges change over persistence, activity over substance, process over product, and novelty over continuity. It emphasizes the primacy of the *becoming* of things. Second, it views language, and in particular the activities of *naming* and *symbolic representation*, as the perceived cause of apparent orderliness in the world [*ordinary language philosophy*]. It argues that without the acts of naming, classification and the creation of a subject–predicate structure through language and grammar, lived reality is but a 'shapeless and indistinct mass' (Saussure, 1966: 111). In this process of linguistic ordering and representing, however, representations (q.v.) ossify and become dominant and much of our more tacit forms of knowing remain unacknowledged. It is, therefore, the insistent deconstruction (q.v.) of these oftentimes ossified, and hence restrictive, representations which forms a central focus of postmodern analyses. Third, postmodernism seeks to modify the conceptual asymmetry created by privileging conscious action over *unconscious* forces. The elevation of rationality, intentionality and choice in the modernist explanatory schema surreptitiously overlooks the role of unconscious nomadic forces in shaping rational choice and deliberate planned action. Postmodern analyses emphasize the heterogeneous, multiple, *alinear* and mostly *unconscious* character of real-world happenings [*psychoanalytic approaches*]. Events and happenings in the real world do not unfold in a discrete, linear and predictable manner. Instead they 'leak in insensibly' (James, 1909/1996: 399). This means that human action and motives must not be simply explained in terms of actors' choices and intentions, but rather in terms of embedded contextual experiences, accumulated memories and cultural traditions that create and define the very possibilities for interpretation and action. These three axioms and imperatives provide the generative principles for a postmodern approach to social analysis.

Robert Chia

PRACTICE THEORY

Definition

Increasing interest in practice theory within management studies takes place in the context of a wider 'practice turn' in contemporary social theory, originating in the 1980s (Ortner, 1984; Schatzki, 2005a; Schatzki et al., 2001; Turner, 1994). Seminal theorists of this turn include Pierre Bourdieu, Michel de Certeau and Anthony Giddens. Their work offers frameworks and vocabularies that draw attention to the logic and reason of situated human action (Reckwitz, 2002). In addition, management scholars engaging with practice theory frequently cite the influence of Karl Weick's injunction to employ verb rather than noun forms, for example 'organizing' instead of 'organization', 'strategizing' instead of 'strategy'. To a lesser extent, influential work from the field of science and technology studies has, to date, provided a theoretical reference point. Most commonly cited work includes that of Bruno Latour, Michel Callon and John Law, as well as other theorists associated with actor-network theory (q.v.) and ethnographers (q.v.) such as Karin Knorr-Cetina and Steve Woolgar. However, key works, such as those of Pickering (1995), Lynch (1993) and Barnes

(1983), have yet to make a significant appearance in practice-focused management studies. It is important to recognize that practice theory is a substantial field of social theory in its own right with considerable debate among diverse voices within it. Schatzki (2001) offers a useful overview and synthesis of three core themes.

First, practice theory is centrally concerned with activity of all kinds, not just the unique and extraordinary but also the familiar and routine. This attention to the apparently banal is reflected in de Certeau's (1984) sociology of 'everyday life', Bourdieu's (1990) ambition to exoticize the domestic and Giddens's (1987) claim for the importance of making remarkable the unremarked [*postmodernism*]. Second, practice theory situates this activity within fields of practice, in which human actors draw on the shared understandings, skills, language and technologies of broader society, for example, Bourdieu's (1990) notion of the habitus, Foucault's (1977) concern for discursive (q.v.) practices [*dialogic*] and de Certeau's (1984) attention to material artefacts. The third core theme of practice theory is attention to the tacit and improvisatory skills and accomplishments of human actors as they go about the ordinary activities of their daily lives. In this view activities are not dictated or determined by social structures, rather social structures are enacted by skilled and reflexive performers. These are the tricks and stratagems of de Certeau (1984), or the instantaneous responses of Bourdieu (1990), as particularly in Giddens's (1984) structuration theory (q.v.), it is these kinds of performance that reproduce and amend the stock of social rules and resources on which activity depends.

Discussion

In management disciplines, practice perspectives are gaining increasing prominence in fields such as technology (Dougherty, 1992; Orlikowski, 2000), learning at work (Brown and Duguid, 2000), institutional change (Seo and Creed, 2002), marketing (Allen, 2002; Holt, 1995), accounting (Ahrens and Chapman, 2007) and, perhaps most developed in strategy, where a sub-discipline 'strategy-as-practice' continues to gain purchase (Jarzabkowski, 2004; Johnson and Huff, 1997; Molloy and Whittington, 2005; Samra-Fredericks, 2003; Whittington, 2006). The common theme across this work is an emphasis on understanding the various fields in terms of the activity that constitutes them in contrast to abstract representations of 'process' (Pettigrew, 1992).

In the field of consumer marketing, for example, Allen (2002) demonstrates these interrelationships with a study of student college choice. Here, the observation of behaviour is combined with attention to the wider cultures in which it is set. At a marketing event for a low-status college, free muffins and an informal, friendly approach are well received by working-class women students as these resonate with their cultural expectations. In contrast, for middle-class students with different cultural expectations these practices were treated with indifference, demonstrating the reciprocal relationship between culture (q.v.) and choice. The modest ambitions and limited training of the low-status college serve effectively to reproduce the meagre expectations of the working-class women that brought them there in the first place.

In the organization and technology field, Orlikowski's (2000) study of Lotus Notes implementation shows a similar but less smooth linking of activity, people and the wider context. The software was originally inspired by the collaborative ideology of North American universities in the 1970s. Yet, as the study shows, the ways in which people work with Lotus Notes tend to be very different from the original ideals of the designers, with many users ignoring sophisticated collaborative features. Activity in this case is shaped by a contemporary culture of technological scepticism.

In the strategic management field, Whittington (2003) explores the relationships between the work, workers and tools of organizing by building upon the distinction between practices, praxis and practitioners. Broadly in line with the definitions proposed by Reckwitz (2002) and Seo and Creed (2002), 'praxis' is used to refer to the work of organizing meetings, consulting, documentation, presenting, communicating and so on [*dialectic*]. Practices refer to tools, techniques and technologies of strategy making, whether conceptual tools, process tools such as project management or physical tools such as hardware. Practitioners are the individuals who carry out this activity as well as the carriers and skilful adapters of practices to local circumstance (Bourdieu, 1990; de Certeau, 1984). For a more in-depth discussion of the practice turn in strategy research see Chia (2004) and Whittington (2006).

Prospects

In the context of management studies, practice theory has offered the promise of a departure from studies of whole organizations to a focus on the role of human actors, materials and artefacts in strategic and organizational activity (Johnson et al., 2003). Yet, there are grounds for questioning the extent to which the apparent turn towards practice theory is complete in so far as it represents a significant departure from the existing ontological and epistemological positions of the various disciplines. Perhaps the clearest suggestion that this might be the case is the continued use of data collection methods associated with institutional and process research (q.v.). At least within the 'strategy-as-practice' field, the need for a different methodological approach to that of the classic process studies is widely recognized (Johnson et al., 2003; Samra-Fredericks, 2003; Whittington, 2003). Yet, there is a recurring concern among management scholars that while research approaches under the 'practice' umbrella attempt real-time observations, these time-based studies do not consider specific actions, or when they do, that these are only accounts of actions, mirroring the critique levelled by practice theorists at process theorists (Schendel, 1992; Van de Ven and Poole, 1990).

Without a concerted effort to engage in the kind of deep ethnography (q.v.) required to be able to claim to have observed individual actions adequately over a relevant time scale, there is a risk that the practice turn in management theory reflects, in Turner's (1994) terms, a short-cut on the quest for 'the really real'. Further, the question arises as to what extent the ostensive practice turn represents a genuine shift in analytical perspective or a substitution of vocabulary. There is plenty of scope for conceptual slippage here. For example, terms such as 'the practice approach', 'practice perspective', 'micro-activities', 'micro-level processes', 'micro-processual approach' may be used interchangeably. Of course, conceptual shifts within any discipline will be marked by periods of discursive churn and the existence of a standardized vocabulary may be a poor indicator of the intellectual health of a field. Nevertheless there is a risk that existing commitments to particular kinds of methodology within management disciplines such as longitudinal surveys and case studies might limit the extent to which management studies is able to put practice into theory.

Eamonn Molloy

PRACTISE-CENTRED RESEARCH

Definition

The emergent body of work now referred to as *practice-based studies* (Gherardi, 2006) is the latest attempt in social sciences in general (Schatzki et al., 2001) and in management and organization studies more specifically to find ways of expressing the complexity of organizing by focusing on the micro-dynamics of action. The practice (q.v.) concept provides a new lens for engaging with the fluidity of organizing (Antonacopoulou, 2006). It embraces ambiguity, uncertainty and discontinuity as the realm of the unknown and the foundation of emerging/becoming/organizing (Clegg et al., 2005) [*antenarrative*]. Practice-based studies focus predominantly on the situated nature of action as this is enacted by actors and manifested in language, the physical environment and the interactions between actors [*structuration theory*]. This is consistent with the view of the dynamic nature of routines articulated by Feldman and Pentland (2003).

Both practice-based studies and re-conceptualizations of routines draw heavily from actor-network theory (q.v.) (Law, 1999) and concentrate on the 'power of association' (Latour, 1986) to account for the importance of connections between actants in the process of creating and recreating both agency and structure. Yet, we have still to identify ways of capturing multiple associations, and the forces that underpin the interconnections that drive these associations. This is consistent with wider calls in social sciences in general (Emirbayer, 1997) for a relational analysis of action as not the product of inter-actions, but action as emanating from trans-action, where the relations and the entities creating these actions are not isolated but are seen to co-evolve in ongoing negotiation as constitutive of each other and of the possibilities their interrelationships can productively create [*constructivism; individualism*].

It is this emphasis on connectivity and relationality that practise-centred research seeks to capture by focusing on the *dynamics* of phenomena. Connectivity draws attention to the relationships within and between agents, their actions and their governing structures. Connectivity therefore consists of both co-ordination (*interdependencies*) and collaboration (*interrelationships*). Beyond network theory (Granovetter, 1973), collaboration theory (Huxham and Vangen, 2005) and co-ordination theory (Crowston, 1997), however, our understanding of what governs the nature of connectivity between human and non-human artefacts is limited (*activity theory; autopoiesis; complexity theory*]. This perspective would also seek to extend systemic theories (Beer, 1972; Luhmann,

1984/1995) as the focus would need to shift from the connections themselves to the conditions that underpin these connections [*soft systems methodology*]. If we are to understand the dynamic nature of social phenomena, we need to make interconnections as the focus of our attention and the conditions that underpin the interrelationships between different forces or actants as the core of our inquiry.

Discussion

Understanding relationships and connections calls for a focus on *what* relationships are and who the key actors are. It also calls for an examination of *how* these relationships are formed, *why* they are formed, *where* they are formed and *when* they are formed. Figure 5 represents diagrammatically the integration of these questions in forming the compass of relational, process and practice research. All these questions reveal a number of potential *tensions*. These tensions in turn can provide valuable clues about the conditions that underpin the connections that underpin dynamic phenomena.

In management research, tensions have been a topic of significant debate (Huxham and Beech, 2003; Quinn, 1988). Consistent with Glaser and Strauss's original (1967) notion of negotiating order [*inductive analysis*], tensions typically represent inconsistencies between often conflicting interests and priorities. This view has been central to the perspective that has informed much critical theory (q.v.) (Alvesson and Willmott, 1992), where hegemony and dependency conditions have tended to colour tensions as routed in the struggle for power and control.

More broadly, however, tensions have also sought to capture inconsistencies between 'espoused theory' and 'theory in use' [*action science*] (Argyris and Schön, 1978b), 'rhetoric' (q.v.) and 'reality' (Legge, 1995), 'exploration' and 'exploitation' (March, 1991). Tensions generally describe internal conflict in balancing competing priorities and generally paradoxes that cannot be resolved (Antonacopoulou, 2004).

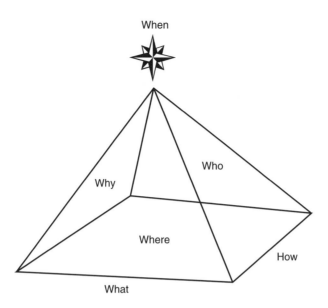

Figure 5 *The compass of relational research*

In general, tensions tend to be presented as problematic mostly because a dialectic logic governs the way tensions are represented. Yet, if one adopts a 'trialectic logic', contradictions and conflict give way to multiple possibilities as different sources of attraction are explored (Horn, 1983) [*dialectic*]. Adopting this logic of tension can also be seen as reflecting *flexibility* and *elasticity* to bend in different directions like an elastic band would do.

Therefore, tensions also provide us with clues about the inherent *dynamics* as forces transact and as their transactions create strain, stress and deformation of the original shape. Similar to a mechanical spring, tensions reflect an inbuilt *energy* that shapes the direction taken through the balancing acts performed. Equally, tensions also provide us with clues about the inbuilt flexibility and elasticity that balancing acts also reflect. Tensions lead to *ex-tensions* through ongoing transformations. Therefore, elasticity can take different forms both in linear and non-linear interactions between tensions and their resulting deformation.

Practise-centred research has been applied as a new approach developed in studying the dynamic nature of practices within organizations. The focus is not only on actions, activities, modes of knowing or indeed the language and symbols (Turner, 1994) reflective of practice as a structure underpinning the wider social context (Lave and Wenger, 1990/1991). Instead, the focus is on how all these dimensions of practice create tensions at a number of levels – *intra-practice, inter-practice, inter-temporally* – thus, reflecting the dynamics of practice.

Within a practice tensions would reveal the range of internal contradictions between intentions and actions and highlight the difficulties of balancing competing priorities in the internal and external goods that constitute a practice (McIntyre, 1985). Therefore, tensions, on the one hand, may reflect instances when a practice seeks to address many equally viable intentions at the same time, potentially resulting in confusion and inertia. This would be the case when the internal goods of a practice may be driving one set of intentions and the external goods may be driving another set of intentions. On the other hand, tensions may create ex-tensions when a practice seeks to expand the remit of activities it entails to embrace new actions that can lead to better performance, efficiency and effectiveness. This would be the case when external goods may provide the boundaries and infrastructure for action but internal goods may provide the energy to pursue new ends in the search for excellence.

Through this lens of tensions, practice can be conceptualized as a flow of connections between multiple dimensions that define the workings of a social group in relation to wider contextual forces that shape interpretations and reconstructions of reality. This new ontological stance on practice also calls for a consistent epistemological position. This would call for studying practice in *practise* (i.e. the ongoing reconfiguration of practice – (Antonacopoulou, 2004, 2006)).

Practice therefore, exists because it is in *practise*,[1] not simply performed, but formed, performed and continuously transformed through the deformations created by the ongoing tensions and ex-tensions. Practise reveals the process of a practice as this unfolds in time and space. This phenomenon of elasticity and plasticity of practices is embedded in practising attempts, which reveal different aspects that configure and reconfigure a practice. *Practise* and *practising*, therefore, focus on the dynamic and emergent nature of practice by drawing attention to *repetition, rehearsal and learning as* central to *practising* attempts.

Examples of practising are to be found when we focus on the way different aspects of practice interconnect within a practice as they are rehearsed by practitioners in action and interaction. Practising also takes place

when a practice interacts with other practices in a nested process that interlocks practices in a viable system of organizing. It is in different forms of practising where we can begin to locate one of the most powerful consequences of practice, namely the emerging *promise* they hold to make a difference to organizational functioning. Table 5 presents the application of a practise-centred approach in revealing different aspects of practice.

Prospects

Practise-centred research invites us to rethink our roles as researcher practitioners but also the tools we employ and the purpose which our research seeks to serve. This calls for methodological tools that can afford to engage with the fluid and relational nature of phenomena *in practise*. Some of the existing methodological tools we employ, such as interviews (q.v.), questionnaires, attitudinal surveys and so on, remain helpful, yet they predominantly account for snapshots of a process. Clearly some processes lend themselves more than others to ethnographic (q.v.) and longitudinal approaches. Increasingly, the use of autobiographical diaries (q.v.) [*oral history*] (Antonacopoulou, 2006) and videos (q.v.) (Binders et al., 2006) provide new innovative approaches for capturing the unfolding nature of phenomena. The reliability of findings in autobiographical accounts through diaries remains a big challenge.

However, acknowledging the power of capturing accounts and reflections in the practitioners' language may help overcome issues of translation, which might address the problems of accurate interpretations of finer meanings, particularly in the context of complex social interactions. Moreover, practitioners' accounts of their practice could enable us

---

[1]A trivial but important distinction between practice and practise is made here drawing on the *Oxford Dictionary* (2001) which emphasizes that this as an important distinction between the verb (practise) and the noun (practice). Beyond verb and noun, practise also reflects the process of practice as this constantly unfolds over time and space. It should be noted that the American spelling does not make this distinction and the dictionary cautioned about the confusion this often creates.

Table 5   *The 12 Ps of reconfiguring practice*

Who	*Practitioners* and their *Phronesis*
What	*Procedures*, rules, routines, resources, actions
How	*Principles*, values and assumptions
Why	*Purpose*, intentions (competing priorities, internal conflict, telos)
Where	*Place*, context, cultural and social conditions
When	*Past, Present, Pace*, time boundaries, history and future projections, rhythm
What	*Patterns* of connecting different aspects of a practice as this is performed
How	*Practice* and practising attempts reveal the internal and external goods at play during different performances of practice, creating new images of practice
Why	*Promise* of a practice emerges, intended and unintended consequences and outcomes of practice

to enhance the relevance and impact of management research on management practice by engaging practitioners in the *co-creation of knowledge* which can usefully enrich the boundaries of *re-search* as a practice.

Elena P. Antonacopoulou

PRAGMATISM

Definition

Pragmatism emerged from mid-nineteenth-century American philosophy. The classical proponents of pragmatism were Charles Sanders Peirce (1839–1914), William James (1842–1910), John Dewey (1859–1952), and George Herbert Mead (1863–1931), and it is Dewey, in his article, 'The development of American pragmatism', who gives one of the most lucid and thorough accounts of its historical founding as well to some of its core principles (Dewey, 1925/1984). In pragmatism there are no a priori propositions or categories and no universal cognitive (q.v.) structures or mental models that shape knowledge. Any meaning derives from lived experience in which humans are at work with their environments on a continuous basis. The eschewal of structures means typical dualisms of the kind psychological–physical, fact–value, culture–nature, and theory–action are dissolved. Rather than understand theory and action as two different activities and phenomena, pragmatism regards theories as tools or instruments in the human endeavour to cope with situations and events in life and to construct meaning by applying concepts in an experimental way [*activity theory*]. Any action (which includes mental action like thinking) is to be assessed with relation to its consequences. Pragmatism emphasizes a fallibilistic epistemology in which experience develops through action and thinking in the process of inquiry, critical thinking or reflection (synonymous terms) and a realist (q.v.) ontology stressing the transactional relationship between subject and world [*constructivism*].

Discussion

Currently, the insights from classical pragmatism are being rearticulated and reinterpreted by the neo-pragmatists (Putnam, 1999; Rorty, 1982). Hilary Putnam argues that pragmatism provides an alternative to a positivistic (q.v.) and anti-positivistic meta-theoretical outlook. Within the field of organization and management studies this is picked up by Zald (1993) and later underlined by Wicks and Freeman (1998) as well as Calori (2000, 2002), all of whom understand pragmatism as potentially offering management and organization studies a way out of the positivism/anti-positivism impasse in which organizational reality or 'essence' on the one hand vies against a pluralism of interpretations of organizing on the other. Through a pragmatically based critique of the epistemology incorporated in these two opposing paradigms, Wicks and Freeman point to the need to establish room for ethics (q.v.) in organization and management studies, and as such increase the relevance of organization and management research [*mode 2*]. Calori makes a related point in his application of the epistemology of pragmatism, in which the distinctions between practitioners' knowledge and researchers' knowledge is seen as complementary and necessary in constructing theories within organization and management studies. Calori bases his pragmatic research strategy on grounded theory (q.v.) from Glaser and Strauss (1967) and Strauss and Corbin (1990/1998), itself anchored in a pragmatic epistemology.

Apart from this general ontological and methodological approach to organization and management studies, one can also trace an interest in pragmatism within organizational learning research. Chris Argyris and Donald Schön make explicit references to a Deweyan pragmatism in their early work (Argyris and Schön, 1974/1978a) on action theory and action science (q.v.). They understand learning as a process of inquiry triggered by surprise and mismatch between expected and actual outcome in organizational actions. Argyris and Schön, however, give primacy to individuals and their mental models as governing their actions, and thereby do not draw the full consequence of the pragmatist understanding of the non-dualist understanding of theory and action.

A perspective that has gained momentum during the last fifteen years within organization and management studies is an increasing interest in the concept of practice (q.v.), and proponents of the practice turn in organization and management studies often refer to pragmatism as being one of their sources of inspiration (Nicolini et al., 2003; Schatzki et al., 2001). Organizational learning has been highly influenced by the practice turn that, in opposition to an individual and cognitive foundation, places its focus on interaction and organizing processes within the sociocultural settings of a given organization. The

practice-based approach to organizational learning focuses upon data in the form of language, acts and artifacts, and uses primary qualitative methods such as interviewing and observation as well as documents.

Another action theoretical approach within organization and management studies comes in the work of Anselm Strauss (1993) and his colleagues, outlined in a comprehensive paper by Adele Clarke, *Social Worlds/ Arenas Theory as Organizational Theory* (Clarke, 1991). Strauss and Clarke's positions draw explicitly on Dewey, especially what is sometimes called Dewey's social-psychological account (Dewey, 1922/1988), and on George Herbert Mead. They see themselves as part of the Chicago School of sociology which grew out of the traditional pragmatists work [*field research*]. Strauss focuses upon actions and interactions and how they shape work. Here he coins the term 'social worlds' to understand the processes of organizing in which commitment to action is the central tenet. The combination of Strauss's research on work and organizing and Dewey's theory on learning has been picked up by Bente Elkjaer in her work on organizational learning in which she develops a position inspired by Dewey's understanding of emotion as the trigger of learning and Strauss's understanding of commitment to action as the organizing principle (Elkjaer, 2004).

Prospects

One of the most significant disadvantages in the use of pragmatism within organization and management studies is the lack of a seminal paper or book where the role of pragmatism is elucidated and discussed, as for example it has been the case in the general field of social studies by way of a Special Issue on Pragmatism in the *European Journal of Social Theory* (2004, 7(3)). Pragmatism is often mentioned together with phenomenology (q.v.), hermeneutics (q.v.), critical theory (q.v.), and ethnomethodology (q.v.) as the foundation for the practice-based understanding of organizational and management studies, but there is still a need for an empirical as well a theoretical major contribution within organization and management studies pointing out what pragmatism has to offer to this field.

Ulrik Brandi, Bente Elkjaer

PROCESS PHILOSOPHY

Definition

It has become fashionable in the field of management studies to emphasize the changing and developmental nature of managing. Rather than focusing on 'management' as a clear and firmly fixed economic entity, there has been a growing interest in research that imaginatively explicates continuous *processes of change*, expresses *vitality*, and is realized in creative *acts of organizing*.

Process philosophy, or process thought, is a distinctive sector of philosophical tradition. Drawing on the pre-Socratic cosmology of Heraclitus, whose basic principle was that 'everything flows', the process approach puts processes (becoming) before distinct things or substances (being) [*method; postmodernism*]. For process thinkers, the concrete reality of 'things' is actually characterized by processes of change, movement and transformation. So that *what is* real is change (process) itself. This kind of ontology is logically opposed to the static system of Parmenides, which held the nature of existence to be permanent, unchanging, '*here, now, immediate*, and *discrete*' (Whitehead, 1933: 180, original emphasis). In recent times, the process-inspired worldview has become most closely identified with the British mathematical physicist turned philosopher Alfred North Whitehead and the French radical phenomenologist Henri Bergson. Other intellectual associates include James, Leibniz, and the twentieth-century philosophers Hartshorne and Deleuze.

Discussion

The clearest expression of Whitehead's process philosophy can be found in his assertion that the 'passage of nature' (Whitehead, 1920: 54) or, in other words, its 'creative advance' (Whitehead, 1929b/1978: 314), is a fundamental characteristic of experience. In this continuous advance, or universal becoming, every occasion of actual experience is the outcome of its predecessors. Actual occasions of experience or 'actual entities' have a certain duration during which they arise, reach satisfaction and perish. Nonetheless, they do not simply disappear without trace but always leave behind consequences that have the potential for entering into other passing moments of experience. So, at each step sense making (q.v.) is no longer of things simply as they appear *to be* at any given moment: they are also what they were, even a fraction of a second ago, and what they can become.

Following Whitehead, the experience of the immediate world around us does not obtain in the simple facets of things – for example, managers, and leaders, or followers and even organizations. This simple location, though handy, definite and manageable, is an error of mistaking abstract constructions for substantial processes – *the fallacy of misplaced concreteness*. This abstraction from an actual occasion of experience only arrives at traditional concepts of a 'here' and a 'now', as durationless instants without passage. But each actual occasion of experience is alive; it 'arises as the bringing together into one real context of diverse perceptions, diverse feelings, diverse purposes, and other diverse activities' (Whitehead, 1927: 9). It includes the perception and conceptualization of a situation whose actuality only exists at that moment: its permanence is constituted in its passage. The first two lines of a popular Christian hymn, 'Abide with me/Fast falls the eventide' (Whitehead, 1929b/1978: 209) characterize this nexus. Here, the perceptual permanence of 'abide' and 'me' in the first line is matched by the perpetual passage of 'fast' and 'falls' in the second line, to create a new immanent synthesis (passage *and* permanence; perishing *and* everlastingness).

Bergson's contribution to process thought, like Whitehead's, is ontological. Like Whitehead, he suggests life and nature are not distinct things or substances, but rather sensations, feelings and ideas seized from an original process. Both men assert evolutionary advance as a continuous creation – nature's *élan vital*. They recognize that life is *not* the thing, but the living of life *is* the thing. Living *is* changing, it is inventing, a creative advance into novelty. Unlike Whitehead, however, Bergson (1912: 44) argues that the corresponding process of isolating, immobilizing or securing actual forms from the limitless flow of 'virtual' possibilities is an 'imitation', which, although useful for the apprehension of life, is 'a counterfeit of real movement' and so is a 'distortion' of the actual world.

In doing so, Bergson enumerates two opposing tendencies for apprehending reality. The first is the logic (epistemology) of the *intellect*, which apprehends the world as an already determined series of solids. It forces on us a static conception of the real, which, if taken too far, cannot/does not embrace the continuity of flow itself (ontology). The second is the process of *intuition*, whereby we plunge into the very life of something and identify ourselves with it by a kind of indwelling. Here reality is expressed as 'fluid concepts', quite different from the static abstractions of logic. On its own the intellect's 'spatial' abstraction of things is too deterministic. However, the flow of the actual world without a corresponding logic is too indiscernible, too 'inaudible'. Life is realized by infusing the intellect with intuition and not simply by reducing the intellect to intuition.

Bergson is primarily a philosopher of time, which, he considers, eludes our intellectual spatialization of things: 'In short, the qualities of matter are so many stable views that we take of its instability' (Bergson, 1983: 302). In other words, we conceive immobility to be as real as movement and then mistake one for the other – the fallacy of misplaced concreteness. Nonetheless, time is always going on, it never completes: it is something lived and not merely thought. This is not to deny that time cannot be thought. Clearly it can. Bergson's point is simply that our conception of time as

a series of positions, one then the other and so on, is a matter of abstractive thinking and *not* a property of concrete (living) time itself. Simply located positions are surface effects we employ to give substantiality to our experience, but under whose supposed 'naturalness' the fluxing nature of reality is neglected.

For us to grasp this principle, Bergson argues, we must reverse our mental habits to see that mobility is the only actual reality. We must detach ourselves from the 'already made' and attend to the 'being made' (Bergson, 1983: 237). The *modus vivendi* between the intellectual force of the already made and the instinctual force of the being made is a focus on *acts of organizing*, 'it is the very flux of the real that we should be trying to follow ... the flux of time is the reality itself, and the things which we study are the things which flow' (Bergson, 1983: 343–344).

Certainly, theorizing 'acts of organizing' is not new in management studies. Karl Weick (1969/1979, 1995) has been writing about acts of organizing as the means by which participants make sense of their social interactions for over thirty years, and Robert Cooper's philosophical and sociological explorations of dis/organization, have articulated a processual style of thinking since at least the mid-1970s (see, for example, Cooper, 1976) [*relativism*]. More recently, organizational theorists (Linstead, 2002a; Tsoukas and Chia, 2002), have begun to advocate a need for better appreciations of process philosophy.

It is interesting, therefore, to find how insights from two leading process thinkers such as Whitehead and Bergson resonate with these contemporary concerns. The latest developments in the field consist of contributions from scholars who believe process philosophy is congenial to understanding the dynamic nature of management practice. Drawing substantively, though not exclusively, on Whitehead and Bergson, process thought has been applied across such fields as organization theory and development, group behaviour, new product innovation, organizational knowledge, social organization and business cultures.

Prospects

Finally, of course, there remain many dilemmas, challenges and debates surrounding the uses of process thought in management studies. One 'hot topic' relates to the different views scholars hold about whether organizations consist of things *or* processes, or whether these are complementary ways of viewing entity *and* flux. A second topical issue of concern is the difference between process theorists purporting to explain organizational development and change by making expedient use of longitudinal case studies (q.v.) (see, for example, Langley, 1999; Ropo et al., 1997; Van de Ven and Poole, 1995) [*process research*] and those accepting the metaphysical centrality of a process-relational outlook (Chia, 1999; Wood, 2005), but as yet unable or unwilling to fix 'gangways' to practice or only now beginning to fabricate methodological 'railings' that respond to the perceived demand of organization and management studies (Tsoukas and Chia, 2002; Van de Ven and Poole, 2005; Wood and Ferlie, 2003). Then again, perhaps these different views are problems only if we retain a static vision of things? Thus, by my reading at any rate, spoke Zarathustra (Nietzsche, 1885/1969: 219):

> O my brothers, is everything not *now in flux*? Have not all railings and gangways fallen into the water and come to nothing? Who can still *cling to* 'good' and 'evil'?

Martin Wood

PROCESS RESEARCH

Definition

Process research involves an explicit and direct focus on processes as the object of empirical investigation. Put simply, its aim is to develop an understanding of how and why phenomena evolve over time (Langley, 1999; Van de Ven, 1992; Van de Ven and Poole, 2005). Process research is obviously of particular relevance for the study of topics such as organizational change, decision-making, learning, innovation, implementation – phenomena that, by definition, imply action, change and temporal flux or 'organizational becoming' (Tsoukas and Chia, 2002).

Discussion

In his classic work on organization theory, Mohr (1982) made a clear distinction between what he calls 'variance theory' and 'process theory'. While variance theories provide explanations for phenomena in terms of relationships among dependent and independent *variables* (e.g. more of X and more of Y produce more of Z), process theories provide explanations in terms of the pattern of *events* leading to an outcome over time (e.g. do A and then B to get C). Understanding patterns in events is thus central to developing process theory. This suggests a completely different, yet complementary, causal logic from that used in variance research, one based on narrative sequence and ordering (Pentland, 1999), rather than on correlation.

Figure 6 provides a visual illustration of the distinction between variance and process theories applied to the topic of strategic change. As can be seen, the variance approach tends to either ignore or freeze temporal flows into scaled variables (e.g. decision processes as more or less rational, or more or less political), while the process approach takes these flows as its principal object. Process researchers who are interested in examining these flows and in testing or developing process theories will thus collect data that consist largely of stories (q.v.) about what happened and who did what when: that is, events, activities and choices ordered over time.

Process research is also associated to a greater or lesser extent with a philosophical tradition and ontological perspective in which the world is viewed as composed first and foremost of fluid 'processes' rather than of immutable 'things' (Chia, 2002; Rescher, 1996b; Van de Ven and Poole, 2005/1998; Whitehead, 1929b/1978) [*complexity theory; process philosophy*]. In relation to this, Chia

173

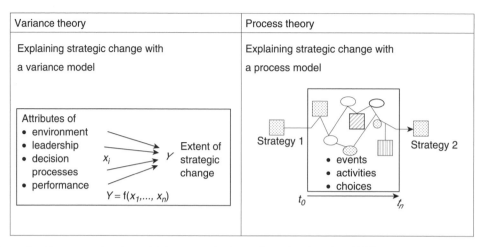

Figure 6 *Two approaches to explaining strategic change (based on Langley, 1999)*

and Langley (2004) distinguished between what they call 'strong-form' and 'weak-form' process thinking. They note that 'the "weak" view treats processes as important but ultimately reducible to the action of things, while the "strong" view deems actions and things to be instantiations of process-complexes' (Chia and Langley, 2004: 1466). The more radical strong view is attractive in the way it unmasks the socially constructed nature of habitual conceptions of organizations and other phenomena (e.g. structure, culture) as stable objects, focusing attention instead on the way they are continuously constituted, reproduced and adapted through everyday actions and interactions. Strong-form process thinking problematizes what is taken for granted in much of management research. Such a view also lies behind Weick's (1969/1979) recommendation to think in terms of gerunds – for example, to consider 'organizing' rather than 'organization', 'structuring' rather than 'structure'. Process philosophy thus provides inspiration for process research. However, in practice, most empirical studies in this tradition have tended towards the less radical end of the process thinking spectrum, at least partly for pragmatic reasons associated with the need for

some form of clarity in the bounding of research objects and units of analysis (Van de Ven and Poole, 2005).

Indeed, once the decision has been made to adopt a process perspective to empirical research, the execution of the research, and more particularly the derivation of theory from process data, can constitute something of a challenge. As Langley (1999) notes, process data are messy. They are generally based on real-time observations, interviews (q.v.) and documentary traces of various kinds. They deal with variably time-embedded incidents, events and trends. Their units of observation and analysis are often multiple and ambiguous [*template analysis*]. Moreover, despite the focus on actions, choices and events, process data tend to be eclectic, drawing in less concrete phenomena, such as changing relationships, thoughts, feelings and interpretations.

Based on a review of exemplary process studies, Langley (1999) identified a set of seven generic strategies for making sense of process data that each have complementary strengths and weaknesses in terms of accuracy, parsimony and generality (Weick, 1969/1979) and that are likely to generate different forms of theory. These are labelled the narrative (q.v.), quantification, alternate templates, grounded theory (q.v.), visual (q.v.) mapping, temporal decomposition and synthetic strategies [*causal cognitive mapping; cognitive mapping; composite mapping*].

The 'narrative' and 'quantification' sensemaking (q.v.) strategies lie at opposite poles of a continuum. The narrative approach involves the reconstitution of events into an extended verbal account or 'thick description' and is associated with ethnography (q.v.) (Van Maanen, 1988) or organizational history (e.g. Chandler, 1964) [*historical analysis; oral history*]. It is high on accuracy to the extent that it reflects the detail and ambiguity of particular events, but theorizations derived from it may be lower on parsimony and generality. In contrast, in the quantification strategy, processes are decomposed into microincidents that are coded into a limited number of quantitative categories which can then be analyzed using statistical methods. This approach was extensively used in the Minnesota studies of innovation (Garud and Van de Ven, 1992; Van de Ven, 1992). It offers higher parsimony and generality, but at the expense of accuracy in reflecting the richness of particular events.

The other strategies identified by Langley (1999) lie somewhere between these two extremes. For example, the 'alternate templates' strategy involves the application of multiple a priori theoretical frames or lenses to the same process database. Allison's (1971) study of the Cuban missile crisis is a classic exemplar of this strategy. In the 'grounded theory' strategy, theory is derived by inductive bottom-up coding from the data rather than through top-down deduction based on a priori theory. Classic exemplars of process research using grounded theory in the organizational literature include Gioia et al. (1994) and Isabella (1990). The 'visual mapping' strategy involves the representation of processes using diagrams, tables and other kinds of visual (q.v.) displays [*drawings and images*]. This approach is illustrated in the work of Mintzberg et al. (1976) and Langley and Truax (1994).

Sensemaking of process data can also be stimulated by comparison. The 'temporal bracketing' strategy involves the generation of comparative units of analysis in the form of distinct time periods. Decomposition into successive adjacent periods may sometimes result in process models based on sequential progression (as for example in Isabella, 1990). However, this is not the only possible result. Decomposition may also be used to examine dynamic structuration (q.v.) effects – in particular, how actions of one period lead to changes in the context that will affect action in subsequent periods. Barley's (1986) study of structuring in two radiology departments following the acquisition of CT scanners is a classic exemplar of this approach that does not suppose deterministic progressions. In contrast to the temporal bracketing approach, the 'synthetic strategy' involves the comparison of processes as wholes across different cases. Because of its focus on whole processes and the attraction of relating processes to outcomes, such an approach many tend to lead to variance theoretic formulations of processes, as in the case of Eisenhardt's [1989b] study of decision-making. The seven strategies for theorizing from process data are not exhaustive of all possibilities nor are they mutually exclusive. However, they offer a series of complementary angles for deriving useful insights about process phenomena.

Prospects

In summary, process research focuses attention directly on change, flow and movement in and around organizations, what Pettigrew (1990) has called 'capturing reality in flight'. Beyond its intrinsic academic interest, the importance of process research and thinking for management practice is undeniable. The static nomothetic generalizations of traditional variance-based management research give hints about the systemic patterns surrounding organizational phenomena, but they do not provide the temporally embedded accounts that enable us to understand *how* such patterns come to be. Yet, in pragmatic terms, and especially for lower-performing organizations that want to move towards more favourable positions, this is perhaps the most pressing issue. Variance-based generalizations can even sometimes be misleading because they ignore the non-linear effects of action under complexity: actions to improve performance engender reactions that feed back into further actions, often with unexpected consequences that such models do not capture. A direct focus on the processes of change can contribute to generating more actionable knowledge.

Ann Langley

PROJECTIVE TECHNIQUES

Definition

In the narrowest sense projective techniques involve the presentation to respondents of frequently ambiguous stimulus material, for example pictures or drawings (q.v.). A well-known example is the Thematic Appreciation Test (TAT). The TAT (Morgan and Murray, 1935) was originally developed for use in clinical work in psychotherapy and psychoanalysis (q.v.). It comprises a number of cards (up to 31), the majority including photographs or drawings. Respondents are invited to construct a story (q.v.) or otherwise elicited by the image. Hansemark (1997), building on work from McClelland et al. (1953) and the TAT manual, neatly identifies both the rationale and benefits:

> The supporting theory, with its roots in psychoanalytic theory, argues that a person will project his own feelings, needs and motives in to the picture: the projective hypothesis. [It will] ... expose the underlying tendencies which the subject ... is not willing to admit, or cannot admit because he is not conscious of them. (Hansemark, 1997: 280)

Discussion

Hansemark (1997: 281) notes potential criticisms of the TAT in terms that it is time-consuming in administration and scoring, of low predictive validity and reliability (q.v.)

and, given the subjectivity and difficulty of interpreting the resulting stories, it requires an interpreter with clinical experience. McClelland and colleagues developed a modified and simplified version of TAT for research use which involved a reduced number of pictures and an objective coding model (McClelland et al., 1953; see also Atkinson and McClelland, 1948).

However, the range of techniques that can be considered as 'projective' can be extended. Consideration of the methodologies of 'projective drawing and metaphorical analogy fantasizing' (Nossiter and Biberman, 1990) expands the range to include visual images (q.v.) and metaphors generated by respondents. Moreover, Jacobs and Heracleous (2006: 207) extend the use of metaphor beyond a 'dominant semantic-cognitive dimension' to include 'spatial and embodied dimensions' [*aesthetics; postcards; space*]. Within this 'novel metaphorical approach', they describe a number of methods of constructing or creating images or objects that act as embodied metaphors. The physical, tactile and spatial elements of the construction and the physical, often group, activity of 'doing metaphor' add to the semantic-cognitive aspects of metaphor (Jacobs and Heracleous, 2006: 205).

Metaphor-based (q.v) inquiry has as 'a central premise' the process of projecting on to the subject or object the characteristics of an alternative subject or object to produce or expose new ways of thinking about the subject (Oswick et al., 2001). A similar point is made by Schön (1993), who characterizes 'generative' metaphor as providing novel perceptions, explanations and inventions. Conversely, Jacob and Heracleous (2006: 210) summarize critiques that, among other concerns, give emphasis to the potentially conservative impact of metaphor (through high-lighting similarity rather than difference).

Visual metaphors, along with photographs and projective techniques (limited by example to the TAT), have been identified as useful in situations where 'data are limited, the generation of rich ideas is proving difficult and where a means is needed to engage individuals in a discussion of issues that are viewed as contentious or problematic' (Thorpe and Cornelisson, 2003: 70).

The use of respondent generated drawings can be illustrated through examples of organization-based studies (Kearney and Hyle, 2004; Meyer, 1991; Nossiter and Biberman, 1990; Reddiford, 1996). The foci of the research included views of organizational culture, approaches to change, emotional responses to change and 'diffusion of information technology'. Meyer suggests the 'collection of visual data involves two stages:

- Encoding information to produce graphic representations of organizational life
- Decoding the graphic representations to produce visual data for analysis' (1991: 224).

A similar analysis of the stages of the process is captured in a description of 'change drawings' (Jacobs and Heracleous, 2006: 215).

Approaches to the use of metaphor 'as a vehicle for, rather than a target of, research' (Oswick and Montgomery, 1999: 201) can be illustrated by reference to two studies. In their study, Oswick and Montgomery invited respondents to compare an organization to an animal and to part of a car and to explain why the metaphor chosen was seen as appropriate. Erdem and Satir (2003) incorporated a range of metaphors, drawn from a dictionary of metaphor common in the Turkish language and from previous studies, into a questionnaire administered in three separate organizations.

The value of metaphor as a means of creating insight and consideration of the challenges to their use has been examined at a theoretical and practical level (e.g. Jensen, 2006; Morgan, 1986/1997; Oswick and Montgomery, 1999; Pesqueux, 1999; Tsoukas, 1991). Similarly, useful discussion of the construction, nature and analysis of metaphor can be found in, for example, Schmitt (2000), Tsoukas (1991, 2005), Jensen (2006) and Cornelisson (2005).

Drawing on their own work and a review of the literature of using visual approaches, Kearney and Hyle (2004: 376–380) identified a number of practical considerations for

researchers, building on their analysis and extending it to illustrate the use of metaphor as a vehicle for research:

- Participant-produced drawings and metaphor appear to create a path towards participant perceptions, attitudes, feelings and emotions, also noted by Reddiford (1996: 38), where participants captured emotions not previously recognized or acknowledged. Tsoukas (1991: 570) notes that metaphors 'more than literal assertions, do not simply describe an external reality; they also help constitute that reality and *prescribe* how it ought to be viewed and evaluated' (emphasis in the original).
- The cognitive process required to draw leads to a more succinct presentation of the key elements of participants' experience. Similarly, metaphors are noted for their 'vividness and compactness' (Ortony, 1975: 45).
- The personal experience (depicted in the drawings) could only be considered complete with additional interpretation of the drawing by the participant. Several studies supplemented the graphical data and respondent interpretation with data gathered through other means, such as questionnaires and interviews, both structured and unstructured. The use of visual representation supported the expression of incomplete or otherwise 'difficult to voice' thoughts and enabled them to be put into words (Bryans and Mavin, 2006). Jensen (2006: 6) notes an 'act of co-creation' between researcher and respondent to ensure 'similar language meaning is derived after the metaphoric statement is made'.
- The extent to which drawing activity encourages or discourages participation is unpredictable and dependent on individual and situational factors.
- The amount of structure imposed on the drawing process or the scope allowed in the generation of metaphor is a key consideration in the design of the research approach. Little structure allows participants

to identify key components of the research topic, free from preconceived biases of the researcher. Alternatively, a greater degree of structure is helpful where inter-organizational comparison was sought. The nature of the metaphor suggested by researchers can itself focus respondent attention on particular characteristics of the phenomenon under study. Oswick and Montgomery (1999: 519) note that animal metaphors tended to focus attention on aspects of change (for example, species adaptation) while the car metaphor was associated with issues of strategy (for example, issues of movement, direction and vision).

Although visual approaches of the kind described are acknowledged to be non-traditional (Kearney and Hyle, 2004: 362), there is a clear potential for these techniques to add to the range available to the qualitative researcher.

Brian Simpson

PSYCHOANALYTIC APPROACHES

Definition

The application of psychoanalytic ideas to the study of management and organizations is linked to what is commonly referred to as the 'Tavistock Tradition' which, in its early days, drew upon open systems thinking and Kleinian psychoanalysis. In contrast to behavioural, technicist or economic approaches, psychoanalytic thinking has tended to remain at the periphery of management education and has had relatively little impact on mainstream management and organization science [inductive analysis]. In some part the fault lies with the originators of the tradition: by placing itself largely outside the academy, particularly during the last three decades, this tradition has largely immunized itself from developments in organizational, management

and social theory. On the other hand, this location has enabled it to sustain a commitment to learning from here-and-now experience and a valuation of 'personal knowledge' which constitutes a profound challenge to the instrumental models of knowledge which dominate business schools and social sciences (or anywhere where there is a deep cultural suspicion and distrust of the idea that rational processes alone are not enough to understand management) [positivism and post-positivism].

In general terms, a psychoanalytic approach takes seriously the idea that the life of organizations and work groups has irrational, passionate and, above all, unconscious dimensions which function in unpredictable ways alongside or contrary to the task. It also recognizes that the role of manager invites intense and sometimes disturbing projections and is an emotionally charged function. Finally, psychoanalytic approaches to management work at the level of understanding unconscious processes in groups and systems – among role-holders – rather than in terms of the personal histories of individuals. The focus is on the internal life of organizations and unconscious currents in an organization's psyche.

Discussion

While Freud (1921) never wrote about the management of organizational work, a great many of his insights into the emotional life of groups and leaders form the basis of this approach. Among these come the following ideas: (1) life in groups, and by extension organizations, is conflict-driven with an irreconcilable tension between the narcissism of the individual and the pull towards group membership; (2) there is constant regressive pull in the life of groups back to primitive, childish and instinctual behaviours; (3) group leaders (management) invite and attract oedipal projections and identifications; (4) the group is bound together by libidinal ties and networks of identification – follower to follower and followers to leader. In sum, a certain amount of anxiety is inherent in group life.

The work of Melanie Klein (1948, 1952), in elaborating depressive and psychotic anxiety in the lives of individuals, was a crucial bridge to what later became known as the Tavistock Tradition – a set of theories and techniques to understand group and organizational life which emerged in the UK in the decades following the Second World War. Key psychoanalytic concepts such as the unconscious, repression, resistance, transference, splitting and projection were used to understand ways in which work groups as a whole operate in self-defeating, neurotic or psychotic ways. Jaques (1953) was the first to apply Klein's work on anxiety to the study of organizations, Menzies Lyth (1959) studied the defensive practices and culture in the nursing service and Bion's (1961) work on basic assumption mentalities explored the ways in which powerful unconscious drives interfere with the functioning of work-groups taking them 'off-task'. A body of writing has since developed which focuses on the ways organizations, especially in times of acute crisis and change, deal with the anxieties evoked by the work itself and anxieties evoked by wider organizational crises and threats to survival (e.g. Obholzer and Roberts, 1994) [action science].

Alongside theory, there is a specific approach to technique – psychoanalytic consultancy – the purpose of which is to identify and transform the emotional currents which provoke symptoms and dysfunction in group life [action learning; action research; interactive phenomenological analysis]. Consultancy can be at the level of one-to-one role analysis (as developed by Harold Bridger), but is more usual with larger staff groups. Particular attention is paid to the unspoken assumptions and phantasies which seem to be operant in group life and to the here-and-now lived experience of the consultant as she is used (or 'mobilized') in the emotional processes of the group. In this respect, there is some overlap with popular notions of 'emotional (q.v.) intelligence' which operate at the periphery of management education. More specifically, it is the pre-conscious and unconscious realities of organizational life, the 'unthought knowns' and resistances to the primary task which are brought to the surface.

Prospects

This tradition is now over fifty years old and has had some difficulty in renewing itself in terms of theory and practice. It has spawned a network of sister institutes and trainings[1] all broadly wedded to Kleinian and post-Kleinian thinking and variations on open systems theory. Those in general unsympathetic to psychoanalysis accuse it of political conservatism, seeing it as an institutionalized form of modern power/knowledge which seeks to manipulate the internal worlds of work-groups. On the other hand, those more sympathetic to the Tavistock Tradition point to its theoretical conservatism and its dogmatic adherence to a Kleinian model of the psyche, a model which has proved highly resistant to registering the real political and environmental contexts in which management and organizations operate. In addition, its non-psychoanalytic approach in systems theory now appears crudely functionalist.

There are, however, promising recent developments within the tradition and beyond. These include: a renewed interest in the lateral and sibling dimensions of individual and organizational life; the impact of relational psychoanalytic thinking; politically reflexive (q.v.) organizational consultation; and the use of Social Dreaming as a tool of organizational learning.

Anne-Marie Cummins

---

[1]AK Rice Institute in the USA, OFEK in Israel, The Grubb Institute in London, ISLA in South Africa, CESMA in Italy.

R

READING AS INQUIRY

Definition

As researchers, most of us are inevitably concerned with how our work is read. Provided research is cloaked in the rhetoric of 'objectivity,' 'truth' and 'causal explanation', the presumed reader – the prototypical reader of the manuscript that an author has in mind as she writes – is often assumed to be a passive recipient of ideas. This view of reading assumes that the text carries a message devised by the author that is simply paraphrased in the reading of it (Monin et al., 2003). Thus, many foundational management texts give the appearance of straightforward objectivity, whereby the writer *instructs* the reader.

During the latter half of the 1960s, literary critics began to study reading not only as a process of consumption and use, but also as reception: the process by which texts receive their meaning (Eskola, 1990). In Europe the new school of research became most commonly known as reception aesthetics (q.v.) (e.g. Iser, 1978) and in the USA it was called reader-response criticism (e.g. Fish, 1990). In contrast to New Criticism, which emphasized that only that which is within a text is part of the meaning of a text, these perspectives affirm a role for the reader as *writer* of her own text. To 'read' is to discern or construct meanings. Through the act of interpretation, reading itself becomes a method of inquiry [*deconstruction*].

Discussion

Scholars of reader-response criticism and reception aesthetics do not represent a unified tradition, but are a collection of critics who share an agenda of bringing to centre stage the process of reading rather than a focus on the written word alone. The role of the reader is cast as a creative agent actively *participating* in her own meaning-making as she responds to the text, rather than a passive recipient of what an author writes. This holds implications for the sense in which a text exists, to what extent reader interpretation is a public act conditioned by the cultural circumstances of the reader as opposed to a private act governed by a response to relatively independent codes of a text, and the nature of knowledge [*hermeneutics*].

For example, in Iser's (1978) phenomenological (q.v.) approach to reading, the text functions as a set of instructions for its own processing. Texts are, however, never complete: there are always missing details, gaps that could be filled in. These areas of indeterminacy are open to being filled in a variety of ways. The 'reality' of the text lies between the reader and the text in the creation of a 'virtual text' (Iser, 1978); it is the result of the dialectic (q.v.) between the author's text and the subjectivity of the reader. Each reading of the text may result in a new meaning: a reader who engages with the text brings to it her past experience, her present context, and projections for the future. Reading is thus an event in time (Rosenblatt, 1978).

In contrast, Fish (1990) argues that there are no formal structures in a text that are independent of its reader; meaning does not inhere in the text, but is fully located within the reading (interpretative) community. The interpretative community is a reading public that shares a strategy or approach to interpretation. While individual readers bring their idiosyncratic interpretations based on personal experience to bear on a text, we inherit shared systems of intelligibility (Fish, 1990) [*semiotics; structuration theory*]. These symbolic systems and cultural rules are socially constructed (q.v.) rather than purely subjective, individual interpretations. From this perspective, the very properties of the text are constituted by the strategies the reader brings to bear on the text. The possible meanings constructed through a reading of a text have a communal basis, allowing for shared responses or similar readings within that community.

Versions of reader-response criticism/ reception aesthetics have been adopted in organization studies as a way to understand authorial intent and the construction of meaning by readers, to inspire different readings, and to recover the polysemic and polyvocal qualities inherent in texts [*dialogic*]. Examples from management studies include Monin et al's (2003) horizontal (i.e. rhetorical) and vertical (i.e. philosophical) readings of excerpts of Frederick Taylor's *The Principles of Scientific Management* (1912), and Monin and Monin's (2005) re-reading of Blanchard and Johnson's *The One Minute Manager* as a fairytale – a narrative (q.v.) genre that predisposes the reader to certain reading strategies. In the field of international management, I offer three readings of a comic strip that depicts the early internationalization of a firm, drawing on Deetz's (1996) characterizations of research programmes to delineate distinct 'interpretative communities' that inform each reading (McGaughey, 2006). Sherry and Schouten (2002) examine the reading and writing of poetry in marketing, while Scott (1994) advocates reader-response theory to explore the link between advertising text and consumer responses, and Hirschman (1999) uses it to examine consumer-generated understandings of a television programme across two interpretative communities.

Prospects

While many of us will read a text primarily using the reading strategies of the interpretative community (or communities) to which we belong, if, as researchers, we can begin to develop awareness of our own and sensitivity towards other reading strategies or effects [*reflexivity*], this brings with it the ability to 'toggle' between readings. One potential of such toggling is the fostering of generative discourses – edifying ways of reading that both challenge existing traditions of taken-for-granted conventions, prompt us to ask new questions and offer new ways of describing and explaining the world (Gergen, 1999: 116–117) and to better create spaces for alternative readings, their critique and their contribution to conversations. This also draws attention to creating texts through writing that fosters multiple interpretations [*postcards; representations*].

Sara L. McGaughey

REALISM

Definition

Modern, scientific realism has its roots in the early twentieth century idealism–realism debate, in which the realists Moore (1903) and Russell (1929) staunchly defended the position that the world exists independently of its being perceived. It is from this classical realism that modern realists get the view that there really is something 'out there' for science to study and theorize about. Classical realism thus contrasts with both idealism and postmodernist relativism, which hold that all reality is 'in here' (the mind) and, therefore, all reality is relative to the mind that knows it [*positivism and post-positivism; postmodernism; relativism*].

Discussion

Among philosophers of science today, *scientific realism* is probably the most commonly held philosophical position (e.g. Bhaskar, 1979b; Boyd, 1984; Harré, 1986; Leplin, 1984; Levin, 1984; MacKinnon, 1979; Manicas, 1987; McMullin, 1984; Niiniluoto, 1999; Putnam, 1990; Searle, 1995; Siegel, 1983, 1987; Suppe, 1977). Also, scholars in management, marketing, and economics are turning towards realist positions (e.g. Azevedo, 2002; Easton, 2002; Fleetwood, 1999; Hunt, 2003, 2005; Kwan and Tsang, 2001; Lawson, 1996; McKelvey, 1999, 2002; Meckler and Baile, 2003a, 2003b; Tsoukas, 1989). Modern, scientific realism encompasses *fallibilistic* realism, *critical* realism (q.v.), and *inductive* realism. These three positions hold, in turn, that first, though the job of science is to develop genuine knowledge or *truth* about the world, such knowledge will never be known with certainty. The concept of 'know with certainty' belongs in theology, not science. For scientific realism, there is no 'God's eye view' nor does science need one to fulfil its goal of being a truth-seeking enterprise. As Siegel (1983: 82) puts it, 'To claim that a scientific proposition is true is not to claim that it is certain; rather, it is to claim that the world is as the proposition says it is'. Second, because of the fallibility of our perceptual (measurement) processes, science must critically evaluate and test its knowledge claims to determine their truth content. 'Direct' or 'naïve' realism, which holds that our perceptual processes always result in veridical representations of external objects, is rejected. Third, the long-term success of a scientific theory gives us reason to believe that something like the entities and structures, observable or non-observable, tangible or intangible, posited by the theory actually exist. Thus, the (often implicit) Humean scepticism underlying logical positivism, logical empiricism, and Popperian falsificationism is rejected [*method*]. Contrary to logical positivism and logical empiricism, concepts that are *unobservable* are appropriate in theories that purport to explain phenomena that are *observable*. Contrary to Popper, the positive results of empirical tests – not just falsifications – provide evidence as to the truth content of the theories tested.

In current social science, the 'critical' in *critical realism* is used in two very different ways. First, as discussed, scientific realism is critical in that science must both critically (1) evaluate and test its knowledge claims to determine their truth content and (2) evaluate and re-evaluate the methodologies and epistemologies that inform extant scientific practice. Most scientists and realist philosophers of science accept this kind of *critical* realism. However, the 'critical' in critical realism is also often used in the manner of Sayer (1992: 6), who states: 'Social science must be critical of its object'. For Sayer's and others' versions of critical realism, therefore, it is not enough that one be critical of science's knowledge claims, methodologies, and epistemologies. Researchers must also be critical of society and become social activists because social scientists 'should develop a critical awareness in people and, indeed, assist in their emancipation' (1992: 42). Therefore, those researchers who are interested in explaining, predicting, and understanding phenomena, but who do *not* want to assume the role of the social activist involved in transforming society [*action science*], should be cautious about self-describing their research as 'critical realist' in the Sayer sense.

Although scientific realism views science as a truth-seeking enterprise, it conceptualizes *truth* as not an entity in the world to be studied, but as an *attribute* of beliefs and linguistic expressions, such as those denoted by the labels 'theories', 'laws', 'propositions', and 'hypotheses'. Recall that the inductive realism tenet maintains that the long-run success of a theory gives reason to believe that something like the entities and structure postulated by the theory actually exists. The 'something like', then, equates with a theory or proposition being 'approximately true' or 'having truth content'. By 'long-run success' we mean that a theory that has consistently, through time, made correct predictions, provided systematic, defensible explanations, and supported successful interventions in the real world.

Consider the concept 'organizational commitment' (hereafter, OC). Is OC real? Does it refer to something in the real world or does it not? Is the proposition true that 'firms whose employees have high OC tend to be more profitable than those whose employees do not?' For scientific realism, OC is likely real and the OC proposition is likely true if, through time, there is a high ratio of successes to failures. That is, truth (falsity) is inferred from a high (low) frequency of successful (unsuccessful) predictions, explanations, and interventions. However, scientific realism does not imply that one can make claims as to the *probability* that the OC proposition is true. Evaluations of theories and their concepts involve a 'weighing' of the evidence (Bunge, 1967). However, scientific realism does not imply that 'a high proportion of successes, relative to failures' means 'true with probability "p"'. Nor does it imply that 'a high proportion of failures, relative to successes' means 'false with probability "p"'. Indeed, most scientific realists are highly sceptical of efforts that attempt to apply the logic of probability to the weighing of evidence involved in the empirical testing of theories.

Can we say that we *objectively* know that the OC proposition is likely true? Anti-realists have put forth five arguments that are claimed to defeat the objectivity of science. First, the *linguistic relativism* argument claims that objectivity is impossible because the language of a culture determines the reality that members of the culture will see. Second, the *incommensurability* argument claims that objectivity is impossible because the paradigms that researchers hold are non-comparable. Third, the *Humean scepticism* argument claims that objectivity is impossible because theories are underdetermined by facts (i.e. no conceivable number of facts conclusively proves a theory's truth). Fourth, the *psychology of perception* argument claims that objectivity is impossible because researchers see what their theories tell them is there (which makes theory-neutral observations impossible). Fifth, the *epistemically significant observations* argument is: (a) though 'percepts' or 'raw' observations are objective, (b) these percepts must be informed by theories in order for them to play their designated role in theory testing, (c) which makes all epistemically significant observations theory-laden, (d) which defeats objectivity. In the scientific realism literature, all five of the arguments against the possibility of objective science have been discredited. Interested readers should see Hunt (2003) for a review of the refutations.

Prospects

The prospects for realist perspectives in management and organization studies are inextricably bound with the presence of trust. Trust is essential because scientific knowledge is a shared form of knowledge; it is shared with its clients. The clients of academic management researchers include not just other academics, but also practising managers, students, government officials, and the public in general [*action research; mode 2*]. In essence, all researchers who share their research with others state implicitly: 'trust me'. One consequence of the realist recognition of the importance of trust in science concerns those whose research projects are claimed to be guided by philosophies maintaining that *no* research 'touches base' with a reality external to the researcher's own linguistically encapsulated theory, or paradigm, or research tradition. Such researchers are stating: 'don't trust me'. In contrast, research guided by realist philosophy, with its emphasis on truth and objectivity as research objectives and regulative ideals, is a worthy candidate for our trust. It 'touches base' – and that's a good start.

Shelby D. Hunt

REFLEXIVITY

Definition

Reflexivity entails the researcher being aware of his effect on the process and outcomes of research based on the premise that 'knowledge cannot be separated from the knower' (Steedman, 1991) and that, 'In the social sciences, there is only interpretation. Nothing speaks for itself' (Denzin, 1994). In carrying out qualitative research, it is impossible to remain 'outside' our subject matter; our presence, in whatever form, will have some kind of effect. Reflexive research takes account of this researcher involvement.

Discussion

The concept and practice of reflexivity have been defined in many ways. Alvesson and Sköldberg (2000) describe it as the 'interpretation of interpretation' – another layer of analysis after data have been interpreted. For Woolgar (1988), reflexivity is 'the ethnographer [q.v.] of the text' (p. 14). Here we distinguish between 'introspective' reflexivity (Finlay, 2002) 'methodological' reflexivity and epistemological reflexivity (Johnson and Duberley, 2003).

Introspective reflexivity

This approach to reflexivity involves a high degree of self-consciousness on the part of the researcher, especially in terms of how his identity affects the design and process of his work. Introspective reflexivity has been likened to reflection whereby we simply 'think about what we are doing' (Woolgar, 1988: 22) For some, this is more likely to be reflection-in-action as per Schön's (1983) model of the skilled practitioner [action learning; action research] who incorporates reflection into their everyday activities rather than deliberately and consciously reflecting as part of a post hoc rationalization of events.

Steier (1995: 75–76) characterizes the personal engagement of the researcher in three ways:

- Research as both invention and intervention: As researchers we can view ourselves in two ways: either as inventors of order in our interpretation of the social processes we are observing or as co-constructors of that situation by virtue of our presence.
- Emotioning in research: Our own engagement with what happens in the group is not entirely rational and our translation of it will be affected by our own emotions (q.v.).
- Research as mutual mirroring: Rather than reflecting real images, the researcher may help to frame the behaviour of the group or vice versa.

This approach can be criticized for giving too much focus to the researcher rather than the subjects in that it can be highly self-referential with an emphasis on self-disclosure rather than on presenting 'meaningful' research.

Methodological Reflexivity

A focus on the methods (q.v.) deployed in research as well as an acknowledgment of the role of the researcher result in a more technically-oriented reflexivity. The design of the research is of paramount importance; so while the researcher may have been actively involved in co-constructing meaning and does not deny this intersubjectivity, there is a clearly articulated methodology which emphasizes the researcher's closeness to the subject matter yet a conscious professional distance is maintained.

It could be argued that both of these approaches to reflexivity work on a relatively superficial level: the first at the level of the individual, in the form of the researcher, and the second at a theoretical level, setting out to prove that acceptable standards have been adhered to in the conduct of the research. Neither approach questions the epistemological or meta-theoretical assumptions underpinning the research.

Epistemological reflexivity

The conundrum of epistemological circularity (Johnson and Duberley, 2000) means that we cannot hope to find the 'best' way of carrying out research in order to produce new knowledge; we can only produce this knowledge from a stated perspective [positivism and post-positivism]. However, we, and our readers [reading], must be clear about what this meta-theoretical perspective is. It is only in being as clear as we can about what our epistemological and ontological convictions are that we can produce truly reflexive research. It is not enough to merely state our epistemological stance but to question it and perhaps reframe it as we proceed. Consciousness here is not so much of self *per se* but of 'becoming more consciously reflexive by thinking about our own thinking' (Johnson and Cassell, 2001: 127).

Reflexive research should be *language-sensitive* (Alvesson and Deetz, 2000) and the linguistic turn in management studies has emphasized the need for reflexivity [*practice theory; practise-centred research*]. For example, research undertaken with a social constructionist (q.v.) epistemology is likely to focus on language as the mediating influence in the co-creation of meaning. There is a heavy focus on 'dialogue' (q.v.), 'conversation' (q.v.) and 'talk'. It will have a critical, reflexive focus in that it questions taken-for-granted assumptions. The collection of qualitative data normally forms part of an iterative process as opposed to a positivist linear approach. Induction, rather than deduction and discovery, is the guiding principle that goes hand-in-hand with researchers being aware of the effects of their presence and influence on the subjects and the data. Reflexivity, from a postmodern (q.v.) perspective, questions assumptions and does not treat knowledge as the domain of a chosen few in an intellectual elite. Lyotard (1979/1984) proposes that scientific knowledge does not represent the totality of knowledge; narrative knowledge is significant because, in this case, knowledge is not separated from the knower. Thus, as researchers we must examine the effects of our own lives and thoughts on the knowledge that we seek to capture and use.

Lisa Anderson

RELATIVISM

Definition

Relativism sees the world as a dynamic and fluctuating field of *interactions* as distinct from a collection of singular things and categories in movement. The interaction of relativism stresses the action *between* singular things and categories rather than the things and categories themselves. This means, for example, that relativism sees the human individual less as a self-contained person in a social context and more as a constituent part of an ongoing field of interactive relationships in which the human body moves as a propulsive reflection of the forces that surround it. Relativism in this context reveals human action to be the existential continuity between the body and its environment since its movement is always *between* the two [*dialogic*], so that the action of the body continues beyond its edges [*process philosophy*]. Relativism makes us see human action as an interactive network of *events* rather than the actions of singular social terms such as 'individual' or 'group' [*complexity theory*].

An event is a complex, dynamic interaction of parts that are forever subject to change and transformation. It is a temporary unit of the world as a field of diverse, flowing parts. The event is a transient bringing together and grasping of this diverse, fluid field in much the same way as we see the co-ordinated, moving images on the television screen that disappear just as soon as they have appeared. The event itself originates in an ungraspable space and time that lie beyond the immediacy of the everyday world of practical comprehension [*process theory*]. The relativity theory of modern physics reminds us that space and time are not static categories or structures but are more like an invisible background of mutable matter from which life engenders its ceaseless flow of multiple events. The event (from the Latin *evenire*, to come out) is an extraction from this invisible, ever-flowing background, comparable perhaps to the cinematic capturing by movie camera of an event that occurs as a transient action in the flow of everyday life. In relativity theory everything is relative so that 'both observer and observed are merging and interpenetrating aspects of one whole reality, which is indivisible and unanalysable' (Bohm, 1980: 9). No longer an objective and independent observer of the world, the scientist does not merely act *on* an object of research but is also constituted by the particular object and methods used in the research [*actor-network theory*]. In the field of relativity, 'mind and matter are not separate substances. Rather, they are different aspects of one whole and unbroken movement' (Bohm, 1980: 11). The event is a transient and temporary extraction of this whole and unbroken field in which everything is dynamically relative to everything else [*dialectic*].

Discussion

Social structures such as organizations are also relative events because social structures, such as organizations, are also relative events. Relativism reminds us that all social structures are constituted by the relationships between their constituent parts [*activity theory*]. Parts are always relative to other parts with which they constitute a whole. Relativism tells us that a whole is not just an overall container of its parts but that the parts constitute the whole just as the whole constitutes the parts. The scientist exemplifies this reciprocal relationship in that he or she is as much a part and product of the research process as are the object and data of the research. Part and whole thus always actively reflect and relate to each other in an act of 'undivided wholeness' (Bohm, 1980); they are like the reversible structure of a palindrome in which a word or sentence is the same whether read forward or backward. Relativism as the 'undivided wholeness' of parts means that parts are always on the move, always in transit. Parts express the relationship of relativism inasmuch as they are always *partial* and incomplete, always seeking connections. Parts thus express movement and action; they are always ready to de-*part*; they remind us that human agency is the perpetual movement *between* terms rather than the movement of individual things. Relativism suggests that the 'undivided wholeness' of relativity theory is a latent power that moves through the parts (from the Latin *partire, portare,* to bear, carry,

share, distribute) that reflect and relate it. An event is thus not merely a transient extraction from this latent field of 'undivided wholeness' but is also carried and projected by its ceaseless movement of *betweenness*. In this sense, an event is the coming together of parts in their search for some sense of completion. Human products are events that express the relativity and existential (q.v.) continuity of the body's parts with the external world. The body's organs and senses are parts that reproduce and reflect themselves in the material products of human culture. Products are physical re-enactments of the body's need to relate and reflect itself through its sentient connections with the outside world. The chair, for example, speaks back to its human complements to say it is always here as a friendly and supportive extension of the body [*affordances*]. The computer can be interpreted as part of the reaching out of the central nervous system beyond the body to complement its immanent sense of partialness. Chair and computer are thus objectified acts of relativity and movement which underline the essential betweenness of the human agent and its products which constitute each other like the pieces of a jigsaw puzzle in composition (Scarry, 1985).

Relativism makes us see human systems such as formal organizations less as self-contained, autonomously enduring institutions and more as temporary and transient products that are continuously and repeatedly put together as coherent structures and thus extracted from the 'undivided wholeness' of space and time that moves and sources them as a latent but dynamic background. Human systems and their products are thus more like events that are grasped and captured, however briefly, from this ceaseless flow of interlocking relativities. As an event, a human system cannot be seen. We can never see the supermarket or the university as such since they are essentially constituted by the active relativities and relationships *between* their parts. We may see the supermarket's display of products, its customers, its working staff and its building, but the total field of active and changing relationships between these various parts always exceeds our conceptual grasp. As a field of relativity, the supermarket exists through the active connections between its multiple parts and elements [*phenomenology*]; its products relate to its customers as objectified acts of relativity and movement which tell us that the supermarket exists only as a dynamic network of interactive parts in a general process of human composition and never simply as a static collection of consumable and useful objects.

Relativism persuades us to think in terms of the movement of relationship rather than the self-consistency of individual things and objects. The things and objects of the human world are themselves materialized expressions of the body's needs and desires to reach out in order to experience itself. It's in this sense that the body along with its things and objects are more appropriately seen as *parts* that are always *partial*, that are always ready to *de-part*, to move on and connect with other parts in a wider, more comprehensive, mobile space. Relativism thus underlines acts of *relating* in the double sense of connecting parts together and making manifest that which is latent yet potentially realizable. Relating thus reminds us that all acts of connection take place against a background source of variable and possible relationships which, like the letters of the alphabet or the words of language, can be combined and permutated to create an infinity of events and forms. It is this background source of latency that moves and motivates the work of the human world as a suspended space of multiple possibilities. Latency is a version of 'undivided wholeness' which can never be fully expressed but only alluded to through the partial events that make up the human world. In the context of latency, every part is incomplete, ever ready to de-part in an evolving field of composition and permutation (Cooper, 2005). Relativism now appears not simply as a field of dynamic and fluctuating interactions but also as the *re-lating* of the latent and virtual possibilities of the world. The re-lating of relativism is like the hypertext of computer technology which collates

text, sound, images, diagrams and maps and allows them to be variously combined on a computer screen. Hypertext re-lates the virtual and latent potential of the informational world through its capacity to make available the vast resources of libraries, museums, art galleries and other information sources to a single computer user. Hypertext tells us that we are permanently suspended in a relational field that lies always *between* the manifest, taken-for-granted forms of the world and the elusive and allusive call of the 'undivided wholeness' of latency which hints and taunts all human relationships while forever receding from human capture. Relativism is the continuous *re-lating* of the suspended space and time of immanent *betweenness*.

Robert Cooper

RELIABILITY

Definition

In terms of qualitative research, objectivity refers to the attempts of researchers to secure a solidity of meaning from qualitative data that are often a complicated and opaque process. There are no agreed or precise methods for 'teasing out' themes or theories that can lead to objective understanding. In addition, the wide variety of qualitative data, or 'texts', that can be incorporated into a research project further complicates the process. Generally, the aim is to develop categories and codes that reflect similar issues or ideas in the data under review; meaning objectivity is entwined with the gerund objectifying; it is a research activity in which the researcher aims to convince the reader (q.v.) of the soundness and sense of their research [*case study; process research*].

Discussion

The particular nature of objective qualitative research was given extensive consideration with the development of grounded theory (q.v.) by Glaser and Strauss in 1967. They proposed that researchers immerse themselves in the data and let the issues 'emerge' as they start to understand the patterns in the data. There is an iterative interplay between the collection and analysis of data and, in this way, the researcher is able to unravel the complexities of the social phenomena under review and so provide increasingly objective understandings. There is a specific assumption in Glaser and Strauss's original work on grounded theory that the researcher can approach the data without a priori assumptions; themes are identified only with recourse to the data. As such, the researcher inductively builds theory from the data as themes are refined, connected and categorized [*inductive analysis*]. While Glaser remained an advocate of an open and flexible approach to data analysis, Strauss changed his views and, in Strauss and Corbin (1990/1998), advocated a more technical process of pre-scriptive 'steps' through which the researcher proceeds in order to apply and verify themes and categories. They have provided a list of 'tools' that can used to support the analysis process. Both approaches, however, consider that the researcher provides a rational analysis of the text and that data classification is a rigorous and hence objective process.

Others are more sanguine about the possibility of the researcher being able to maintain objectivity. Charmaz (2000/2003: 250), for example, suggests that it is more important to attend to and interpret the subjects' meanings in the data, while at the same time acknowledging the potential for different interpretations and 'the mutual creation of knowledge by the viewer and the viewed'. From this perspective, searching for themes and building theory is not an objective process, but emergent and open-ended. Meaning-making does not necessarily need to follow a prescriptive process, and it is a collective, rather than solitary, endeavour. As participants in social life we already hold prior assumptions and theories about how and what influences the conduct of any particular activity. Even if we have not participated in that particular event, we make sense out of it by creating and applying categories based on our prior experiences and knowledge. To be able to suspend belief and approach any social situation in an objective and dispassionate manner is difficult, if not impossible. Thus, the categories do not so much 'emerge' from the data as they are formed, in part at least, from the application of a pre-existing typology, and perhaps even through engaging the subject in the analysis process [*mode 2*]. So, for example, it is accepted that a literature review [*systematic literature reviews*], or pre-existing theory, can be used to develop a template (q.v.) or codebook, which is applied, refined and developed through the analysis process [*matrices analysis*]. The main categories developed a priori only sensitize the researcher's perception to the data. They provide a starting point, but analysis is still an interpretative process where new themes are identified, sub-themes are generated, new connections acknowledged and new theories are developed. Themes and theories thus still 'emerge' through the close reading and interpretation of texts.

Despite the debates about the correct way to analyze and search for objective themes in data, the general aim of this type of analysis is to convince the reader that the process has been rigorous, reliable and that the issues of researcher bias have been addressed [*reflexivity*]. However, given the variety of epistemological positions taken in qualitative research, the definitions of rigour, reliability and bias are much debated [*phronetic organizational research; realism*]. Indeed, since thematic analysis requires that the researcher interprets the data, it is, ultimately, a sensemaking (q.v.) process. Thus, convincing others of the credibility and dependability of the data and their analysis is significantly different from the standards applied in quantitative research, where standard errors and degrees of significance are generally agreed. Verification, reliability and bias are addressed by acknowledging prior assumptions, by making the researcher's role in the project clear, by describing how codes were developed, how links were made and how concepts were defined and applied. By exposing the process of interpretation for review, the researcher invites the reader to believe that the approach adopted is consistent with the aims of the research, and that the interpretation applied, while not necessarily the only one available, was at least conducted in good faith.

In this regard, most researchers define the concepts and themes that they generate and provide examples of 'texts' that support their interpretation. The reader (q.v.) is shown how a deep analysis of the data has generated ideas about the subject under review and they are invited to 'see' how the themes identified are linked through narratives constructed by the researcher. To back up their 'story' the researcher provides a description of how coding records were analyzed and the process by which links in the data were established. There is a variety of ways to authenticate the analysis, such as word counts, example speech acts, or references to coding densities. Increasingly, thematic analysis is being conducted using computer-aided qualitative data analysis software [*CAQDAS*] in order to support claims for 'rigour' and 'transparency' [*mixed methods in management research*]. Ultimately, however, acceptance of claims to objectivity depends on the philosophical position taken in the research. The researcher will have to show that the way he/she has conducted his/her thematic analysis is consistent with both the underpinning epistemological assumptions, and that it usefully addresses the research questions posed.

Allan Macpherson

REPERTORY GRID TECHNIQUE

Definition

The repertory grid technique is based on George Kelly's (1955a, 1969) personal construct theory – also known as personal construct psychology (PCP) – which assumes an individual understands his world in terms of his own personal constructions. These constructs are developed through social interaction and represent the 'templates' through which the individual views his world (Stewart and Mayes, 1997-2006). This set of constructs helps an individual cope and manage his environment. It follows that an understanding of a person's set of constructs enables the inquirer to gain insight into a person's psychological space (Fransella, 2004; Gammack and Stephens, 1994; Stewart and Stewart, 1981). This, in turn, provides insight into how a subject experiences phenomena and how he is likely to act to particular situations [*phenomenology*]. Kelly argued that for every positive way of seeing the world there is the negative opposite. He therefore proposes that personal constructs are bipolar in nature as well as being finite in number (Kelly, 1955a). This belief is at the heart of the creation of a repertory grid.

Discussion

The technique has its roots in clinical psychology [*inductive analysis*] and gained tremendous support and breadth of application in areas such as organizational management and management training; anywhere where there was an emphasis on using robust intervention tools to help understand and improve another's condition (Raskin, 2001; Stevens, 1998). So beyond clinical psychology (Leach et al., 2001), the technique has been applied to research in human resource management (Bell, 2000), knowledge management (Stumpf and McDonnell, 2003) and marketing (Caldwell and Coshall, 2000; Schoenfelder and Harris, 2002).

The repertory grid interview technique was originally called the 'Role Construct Repertory Text'. The term 'repertory' derives from 'repertoire' – the repertoire of constructs which the subject develops during an interview (Stewart and Mayes, 1997–2006) [*dramaturgy*]. The grid is the resulting tool of an interview that helps to display an individual's perception of a specified problem or situation as free as is possible from interviewer bias. A repertory grid consists of three features.

- The elements: these are the objects upon which the subjects are asked to focus. These are often people or skills they possess when the method is used in psychology or training, but can equally be products if applied, for example, to marketing.
- The constructs: these are the personal criteria the individual uses when describing the differences between the elements. They consist of positive and negative poles which are often not the semantic opposites of one another.
- The correlations: the analysis of the grids allows various relationships to be discovered that exist between the constructs and elements. This can be between constructs and constructs, elements and constructs and elements and elements.

The elements, or objects of consideration of the interview, can be defined in advance by the researcher, such as specific product comparisons in marketing (Schoenfelder and Harris, 2002), or may be selected as being relevant to the research focus together with the interviewee. Teasing out the personal constructs of the interviewee follows according to Kelly's preferred construct elicitation technique. This is known as the triad method and it is combined with the 'laddering' technique that is commonly used in qualitative research (Neimeyer et al., 2001) [cognitive mapping]. The triad method is applied, in practice, by presenting the interviewee with the elements (the objects of the research) on cards [interviewing; stimulated recall]. Keeping the focus of the research in mind, the interviewee is asked to find a word or phrase to describe how two objects are more similar and different than the third. The interviewee is also asked to provide a phrase that would describe the negative opposite. This is not always the semantic opposite (Caputi and Reddy, 1999). For example, if the focus was to find out how consumers select between mobile phones, this might start with two mobile phones being perceived as having a futuristic design and one having an old-fashioned design (Schoenfelder and Harris, 2004). This is the beginning of a ladder. The laddering technique acknowledges

that subordinate values or constructs tend to be more rational and easily elicited in a verbal form. The technique accesses constructs via an easy cognitive route and moves to underlying high-order, more emotionally-based constructs that are more difficult to elicit (Wansink, 2003) [emotion research].

The repertory grid process results in a repertory grid that consists of personal constructs (usually between 10 and 20) and a specified number of elements (between 5 and 10). The grid is created by asking the subject to evaluate the elements in terms of the constructs that have been elicited. This may be done using ticks and crosses, or using a mathematical rating often ranging between 1 – as being the strongest rated – to 7 – being the weakest rating. Small grids can often be evaluated by eye, whereas for larger grids, such as larger than five constructs by five elements, it is helpful and more common to use a software package for support (Easterby-Smith et al., 1991/2002; Evans, 2006; Scheer, 2006). The grids can be analyzed interpretatively or mathematically [mixed methods in management research]. There are several ways of analysing the content of a repertory grid using a mathematical representation. These are: cluster analysis or principal component analysis. The first method groups together constructs or elements that are similar to one another and presents them visually in a tree diagram called a 'dendrogram'. This analysis is simple to read but has the disadvantage that it does not show the relationship between constructs and elements, nor does it give insight into the relative importance of the constructs to the individual. The second method, principal component analysis, has the advantage that is able to meet these requirements. Using this type of analysis to support interpretation, the constructs and/or elements will be clustered where the algorithms of the construct comparison are similarly high or similarly low. Clusters that are furthest from the centre of the resulting principal component map (PCA map) are most strongly linked to the emerging component or dimension of criteria important to the individual. In this way, the researcher is able to discover visually which types of criterion or construct are most important to the individual and also gain information about their relative importance. Different forms of analysis can be informative for different types of inquiry.

Prospects

The repertory grid technique has a number of advantages and disadvantages (discussed in more depth in Stewart and Stewart (1981) and Fransella (2004)). The advantages are:

- It builds on a technique that can work with cognitive and affective statements given by the research subject.
- The interviewing technique teases out constructs that otherwise may remain hidden.
- The visual (q.v.) presentation of results means it is relatively easy for the researcher to gain an initial overview to help interpretation.
- Repertory grid analysis is one of the few qualitative research techniques that provides analytic information rather than staying on the descriptive level.
- The technique has low researcher involvement (and hence bias).

However, there are two significant disadvantages.

- The movement from a highly qualitative, in-depth interview to a data analysis with a mathematical base is seen by some as critical, hence it is important for the researcher to remain involved in the data collected in the interview process and interpret any form of analysis of the grid in the light of the information that he has gained through the interview (q.v.). The epistemological obstacle may also be combatted by increasing the validity of the results by using an additional qualitative analysis method, such as transcript analysis, to compare and support the results of the grid.
- The researcher must resist the temptation to overlook the methodological principles in favour of a purely mechanistic analysis.

In addition, as with all qualitative research, the repertory grid technique demands an involved and sensitive researcher [*reflexivity*]. Also, the creation and filling in of the grid are sometimes complicated and demands a high level of concentration, meaning sample groups using repertory grid technique are relatively small – usually no more than 30 (Tan, 1999).

Julie Schoenfelder

REPRESENTATIONS

Definition

Our choice of research representations plays a critical role in conveying context and meaning as we seek to disseminate our research to others, including scholars of organization studies, policy makers, students, practitioners, and participants in the research process itself. *'Research representations'* refers to the portrayals of our approach to inquiry and related outcomes that we construct and present to others or ourselves. The term captures both initial presentations and *re*-presentations over time and across communities. Management and organization research has been characterized by increased attention to the construction and consumption of these texts. 'Text' is used here to designate a set or series of visual or auditory signs interpretable as *symbols*, rather than simply ink dots on a page, a string of sounds, or observed physical objects or movement. These signs become symbols for the reader by virtue of them pointing to something beyond themselves (Rosenblatt, 1978).

Discussion

In much management and organization research, texts that are research representations remain written in the passive voice, as though they are not objects constructed by authors perceiving phenomena. Indeed, the objectivism that underpins the dominant positivist thinking holds an assumption that truth or reality can be carried by language, and that 'scientific' languages are closer to the truth than others. Dispassionate, passive and 'objective' rhetoric – what Van Maanen (1995b: 9) has called 'the style of non-style' – characterizes scientific writing through which knowledge is constituted as problem (hypothesis)-centred, linear and straightforward [*phronetic organizational research; positivism and post-positivism*]. When a text violates this dominant convention, it is 'vulnerable to dismissal and to trivialization' (Richardson, 1993: 704–705).

The literary turn in the social sciences (Czarniawska, 1999; Richardson, 1990) brings with it attentiveness to the narrative (q.v.) and rhetorical (q.v.) structures in writing, and makes explicit the notion that the 'facts' in a text cannot be kept separate from their means of communication. What is true, right or proper is determined within a community with shared conventions [*social poetics*]. Beyond that community, the convention loses its power to command conformity or silence. Scientific writing is only one way of putting things, a 'truth by convention'. As Richardson (1990: 13) points out, science writing is a 'socio-historical construction that is narratively driven and depends upon literary devices not just for adornment but for *cognitive* meaning'. Even an economic text can be 'analyzed like a poem, to see how it achieves its purposes through [literary devices]' (McCloskey, 1995: 11). Of course, a richness of rhetorical devices intended to guide readers to the author's desired conclusion permeates quantitative studies in management; numbers do not speak for themselves [*reading as inquiry*].

Denied, then, in the literary turn is any special privilege between the 'world' and the 'word' (Czarniawska, 1997: 55–56). Qualitative researchers can no longer (or ever could) capture the complexity, subtlety and transience of lived experience. Denzin and Lincoln (2005) refer to this as the 'crisis of representation' [*postmodernism*]. Concerns for authorship and authority (i.e. whose truth?) and the rhetorical style used in texts to convey meanings lead to the creation of texts that blur the boundary separating 'art' and 'science' (Clifford, 1986) [*aesthetics*]. Such representations may better convey a sense of partiality, and give space to incongruent voices, polysemy, and the ambiguity and indeterminancy that are often lost in the 'narrative smoothing' of more normative discourses.

Examples of texts that depict or explore this blurring have include literary works such as Sherry and Schouten's (2002) exploration of poetry in marketing, Jerimer's (1985) short story of Mark Armstrong's work life from two perspectives, and dramatic scripts involving organizational actors and researchers (e.g. McGaughey, 2004); performance works such as chamber theatre (e.g. Paget, 1995) [*dramaturgy*]; and comic strips where conventions blur the word/image gap and create an ambiguity that permits many interpretations (e.g. McGaughey, 2006).

Prospects

The dangers of experimental representations have also been highlighted, and include: an inappropriate division between fieldwork and writing (Richardson and St Pierre, 2005) [*ethnography; field research*]; the shifting of the reader's focus from the organizational members and their activities towards the representational efforts of the researchers themselves; the creation of a new basis for authorial privilege; and the risks of depending on the personal authorial abilities and the elevation of aesthetic criteria of legitimation (Atkinson and Delamont, 2005). Closely linked to the crisis of representation is a 'crisis of legitmation' that raises questions about a text's authority and how it should be evaluated, and the 'crisis of praxis' (Denzin and Lincoln, 2005).

For an overview of science and literary writing in historical context, see Richardson (1990). Czarniawska (1999) uses literary theory to help problematize organization theory, and Polkinghorne (1997) encourages researchers to experiment with narrative approaches when reporting their endeavours.

Richardson and St Pierre (2005) explore writing as a method of inquiry and provide some practical exercises for researchers to develop writing skills. Denzin and Lincoln (2005) discuss the triple crisis of representation, legitimation and praxis, including different criteria of evaluation

Sara L. McGaughey

RHETORIC

Definition

The art of rhetoric has been taught and studied since the time of the ancient Greek philosophers. However, a revival of interest in the examination of rhetoric has recently been stimulated both by work in philosophy on the New Rhetoric (Perelman, 1987) and by the recent 'linguistic turn' of the social sciences that has focused on detailed analyses of language and discourse (Billig, 1987/1996; Potter, 1996). An interest in rhetoric is shared by scholars from many different disciplines, including philosophy, communication studies, psychology, linguistics and management/ organization studies.

The study of rhetoric concerns itself with how an orator's (or speaker's) argument is constructed to be persuasive. In this sense, rhetoric is viewed as a particular kind of *instrumental discourse* (q.v.) As a consequence, rhetoric has in the past often been contrasted with 'reality' as 'empty' speech that is all art and no substance. Rhetorical scholars, however, view rhetoric as rather the *creation of particular understandings of reality* through argument (for critiques of the rhetoric/reality dichotomy, see Hamilton, 2001; O'Neill, 1998; Watson, 1995b). Rhetorical scholars do not view rhetorical talk as distinct from action but rather as part of the 'social accomplishment of organization' (Grant et al., 1998: 5) and emphasize its *dialogical* (q.v.) *nature* (Billig, 1987/1996; Shotter, 1993; Watson, 1995c), involving both argument and counter-argument.

This may be between groups or individuals but also within individuals as we debate with ourselves about courses of action and the interpretation of events (Billig, 1987/1996; Hayes and Walsham, 2000). Important also to our understanding of rhetoric is the role of the *audience* in shaping and evaluating rhetoric [*reading*]. In addition, many rhetorical scholars are *reflexively* (q.v.) *aware* of and draw attention to their own rhetorical strategies in their academic writings (e.g. Symon, 2000; Watson, 2005c).

In general, a rhetorical analysis may proceed by initially identifying: the orator of the rhetoric and his/her potential credibility (e.g. senior manager, trades union official, researcher); the genre of the rhetoric (that is the nature of the text, e.g. written corporate documentation, individual interviews, public speech, etc.); the audience for the rhetoric (e.g. researcher, organizational members, specific employees, etc.); and the exigence or argumentative context (that is the problem or issue being addressed, e.g. the nature of an organizational change). The analysis itself will often be a detailed deconstruction (q.v.) of specific texts that demonstrates how the orator creates a credible identity for him/ herself, orients his/her arguments to this context and audience, and undermines the arguments of possible opponents, with the aim of seeking to persuade the audience of a particular version of reality.

Of the five classic 'canons' of rhetoric (or 'stages in the composition and delivery of the speech', Gill and Whedbee, 1995: 158), most academic emphasis has probably been on expression/style as scholars have investigated specific 'tropes' or figures of speech. These include: metaphor (q.v.), metonymy, synecdoche and irony (for more details on the nature of these, see Hamilton, 2003; Oswick et al., 2005) [*projective techniques*]. However, there is also a growing interest in the art of invention, which encompasses three possible modes of persuasive speech: rational appeal (logos); emotional appeal (pathos); and the appeal of the orator (ethos). There has been particular interest in one specific form of rational appeal, the enthymeme, in recent management writings (Hamilton, 2005b; Heracleous and Barrett, 2001).

Interest in rhetoric within management research specifically has particularly developed over the last fifteen years. Management scholars interested in rhetoric are exploring such issues as:

- How does rhetoric facilitate processes of change and legitimate new organizational forms and practices?
- What rhetorical strategies are adopted by organizational members in seeking to make their arguments persuasive?
- How do the rhetorical strategies of opponents and proponents of organizational change compare?

Both Legge and Watson have explored the rhetoric of human resources management (HRM) discourses and practices (Legge, 1995; Watson, 1995c; and see Carter and Jackson, 2004), and Hamilton has written extensively on rheorical discourse in employment relations (1997, 2001). A variety of authors have examined the rhetoric of organizational change (e.g. Mueller et al., 2003; Suddaby and Greenwood, 2005), some focusing specifically on technological change (Hayes and Walsham, 2000; Heracleous and Barrett, 2001; Symon, 2005). Others have examined the rhetorical features of specific organizational interventions (e.g. Zbaracki (1998) on total quality management; Case (1999) on business process re-engineering) and of consultancy practice more generally (Berglund and Werr, 2000). From communication studies, there is also interest in rhetoric as formal organizational presentation, for example, within corporate manifestos (e.g. Cheney et al., 2005). More broadly, Sillence (2002, 2005) has tried to identify and model general features of effective argumentation in organizational settings, emphasizing the interrelationships between and contextual contingency of many of these features. Taken together, such work has provided insight into the processes of controversy and debate within organizations; illuminated the strategic use of language as a means of initiating, directing, legitimating and resisting change; and has led to the demystification of the appeal of specific managerial 'fads' and consultancy advice.

Prospects

As research progresses, we are likely to see the application of rhetorical analysis to a greater variety of management topics and the integration of findings from individual empirical studies into a more coherent theoretical view on rhetoric in organizations. However, differences in epistemological perspective are also likely to become more obvious. Currently, the most obvious issue of debate is the extent to which rhetoric is contrasted with reality [*realism*]. Although rhetorical scholars generally reject the association of rhetoric with mere linguistic flourishes, some commentators still have recourse to a 'reality' with which rhetoric is compared (e.g. Zbaracki, 1998), while others argue for a more rigorous relativism (q.v.) (e.g. Symon, 2005; Watson, 1995a). Emerging debates may concern whether we can identify generalizable (effective) rhetorical strategies, whether we can identify contingencies (q.v.) for the use of particular strategies or whether rhetorical analyses should be focused on localized, detailed deconstructions of particular texts. Given rhetoric's focus on argument and counter-argument, it will not be surprising to see some constructive debate continue within the organizational rhetoric literature.

Gillian Symon

S

SEMIOTICS

Definition

The subject of semiotics is extremely complex and not easily reduced to simple definition. Whether in spite of or because of this complexity, semiotics has been highly significant in terms of its impact on twentieth-century thought and its legacy continues to inform current thinking in all branches of knowledge. In this respect management and organization studies are not immune to this influence.

The twentieth century saw a considerable fascination with language: a phenomenon which is sometimes referred to as *the linguistic turn* in philosophy [*ordinary language philosophy*]. This concern with language had its origins in the work of the Swiss linguist Ferdinand de Saussure. In his work, *Course in General Linguistics*, which was published in 1916 a year after his death, he had argued for a *science of signs*, which he termed 'semiology': a term which is still used in preference to semiotics outside the English-speaking world. Semiology, literally the science or study of the sign, he maintained, would permit the analysis of signs, linguistics, rituals and what he termed *systems of convention*. According to Saussure, semiology is 'a science which studies the life of signs at the heart of social life' (1916/1971: 33). Such analysis has proved to be extremely useful, particularly in critical organization studies. Semiotics provides a way of understanding meanings in organizations, of looking at cultures, understanding marketing and for the examination of gender construction.

Nowadays, semioticians talk about 'reading' (q.v.) signs so that a semiological analysis addresses itself to the language of signs. This can mean reading or decoding such diverse texts as an advertisement for a supermarket, a song by a popular band or a cereal packet. Films, books and cultures can also be read in this way. Signs are not only words but also images, sounds, colours, actions and objects, and every sign has its own *denotation*, that is to say, it refers to something in the world: an object, a feeling, a state. Anything can be a sign as long as it signifies something. However, despite the way in which semiotics has developed and *rematerialized* the sign, Saussure's primary interest was in the sign as a psychological construct. He was concerned not with the relationship between a thing and its name but rather between a concept and a sound image.

Saussure proposed a two-part model of the sign in which the sound image of the sign was called the *signifier* and the concept to which it referred was termed the *signified*. It makes no sense to speak of a meaningless signifier. Something must be signified. By producing his two-part model, Saussure made an important distinction. For example, the *sound image* or signifier for 'mother' relies on the reader understanding the *concept* 'mother', the signified. However, as is immediately apparent, the concept mother has multiple connotations. Beyond the simple meaning of the term, what is signified will depend on the relative experiences of the concept 'mother'. A mother might be kind or cruel, might have abandoned her child, might be dead. The concept will vary according to a person's experience of 'mother'. Saussure's contribution is highly significant here because by giving emphasis to the individual interpretation of signs, he implicitly challenged the idea of a 'real' external world and, in turn, contributed to the notion of the world as a social construction (q.v.) [*activity theory; constructivism*].

For Saussure, language is a system of convention in which there is a degree of consensus about the use and meaning of words. However, he is concerned to argue that the first principle of semiology is the arbitrariness of the sign. What Saussure meant by this is that, for example, the word 'cat' as the English word for a particular type of domestic pet might just as readily be rendered *chat* in French, or *Katze* in German. In other words, the allocation of the sound image is arbitrary. However, once allocated, the signifier becomes consensually applied. It is not possible to say 'dog' and to mean 'cat'. It is impossible in this brief entry to provide a more comprehensive introduction to semiotics. However, it is possible to give some indication of the influences which semiotic analysis has had on the study of organizations by tracing some of the key theorists whose work has been crucial to the development of the field.

Discussion

In this respect, one of the earliest writers to bring semiotic analysis to a wider audience was Roland Barthes (1915–1980). Barthes was a philospher, social theorist and literary critic. His early work was mainly in semiology and structuralism and in the 1960s he produced his well-known essay, 'The death of the author', which argued that the author was not the sole authority on the meaning of a text. This proved to be a highly influential notion and in organizational theorizing led to a challenge to notions of authority. Barthes' work was extended and developed by his doctoral student Julia Kristeva, who is arguably one of the most

important figures in poststructuralist philosophy [*postmodernism*]. She was particularly influenced by Barthes, who, as one of the foremost champions of structuralism, had sought to reveal the ways in which bourgeois ideology was embedded in French language and literature. A concern with semiotics and the implicit regulation of language has been significant in her writing. Her best-known work is probably *Revolution in Poetic Language* (1974/1984) in which she takes the view that poetic language puts the subject in crisis and disrupts the unity of the symbolic. Her argument that the poetic subverts the dominant social discourse to challenge order, rationality and patriarchal regulation is clearly influential in critical (q.v.) and feminist (q.v.) theories of organization.

There are perhaps two main writers whose work has been taken up by organization and management theorists: Jacques Derrida and Jean Baudrillard. It is not easy to comment on the considerable volume of work by Jacques Derrida (1930–2004). Yet his work on deconstruction (q.v.) has made a phenomenal impact on literary criticism and continental philosophy in general. Derrida described traditional philosophy as logocentric and argued that this logocentrism made other forms of writing, such as poetry and literature, secondary to its command of meaning and 'truth'. In 1966 Derrida gave a conference paper at Johns Hopkins University in the USA on 'Structure, sign, and play in the discourse of the human sciences'. This paper, which is published as part of *Writing and Difference* (1978/2001), gave impetus to the notion of *post*structuralism with its emphasis on the problem of language and text, with meaning, authorship and interpretation. It was Derrida who famously said 'There is nothing outside the text' [*Il n'y a pas de hors-texte*].

Baudrillard's work, emerging from structuralist semiotics, has provided a range of commentaries on patterns of consumerism, the meaning of history and gender relations. Baudrillard's interest in semiotics is concerned with self-referentiality and the problem of an excess of meaning. For Baudrillard, this has resulted in an absence of meaning. In particular, he has sought to challenge the power of the sign in relation to commodities and commification. Of his many books, perhaps the most relevant here are *Symbolic Exchange and Death* (1993) and *For a Critique of the Political Economy of the Sign* (1981), in which he attempted to bring together structural semiotics with the works of Marx (q.v.) [*dialectic*]. His work is predominantly about the relationship between power and meaning [*phronetic organizational research*]. For this reason, he has had a significant influence on organizational theory and analysis.

Apart from these, there are a number of writers who could be said to have been influenced by semiotics and the problem of meaning and language. These are Gilles Deleuze and Felix Guattari [*process philosophy*], Georges Bataille, Jean-Francois Lyotard, Jürgen Habermas and Richard Rorty to name but a few. Luce Irigaray and Hélène Cixous, in particular, have given specific attention to the relationship between self and language. Overall, semiotics has had an enormous influence in a wide range of areas but perhaps most notably in literary criticism, feminist theory, psychoanalysis, sociology and latterly in organization theory. These developments have, in turn, spawned a whole range of theoretical perspectives such as post-colonialism (q.v.), queer theory, feminism and cultural studies. From its inception, semiotics challenged authorship and authority, regulation by language, power, and the creation of meaning. Consequently, it has considerable appeal to management and organization theorists.

Heather Höpfl

SENSEMAKING

Definition

The most comprehensive statement of what sensemaking in organizations is is found in Weick's 1995 book of that name. Dictionaries are comprised of definitions and with Weick we find a straightforward one: 'sensemaking is what it says it is, namely, making something sensible. It is to be understood literally not metaphorically' (1995: 16). This plain-speaking definition distances itself from fancy metaphor (q.v.) and in doing so appeals directly to common sense. But it would be a mistake to understand sensemaking as commonsensical.

Discussion

There is more to sensemaking than Karl Weick, but it doesn't make much sense without him. Weick is the chief proponent and exponent of the sensemaking perspective and as such any entry has to begin with an appreciation of his ideas. However, if sensemaking does not amount in time to a good deal more than Weick, then the future and legacy of the perspective will be curtailed. The days in which grand narratives are associated with individuals (e.g. Freudian or Marxist (q.v.)) are disappearing; no one can be a paradigm entirely to his or herself. A recent contributor to a special edition of *Organization Studies* dedicated to sensemaking and Weick described his reaction on first reading Weick as like reading someone 'who had just popped in to earth on his way to another planet' (Gioia, 2007). It would not, however, be mistaken to understand sensemaking as the process by which people in and through interaction generate plausible versions as to what they are confronting and how best to proceed. That is, sensemaking is concerned with how people create common sense that allows them to go on. The mistake is to confuse common sense with the process of common-sensemaking, which is not commonsensical.

This line of thought provides a link with the origins of sensemaking which are to be found in Weick's *The Social Psychology of Organizing* (1969/1979). Organizing was formally defined as 'consensually validated grammar for reducing equivocality by means of sensible interlocked behaviours' (1979: 3). This is not as opaque as it reads. All it says is that there is a deal of uncertainty (equivocality to be exact) as to what is going on and it can be difficult to figure out what to do. When you are in uncertain situations you generally turn to someone else and talk to them to see if you can jointly make sense of what is happening and how to proceed (inter-locked behaviour). Consensual validation is described as 'common sense of a high order' or simply agreements as to what is real and illusory (1979: 3). In constructing these agree-ments grammar is used that consists of recipes for getting things done when one per-son alone can't do them and recipes for inter-preting what has been done (1979: 4). Put differently, grammar is organizational com-mon-sensemaking or 'the way we do things around here' or, at a pinch, 'culture' [cross-cultural research]. What else is culture but a system of recipes which tell you how to act in particular situations while at the same time providing others with a yardstick for evaluat-ing this acting?

The ideas that inform sensemaking are thus rooted in wider social scientific literatures dealing with how people create sense of experience. These include: social psychol-ogy (e.g. Festinger); micro-sociology (e.g. Goffman) [dramaturgy]; ethnomethodolgy (q.v.) (e.g. Garfinkel); social constructionism (q.v.) (e.g. Berger and Luckman); and cultural anthropology [ethnography] (e.g. Geertz). Philosopically, there are strong resonances with European phenomenology (q.v.) and North American pragmatism (q.v.) while sym-bolic interactionism (Mead/Blumer) is described as the 'unofficial house theory' of sensemaking (Weick, 1995). Ironically, when these ideas were being formed and written, the world of business was not a consideration. *The Social Psychology of Organizing* was written for social psychologists: 'Business school and businesss applications were not even salient in the thinking of the book' (Colville et al., 1999). So why have the ideas and the sensemaking perspective been so influential in organization and management studies?

First, the ideas provided a counter to the prevailing assumptions of the then positivis-tic (q.v.) orthodoxy in the field. Sensemaking showed how organizations were not necessarily goal-oriented. The idea that organizational plans were retrospective reconstructions of elapsed actions that had functioned earlier like blind variations was new to academic organization studies.

Second, the ideas were translated by Peters and Waterman in *In Search of Excellence* (1982) – still the best selling management book of all time – and thus found a popular outlet in general management (Colville et al., 1999). Word spread and the ideas travelled.

Third, Weick is a wordsmith. Van Maanen says the purpose of organization theory is to communicate understandings and to per-suade readers, the more the better, that not only do we have something to say but what we say is important and worth heeding (Van Maanen, 1995a). Sensemaking has been heeded because Weick writes with style and is persuasive. Van Maanen lauds style as theory, but others argue that theory must transcend the style of the writer to be scien-tific (Pfeffer, 1995) [representations]. To this end Weick is writing with others to embed the style in wider social scientific activities, and as the ideas are taken up and used by others independently of Weick, they accrue their own epistemological and methodologi-cal status The most recent statements con-cerning the use of sensemaking from Weick himself appear in *Organization Science* (Weick et al., 2005). Furthermore, sensemaking is currently being conducted in more main-stream organizations and situations (rather than in more esoteric contexts, e.g. firefight-ers, aircraft carriers and flight decks) such as middle-management change (Balogun and Johnson, 2004), while writers such as Brown (2004) link sensemaking and the ideas and approaches found in narrative (q.v.) and dis-course analysis (q.v.).

Prospects

In the future, for the sensemaking perspec-tive to progress it will also have to deal more clearly with issues of power [actor-network theory; critical theory] and emotion (q.v.). Supporters have claimed these issues are considered, but those of a more critical perspective fail to be convinced. This is a challenge which should be taken up. Another branch of critique comes from advocates of practice theory (q.v.) who argue that sense-making tends to overlook the role practices play in influencing emergent patterns of activity; organizing is not simply the product of collective minds (Schatzki, 2005a).

But it should not be forgotten that sense-making is 'a low paradigm best described as a developing set of ideas with explanatory possibilities, rather than as a body of knowl-edge' (Weick, 1995: xi). That means don't get too hung up on paradigm wars, arguments over style versus content and definitions underlined with magic markers. Tom Wolfe never defined 'The Right Stuff' but kept giv-ing instances and examples in varying con-texts such that the reader knew what it meant (i.e. the idea had presence) (Van Maanen, 1995a). Indeed, all over the world people know what 'The Right Stuff' means and every dictionary includes it. That is what sensemaking is – the right stuff – and every dictionary should include it.

Ian Colville

SERVICE USER RESEARCH

Definition

The push to involve service users in research has come from both the consumerist tradition of the 1990s and the democratic tradition of developing participation in order to improve the quality and effectiveness of services. In the UK, for example, service user and carer involvement have been central themes in the modernization agenda of the ruling Labour Party which put service users at the heart of health and social care research (Department of Health, 1998, 1999, 2000a, 2000b) and can be seen in their aspiration for activity associ-ated with the young (Children and Young People's Unit, 2001: 2). The assumption is that by involving users in research there is

the potential for different perspectives; a focus on existing problems; accountable expenditure; a higher profile for academic activity, notably among marginalized commu-nities who are often significant users (Hanley et al., 2004: 2–4). Alongside such compelling reasons for involving service users in research is the increasing requirement by research commissioners in the UK who have made 'user involvement' an important aspect of funding applications (Roberts, 2004) [*ethics; mode 2*].

Discussion

In seeking to involve service users in manage-ment and organization research there is a need to develop new approaches. To date, most efforts have concentrated on public sector service provision. Here service users need to be viewed not as objects or merely as subjects but as social actors acting, changing and being changed by the world they live in. Arnstein (1971) famously identified an eight-rung model of citizen participation but McLaughlin (2006a) reduced this to four, building on the work of Hanley et al. (2004). The continuum consists of: tokenistic involvement, consultation, collaboration (q.v.) and service user controlled research.

- Tokenistic involvement occurs when the researcher says they are involving service users but organizes the project in such a way that their involvement is a sham.
- Consultation is the first and safest level of participation; it does not require those consulting to act on what is heard, only to ask. McLaughlin et al. (2004) have shown how consultation can be viewed as a 'use-fully ambiguous' concept meaning differ-ent things to different people.
- Collaboration implies an ongoing relation-ship with the research project and the resultant power to affect decisions. Service users may participate in all or just one of these ways: as members of a steer-ing group, collaborators on the research question, assisting with the research design, undertaking interviews (q.v.),

analysing and interpreting data, writing up the research report and disseminating the results.

- User-controlled research refers to those research projects where power resides with the service users. In contrast to the consultative or collaborative approaches, the user-controlled model locates decision-making and power with the service user. Although this is a relatively new area of research, one example is the Wiltshire and Swindon User's Network Best Value Review of the implementation of direct payments (Evans and Carmichael, 2002).

One of the key benefits of involving service users as co-researchers, identified by Smith et al. (2002) and McLaughlin (2005, 2006b), is ensuring that research tools like questionnaires, consent forms or other leaflets are accessible to the target population [*access*]. Service user researchers may have a view as to which questions should be asked and in what order, may be able to identify where hard-to-reach groups congregate and may also be able to communicate with such groups more effectively than an academic researcher.

There are also considerable benefits for the service user in becoming involved in research as service users can gain new skills and increased self-confidence and become more employable, while at the same time contributing to the improvement of services they use.

Prospects

Currently, service user involvement in research is more honoured in the rhetoric than practice. Results are often measured by what the service user got out of the experience and the degree of participation, than by changes to service delivery. This type of research is resource and energy intensive; service users need to be trained, provided with support and to receive a fair return for their participation. Ethical considerations need to be addressed fully, including issues such as the 'informed consent' of service user researchers, and their responsibility to maintain confidentiality may need addressing

on a regular basis (Smith et al., 2002) [*participant observation*]. Alongside this, there is the increased challenge to navigate such approaches through research ethics and governance frameworks (Department of Health, 2001; Scottish Executive, 2002).

Following these practical and ethical considerations there is a debate to be had as to which research tasks, stages and types of research service users can reasonably undertake and how these will add value to addressing the research question. The more complex qualitative research approaches are likely to be beyond the skill and knowledge level of service user researchers and this may limit the types of research question that can be pursued. Also, the term 'service user' is not uncontested and is not an homogeneous term; it is quite possible for researchers to work with service users while being a service user themselves. This type of research is not a panacea, but if used properly represents another tool and approach for management and organization researchers to consider when looking to involve third-party users in some form of collaborative venture, whether within the public sector or beyond. Knowledge about service users or the services they use is incomplete if it does not include the knowledge that service users have of themselves or the services they experience.

Hugh McLaughlin

SOCIAL CONSTRUCTIONISM

Definition

Over the last twenty years, organizational researchers have expanded the repertoire of qualitative methods to include those embracing a linguistic perspective. These methods draw on social constructionist assumptions that language is a means of constituting reality. The philosophical underpinnings of this approach can be traced back over forty years to the work of Berger and Luckmann, who, in their seminal book *The Social Construction of*

Reality (1966), suggested that our social world is produced and maintained between people in their ongoing activities and interactions. They suggested that we experience social reality as objective – as being already there – because we encounter other people and institutions and are socialized into their definitions of the world. Yet that world is shaped in human interaction. As Berger and Luckmann said, 'Society is a human product. Society is an objective reality. Man is a social product' (1966: 61). They also emphasized the importance of language and conversation as a crucial part of reality construction and maintenance. Thus, the main premise of social constructionism is that social realities, identities and knowledge are created and maintained in interactions, and are culturally, historically, and linguistically influenced.

Discussion

While scholars working from a constructionist orientation commonly reject essentialist explanations of the world, there are various orientations, including radical constructivism (q.v.) (e.g. Von Glasersfeld, 1987), cognitive constructivism [*cognitive mapping; repertory grid technique*] (e.g. Kelly, 1955b), social constructivism (e.g. Bruner, 1990; Watzlawick, 1984) and social constructionism (e.g. Gergen, 1994a; Shotter, 1993). These versions differ for a number of reasons: for example, whether reality construction is seen as a cognitive or discursive process (occurring in the mind or in linguistic practices); as situated in 'I' or 'we' (in the individual or relationships between people); and whether the researcher creates theoretical generalizations or insights into particular contexts. For example social constructivists focus on construction as an individual cognitive process influenced by social relationships, and explore how individuals make sense of their social situations – Schön's (1983) work on the reflective practitioner illustrates this perspective. While constructivists often include the subject's voice in the research process through participative data collection methods, they are still interested in generating theoretical explanations

from practice and they often do not see themselves as apart of the constructing process. Social constructionists focus on how meaning and a practical sense of a situation are created between people in their taken-for-granted ways of talking, and in responsive dialogue. Many embrace reflexive (q.v.) approaches to research, seeing themselves as part of the process of constructing meaning (Gergen, 1999 for fuller discussion). Social constructionism not only encourages researchers to challenge taken-for-granted realities, but also can form the genesis for change by emphasizing the emergent nature of life and knowledge and therefore the possibility of creating alternative realities.

Organization theorists working from a social constructionist perspective see organizations and organizing as continually constructed in social interactions and talk. Notable work on this area includes Watson's (1994b) ethnographic study of organization culture and Weick's (1995) work on sensemaking (q.v.) in organizations. Organization theory has also been influenced by work in the sociology of knowledge and technology studies. In *Laboratory Life: The Social Construction of Scientific Facts*, Latour and Woolgar (1979) argued that scientific knowledge and facts are social products created from the many interpretations of people involved in scientific work [*actor-network theory*]. These ideas have been taken up by social construction of technology (SCOT) theorists who explore how technologies are influenced not just by technical considerations, but also by social and cultural factors as well as the interactions and interpretations of people using it.

Berger and Luckmann's ideas have been developed within organization studies in sociologically-based studies [*ethnography; field research*], language-based work, critically-based work, postmodern (q.v.) and poststructuralist-influenced work, and relationally-oriented work [*individualism*]. Some researchers take a macro-perspective, focusing on how, for example, organizational culture, identities, or ways of categorizing (e.g. gender and race) are discursively produced. Others interpret interaction and language in a particular context to explore how meanings emerge and what that might tell us about the process of socially constructing experience. Researchers taking a social constructionist perspective use a range of methods, including conversation analysis (q.v.), discourse analysis (q.v.) (both critical and non-critical), interviewing (q.v.), document and textual analysis, social poetics (q.v.), and narrative analysis (q.v.).

Prospects

One risk with the emphasis on constituting social relations between people is a tendency to preclude an understanding of social institutions and human identity still in touch with, and influenced by, a reality that is beyond such relations. The recognition that the meanings and status accorded to social phenomena are steeped in prevailing modes of interaction (language and tradition) is not to argue that material reality is equally beholden to historically-situated interactions – what is situated is status, not existence *per se* [*critical realism; realism*]. Another risk is the tendency of social constructionist declarations to be just that, statements of approaches to research whose certitude, deliberateness and sense of purposeful goal belie the primal background conditions of basic human action from which language and its constructions emerge. Language is not all there is, nor is it entirely within our gift to conventionally decide upon the meaning constructed through the words and grammar of language. In every meaning there is potential for its being upset [*relativism*], including the knowledge emerging from social constructionist approaches.

Ann L. Cunliffe

SOCIAL POETICS

Definition

Social poetics draws on social constructionist (q.v.) assumptions that we shape our realities,

meaning and selves intersubjectively through our everyday conversations (q.v.). The history of poetics can be traced back to Aristotle, who noted that 'poetic' work is concerned with imitating and learning from life in artistic ways, including language, storytelling (q.v.), rhythm, harmony, colour and form. A number of scholars have built on Aristotle's notion, suggesting that poetics is not purely imitation but also the creation of social realities (Fergusson, 1961). In particular, Shotter (1996), Katz and Shotter (1996), McNamee (2000) and Cunliffe (2002) draw on a variety of disciplines (linguistics, discursive psychology, existential phenomenology (q.v.), poststructuralism, etc.) to develop social poetics in the fields of medicine, therapy and management respectively.

The research method or practice of social poetics explores how meaning is created between people as they utilize discursive resources in imaginative and improvisational ways. McNamee (2000) suggests researchers should focus on the moments of relational engagement to explore how participants engage in conversations, craft meaning, and open up possibilities for co-ordinating action.

Discussion

Three crucial differences exist between social poetics and many other social constructionist-based research methods (Cunliffe, 2003):

1. Social poetics draws on the notion of language-as-ontology.
2. Researchers study poetic and imaginative rather than theoretical ways of talking.
3. Researchers believe that they are part of the process of constructing meaning and therefore take a radically-reflexive (q.v.) approach to research.

1. Language-as-ontology

Language and discourse-based research methods can be situated in two broad frames (Cunliffe, 2002): those which essentially view *language-as-epistemology* (as method), and a second, less developed approach which views social experience and identities being constructed through language, that is, *language-as-ontology* (as being). The former assumes that meaning is relatively fixed and lies in individual words, has an essence that can be captured and is consistent across contexts. Researchers working from this perspective study, and often codify, the type of language used and stories told by organizational members to draw conclusions about structure, culture, leadership and other aspects of organizational life (e.g. Boje, 1991; Watson, 1994b). Language-as-ontology presupposes language is a form of being; that we come to know and create ourselves and our experience through embodied speech. Our feelings, reactions, sensing, words, gestures, touch, movements, etc. all hold possibilities of meaning that we may experience in precognitive and cognitive ways. Therefore we articulate and create relationships with our surroundings within our embodied, moment-to-moment, responsive dialogue, and in doing so (re)create ourselves, others, and possibilities for action. Such meaning is not necessarily straightforward, nor shared, but can be indeterminate, self-contradictory, and contested as people struggle with the tensions and interplay of voices and interpretations. In summary, whereas language-as-epistemology focuses on codifying or thematizing talk, language-as-ontology emphasizes a practical, embodied, involved understanding from within the moment of conversation.

2. Poetic ways of talking

Poetics is derived from the Greek word *poiesis*, which means to create something, often in an artful way. Meaning is created as language plays through us, as words, sounds, rhythm and gestures evoke connections and verbal and emotional responses. Whereas many discourse-based research methods assume language is representational (i.e. describes reality), researchers working from a language-as-ontology perspective believe that language is: (a) creative – social realities unfold and take on images from language itself as we speak, write, read, and listen,

that is we improvize meaning; (b) metaphorical (q.v.) [*projective techniques*] – meaning is grounded in root metaphors and through the use of metaphors; (c) allusive – meanings emerge in indirect ways as we grasp a responsive sense of situations through imaginative forms of talk, including metaphors, storytelling, irony and gestures.

3. A radically-reflexive approach to research

Language-as-ontology assumes researchers cannot separate themselves from the process of creating meaning. Any research conversation incorporates relational engagement where impressions and a sense of the situation are constructed intersubjectively between researcher and organizational members. The practice of social poetics means examining reflexively how all research participants (including the researcher) contribute to meaning-making. This embraces a radically-reflexive approach to research, which builds on work in sociology, anthropology and linguistics to suggest that we as researchers need to take responsibility for our own theorizing (Cunliffe, 2003; Pollner, 1991).

Social poetics therefore explores how we create meaning between us in our everyday conversations in particular social contexts, and emphasizes a kind of practical understanding that consists of 'seeing connections' between aspects of our surrounding circumstances, between ourselves and others, and between our sense of the situation and action (Bakhtin, 1986; Wittgenstein, 1953, 1980) [*ordinary language philosophy*]. These connections often consist of gestural and poetic aspects of our dialogue which create 'arresting moments' in which we are struck, oriented or moved to respond to our surroundings in different ways (Shotter, 1996). The focus lies on the responsive speech of research participants; how connections and meanings emerge as we feel the rhythm, resonance, and reverberation of speech and sound. Research conversations can be audio or video (q.v.) taped to allow the researcher and organizational members to watch the tapes and explore what 'strikes' them about what was said, the language used, how meaning was created, and the implications for making meaning within their organization. For example, participants might explore how the metaphors and images [*drawings and images; visual data analysis*] used in the conversation provoked participants into making connections; how the use of irony and contradiction evokes oppositional meanings; how gestures emphasize meaning; and how imaginative forms of talk ('imagine what would happen if...') created new ways of interacting. In this way, organizational members themselves engage in radically-reflexive practice and begin to realize how they constitute their organizational experiences as they talk with others, and how they might articulate new, more responsive organizational realities.

Ann L. Cunliffe

SOFT SYSTEMS METHODOLOGY

Definition

Soft systems methodology (SSM) is a way of organizing the exploration of the problematical situations which we continually encounter in everyday life, both inside organizations and in our personal lives, situations about which we feel: 'something needs to be done about this'. The approach enables deliberate action-to-improve such situations to be defined and implemented [*action learning; action science*]. The SSM process *learns* its way to deciding upon and taking action, so the methodology is itself a *learning system*.

We experience everyday life as being immensely complex and far from static. But the complexity we experience has some stable characteristics. Every situation in real life, while being ever-changing, will show much connectivity between the elements it contains; and it will also reveal multiple ways in which different people are 'seeing' and interpreting

the world: one person's perceived 'terrorist' being another's 'freedom fighter'. These people have different *worldviews*. Also, because human beings are capable of consciously forming intentions, and acting in the light of those intentions, every real-world situation will display, in addition to aimless messing about, would-be *purposeful action*. SSM's learning system is built upon this image of everyday life in the human tribe, with its elements of: a changing dense connectivity, multiple worldviews and the possibility of purposeful action [*complexity theory; practice theory*].

SSM's process starts by finding out about both the situation addressed and the intervention intended to 'do something about it', to improve it. (Techniques for different kinds of finding out are provided, including cultural and political analysis.) In the light of this knowledge some different worldviews, which might be associated with different relevant stakeholders, are defined. Models of 'purposeful activity systems' which, seen through these worldviews, would be regarded as sensible, are then constructed. Each model consists of a monitored cluster of linked activities which make up a purposeful whole. (If, for example, you were examining issues in managing the UK's National Health Service, you might sweep in worldviews attributed to many different stakeholders: NHS managers, doctors and nurses, the Department of Health, commercial providers of healthcare services, patients, etc. These would produce different models relevant to discussing the NHS, seen through these worldviews.) The models are used as devices which act as a source of questions to ask of the real-world situation, questions such as: does this activity in the model get done in the real world? Who by? How? How is it judged? Etc. [*activity theory; composite mapping; repertory grid technique; visual data analysis*]. Asking these questions serves to provide a coherent structure to discussion or debate about the situation and how it might be changed. Such discussion surfaces worldviews and generates learning leading to context-dependent ideas for change and improvement.

As the discussion/debate progresses the SSM practitioner(s) will be seeking either consensus (which in real life is a rather rare, occasional outcome) or, more usually, *accommodations* between different worldviews which enable action-to-improve the situation to be taken, action which different people and groups having different worldviews can nevertheless live with. (Indeed, ongoing social life can be seen as a process of continuously finding such accommodations.) The changes need to be both (systemically) desirable, given that these models are thought to be relevant, and also feasible for these particular people in this unique situation with its particular history, now.

Since the implementation of changes will create a modified or new situation, it is clear that the learning process could in principle continue. In this sense, SSM can be seen as a way of *managing* through time any situation in which purposeful action is relevant. For a recent introduction, see Checkland and Poulter's (2006) *Learning for action*. Figure 7 illustrates the overall process of SSM.

Discussion

SSM was developed in a programme of 'action research' at Lancaster University in the UK (Checkland, 1981). The vehicle for its development was a Masters course which attracted experienced students in their early 30s, together with a consultancy company wholly-owned by the university. In the 'action research' (q.v.) process, the researchers entered real-world problem situations, *took part* in the 'managing'/'problem-solving' going on, and used the experiences as the source material for the SSM's development.

At the initiation of the programme, the research took an existing systems methodology as a given. The approach chosen was the Systems Engineering (SE) which Bell Telephone Laboratories had generalized from case histories of their own technological developments. This SE entailed carefully defining a need and then creating a system to meet that need based on a precise definition of system objectives. This approach is demonstrably successful in *technically-defined* problem situations (e.g. 'We need a better short-wave radio network'). So the initial research question at Lancaster was: 'Can SE, which works in technical situations, be transferred to and used in *management* problem situations?' The answer to that question was 'No'!

Action research experiences quickly showed that the thinking entailed in SE was simply not rich enough to cope with the buzzing complexity and confusion in management situations. SE had to be transformed to cope with this level of complexity, and SSM is the re-invented and extended approach which experiential learning in many studies, large and small, in both companies and in the public sector, eventually produced. The action research programme entailed more than 300 studies, and ran for thirty years. The university-owned consultancy company operated for 20 of those. Thus SSM – though clearly never 'complete' – is now a mature and well-tested approach.

The shift from SE to SSM was not a single once-and-for-all change, made overnight. Rather, the transformation evolved as experiences accumulated; and as changes were made they were tested in new experiences. In this process it took some time for those developing SSM to realize that the intellectual gap between 'engineering' a 'system' to meet declared objectives and learning your way to defensible action-to-improve a situation was huge. It was a much more significant shift than had ever been imagined at the start of the action research programme (Checkland and Scholes, 1990/1999).

Systems Engineering resembles a number of the approaches developed in the field of Management Science in the 1950s and 1960s: classic Operational Research, RAND Systems Analysis, early Systems Dynamics, the Viable Systems Model, early computer systems analysis. All these approaches treat the word 'system' as the name for some real entity out there in the world which can be designed and

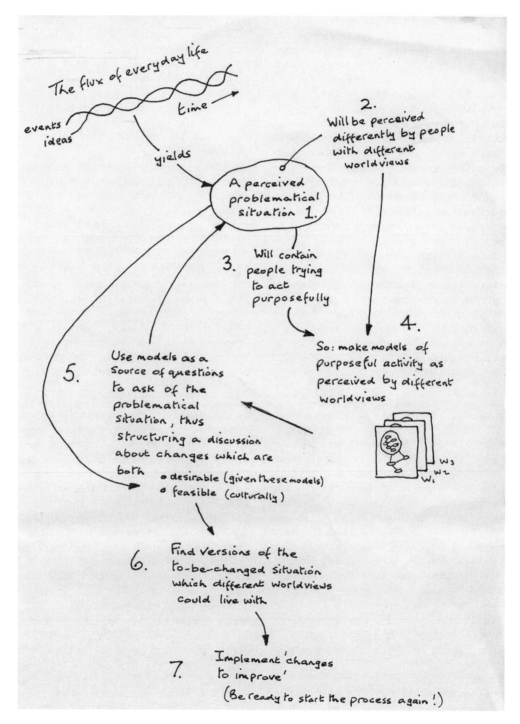

Figure 7   *SSM's cycle of learning for action (from Checkland and Poulter, 2006)*

engineered. This imprecise use of the word 'system' (taken from casual everyday language – as when we speak of 'the transport system', etc.) indicates the assumption, consciously or unthinkingly, of a positivist (q.v.) view of a designable external reality, in partnership with a functionalist sociology. The experiences in real situations in the action research programme made it impossible to see SSM as fitting into this positivist/functionalist framework (Checkland and Holwell, 1998).

To understand, appreciate and make sense of the research experiences, it was necessary to see 'social reality' not as systemic but as the outcome of a process in which human beings, the product of their genetic inheritance and previous experiences in the world, continually negotiate and re-negotiate with others their perceptions and interpretations of the world. This placed SSM in a phenomenological (q.v.) rather than positivist framework, and the sociology which makes sense of the structured discussion/debate in SSM is the interpretative sociology which Schutz [ethnomethodology] developed from Husserl's phenomenology.

Prospects

There is clearly a big step from what is now thought of as the 'hard' systems thinking of the 1950s and 1960s to the 'soft' systems thinking which SSM exemplifies. The step involves moving from seeing the *world* as systemic (as a set of interacting systems) to seeing *the process of inquiry into the world* as being capable of being organized as a learning system. This difference between 'hard' and 'soft' systems thinking is, for many people, difficult to take on board. The reason for this is that the casual everyday language use of the word 'system' is so deeply embedded in our consciousness. It is always a mistake to take everyday language to be precise enough for scholarship! However, that progress is being made is indicated by the fact that in the communities of practice in Operational Research and System Dynamics the phrases 'Soft OR' and 'Qualitative System Dynamics' are, respectively, now taken to be meaningful. This

signals the beginnings of a shift of focus from 'hard' to 'soft' systems thinking (Checkland and Holwell, 2004).

Peter Checkland

SPACE

Definition

Bachelard (1969) writes 'that space seized upon by the imagination cannot remain indifferent space subject to the measures and estimates of the surveyor' (1969: xxxvi). His is a notion of space that draws attention to the subjective and intensive dimensions of space. This view of space as *experienced space*, as subjective and partial, can be contrasted with accounts that attempt to operationalize the components that make up space. A spectrum extends between more positivist treatments of space and more phenomenologically oriented perspectives, in which space is constructed through experiential intensity, symbols and meaning [*phenomenology; positivism and post-positivism; realism*].

Discussion

From a positivist perspective, space becomes an independent variable: a modality that can be seen to influence working practice in varying ways depending on its multiple dimensions. Research in this tradition addresses the relation between workspace and its effect on stimulating the workforce (e.g. Vischer, 1999) or striving to measure workspace satisfaction more generally [*contingency theory*]. Other, more functional accounts build on Allen's seminal (1984) research on distance-interaction relationships in R&D projects. Here, distance is measured between different actors and is seen as one factor mediating the nature, essentially the frequency, of interpersonal exchange. Other studies in this vein focus on the distance and co-location of individuals as spatial factors affecting interpersonal interactions and information flow in organizations (Moenaert and Caeldries, 1996). Factors like strong visual and physical connections between spaces are seen to facilitate chance encounters and information flow between individuals (Bonetta, 2003). Furthermore, Brill's (2001) work shows that the two most important issues for productivity in regard to workspace are support for concentrated work and support for impromptu interactions.

The aim of objectively measuring spatial features, such as configuration of rooms, work stations or bays, and the modes of exchanging information, is also evident in design research aimed at exploring organizations (Penn et al., 1999). From a design perspective, researchers have investigated the relation between workspace and work patterns (Duffy, 1997), the role of distance (Moenaert and Caeldries, 1996) and spatial configuration (Hillier and Penn, 1991). These questions are relevant to debates on organizational performance. Effective workspace design that supports both concentrated work and the productive exchange of information can increase productivity and innovative performance.

In this line of scholarship, the aim is to disintegrate workspace into multiple features so as to explore their relationship with multiple work process variables that are critical to organizational performance. Attempts to operationalize the complexity of spatial practice build on elementary taxonomies such as Hall's (1966) proxemic framework, which identifies three categories of spatial features: fixed-feature space, semi-fixed feature space and non-fixed feature space. Fixed features involve firm building elements such as walls, doors and slabs. They resemble material limits for space use and human activities. Semi-fixed features are defined by semi-movable and movable objects like plants and furniture, which can be perceived differently in different contexts. Finally, non-fixed features are constituted by symbolic characteristics of space shaped by human behaviour, for example perceived boundaries that subtly divide up office spaces.

The positivist-empiricist interest at the heart of these studies leads to certain kinds of research method. For data collection on space use, information consumption and space–information consumption relationships, the use of logs, shadowing, survey tools, activity logs and observation through the use of video (q.v.) are proposed. The challenge is to collect data on consultation frequencies, types and location, without a burden to the practitioners but with precision (Toker, 2006).

This line of thinking stands in stark contrast with the subjectivist approach looking at the experience of space, and a socio-cultural view on how discourse and meaning structure the activity within space. The former is positivistic; it is about measurement and scientific rationalism. The latter involves spatial symbolism, poeticism and an emphasis on lived experience [*aesthetics; semiotics*].

From the subjective-experiential perspective, a different sense of space unfolds. Bachelard (1969), Lefebvre (1991), de Certeau (1984), Foucault (1984), Augé (1995) and others in this tradition focus less on constructing valid measures for space and instead concentrate on how space itself is socially constructed. Bachelard (1969) explores how space is shaped through the intensely subjective emotional experience of experiencing and dwelling in spaces like the family home. He charts an intimate poetic intensity of certain spaces and offers his own classification of space, ranging from the miniscule to the immense. Lefebvre (1991) focuses on how space is contested and produced variously as a lived space full of intensity and possibility or as a reified and commoditized space shaped by market and administrative forces. De Certeau (1984) connects with Lefebvre's themes and charts not just the homogenized places conjured up by planners and bureaucratic elites, but notes how they can be subverted and resisted through so-called tactics and ruses that are part of the practices of everyday life. Foucault (1984) equally underscores the role of discourse, power and authorized knowledge in shaping the nature of space. However, he also points to so-called heterotopic spaces, which are inherently contradictory, at once real and imaginary, which eschew dominant conceptions of space [*postmodernism*]. Finally, Augé (1995) introduces the notion of non-place, which adds to the existing classifications of space by denoting those generic, anti-historical and fundamentally homogenized spaces such as supermarkets and car parks, airport lounges and the many cubicles of contemporary office work.

Problems and prospects

Understanding space, particularly its emotional, imaginative and intuitive influence, is difficult because, by definition, its materiality is one of absence; space is no frontier at all. Moreover, variations in the use and appeal of space are configured by a multiplicity of influences [*ethnography; ethnomethodology*] that are temporally bound [*activity theory*] and which are never monolithic – appropriateness is always contested [*relativism*]. Moreover, it is also important to think of both material and symbolic approaches as providing an analytical language and a set of conceptual metaphors [*metaphor*] with which to think about space rather than a set of tools with which to measure it. Those interested in researching space should be aware of the spectrum of existing work, extending from subjective and interpretative accounts to more positivist accounts. Aligning a suitable conceptual and methodological armature will necessarily depend on the aims of research and the ensuing research questions. In defining one's conceptual position, however, it can be useful to take the contrasting traditions into account, creating a more qualified and nuanced space for inquiry itself.

Boris Ewenstein

STAKEHOLDER THEORY

Definition

The term 'stakeholder', first used in 1963 by the Stanford Research Institute's Long Range Planning Service, is 'an obvious literary device meant to call into question the emphasis on "stockholders"' (Freeman, 1999: 234). Stakeholders are classically defined as 'any group or individual who can affect or is affected by the achievement of the organization's objectives' (Freeman, 1984: 46) and are taken to include shareholders, employees, customers, suppliers and society, at a minimum. The stakeholder theory of the firm was initially conceived as a theory of strategic management (Freeman, 1984) but developed as a theory of business ethics in the subsequent years (Phillips, 2003). From a research perspective, it broadens the unit of analysis to cover all of those who have an interest in an organization's activity, suggesting that to understand management and organizational life it is not sufficient to simply limit attention to the study of managers and organizations *per se*.

Discussion

If the word 'stakeholder' were a person, it would be just coming into its prime. Born in 1963, it has accumulated experience in influential positions and ought to be prepared for some serious responsibility. (Slinger, 1999: 136)

By now it is evident that 'the term stakeholder is a powerful one' (Phillips et al., 2003: 479). The stakeholder concept has grown in prominence over recent years due to public interest, increased coverage in the media, concern about corporate governance, and its adoption by 'third-way' politics.[1] According to Freeman and Phillips (2002: 332), 'the past 15 years has seen the development of the idea of stakeholders into an "idea of currency"'. This represents a rare case where philosophical terminology has become part of the popular lexicon (Bowie, 2002).

The appeal of stakeholder theory for management theorists is both empirical and normative. Empirically, stakeholder theory 'rests on an observation or what we might call a

---

[1] The popular use of the term culminated in its use in a speech given by Tony Blair while he was leader of the UK opposition Labour party in January 1996.

fact' (Cragg, 2002: 115), that is, that managers should attend to stakeholders, and hence so should researchers. Normatively, stakeholder theory conveys the notion that fundamental moral principles influence corporate activities (Cragg, 2002). Stakeholder theory involves researchers addressing morals and values explicitly as a central feature of managing organizations (Phillips et al., 2003). The distinction of stakeholder theory does not lie in its moral content *per se*, but rather in the acknowledgement and centrality of moral content; the researcher cannot invoke a scientifically neutral or dispassionate stance [*critical theory; positivism and post-positivism*].

As a consequence of the ubiquity of the stakeholder idea, the concept has become everything to everyone and has been put at risk of being diluted to the point that it holds little meaning (Phillips et al., 2003). Unsurprisingly, critics have swooped to attack stakeholder theory as friend and foe (Phillips, 2003) and from both the right and the left (Stoney and Winstanley, 2001). The right has criticized stakeholder theory for being destructive of the purpose of the corporation (Barry, 2002), distracting researchers and being tantamount to socialism (Sternberg, 1997). The left has criticized stakeholder theory as being apologist to managerialism (Banerjee, 2000) and encouraging researchers to neglect the fundamental issue of structural power differences between owners and non-owners of capital (Stoney and Winstanley, 2001) [*actor-network theory; phronetic organizational research*].

Among researchers advocating the importance of recognizing stakeholders, three concerns are consistently raised: the lack of a normative core defining their approach; the inability to properly identify stakeholders; and the lack of a method for balancing competing stakeholder interests. Developments in stakeholder theory have sought to address these shortcomings, some of which are described forthwith.

Differentiating stakeholder theory by its normative core

Stakeholder theory is best understood as a rubric of theoretical approaches rather than as a single unified theory. Donaldson and Preston (1995) posited that stakeholder theory comprises three strands of theory: descriptive, instrumental and normative, all of which are interrelated. Researchers split into two camps, some supporting the notion of divergent stakeholder theories and others supporting the notion of convergent stakeholder theory. Freeman (1999) cautioned against the 'separation thesis' – that the moral side of business can be divorced from the pragmatic side of business (Jones et al., 2002). Kaler (2003), however, prefers a typology of stakeholder theories based on the extent to which serving the interests of non-owner stakeholders is accepted as a responsibility of the organization being researched.

Identifying stakeholders

Stakeholder theory offers a 'maddening list of signals' on how the question of stakeholder identification can be answered (Mitchell et al., 1997). Researchers looking to identify stakeholders tend to distinguish primary or direct stakeholders, such as employees or customers, from secondary or indirect stakeholders, such as the natural environment or future generations. It is tempting to see the broader definition of stakeholders as the more moral or responsible definition and that which looks to advance understanding of what constitutes the subject matter of management and organizational research. However, Phillips (1999: 32) holds that that 'stakeholder theory is meaningless unless it is usefully delineated'. Hence, it may be more useful to consider definitions as depicting stakeholders either in an influential relationship with an organization (influenced by or influencing it) or in a moral relationship (having a moral claim) (Kaler, 2002). Circumscription is needed not only for sound theorizing – demarcation of stakeholders allows for a moral relationship between the organization and its stakeholders by excluding those stakeholders without a moral stake – but also for defining the limits of the discipline itself. Clearly, not all social phenomena can fall into the rubric of stakeholder research without undermining the distinctiveness of the field.

Balancing conflicting stakeholder needs

Managers balance conflicting stakeholder interests according to their perception of the importance of the various stakeholders. Mitchell et al's (1997) instrumental model of stakeholder salience is based on both influence (power) and moral claim (legitimacy) as well as the urgency of the claims. Phillips's (1997) normative principle of fairness claims that stakeholders should be returned benefits, or be protected from harm, in proportion to their contribution to the firm.

Prospects

There are many possibilities for the future of stakeholder theory. With a rise in the standing of moral pluralism (Nieuwenburg, 2004), stakeholder theory has a distinct role as a pragmatic (q.v.) pluralist theory of business ethics. Stakeholder theory may drive the application of business ethics to various fields of management studies, such as human resource management (Greenwood and De Cieri, 2007) and social and environmental reporting (O'Dwyer et al., 2005). Some important challenges that stakeholder theory faces are the presence of systemic control and power in the organization–stakeholder relationship and the corresponding need to address the position of powerless stakeholders such as indentured workers (Van Buren, 2001) and indigenous owners of devastated natural environments (Banerjee, 2000).

Michelle Greenwood

STIMULATED RECALL

Definition

Simulated recall (SR) as a research approach falls into the group of research methods that are often referred to as introspective methods. In general it is considered to be an approach that is particularly suitable for examining processes and has most frequently been used to study learning processes, interpersonal skills and decision-making processes [*action learning*]. As a method it has some similarities to protocol analysis, as originally developed by Newall Simon, to examine decision-making processes. Protocol analysis is, however, increasingly utilized more by software developers and information scientists for both designing and managing, in particular, design support systems (DSS), but also information systems and computer networks more generally. Stimulated recall, on the other hand, continues to be used by, in particular, educational and medical/clinical researchers as well as by second language researchers. Within medical research, for example, it is frequently applied as a method for examining the clinical reasoning processes of medical students, doctors and/or consultants.

In general, as Howard Barrows comments in his book *Stimulated Recall (Personalized Assessment of Clinical Reasoning)* (Barrows, 2000), stimulated recall remains an underutilized research method because, he claims, its existence is generally not widely recognized nor its usefulness appreciated. Indeed, its application in the field of management has been limited. The early study by Burgoyne and Hodgson (1983), where it was used in a study of natural learning and managerial action, remains one of the few applications of the method for management research purposes. Within education, however, it has been used for researching educational leadership issues and decision-making.

Discussion

As an approach, stimulated recall involves playing back a recorded protocol of a situation, interaction or event to a person(s) in order to stimulate the thoughts or feelings that they were having at the time of the event. It is an approach that was originally developed by B.S. Bloom to compare students' thought processes in lectures and discussion groups (Bloom, 1953).

Bloom audio-taped the teaching situation and then, within two days, played back to the individual students extracts from the session. Each student was then asked to recall the thoughts he or she had during the original situation, the idea being to use stimuli and cues to allow a subject to relive and account for an experience [*inductive analysis; interviewing; interviews; psychoanalytic approaches*].

Bloom's use of stimulated recall was further developed by Siegel and his colleagues in a later study in which the students attended not a live lecture but a video-recorded (q.v.) lecture. Immediately after watching it they were tested on the content of what had been lectured on. Then extracts were played back to them (still as a group) and they were asked to write down what they had been thinking during the original presentation (Siegel et al., 1963).

Siegel et al. found a correlation between the test score (assumed to be a measure of knowledge gained from the original presentation) and the relevance of the thinking recorded by students. They argued they were improving upon Bloom's approach in three ways:

1. The recall is better the sooner it is done.
2. Audio tape reproduces only a portion of the original classroom experience.
3. Their version is less laborious than collecting data on an individual basis [*interviews – groups*].

Bloom himself tested the adequacy of playing back extracts to students who were then asked what overt events (i.e. activities, specific talk or particular gestures and mannerisms) followed immediately after that particular point in the recording. He found that recall of the events was 95 per cent accurate provided this was done within two days of the original experience. It might be assumed from this that students can recall their own thoughts and feelings during the extract with similar accuracy.

When using stimulated recall Bloom and Siegel et al. chose the extracts (critical incidents (q.v.)) to play back to students. Bloom gives no indication of the criteria he used for

his choice, but in their research Siegel et al. suggest a link between critical incidents and when the lecturer asked a question or defined terms.

An alternative approach was developed by Kagan et al. (1967) who video-taped a number of interactive situations. They then played back the tapes to the participants, who, with the help of a trained recall interviewer, were encouraged to ask for the tape to be stopped when they had something to recall. The key difference in this approach is that the participants themselves are mainly responsible for the selection of extracts. Kagan et al. believed that given enough cues and clues to help them relive an experience, a person's feelings and thoughts could be explored in depth and with reasonable accuracy.

Prospects

The paper, 'Stimulated recall: A report on its use in naturalistic research', by Lyle (2003), gives a good account of some of the criticisms that exist about the method. The accuracy in terms of validity and reliability (q.v.) of people's accounts has been one of the criticisms of the approach [*non-participant observation*]. The main criticism, however, is that the subject may be reacting/describing his or her feelings to what they currently see or hear and not recalling the thoughts or feelings at the time of an actual episode or interaction. It is also important to acknowledge the distinction between recall of an event and reflection on an event and for this reason questioning is considered a significant issue when using SR, as inappropriate probing leads to additional reflection and analysis rather than recall.

In general, it has to be said, those studies that have adopted stimulated recall as a research approach have found that it produces both insightful and useful data for examining the way people experience a specific event of interaction. It does, I still believe, offer enormous potential as a method for management researchers.

Vivien Hodgson

STORYTELLING IN MANAGEMENT RESEARCH

Definition

The *storytelling turn* in management and organization research occurred over the last thirty years. It began by treating story in the 1980s as static text, turned in the 1990s to the *in situ* dynamics of co-producing stories, and in the 2000s to the systemic complexity of *storytelling organization*. There are numerous ways to define storytelling and each takes research in a different direction. Definition is important to researchers; to decide to privilege narrative or story, sample terse or coherent text, look at text with or without context, and if, in context, to sample only the managerialist story or include the marginal counter-stories of less powerful stakeholders (q.v.).

Narrativists (q.v.) marginalize the story. Czarniawska (1997, 1998) defines stories as must-have plots, but later (1999) discounts the story to plotless narrative: 'A story consists of a plot comprising causally related episodes that culminate in a solution to a problem' (Czarniawska, 1997: 78), then discounts the story to 'texts that present events developing in time according to (impersonal) causes or (human) intentions' (Czarniawska, 1998: vii). And back to plot: 'For them to become a narrative, they require a plot, that is, some way to bring them into a meaningful whole' (Czarniawska, 1999: 2).[1]

Gabriel marginalizes narrative and debates what is a story. For Gabriel (2000: 20), a *proper* story does more than recount facts or describe experience; it must have emotion, poetic embellishment, and be cohesive, plotted with a beginning, middle, and end: 'I shall argue not all narratives are stories; in particular, factual or descriptive accounts of events that aspire at objectivity rather than emotional effect must not be treated as stories' (Gabriel, 2000: 5). Gabriel's definition is

the opposite to Czarniawska's (1999). '*Stories are narratives with plots and characters, generating emotion in narrator and audience, through a poetic elaboration of symbolic material*' (Gabriel, 2000: 239, italics in original).

An early story definition, 'an oral or written performance involving two or more people interpreting past or anticipated experience' (Boje, 1991: 111), is not so restrictive as Gabriel's or Czarniawska's. This approach is to include stories that are terse, fragmented, disputed with counter-stories to dominant ones, and antenarrative (q.v.) (Boje, 1991, 1995, 2001). Antenarrative is defined as a pre-story, and a bet that you can create a story that will change organizations (Boje, 2001: 1), and can be theatrically performed to 'enroll stakeholders in "intertextual" ways transforming the world of action into theatrics' (Boje et al., 2004a: 756). This research has led to systemics of *storytelling organization* (Boje, 1991, 1995; Boje et al., 1999; Boyce, 1995; Gephart, 1991; Kaye, 1996).

I propose a way out of Czarniawska's, Gabriel's, and Boje's debates by looking at how story *and* narrative interact in complex organizations. Why not treat improper stories (and antenarrative) that are pre-plotted, terse, and even emergently incoherent in their *in situ* interrelationship to proper stories and narratives that are plotted and coherent? The advantage is looking more precisely at the relationship between storytellers and listeners.

An *inclusive* storytelling turn invites researchers to recognize how story listeners are no longer static story-consumers, but producers of story space, defined as systemic interactivity of stories, narratives, and antenarratives co-produced, co-shared, co-remembered, and otherwise co-organized in *storytelling organizations* [*reading*]. One type of storytelling organization is the *Tamara*. *Tamara organizing* is defined as the plurality of simultaneous, performative story spaces and the networking of co-producers in complex

---

[1]Her definition recalls Polkinghorne's (1988: 36): story: 'serves as a lens through which the apparently independent and disconnected elements of existence are seen as related parts of a whole'.

organizations (Boje, 1995). Instead of seated spectators statically watching the theatre on stage, consumers of Krizanc's (1989) *Tamara* become co-producers, by moving around a mansion with ten rooms, deciding which simultaneous action to join into; the audience fragments, small groups running from room to room, chasing storylines, and becoming actor and spectator (spect-actor).

Discussion

The first trend looks at stories-out-of-context. Stories in laboratory, interview (q.v.), and survey research generally have been wrenched from their natural performance contexts and treated as objectified social facts, mere texts, with little empirical attention given to the natural linguistic context in which stories are being performed. Researchers must decide if they are looking at the relationship between the story and the *in situ* performance context or just at story text as an in-place metering device to measure some other phenomena such as culture, tacit knowledge, or sensemaking (q.v.).

A second stream of research looks at stories in their performance context, but from a functionalist point of view. O'Connor (2002), for example, identifies studies that analyzed storytelling in functionalist managerialist studies (especially the organizational culture work of the 1980s). This would include stories elicited in researcher-led interviews (e.g. Martin et al., 1983) to demonstrate functional uses of storytelling such as socialization (Knowledge Socialization Project at IBM Research),[2] control (Wilkins, 1983), change (Denning, 2005), typologies of strategy-stories (Barry and Elmes, 1997), entrepreneurship (O'Connor, 2000), and story-leadership ethnography (Boje, 1991).

A third stream is managerialist, but restricts a story to the status of a 'tool' (Denning, 2001; Gargiulo, 2002; Parkin, 2004). Denning ignores context, and coaches CEOs to construct tool stories that are explicitly familiar to

listeners, single-protagonist, and positive with a happy ending; the 'springboard' story is defined as 'a story that enables a leap in understanding by the audience so as to grasp how an organization or community or complex system may change' (Denning 2001: xviii). Gargiulo (2002: 35–36) includes the negative story. He cautions that stories can be weapons, propaganda, and what con artists do. He coaches CEOs (and HR trainers) to create a tool box of many stories. For CEOs who find crafting a springboard story or an entire box of them, Parkin (2004) just assembles 50 folktales and spiritual stories. Left unanswered in management research is the effectiveness of tool stories, and the differences between ones built in context and those imported from some foreign context.

The fourth stream steers clear of functionalist/managerialist story study. This includes studies in critical theory (Mumby, 1987) and postmodernism (Boje, 1995; Boje and Rhodes, 2005), poststructuralist/deconstruction (q.v.) (Martin, 1990), intertextuality studies (O'Connor, 2002), and feminism (q.v.) studies (Calás and Smircich, 1991). The focus is on pluralism of narrative form, multiple ways of interpreting stories, and uncovering suppressed, marginalized, or hidden stories as a counter-narrative to the conventional storyline of a particular organization and its spokespersons.

In terms of knowledge and networking, the four streams approach story quite differently. The managerialist/functionalist researchers focus on how storytelling is used to transfer knowledge from network participants (individuals) to the system (institution). A critical theory (q.v.) study sets out to find ways to liberate individuals (classes or gender/race) from exploitative knowledge transfer. Critical postmodern (q.v.), poststructuralist, feminist, and intertextual studies look at a plurality of knowledge constituted by a variety of storytellers, some more powerful than others, and at counter-story. Finally, future research can

---

[2] www.research.ibm.com/knowsoc/index.html

benefit from looking at the emergent system complexity (q.v.) aspects of the storytelling organization. This includes the interaction of antenarrative and narrative as well as proper and improper story forms, in acts of co-production, co-consumption, and co-distribution in storied systems.

In sum, the storytelling turn is from static story consumers, or story treated as an in-place device to meter some other construct, to story co-production and story hegemony – that is what complexity and organizing are all about.

David M. Boje

STRUCTURATION THEORY

Definition

Structuration theory proposes that the social sciences investigate neither human agency nor social structures but the social practices by which both agency and structure are created and sustained; the emphasis is on their relational, co-constituting complicity in action.

Discussion

The relationship between agency and structure is among the most pervasive and difficult issues in social theory. How are actions of individual agents related to the structural properties of societies and social systems, and vice versa? Trying to understand such a relationship, researchers very often tend towards a dichotomist view, giving primacy to agency (voluntarism) or to structure (determinism). Therefore, researchers are skilled in creating dichotomies (other classical examples are meaning/cause, autonomy/tradition and micro/macro) that, once established, end up hiding the emergence of other ways of thinking, which are sometimes more creative, opportune, less confined to institutionalized meanings, or simply different [practice theory; pragmatism]. It is from the above perspective – the openness to alternative views – that the

potential of Giddens's propositions, which have been adopted by a number of management researchers since the 1980s, can be interpreted. In a number of articles in the late 1970s and early 1980s, culminating with the publication of The Constitution of Society in 1984, British sociologist Anthony Giddens addressed fundamental problems in the social sciences in a way that was unconventional at the time. He challenged the premise of mutual exclusivity and assumed the duality of structure and action, proposing a form of social analysis that avoids the historical division between determinist and voluntarist views, and that helps to bridge micro- and macro-levels of analysis.

Giddens is not alone in proposing alternative forms of social analysis and avoiding dualist logic. Other examples are Bourdieu's (1977) interplay between objectivism and subjectivism, Bernstein's (1983) move beyond objectivism and relativism (q.v.), Bhaskar's (1979a/1989) account of positivism (q.v.) and postmodernism (q.v.) [critical realism], and Fay's (1996) discussion of science versus hermeneutics (q.v.). Examples of the extensions of such a debate into management and organizational studies are Reed's (1997) discussion of duality and dualism, Willmott's (1993a) break from paradigm mentality and Weaver and Gioia's (1994) incommensurability versus structurationist inquiry. All these alternative accounts represent efforts to overcome 'narrow' dualistic thinking and to explore new interpretations of renowned sociological dilemmas. Most of them are not 'competitors' but 'alternatives', and the choice among them is often a matter of 'ontological affinity' (Pozzebon, 2004).

To examine the dualism between structure and agency, Giddens departed from the conceptualization of structure as some given or external form. Structure is what gives form and shape to social life, but it is not itself the form and shape. Structure exists only in and through the activities of human agents (Giddens, 1989). Similarly, he departed from the idea of agency as something just 'contained' within the individual. Agency does not refer to people's intentions in doing things but rather to the flow or pattern of people's actions. Giddens deeply reformulated the notions of structure and agency, emphasizing that 'action, which has strongly routinized aspects, is both conditioned by existing cultural structures and also creates and recreates those structures through the enactment process' (Walsham, 1993: 34). He suggested that while structural properties of societies and social systems are real, they have no physical existence. Instead, they depend upon regularities of social reproduction (Giddens and Pierson, 1998). As a consequence, the basic domain of study in the social sciences consists of social practices ordered across space and time (Giddens, 1984: 2).

Complementary to the notion of duality of structure is the concept of knowledgeability. For Giddens (1984), all actors are socially competent. The core idea is reflexivity: the capacity of humans to be reflexive (q.v.) – to think about their situation – entails the ability to change it. The concepts of duality of structure and knowledgeability are, indeed, interrelated. In fact, the structurationist way of interpreting the interplay between structure and action requires competent and reflexive actors. Additional key concepts in structuration theory are: structures of signification, domination and legitimation; structuring modalities (interpretative schemes, facilities and norms); elements of interaction (communication, power and sanction); consciousness (discursive and practical) and unconsciousness; and time–space distantiation (Giddens, 1984).

Prospects

By providing an account of the constitution of social life that departed from and challenged established theoretical positions and traditions (Giddens, 1976, 1979, 1984), structuration theory drew significant attention, and numerous books and papers promptly emerged discussing, scrutinizing, supporting or criticizing (Held and Thompson, 1989). However theoretically promising, the applicability of Giddens' concepts is not without difficulties. Structuration theory is conceptually complex, articulating concepts from

psychoanalysis (q.v.), phenomenology (q.v.), ethnomethodology (q.v.), and action theory [*action science*], among others. Based on general propositions and concepts that operate at a high level of abstraction, structuration theory gives rise to diverse and sometimes contradictory interpretations (Pozzebon and Pinsonneault, 2005).

Despite all the obstacles and criticism, structuration theory has played a relevant role in investigations concerning organizations and their management, and individuals and their choices. Since the publication of *The constitution of society* (Giddens, 1984), researchers in diverse fields have made use of concepts drawn from structuration theory in pursuing both conceptual discussions and empirical inquiries. However, much of structuration theory's potential for helping to increase the understanding of management issues remains to be developed.

Marlei Pozzebon

SYSTEMATIC LITERATURE REVIEWS

Definition

Systematic literature reviews (SLRs) are methods for making sense of large volumes of information. They are used to interpret this information in order to explain 'what works' and 'what does not work' when exploring specific research themes, social policy or practical issues (Petticrew and Roberts, 2006). SLRs are designed to identify existing gaps in a field of research and to make recommendations for closing these gaps. The point is to bring together the evidence base on a particular theme in order to make credible policy, research or practical recommendations [*reliability*].

SLRs originated in medicine where they were used to bridge the gap between research knowledge and practice. The method has since filtered into many science and social science disciplines and it is often used to help inform policy-making. In many cases, when conducting a review, an SLR uses citation indices, a research protocol, search strings, inclusion and exclusion criteria and quality assessment criteria (Tranfield et al., 2003). There are a number of key principles behind SLRs (Pittaway et al., 2004; Thorpe et al., 2005):

1. Transparency – the approach used when undertaking the review is recorded and made available when reporting the study.
2. Clarity – there is a clear series of steps through which the researcher proceeds and these steps present an 'audit trail' that can be scrutinized.
3. Focus – the review ensures a focused approach around a clearly formulated question.
4. Integration – SLRs are designed to link research communities with practitioners and policy-makers.
5. Equality – there is no distinction made on principle between different forms of publication output (e.g. between policy reports and academic journals).
6. Accessibility – SLRs seek to make the output from reviews more widely available outside the research community.
7. Coverage – the systematic nature of the review should ensure extensive coverage of the theme, in many cases across disciplines and subjects.
8. Synthesis – SLRs seek to compare, contrast and draw conclusions across a number of fields to present the current 'evidence base'.

Discussion

The method is relatively new in management and organization research and has been developed and argued for by researchers at Cranfield School of Management (Denyer and Neely, 2004; Tranfield et al., 2003). The 'Cranfield method' of SLRs mirrors in many respects common practice in other social sciences. It involves a number of stages and processes which are followed by the researcher. Stage 1 involves planning the review: identifying the need; preparing a proposal; and developing the review protocol.

Stage 2 involves conducting the review: identifying the publications; selecting the studies; assessing quality; extracting data and conclusions; and synthesizing the data. Stage 3 involves reporting and dissemination: developing the report and recommendations; and making use of the evidence in practice. Underpinning these stages are some key elements that are often applied in the Cranfield method. For example, this method of SLRs usually requires a review panel to be formed, including the research sponsors, the researchers and other experts. The panel provides a narrative cross-reference, checking through knowledgeable experience that the SLR is picking up appropriate work and not missing anything important. The SLR method also uses inclusion and exclusion criteria. These are criteria set from the outset that define what is to be reviewed. In addition, quality criteria are set and used to judge the weight that is given to certain findings as they emerge, for example, influenced by the robustness of the method used to conduct the research [*inductive analysis*]. In setting such criteria, the review process seeks to enable effective but clear synthesis of findings related to the subject in order to provide practical or policy recommendations [*mode 2*].

The Cranfield method, as outlined above, has been used in a number of studies. Most notably, the Advanced Institute of Management Research (AIM) used it in three studies designed to explore innovation and productivity on behalf of the Department and Trade and Industry (DTI) (Denyer and Neely, 2004). These studies on networking and innovation (Pittaway et al., 2004); the adoption of promising practices (Leseure et al., 2004); and value creation (Edwards et al., 2004) were followed by a study conducted on behalf of the Economic and Social Research Council (ESRC) on knowledge within small and medium-sized firms (Thorpe et al., 2005) and small firms and growth (Macpherson and Holt, 2007). In many of these studies, the SLR method was used to expand both the thematic understanding and conceptual treatment of the subject as well as providing a current picture of the status of research in the field (Pittaway et al., 2004; Thorpe et al., 2005).

Prospects

The SLR method is at an early stage in its development within management research. It is an extremely valuable tool, providing a *method for conducting literature reviews*. SLRs are improvements on the traditional 'narrative' method because they provide a transparent and clear approach which is reported to the reader, who can then critique it. They also provide a thematic understanding (rather than a subject-based one) which enhances conceptual understanding (Thorpe et al., 2005). Currently, the process behind a narrative review is often ambiguous and, therefore, less open to scrutiny. The SLR method is most valuable when it is seeking to translate and synthesize academic research so that it can be applied in policy or practical contexts. SLRs do not, however, replace narrative methods, or expertise in a given subject, because they do not necessarily provide the same 'intuitive'

qualities and are best viewed as supporting methods. Inevitably, however, it is expected that the use of SLRs will expand. It is likely to become a more central feature in doctoral programmes and a common requirement in publicly sponsored research. The Cranfield method of SLRs, however, is one method for conducting a literature review and it is one form of systematic method. As the concept of using and reporting a 'method' for doing a literature review becomes more widespread, it is expected that a wide range of alternatives (usually based on different epistemological assumptions) will emerge. These may include 'narrative' or 'interpretative' methods where the approach is more openly reported than in current practice, and alternative methods which are equally systematic but very different from the Cranfield method. A particular issue that faces these future approaches is how to integrate the intuitive benefits of narrative methods with the systematic benefits of SLRs.

Luke Pittaway

TAYLORISM

Definition

Taylorism relates to sets of techniques associated with standardization, planning and measurement designed to control the behaviour of employees in workplaces. Named after Frederick Winslow Taylor – or 'Speedy Taylor' as he became known – who, in his books *Shop Management* (1903) and *Principles of Scientific Management* (1911), recognized that, with technological advances (beginning almost a century earlier with machinery such as Hargreaves's 'Spinning Jenny' and Arkwright's 'Waterframe') and the growth in organizational size, there was an increasing shift in the way work was being done. No longer tied to a skill or craft, workers' sense of autonomy and self-identity was becoming increasingly associated with the contractual arrangements by which they were employed [*modernism and scientific management*]. The actual task was secondary to their legal rights. This lessening of association between what a worker *did* and who a worker *was* opened up the possibilities of controlling the nature of work through management; an interference that would be tolerated provided the wages stemming from contractual undertakings were sufficient compensation. The problem Taylor then recognized was that of equipping managers with tools to bring about such control and order, thereby increasing efficiency and combating the restrictive control of output levels by groups of workers commonly referred to as 'systematic soldiering'. The chosen tools were those such as time and motion studies and information management systems, tools whose application divided work practices into their barest component elements, thereby making the nature of work transparent and malleable. Workers became embedded in the minutiae of tasks, components in organizational processes, and would tolerate such deskilling and repetition because of higher wages. Organizations themselves would lose any mystery or even tradition, becoming identified by clear lines of authority, responsibility, the separation of planning from operations, and procedurally governed by the use of incentives and management by exception.

Discussion

Guillén (2006) reminds us that the origins of scientific management stem from the latter half of the nineteenth century, although others have identified the same focus on order and standardization as far back as Mencius (372–289BC), whose models and systems pointed to the advantage of the division of labour [*Confucianism*]. So it would be a mistake to view Taylorist principles as entirely down to Taylor. Adam Smith's *The Wealth of Nations* (1776) envisaged the possibilities of improved efficiency through specialization and the division of labour, though it warned of their corrosive influence on the human moral sentiments. Similarly, in 1798, Eli Whitley, a musket maker, produced muskets containing interchangeable parts and used cost accounting techniques to control quality. Charles Babbage's *On the Economy of Machinery Manufactures* (1832) brought Smith's insights on the division of labour into line with payment systems, arguing that only that amount of skill needed to undertake the hardest of any specialized task needed to be paid for at the highest rate, with the lower skilled tasks being able to be completed and paid for at a lower rate.

Taylorism in the way it is used today stems from the aftermath of the American Civil War when the growth of American industry led to all manner of difficulties associated with the management of ever more complex tasks and the need for managers to bring a sense of order into the workplace. Bendix (2001) talks of the 'American System' where innovation met the challenge of complexity and where mechanization and standardization and the move to systematic management were seen as the means of bringing much needed economy and efficiency into being. Taylor's response to these challenges was to propose a 'science' of management in which every organizational activity would be parsed into its tightest algorithmic form, linking movement with output and remuneration in a neatly ordered, orchestrated whole. Coupled to this was the 'scientific' selection, training and development of the workforce, including foremen and managers – very much the forerunner of today's systematic use of job descriptions and person specifications. The ethic informing this tightly controlled integration was known as a 'spirit of hearty co-operation', extending between workers and managers, coupled to a rational choice logic in which motivation was associated with monetary reward. The assumption was that employees came to work to earn money and that they would work harder if they were given more money for better work.

Taylorism is rightly associated with such names as Gilbreth (1911), who developed time and motion applications for both motion economies and micro-motion studies; Gant, who examined aspects of scheduling work through visual process charts; and Ford, who took on Taylor's mantle and extended his ideas to perfect the moving assembly line. Both before, during and after the Second World War ever more sophisticated methods of scientific management came into use, for example inventory control systems in the 1930s, statistical quality control methods in the 1950s and the whole field of operational research in the 1950s and 1960s.

Prospects

There are decidedly objectivist and positivistic (q.v.) notions in Taylorism; a belief that there is *one best way* (a term coined by Gilbreth) and that there are procedures that can be designed and followed to optimize human work so as to realize such a way. What Taylor and his contemporaries created is still commonplace today in beliefs about what counts in terms of performance and efficiency (Lupton, 2000). These include, notions of lean thinking, business process re-engineering, management by objectives, downsizing and even the emergence of group incentives and company-wide gainsharing schemes. Yet it is also clear, at least from the first studies of managerial work published in Sweden in 1951, closely followed by other studies in the UK and the USA, that the managerial task was far from being just a matter of planning, decision-making and directing, but was much more 'messy', involving trouble-shooting, negotiating and 'politics'. No matter how controlling the overt procedures, there is always room for briccolage and spillage. Hence calls for control have taken on a more cultural spin, meaning Taylorism itself has become one active component of a wider philosophy of social control.

Richard Thorpe and Tom Lupton

TEMPLATE ANALYSIS

Definition

One of the key issues facing the qualitative researcher is how to effectively manage the volume of text that is generated by qualitative research. Evidence suggests that this issue is the source of some anxiety, particularly for new qualitative researchers who may be somewhat daunted by the sheer amount of data produced in a qualitative study (Cassell et al., 2005) [*process research*]. The primary concern is where to start in the long and involved process of making sense of the data collected. Template analysis is a structured technique for analysing qualitative data that enables researchers to place some order on their data from the start of the analytic process. The key advantage of the technique therefore is that through its application, researchers have a relatively clear path to follow in creating a structure for the analysis of their data.

Discussion

Template analysis is not a new form of analysis, the label first being used by Crabtree and Miller (1992) with regard to the use of 'codebooks' for the analysis of text. The recent expansion of interest and use in the technique in the management field can be attributed to Nigel King. As well as producing two influential chapters about how to conduct template analysis in the management and organizational field (King, 1998, 2004), King has also established a website at the University of Huddersfield which contains resources for those interested in using this particular technique (www.hud.ac. uk/hhs/research/template_analysis/index. htm).

The technique relies upon the coding of text in a thematic way to produce a given structure, or template. Other authors have also outlined different ways of thematically categorizing and analyzing text, without the use of the word 'template'. For example, Dey's (2003) approach to qualitative data analysis can be seen to advocate the creation of a structure for the data through the assigning of chunks of data to particular categories. Similarly, Robson (1993/2002), when outlining some rules for the analysis of qualitative data, recommends that themes, categories and codes should be generated as the analysis progresses [*inductive analysis; matrices analysis; systematic literature reviews*]. Additionally, the processes to designing a template are similar to the 'classic set of analytic moves' outlined by Miles and Huberman (1994b: 9).

The key component of template analysis is the design of a template into which different chunks of data can be categorized. The process through which the initial template is designed depends upon the approach of the researcher and is influenced by issues such as epistemological preferences, and the extent to which the study has structured research questions. For example, the themes within the template can be defined before the template is constructed. They may be taken from the questions in an interview (q.v.) schedule, for instance, or explicitly link in to the study's research questions. This is a useful approach when a study has clearly defined research questions, and the researcher has some idea about how he/she wants to interrogate the data. An alternative approach, in line with the processes of grounded theory (q.v.), is to generate the themes from the data itself. Once the themes within the template are generated, various extracts from the data are coded into those themes. One of the key strengths of template analysis is that templates are very flexible. Through the coding process, new themes within the template can be created in which to site data that do not appropriately fit elsewhere. Therefore new themes for analysis can be accommodated that were not necessarily conceived at the outset of the research. Templates can be regularly modified as the analytic process develops.

Although a number of published qualitative research studies within the management field have drawn on the principles of template analysis, those which explicitly refer to the term as a way of structuring data as have only just started to emerge. Examples include Cassell et al. (2002); Parry (2003); Canning and O'Dwyer (2003); Waddington and Fletcher (2005); Warnaby and Yip (2005); Cassell et al. (2006); Richardson and McKenna (2006); Duberley et al. (2006); and Yanamanadram and White (2006). These examples illustrate some of the different ways in which templates can be used, and also come from a range of sub-disciplines within the business and management field, for example accounting, human resource management, marketing, and services management. One could speculate that qualitative research informed by template analysis will become increasingly reported within the business and management literature, the flexibility of the application of the technique being a key incentive for researchers to engage with it.

Prospects

Template analysis is clearly not applicable in all qualitative research situations. Although a strength of the technique is that it is epistemologically flexible, and not wedded to a single epistemological position, this may make it inappropriate for some types of qualitative research. As King (2004) suggests, in some of the more constructivist (q.v.) approaches to research where the focus is on analysing discourse (q.v.), the reduction of data into coded segments may conflate with the epistemological assumption that there are multiple meanings and interpretations of one particular piece of text. There is also some concern that the use of templates leads to a reductionist stance on the data collected, and when conducting this technique it is important that the analyst regularly reverts back to the individual data source so that the wholeness of the data is not lost. Furthermore, a template can only serve as a way of facilitating the organization of data, rather than producing any analytic outcomes. There may be a temptation to assume that the extent of text coded within a particular theme has some form of salience. Given that the emphasis is on the 'pragmatic' use of coding (King, 2004: 256), it is important that the number of excerpts within a theme is not conflated with the significance of that theme.

Template analysis is therefore a useful way of structuring qualitative data to make the complexities of the analytic process more manageable. However, once the final template is constructed, and all the relevant data

coded appropriately, there is still work to be done. Researchers then continue the process of interpreting their data to produce the findings of their research.

Catherine Cassell

TRIANGULATION

Definition

In its most literal sense, triangulation is a means for the fixing of a position based on knowledge of the location and distance apart of two other points. It is an approach derived from navigation, military strategy and surveying, and is based on the logic that researchers can move closer to obtaining a 'true' picture if they take multiple measurements, use multiple methods or examine a phenomenon at multiple levels of analysis [*realism*]. In social research, the term is associated with the use of multiple methods [*mixed methods in management research*] and measures of an empirical phenomenon in order to reduce bias and to improve convergent validity, which is the substantiation of an empirical phenomenon through the use of multiple sources of evidence.

In accordance with its derivation, triangulation is typically described through the language of capture and constraint – of fixing, positioning and confining. The implicit assumption in much of the social science literature on triangulation is of developing a more effective method for the capturing and fixing of social phenomena in order to realize a more accurate analysis and explanation [*process philosophy*]. For organization and management studies, the concomitant phenomenal (q.v.) perspective is of organizations as stable empirical entities that exist and can be represented independently of their observers. This emphasis on stabilization derives from positivism (q.v.), which assumes a dualist and obectivist relationship between the researcher and what can be known about the research subject [*practice theory; structuration theory*].

Under such assumptions, triangulation may take several forms. For example, the four types of triangulation distinguished by Norman Denzin (1978) include: (a) data triangulation, where data are collected at different times or from different sources; (b) investigator triangulation, where different researchers or evaluators independently collect data on the same phenomenon and compare the results; (c) methodological triangulation, where multiple methods of data collection are used; and (d) theory triangulation, where different theories are used to interpret a set of data. Within each type of triangulation there are various sub-types, for example, methodological triangulation can include various combinations of qualitative and quantitative research designs. Beyond common paradigmatic assumptions, Marianne Lewis and Andrew Grimes (1999) argued that metatriangulation may be employed to examine relationships among different perspectives on organizational phenomena.

Discussion

A recent example of methodological triangulation is Charlene Yauch and Harold Steudel's (2003) use of both quantitative and qualitative methods in two exploratory case studies designed to assess the organizational cultures of two small manufacturers. They discuss definitional debates and choose to distingush triangulation, which is aimed at corroborating data and reducing bias, from complementarity, which is aimed at deepening understanding. Recognizing these debates but not making such fine distinctions, Melanie Kan and Ken Parry (2004) also used mixed methods in their investigation of nursing leadership in New Zealand. In a grounded theory (q.v.) study they used both questionnaire and qualitative data to make the point that both forms of data may be triangulated within a grounded theory approach. They argued that triangulation within the grounded theory method can assist the researcher to understand complex

leadership processes, while David Buchanan (2003) has questioned the utility of triangulation in processual analysis and suggests that triangulation is a device that has political as well as methodological effects. Drawing on a particular series of case studies on organizational change, Buchanan argued that triangulation may serve to suppress the variety of change narratives and thereby stifle the representation of diversity in organizational life. It is ironic that triangulation, which, in theory, aims to obtain a more complete representation of reality, may, instead, serve to present an impoverished picture.

Prospects

Moving beyond issues of representation (q.v.), the positivist assumptions that underlie triangulation have themselves been the subject of much debate. For example, those adopting postmodern (q.v.) and some social constructionist (q.v.) research methodologies have radically questioned the separation of researcher and subject. Instead, it is claimed, reality is mediated rather than objective, and language constitutes rather than reflects or describes any more essential mental processes. Accompanying such recognition of the research author's stance comes a demystification of the researcher's authority, for concern lies more with questioning taken-for-granted categories and oppositions than with finding answers. Further, if the living subject is no longer understood to be a concrete object, its representation, capture and transmission become more difficult.

Such considerations led Julie Wolfram Cox and John Hassard (2005) to suggest that it is worthwhile to consider not only the triangulation of *distance* to the 'true' subject but also the di*stance* of triangulation: the reflexive (q.v.) *stance* of the researcher. In doing so, their focus was on unsettling assumptions about the fixed metaphorical space within an enclosing triangle and on drawing attention to how and by whom it is drawn or structured. In their analysis, emphasis shifted from observation [*non-participant observation;*

participant observation] and stabilization to an appreciation of organizing and ordering practices and of the very situated and precarious nature of the organizational research endeavour. In particular, they (deliberately) considered three possible research strategies – and their associated impossibilities: following nomothetic lines and searching for convergent patterns based on theoretical propositions; taking an ideographic overview of content generated from research participants, and finding an angle. As attempts to see the whole pose such difficulties, this third option is for the researcher not only to enter the picture but also to choose to adopt a partial view. This may allow for a new way of thinking about the stance of the researcher, for instead of considering triangulation as an approach to closure or capture, it can be seen as an opening or angling. It can be argued, therefore, that as it is never possible to be neutral and dispassionate in attempts to enclose the whole, perhaps researchers should abandon attempts to do so.

Julie Wolfram Cox

V

VIDEO

Definition

Video-based research involves the use of moving film–based, taped or digital imagery (and sound) to 'capture' or create data in ways that can be subjected to analysis.

Discussion

Management research has long privileged verbal forms of communication over visual forms, with most qualitative management research limited to textual data-gathering techniques and representations, such as transcribed interviews (q.v.), verbal observations of visual events published in text-based journals. While there is the occasional example of the use of still photographs (e.g. Buchanan, 2001) [*aesthetics; drawings and images*], rarely is there any evidence of moving images being encompassed into management research designs and representations. Yet, as Secrist et al. (2002) note, despite all the thick description and detail that writers provide, they often suggest that words alone are not enough to communicate the complex social interactions which they encounter and consequently there has been a burgeoning of interest in what visual methods may add to current text-based research. In line with this visual turn, recent technical innovations in the field of digital video are also making it much easier for researchers to consider incorporating the moving image into research designs (Heath and Hindmarsh, 2002). While analogue video

has long been available and used by social scientists in fields such as anthropology, which has a long-standing tradition of using film as part of data collection and representation (McDougall,1997; Mead, 1995; Prins, 2002), until relatively recently manipulating analogue video required specialist equipment and technical expertise (Shrum et al., 2005). Consequently, these practical and methodological problems rendered the use of video prohibitively expensive for the majority of researchers. In contrast, the new digital camcorders are small, affordable and portable and relatively easy to use, offering high-quality audio and video data which can be captured from a camera and transferred on to a desktop computer and then manipulated easily and quickly using a range of digital video editing applications.

Yet despite these new technological developments, there remain a very limited number of examples in the field of management where video data have previously been applied. Also, in the small number of studies which have incorporated moving images, these images are only used in the data collection stage with researchers converting the visual data into text for dissemination. One attempt at applying a video methodology is Cunliffe's (2001) postmodern (q.v.) perspective on management practice, where she video-taped interviews she conducted with a number of managers. She subsequently played these video-taped interviews back to the managers to explore with them how they had co-created meaning together through dialogical practices [*social poetics; stimulated* recall]. In this way the meaning of the interviews was discussed and deciphered in collaboration (q.v.) with the participant, as a form of co-inquiry where 'the manager/reader and researcher would all author meaning'. However, while the author and manager both view and discuss the video tapes, the research is presented to the reader/audience through text alone, therefore the sight, sound and feel of the interview are not available to the readers (q.v.), making it difficult for them to 'co-author, the interaction in the same way. In another vein, a body of research known collectively as 'workplace studies' (Heath and Hindmarsh, 2002; Luff et al., 2000) has made use of video-tape to examine the effects of the material environment on action and interaction. Such studies focus on interaction and technology in a variety of organizational settings. While interesting in that such studies illustrate the importance of material/visual features, the results are highlighted through verbal discussion and the visual is never presented to the audience. Strecker (1997) criticizes research that uses visual images in this manner, proposing that researchers are standing between their informants and audiences by translating images into words. Pink (2001) argues if researchers continue to translate the visual into text, they are imposing their own interpretations on the images and dismissing the possibility that images may have more than one potential meaning [aesthetics; semiotics; visual data analysis]. Indeed, if video plays a key role in the research, it seems appropriate to incorporate video in the representation of results, providing the opportunity to show the data upon which observations are based to other researchers and subject the author's analysis to academic scrutiny.

In addition to this interesting opportunity to offer audiences an insight into where qualitative results and observations have come from, the type of data which are collected through the use of video tape may offer a very different insight in organizational processes and can also lead to more in-depth analysis compared to text-based approaches alone. In my own PhD research I am conducting visual ethnographies in a number of companies which include video-taped interviews and also images of people performing their everyday jobs. The research focuses on entrepreneurship but aims not to focus exclusively on the entrepreneur but on other actors in his/her environment. Therefore it aims to incorporate a polyphonic [dialogic] dimension through attention to the many others in the entrepreneurial context. The video-taped interactions and interviews have allowed me to 'capture' versions of interaction and behaviour in everyday settings as well as providing me with a visceral experience of the actual events when they occurred which could not be provided by field notes or audio tapes alone. Video therefore provides a unique memory-enhancing dimension, which allows the researcher to experience to some extent the original event once again. As Heritage and Atkinson (1984: 4) argue:

> the use of recorded data serves as a control on the limitations and fallibilities of intuition and recollection; it exposes the observer to a wide range of interactional materials and circumstances and also provides some guarantee that analytic considerations will not arise as artefacts of intuitive idiosyncrasy, selective attention or recollection.

Using video tape in my research has also allowed me to subject the data to repeated examination through the use of slow motion, still frames and zooming features, leading to an enormous amount of unique micro-detail that could not have been caught through text as the situation unfolded. As Heath and Hindmarsh (2002) note, video tape allows micro-analysis of behaviour not observable in any other way, as it records thirty frames of visual data every second, allowing us to track the emergence of gesture, what they are doing, where they are looking and who they are interacting with, which provides unique data not obtainable through any other form.

Prospects

It seems, as Radcliffe (2004) demonstrates, video produces data that can uniquely add to many research designs. Images do not need to be the main focus of attention or topic in order to warrant researchers using visual data in their research. Indeed, as Pink (2001) highlights, the relation of images to other sensory, material and linguistic details of the study will result in the images being of interest to most researchers. As Pink further shows, this is not a suggestion that video and other visual data collection strategies should replace text-based approaches towards research, but rather that it should be used as a complimentary and additional source of data. Indeed, my own research highlights the importance of using visual and textual methods of data collection alongside one another, as the shortcomings of one may at times be able to compensate for the other.

While video adds a unique dimension of the moving image, the use of a video camera, it seems, is unacceptable to informants in a number of organizational situations. For example, in situations of conflict or where tensions where running particularly high I was often asked to turn off the video camera yet allowed to witness the event myself. On other occasions where sensitive material was being discussed, I was invited to join the discussion but once again asked to leave the video camera behind. This illustrates two points. First, it demonstrates the importance of the place of textual field notes (q.v.) and observations [non-participant observation; participant observation] as they allow the researcher to enter into places and make observations where the video camera is forbidden. Second, it also illustrates that organizational participants are often uncomfortable with the use of video in situations that we, as researchers, find interesting and informative. It seems, judging by their aversion to being videoed in difficult or emotional situations, that participants also recognize how informative and insightful the tangible, concrete nature of a moving image can be.

This suggests a raft of ethical (q.v.) and moral questions about video-based research as participants are easily identifiable by visual images and issues such as informed consent and confidentiality need to be examined. It is imperative that such questions are quickly addressed as with the advent of the online journal and the increasing ease with which researchers may incorporate video-based research into published form it seems likely that we will be seeing a considerable increase in the use of image-based research designs.

Jean Clarke

VISUAL DATA ANALYSIS

Definition

Visual methods are techniques that involve the acquisition and creation of images that can be used and interpreted to contribute insights into aspects of social and organizational behaviour. Developments in computing, since the 1960s, have had a major impact on social research methods, permitting the analysis of large survey data sets, and bringing similar capabilities to the analysis of text. Developments in the technologies of image capture and manipulation, however, have not been widely exploited. Documentary photography (still and movie) has a long tradition in visual sociology, anthropology, and ethnography (Banks, 1995; Bateson and Mead, 1942; Collier and Collier, 1986; Harper, 1994, 2000). Applications in organization studies, however, are rare.

Where they have been used, photographs form data in their own right, recording organizational attributes, offering holistic representations of lifestyles and conditions, capturing complex scenes and processes. Depending on usage, photography can also be a non-reactive mode of data collection (Flick, 1998). Researchers may be able to use images in the public domain. Dougherty and Kunda (1990) used photographs of customers in company annual reports in their study of organizational belief systems. Corporate architecture and office layouts may be coded symbolically for attributes of organization culture (Berg and Kreiner, 1990) [space]. Researchers can also produce their own images [postcards]. Complementing observation, questionnaires, and interviews, Liff and Steward (2001) used photographs to capture the contrasts between different kinds of internet cafés ('e-gateways') and their implications for social inclusion. Buchanan (2001) used a visual process map to help understand patient flows through hospital operating theatres, arguing that photography captures data not covered in interviews, and provides a novel channel for respondent validation of findings.

Visual methods are not confined to photography or to images produced by the researcher (Meyer, 1991). Broussine and Vince (1996) asked managers to draw pictures expressing their feelings (mostly negative) about organizational change [*drawings and images*]. As part of her study of the impact of changes in healthcare on professional identity, Parker (2006) asked nurses to bring to her interviews (q.v.) photographs illustrating the effects of those changes; most brought photographs from their own collections rather than take fresh pictures.

Organizational researchers have recently turned to movies for insights based on narrative analysis (Langley, 1999; Monaco, 2000; Pentland, 1999). Critical of the sanitized view of research accounts, Hassard and Holliday (1998: 1) note that film 'plays out sex, violence, emotion, power struggle, the personal consequences of success and failure, and *disorganization* upon its stage'. Phillips (1995) argues that narrative fiction strengthens the links between academic research and the subjective experience of organizational membership. Foreman and Thatchenkery (1996) analyze the film *Rising Sun* (1993, director Philip Kaufman), first as a study of a Japanese transplant in an alien culture, second as a study in cross-cultural communication, third as a depiction of organizational power politics, and fourth as a metaphor for the postmodern (q.v.) view of the negotiable nature of reality. Buchanan and Huczynski (2004) analyze the movies *Twelve Angry Men* (1957, director Sidney Lumet) and *Thirteen Days* (2001, director Roger Donaldson). Where accounts of influencing are dyadic, and management decisions are shown as tidy and information-based, these movies expose processual, political, temporal, and contextual influences, offering a more realistic treatment.

Discussion

Possibly the first application in organization studies was Frank Gilbreth's use of photography in the early twentieth century to study the efficiency of movement. Gilbreth attached lights to workers' hands and filmed their motions at slow shutter speeds to produce 'chronocyclographic' models (Buchanan and Huczynski, 2004: 436–437). Some classic texts, such as Roethlisberger and Dixon (1939) and Blauner (1964), used photographs as illustrations. Photography has also served historical recording and ideological purposes (Bamberger and Davidson, 1998; Hedges and Beynon, 1982). Photograph interpretation is used in family therapy (Berman, 1993), but this has not been applied to organizational problem-solving and development. The main organizational research uses of visual methods today are probably in marketing and advertising research (Bryman and Bell, 2003).

The limited use of visual methods can be explained by the ambiguous status of imagery as empirical evidence. Images are rarely neutral. They tell a story, present a point of view, support an argument, perpetuate a myth, define or challenge a stereotype. Photographs appear to capture reality; the intimidating architecture of a bank; variation in corporate dress codes; the hazardous clutter on the factory floor. But photographs are also social constructs (q.v.), revealing as much about the photographer, who selects the scene, camera, lens, angle of view, and the moment at which to open the shutter. What is outside the frame, and the events before and after the image was captured, remain unseen. And images have always been subject to further manipulation, made easier with developments in digital photography. A further issue is that viewers perceive images in different ways, so there is no single 'correct' interpretation [*reading as inquiry*]. As with language, photography is a medium through which versions of reality are constituted, rather than just a technique for capturing objective truth.

So the mode of analysis depends on research objectives. The interpretation of paintings relies on a rich toolkit, including iconology, semiotics (q.v.), and hermeneutics (q.v.).

Howells (2003) argues that there is a danger of over-interpretation in applying those perspectives to photographs. For some studies, the compilation of a visual record alone may be adequate; pictures of a community devastated by the closure of a manufacturing plant powerfully reveal the implications for redundant employees (Bamberger and Davidson, 1998). Images can also be content analyzed (q.v.) to identify recurring themes (Broussine and Vince, 1996). The technique of photo-elicitation involves showing photographs to respondents in order to trigger, or to elicit, discussion of those images (Parker, 2006). As researcher and respondent explore a shared object, the image, discussion can reach a greater depth across issues not likely to be addressed by more conventional interview formats.

Prospects

Interest in the potential of visual methods across the social sciences is growing (Emmison and Smith, 2000; Hamilton, 2005a; Howells, 2003; Prosser, 1998; Rose, 2001). Visual organization studies, however, has yet to develop as a mainstream movement, either with a distinctive agenda, or by providing tools that complement traditional research methods. It is a notable paradox, for example, that researchers using observational methods often describe contexts, interactions, and event sequences, reporting what they have heard, making little use of visual imagery (Angrosino and Mays de Pérez, 2000; Atkinson and Hammersley, 1994).

It is a cliché to observe that we live in a world saturated with visual imagery, to which we pay little or no attention. As images have the power to define, as well as to unlock intersubjective differences, this neglect is regrettable. Visual methods thus deserve a more prominent position in the researcher's toolkit. Current trends offer the promise of that development.

David A. Buchanan

References

Abernethy, M.A., Horne, M., Lillis, A.M., Malina, M.A., and Selto, F.H. (2005) 'Building causal performance models from expert knowledge', *Management Accounting Research*, 16: 135–156.

Ackermann, F. and Eden, C. (2004) 'Using causal mapping: individual and group; traditional and new', in M. Pidd (ed.) *Systems Modelling: Theory and Practice*. Chichester: Wiley. pp. 127–145.

Ackoff, R.L. (1974) *Redesigning the Future: A Systems Approach to Societal Problems*. New York: Wiley.

Adler, P.A. and Adler, P. (1994) 'Observational techniques', in N. Denzin and Y. Lincoln (eds) *Handbook of Qualitative Research*. London: Sage.

Adorno, T.W. (1973) *Negative Dialectics*. New York: The Seabury Press.

Aggergaard L.J., Allan H.T., Bryan, K. and Smith, P. (2005) 'Overseas nurses' motivations for working in the UK, globalization and life policies', *Work, Employment and Society*, 19(2): 349–368.

Ahrens, T. and Chapman, C. (2007) 'Management accounting as process and practice', *Accounting, Organisation and Society*, 37(1/2): forthcoming.

Ailon-Souday, G. and Kunda, G. (2003) 'The local selves of global workers: the social construction of national identity in the face of organization globalization', *Organization Studies*, 24: 1073–1096.

Albrow, M. (1997) *Do Organizations Have Feelings?* London: Routledge.

Allen, D.E. (2002) 'Towards a theory of consumer choice as socio-historically shaped practical experience: the fits-like-a glove FLAG framework', *Journal of Consumer Research*, 28(4): 515–532.

Allen, P. (1998) 'Evolving complexity in social science', in G. Altman and W.A. Koch (eds) *Systems: New Paradigms for the Human Sciences*. Berlin: Walter de Gruyter.

Allen, P. (2001) 'What is complexity science: knowledge of the limits of knowledge', *Emergence*, 3(1): 24–42.

Allen, T.J. (1984) *Managing the Flow of Technology: Technology Transfer and the Dissemination of Technological Information Within the R&D Organization*. Cambridge, MA: MIT Press.

Allison, G.T. (1971) *Essence of Decision*. Boston, MA: Little Brown.

Althusser, L. (1971) *Lenin and Philosophy and Other Essays*, Trans B. Brewster. Canada: Monthly Review Press. pp. 127–186.

Alvesson, M. (1994) 'Talking in organizations: managing identity and impressions in an advertising agency', *Organization Studies*, 15: 536–563.

Alvesson, M. (2003) 'Beyond neo-positivism and localism. A reflective approach', *Academy of Management Review*, 28(1): 13–33.

Alvesson, M. and Deetz, S. (2000) *Doing Critical Management Research*. London: Sage.

Alvesson, M. and Kärreman, D. (2000) 'On the study of organizations through discourse analysis', *Human Relations*, 58: 1125–1134.

Alvesson, M. and Sköldberg, K. (2000) *Reflexive Methodology: New Vistas for Qualitative Research*. London: Sage.

Alvesson, M. and Willmott, H. (1976) *Making Sense of Management: A Critical Introduction*. London: Sage.

Alvesson, M. and Willmott, H. (eds) (1992) *Critical Management Studies*. London: Sage.

Amin, S. (1974) *Accumulation on a World Scale: A Critique of the Theory of Underdevelopment*. New York: Monthly Review Press.

Amin, S. (1976) *Unequal Development: An Essay on the Social Formations of Peripheral Capitalism*. New York: Monthly Review Press.

REFERENCES

Andersson, B.E. and Nilsson, S.G. (1964) 'Studies in the reliability and validity of the critical incident technique', *Journal of Applied Psychology*, 48(1): 398–403.

Angrosino, M.V. and Mays de Pérez, K.A. (2000) 'Rethinking observation: from method to context', in N.K. Denzin and Y.S. Lincoln (eds) *Handbook of Qualitative Research* (2nd edn). Thousand Oaks, CA: Sage. pp. 673–702.

Antonacopoulou, E.P. (2004) 'On the virtues of *Practising* scholarship: a tribute to Chris Argyris, a timeless learner', *Management Learning*, 35(4): 381–395.

Antonacopoulou, E.P. (2006) 'On the *practise* of practice: in-tensions and ex-tensions in the ongoing reconfiguration of practices', in D. Barry and H. Hansen (eds) *Handbook of New and Emerging Approaches to Management and Organization*. London: Sage.

Argyris, C. (1980) *Inner Contradictions of Rigorous Research*. New York: Academic Press.

Argyris, C. (1982) *Reasoning, Learning, and Action*. San Francisco, CA: Jossey-Bass.

Argyris, C. (1985) 'Making knowledge more relevant to practice: maps for action', in E.E. Lawler III and Associates (eds) *Doing Research that is Useful for Theory and Practice*. San Francisco, CA: Jossey-Bass.

Argyris, C. (1993) *Knowledge for Action*. San Francisco, CA: Jossey-Bass.

Argyris, C. and Kaplan, R. (1994) 'Implementing new knowledge: the case of activity-based costing', *Accounting Horizons*, 8(3): 83–105.

Argyris, C. and Schön, D.A. (1974/1978a) *Theory in Practice: Increasing Professional Effectiveness*. San Francisco, CA: Jossey-Bass.

Argyris, C. and Schön, D.A. (1978b) *Organizational Learning: A Theory-in-Action Perspective*. Reading, MA: Addison-Wesley and New York: McGraw-Hill.

Argyris, C. and Schön, D.A. (1989) 'Participatory action research and action science compared', *American Behavioral Scientist*, 32: 612–623.

Argyris, C. and Schön, D.A. (1996) *Organizational Learning* (2nd edn). Reading, MA: Addison-Wesley.

Argyris, C., Putnam, R.W. and Smith, D.M. (eds) (1985) *Action Science*. San Francisco, CA: Jossey-Bass.

Argyris, D. (1985) 'The ethnographic approach in intervention and fundamental change', in C. Argyris, R.W. Putnam and D.M. Smith (eds) *Action Science*. San Francisco, CA: Jossey-Bass.

Aristotle (1976) *The Nicomachean Ethics*. Trans J.A.K. Thomson. Revised with notes and appendices H. Tredennick. Introduction and bibliography J. Barnes. Harmondsworth: Penguin.

Aristotle (1991) *The Art of Rhetoric*. Trans H. Lawson-Tancred. London: Penguin.

Arndt, M. and Bigelow, B. (2000) 'Commentary: the potential of chaos theory and complexity theory for health services management', *Health Care Management Review*, 25(1): 35–38.

Arnstein, S. (1971) 'A ladder of citizen participation', *Journal of the Royal Planning Institute*, 35(4): 216–224.

Arrow, K. (1994) 'Methodological individualism and social knowledge', *The American Economic Review*, 84(2): 1–9.

Ashcraft, K.L. and Mumby, D.K. (2004) *Reworking Gender: A Feminist Communicology of Organization*. London: Sage.

Ashton, S. (2006) 'Where's the action? The concept of action in action learning', *Action Learning: Research & Practice*, 3(1): 5–29.

Atkinson, J.W. and McClelland, D.C. (1948) 'The projective expression of needs II: the effect of different intensities of the hunger drive on thematic appreciation', *Journal of Experimental Psychology*, 38: 643–658.

Atkinson, P. and Delamont, S. (2005) 'Analytic perspectives', in N.K. Denzin and Y.S. Lincoln (eds) *The Sage Handbook of Qualitative Research*. Thousand Oaks, CA: Sage.

Atkinson, P. and Hammersley, M. (1994) 'Ethnography and participant observation', in N.K. Denzin and Y.S. Lincoln (eds) *Handbook of Qualitative Sociology*. Thousand Oaks, CA: Sage. pp. 248–261.

Atkinson, P. and Silverman, D. (2001) 'Kundera's immortality. the interview society and the invention of self', *Qualitative Inquiry*, 3: 324–345.

Atkinson, P., Coffey, A. and Delamont, S. (2001) 'A debate about our canon', *Qualitative Research*, 1(1): 5–21.

Augé, M. (1995) *Non-places: An Introduction to an Anthropology of Supermodernity*. London: Verso.

Austin, J. (1962) *How to do Things with Words*. Cambridge, MA: Harvard University Press.

Axelrod, R. (1976) *Structure of Decision: The Cognitive Maps of Political Elites*. Princeton, NJ: Princeton University Press.

Azevedo, J. (2002) 'Updating organizational epistemology', in J.A.C. Baum (ed.) *Companion to Organizations*. Malden: Blackwell. pp. 715–732.

Babbage, C. (1832) *On the Economy of Machinery and Manufactures*. London: Charles Knight, Pall Mall East.

Baccus, M.D. (1986) 'Multipiece truck wheel accidents and their regulations', in H. Garfinkel (ed.) *Ethnomethodological Studies of Work*. London: Routledge and Kegan Paul.

Bachelard, G. (1969) *The Poetics of Space*. Boston, MA: Beacon Press.

Bacon, F. (1620/1960) 'Novum organum', in F.H. Anderson (ed.) *The New Organum and Related Writings*. New York: Liberal Arts Press.

Baecker, D. (1999) *Organisation Als System*. Frankfurt am Main: Suhrkamp.

Bakhtin, M. (1929/1973) *Problems of Dostoevsky's Poetics*. Trans R.W. Rotsel (ed.). US: Ardis.

Bakhtin, M. (1981) *The Dialogic Imagination: Four Essays by M.M. Bakhtin*. Trans C. Emerson and M. Holquist. Austin, TX: University of Texas Press.

Bakhtin, M. (1984) *Problems of Dostoevsky's Poetics*. Trans C. Emerson (ed.). Minneapolis: University of Minnesota Press.

Bakhtin, M. (1986) *Speech Genres and Other Late Essays*. Trans C. Emerson. Minneapolis: University of Minnesota Press.

Bakhtin, M. (1990) *Art and Answerability*. Michael Holquist and Vadim Liapunov (eds). Trans and notes by V. Liapunov and K. Brostrom. Austin, TX: University of Texas Press.

Bakken, T. and Hernes, T. (eds) (2003) *Autopoietic Organization Theory*. Abstract. Liber, Copenhagen: Copenhagen University Press.

Balogun, J. and Johnson, G. (2004) 'Organizational restructuring and middle manager sensemaking', *Academy of Management Journal*, 47(4): 523–549.

Bamberger, B. and Davidson, C. (1998) *Closing Down: The Life and Death of an American Factory*. New York and London: DoubleTake/W.W. Norton.

Banerjee, S.B. (2000) 'Whose land is it anyway? National interest, indigenous stakeholders and colonial discourses: the case of the Jabiluka uranium mine', *Organization and Environment*, 13(1): 3–38.

Banerjee, S.B. and Linstead, S. (2001) 'Globalization, multiculturalism and other fictions: colonialism for the new millennium?', *Organization*, 8(4): 683–722.

Banerjee, S.B. and Linstead, S. (2004) 'Masking subversion: neo-colonial embeddedness in anthropological accounts of indigenous management', *Human Relations*, 57(2): 221–247.

Banham, R. (1960/1980) *Theory and Design in the First Machine Age*. Cambridge, MA: MIT Press.

Banks, M. (1995) 'Visual research methods', *Social Research Update*, 11, University of Surrey, UK.

Bansal, P. and Roth, K. (2000) 'Why companies go green: a model of ecological responsiveness', *Academy of Management Review*, 13(4): 717–736.

Barbalet, J.M. (1998) *Emotion, Social Theory and Social Structure: A Macro-Sociological Approach*. Cambridge: Cambridge University Press.

Barge, K.J. (2002) 'Ante-narrative and managerial practice', Working Paper, University of Georgia. *Accepted for Publication in Revised Form at Communication Studies*.

Barley, S.R. (1986) 'Technology as an occasion for structuring: evidence from observations of CT scanners and the social order of radiology departments', *Administrative Science Quarterly*, 31(1): 78–108.

Barn, R. (1994) 'Black children in the public care system', in B. Humphries and C. Truman (eds) *Re-Thinking Social Research: Anti-Discrimination Approaches in Research Methodology*. Avebury: Aldershot. pp. 37–58.

Barnes, B. (1983) 'Social life as bootstrapped induction', *Sociology*, 4: 524–545.

Barr, A.H. Jr. (1995) 'Preface', in H.R. Hitchcock and P. Johnson, *The International Style*. New York: W.W. Norton. pp. 27–32.

REFERENCES

Barrows, H.S. (2000) *Stimulated Recall (Personalized Assessment of Clinical Reasoning)*. Problem-based learning initiative, Southern Illinois University, USA.

Barry, D. and Elmes, M. (1997) 'Strategy retold: toward a narrative view of strategic discourse', *Academy of Management Review*, 22(2): 429–452.

Barry, N. (2002) 'The stakeholder concept of corporate control is illogical and impractical', *The Independent Review*, VI(4): 541–554.

Bartkus, B.R. and McAfee, R.B. (2004) 'A comparison of the quality of European, Japanese and US mission statements: a content analysis', *European Management Journal*, 22(4): 393–401.

Barthes, R. (1977) 'The death of the author', in *Image, Text, Music. Roland Barthes; Essays*, selected and translated by Stephen Heath. London: Fontana Press.

Bartunik, J.M., Rynes, S.L. and Ireland, R.D. (2006) 'What makes management research interesting, and why does it matter?'. Academy of Management journal editors' forum. *Academy of Management Journal*, 49(1): 9–15.

Basch, J. and Fisher, C.D. (2000) 'Affective events–emotions matrix: a classification of work events and associated emotions', in N.M. Ashkanasy, C.E.J. Hartel and W.J. Zerbe (eds) *Emotions in The Workplace: Research, Theory, and Practice*. Westport, CT: Quorum Books. pp. 36–48.

Baszanger, I. and Dodier, N. (2004) 'Ethnography: relating the part to the whole', in D. Silverman (ed.) *Qualitative Research Theory, Method and Practice* (2nd edn). London: Sage.

Batinic, B. (1997) 'How to make an internet-based survey?', *Advances in Statistical Software*, 6: 125–132.

Bate, S.P. (1997) 'Whatever happened to organizational anthropology? A review of the field of organizational ethnography and anthropological studies', *Human Relations*, 50: 1147–1175.

Bate, S.P. (2000) 'Changing the culture of a hospital: from hierarchy to networked community', *Public Administration*, 78(3): 485–212.

Bateson, G. and Mead, M. (1942) *Balinese Character: A Photographic Analysis*. New York: New York Academy of Sciences, Special Publications 2.

Baudrillard, J. (1981) *For a Critique of the Political Economy of the Sign*. St Louis: Telos Press.

Baudrillard, J. (1993) *Symbolic Exchange and Death*. London: Sage.

Baum, J.A.C. and Rowley, T. (2002) 'Organizations: an introduction', in J.A.C. Baum (ed.) *Companion to Organizations*. Oxford: Blackwell. pp. 1–34.

Bauman, Z. (1992) *Intimations of Postmodernity*. London: Routledge.

Bazeley, P. (2006) 'The contribution of computer software to integrating qualitative and quantitative data and analyses', *Research in the Schools*, 13(1): 63–73.

Bechtold, B.L. (1997) 'Chaos theory as a model for strategy development', *Empowerment in Organizations*, 5(4): 193–201.

Becker, H.S., Geer, B., Hughes, E.C. and Strauss, A.L. (1961) *Boys in White*. Chicago: University of Chicago Press.

Becker, M.C. (2001) 'Managing dispersed knowledge: organizational problems, managerial strategies, and their effectiveness', *Journal of Management Studies*, 38: 1037–1051.

Becket, A., Hewer, P. and Howcroft, B. (2000) 'An exposition of consumer behaviour in the financial services industry', *International Journal of Bank Marketing*, 18(1): 15–26.

Beech, N. (2000) 'Narrative styles of managers and workers', *Journal of Applied Behavioral Science*, 36(2): 210–228.

Beer, S. (1972) *Brain of the Firm*. London: Penguin.

Bell, R. C. (2000) 'On testing the commonality of constructs in supplied grids', *Journal of Constructivist Psychology*, 13(4): 303–311.

Bell, E. and Bryman, A. (2007) 'The ethics of management research: an exploratory content analysis', *British Journal of Management*, 18(1).

Bell, E., Taylor, S. and Thorpe, R. (2002) 'Organizational differentiation through badging: Investors in People and the value of the sign', *Journal of Management Studies*, 39: 1071–1085.

Bendix, R. (2001) *Work and Authority in Industry: Managerial Ideologies in the Course of Industrialization*. New Brunswick, NJ: Transaction.

Berg, B.L. (2001) *Qualitative Research Methods for the Social Sciences*. London: Allyn and Bacon.

Berg, P.O. and Kreiner, K. (1990) 'Corporate architecture: turning physical settings into symbolic resources', in P. Gagliardi (ed.) *Symbols and Artefacts: Views of the Corporate Landscape*. Berlin: Walter de Gruyter.

Berger, P. and Luckmann, T. (1966) *The Social Construction of Reality: A Treatise in the Sociology of Knowledge*. Garden City, NY: Doubleday.

Berglund, J. and Werr, A. (2000) 'The invincible character of management consulting rhetoric: how one blends incommensurates while keeping them apart', *Organization*, 7: 633–656.

Bergson, H. (1907/1983) *Creative Evolution*. Trans A. Mitchell. Lanham, MD: University Press of America.

Berman, L. (1993) *Beyond the Smile: The Therapeutic Uses of the Photograph*. London: Routledge.

Bernstein, R. (1983) *Beyond Objectivism and Relativism: Science, Hermeneutics, and Praxis*. Philadelphia: University of Pennsylvania Press and Oxford: Blackwell.

Bertaux, D. (ed.) (1981) *Biography and Society: The Life History Approach in the Social Sciences*. London: Sage.

Berthold-Bond, D. (1993) *Hegel's Grand Synthesis: A Study of Being, Thought, and History*. New York: Harper. Online at www2.pfeiffer. edu/~lridener/courses/HEGEL.HTML

Betts, J. and Holden, R. (2003) 'Organizational learning in a public sector organization: a case of muddled thinking', *Journal of Workplace Learning*, 15(6): 280–287.

Bhaskar R. (1975) *A Realist Theory of Science*. London: Verso.

Bhaskar R. (1979a/1989) *Reclaiming Reality*. London: Verso.

Bhaskar, R. (1979b) *The Possibility of Naturalism*. Brighton: Harvester Press.

Bhaskar, R. (2002) *Meta-Reality: The Philosophy of Meta-Reality*. London: Sage.

Billig, M. (1987/1996) *Arguing and Thinking: A Rhetorical Approach to Social Psychology* (2nd edn). Cambridge: Cambridge University Press.

Binders, T., Björgvinsson, E. and Hillgren, P.A. (2006) 'Configuring places for learning: participatory development of learning practices at work', in E.P. Antonacopoulou, P. Jarvis, V. Andersen, B. Elkjaer and S. Hoeyrup (eds) *Learning, Working and Living: Mapping the Terrain of Working Life Learning*. London: Palgrave. pp. 139–153.

Bion, W. (1961) *Experiences in Groups*. London: Tavistock.

Bitner, M.J., Booms, B.H. and Tetreault, M.S. (1990) 'The service encounter: diagnosing favorable and unfavorable incidents', *Journal of Marketing*, 54 (January): 71–84.

Bittner, E. (1965) 'The concept of organization', *Social Research*, 32: 239–255.

Bjelic, D. and Lynch, M. (1992) 'The work of a (scientific) demonstration: respecifying Newton's and Goethe's theories of prismatic color', in G. Watson and R.M. Seiler (eds) *Text in Context: Contributions to Ethnomethodology*. Newbury Park, CA: Sage.

Black, J.A. (2000) 'Fermenting change: capitalizing on the inherent change found in dynamic non-linear (or complex) systems', *Journal of Organizational Change Management*, 13(6): 520–525.

Blackburn, R. and Stokes, D. (2000) 'Breaking down the barriers: using focus groups to research small and medium-sized enterprises', *International Small Business Journal*, 19(1): 44–67.

Blackler, F. (1993) 'Knowledge and the theory of organizations: organizations as activity systems and the reframing of management', *Journal of Management Studies*, 30(6): 864–884.

Blackler, F. (1995) 'Knowledge, knowledge work and organizations: an overview and interpretation', *Organization Studies*, 16(6): 1021–1046

Blanchard, K. and Johnson, S. (1994) *The One Minute Manager*. London: HarperCollins.

Blauner, R. (1964) *Alienation and Freedom: The Factory Worker and His Industry*. Chicago and London: University of Chicago Press.

Bleicher, J. (1980) *Contemporary Hermeneutics*. London: Routledge.

Blind, K., Cuhls, K. and Grupp, H. (2001) 'Personal attitudes in the assessment of the future of science and technology: a factor analysis approach', *Technological Forecasting and Social Change*, 68: 131–149.

Bloom, B.S. (1953) 'The thought processes of students' discussion', *Journal of General Education*, 111(3): 160–169.

Bloomfield, B. and Vurdubakis, T. (1994) 'Re-presenting technology: IT consultancy reports as textual reality constructions', *Sociology*, 28: 455–477.

Bloomfield, B. and Vurdubakis, T. (1999) 'The outer limits: monsters, actor networks and the writing of displacement', *Organization*, 6: 625–648.

Bloomfield, B., Coombs, R., Cooper, D. and Rea, D. (1992) 'Machines and manoeuvres: responsibility accounting and the construction of hospital information systems', *Accounting, Management and Information Technology*, 2: 197–219.

Bloor, M. (1976) 'Bishop Berkeley and the adenotonsillectomy enigma: an explanation of variation in the social construction of medical disposals', *Sociology*, 10(1): 43–61.

Bloor, M. (1978) 'On the analysis of observational data: a discussion of the worth and uses of inductive techniques and respondent validation', *Sociology*, 12(3): 545–552.

Blumer, H. (1954) 'What is wrong with social theory?', *American Sociological Review*, 19(1): 3–10.

Boddy, C. (2005) 'A rose by any other name may smell as sweet but "group discussion" is not another name for a "focus group" nor should it be', *Qualitative Market Research*, 8(3): 248–255.

Boden, D. (1994) *The Business of Talk: Organizations in Action.* Cambridge: Polity Press.

Bogardus, E.S. (1926) 'The group interview', *Journal of Applied Sociology*, 10: 372–382.

Bogdan, R. and Taylor, S.J. (1975) *Introduction to Qualitative Research Methods.* London: Wiley.

Bohm, D. (1980) *Wholeness and the Implicate Order.* London: Routledge and Kegan Paul.

Bohm, D. (1988) 'Postmodern science and the postmodern world', in D.R. Griffin (ed.) *The Re-enchantment of Science.* New York: State University of New York Press. pp. 57–68.

Boje, D.M. (1991) 'Organizations as Storytelling Networks: a study of story performance in an office supply firm', *Administrative Science Quarterly*, 36: 106–126.

Boje, D.M. (1995) 'Stories of the storytelling organization: a postmodern analysis of Disney as Tamara-Land', *Academy of Management Journal*, 38(4): 997–1035.

Boje, D.M. (2000) 'Phenomenal complexity theory and change at Disney: response to Letiche', *Journal of Organizational Change Management*, 13(6): 558–566.

Boje, D.M. (2001) *Narrative Methods for Organizational and Communication Research.* London: Sage.

Boje, D.M. (2002) 'Critical dramaturgical analysis of Enron antenarratives and metatheatre', plenary presentation to 5th International Conference on Organizational Discourse: From Micro-Utterances to Macro-Inferences, 24–26 July, London.

Boje, D.M. (2006) 'The antenarrative cultural turn in narrative studies', in M. Zachry and C. Thralls (eds) *Communicative Practices in Workplaces and the Professions.* Amityville, NY: Baywood.

Boje, D.M. and Rhodes, C. (2005) 'The virtual leader construct: the mass mediatization and simulation of transformational leadership', *Leadership*, 1(4): 407–428.

Boje, D.M. and Rosile, G.A. (2002) 'Enron whodunit?', *Ephemera*, 2(4): 315–327.

Boje, D.M. and Rosile, G.A. (2003) 'Life imitates art: Enron's epic and tragic narration', *Management Communication Quarterly*, 17(1): 85–125.

Boje, D.M., Luhman, J. and Baack, D. (1999) 'Hegemonic tales of the field: a telling research encounter between storytelling organizations', *Journal of Management Inquiry*, 8(4): 340–360.

Boje, D.M., Oswick, C. and Ford, J. (2004) 'Language and organization: the doing of discourse', *Academy of Management Review*, 29(4): 571–577.

Boje, D.M., Rosile, G.A., Durant, R.A. and Luhman, J.T. (2004a) 'Enron spectacles: a critical dramaturgical analysis', Special Issue on Theatre and Organizations edited by Georg Schreyögg and Heather Höpfl, *Organization Studies*, 25(5): 751–774.

Bolger, N., Davis, A. and Rafaeli, E. (2003) 'Diary methods: capturing life as it is lived', *Annual Review of Psychology*, 54: 579–616.

Bonetta, L. (2003) 'Lab architecture: do you want to work here?', *Nature*, 424: 718–729.

Boshier, R. (1990) 'Socio-psychological factors in electronic networking', *International Journal of Lifelong Education*, 9(1): 49–64.

Bougon, M., Weick, K.E. and Binkhorst, D. (1977) 'Cognition in organizations: an analysis of the Utrecht Jazz Orchestra', *Administrative Science Quarterly*, 22: 606–639.

Bougon, M.G. (1983) 'Uncovering cognitive maps: the self Q technique', in G. Morgan (ed.) *Beyond Method.* Beverly Hills, CA: Sage. pp. 173–188.

Boulding, K.E. (1956) 'General systems theory: the skeleton of science', *General Systems*, 1: 11–17.

Bourdieu, P. (1977) *Outline of a Theory of Practice*. Cambridge: Cambridge University Press.

Bourdieu, P. (1990) *The Logic of Practice*. Cambridge: Polity Press.

Bourdieu, P. (1998) *Practical Reason: On the Theory of Action*. London: Polity Press.

Bowie, N.E. (2002) *The Blackwell Guide to Business Ethics*. Oxford: Blackwell.

Bowker, G., Timmermans, S. and Star, L. (1996). 'Infrastructure and organizational transformation: classifying nurses' work', in W. Orlikowski, G. Walsham, M. Jones and J. DeGross (eds) *Information Technology and Changes in Organizational Work*. London: Chapman and Hall.

Boyce, M. (1995) 'Collective centering and collective sense-making in the stories and storytelling of one organization', *Organization Studies* 16(1): 107–137.

Boyd, R.N. (1984) 'The current status of scientific realism', in J. Leplin (ed.) *Scientific realism*. Berkeley: University of California Press. pp. 41–82.

Braverman, H. (1974) *Labor and Monopoly Capital: The Degradation of Work in the Twentieth Century*. New York and London: Monthly Review Press.

Breakwell, G.M. and Wood, P. (2000) 'Diary techniques', in G.M. Breakwell, S. Hammond and C. Fife-Schaw (eds) *Research Methods in Psychology* (2nd edn). London: Sage. pp. 294–302.

Brewer, J.D. (2004) 'Ethnography', in C. Cassell and G. Symon (eds) *Essential Guide to Qualitative Methods in Organizational Research*. London: Sage.

Bridgman, P. (1927) *The Logic of Modern Physics*. New York: MacMillan.

Brill, M. (2001) *Disproving Widespread Myths about Workplace Design*. Jasper, IN: Kimball International.

Broadbent, J. (1992) 'Change in organisations: a case study of the use of accounting information in the NHS', *The British Accounting Review*, 24(4): 343–367.

Broadbent, J. (1998) 'The gendered nature of 'accounting logic': pointers to an accounting that encompasses multiple values', *Critical Perspectives on Accounting*, 9(3): 267–297.

Broadbent, J. and Laughlin, R. (1997) 'Developing empirical research: an example informed by a Habermasian approach', *Accounting, Auditing and Accountability Journal*, 10(5): 622–648.

Broadbent, J. and Laughlin, R. (1998) 'Resisting the "New Public Management": absorption and absorbing groups in schools and GP practices', *Accounting, Auditing and Accountability Journal*, 11(4): 403–435.

Brodbeck, P.W. (2002) 'Implications for organization design: teams as pockets of excellence', *Team Performance Management: An International Journal*, 8(1/2): 21–38.

Brooks, A. and Watkins, K. (1994) *The Emerging Power of Action Inquiry Techniques*. San Francisco, CA: Jossey-Bass.

Broussine, M. and Vince, R. (1996) 'Working with metaphor towards organizational change', in C. Oswick and D. Grant (eds) *Organization Development: Metaphorical Explorations*. London: Pitman. pp. 57–72.

Brown, A. (2004) 'Authoritative sensemaking in a public inquiry report', *Organization Studies*, 25(1): 95–112.

Brown, C., Guillet de Monthoux, P. and McCullough, A. (1976) *The Access Case Book*. Stockholm: Teknisk Hogskolelitteratur.

Brown, J.S. and Duguid, P. (2000) *The Social Life of Information*. Boston, MA: Harvard Business School Press.

Brown, J.S. and Duguid, P. (2001) 'Knowledge and organization: a social-practice perspective', *Organization Science*, 12: 198–213.

Brown, S.L. and Eisenhardt, K.M. (1997) 'The art of continuous change: linking complexity theory and time-paced evolution in relentlessly shifting organizations', *Administrative Science Quarterly*, 42: 1–34.

Browning, L., Beyer, J. and Shelter, J. (1995) 'Building cooperation in a competitive industry: Semteck and the semiconductor industry', *Academy of Management Journal*, 13(1): 113–151.

Bruner, J. (1990) *Acts of Meaning*. Cambridge, MA: Harvard University Press.

Bryans, P. and Mavin, S. (2006) 'Visual images: a technique to surface conceptions of research and researchers', *Qualitative Research in Organisations and Management*, 1(2): 113–128.

Bryman, A. (1988) *Doing Research in Organizations*. London: Routledge.

REFERENCES

Bryman, A. and Bell, E. (2003) *Business Research Methods.* Oxford: Oxford University Press.

Bryson, J., Ackermann, F., Eden, C. and Finn, C. (2004) *Visible Thinking: Unlocking Causal Mapping for Practical Business Results.* Chichester: Wiley.

Buchanan, D.A. (2001) 'The role of photography in organizational research: a re-engineering case illustration', *Journal of Management Inquiry*, 10(2): 151–164.

Buchanan, D.A. (2003) 'Getting the story straight: illusions and delusions in the organizational change process', *Tamara*, 2(4): 7–21.

Buchanan, D.A. and Huczynski, A. (2004) 'Images of influence: twelve angry men and thirteen days', *Journal of Management Inquiry*, 13(4): 312–323.

Buchanan, D.A., Boddy, D. and McCalman, J. (1988) 'Getting in, getting on, getting out, and getting back', in A. Bryman (ed.) *Doing Research in Organizations.* London: Routledge.

Buchanan, J.M. and Vanberg, V.J. (2002) 'Constitutional implications of radical subjectivism', *Review of Austrian Economics*, 15(2–3): 121–129.

Bulmer, M. (ed.) (1982a) *Social Research Ethics: An Examination of the Merits of Covert Participant Observation.* London: Macmillan.

Bulmer, M. (1982b) 'The merits and demerits of covert participant observation', in M. Bulmer (ed.) *Social Research Ethics.* London: Macmillan.

Bunge, M. (1967) *Scientific Research, Vol. 2: The Search for Truth.* New York: Springer-Verlag.

Burgelman, R. (1983) 'A process model of internal corporate venturing in the diversified major firm', *Administrative Science Quarterly*, 39: 223–233.

Burgess, R.G. (1984) *An Introduction to Field Research.* London: Routledge.

Burgoyne, J. and Reynolds, M. (eds) (1997) *Management Learning: Integrating Perspectives in Theory and Practice.* London: Sage.

Burgoyne, J.G. and Hodgson, V.E. (1983) 'Natural learning and managerial action: a phenomenological study in the field setting', *Journal of Management Studies*, 20(3): 387–399.

Burke, K. (1966) *Language as Symbolic Action.* Berkeley: University of California Press.

Burke, K. (1969) 'Dramatism', in *International Encyclopedia of the Social Sciences* (Vol. VII). New York: Macmillan.

Burkitt, I. (1997) 'Social relationships and emotions', *Sociology*, 31(1): 37–55.

Burnes, B. (2005) 'Complexity theories and organizational change', *International Journal of Management Reviews*, 7(2): 73–90.

Burrell, G. and Morgan, G. (1979) *Sociological Paradigms and Organisational Analysis.* London: Heinemann.

Bushe, G.R. (1998) 'Appreciative inquiry with teams', *Organization Development Journal*, 16(3): 41–49.

Bushe, G.R. (1999) 'Advances in appreciative inquiry as an organization development intervention', *Organization Development Journal*, 17(2): 61–68.

Calás, M. (1993) 'Deconstructing charismatic leadership: re-reading Weber from the darker side', *Leadership Quarterly*, 4(3/4): 305–328.

Calás, M. and Smircich, L. (1991) 'Voiding seduction to silence leadership', *Organization Studies*, 12(4): 567–602.

Calás, M. and Smircich, L. (1992) 'Re-writing gender into organizational theorizing', in M. Reed and M. Hughes (eds) *Rethinking Organization.* London: Sage. pp. 227–253.

Calás, M. and Smircich, L. (1996) 'From "the woman's" point of view: feminist approaches to organization studies', in S. Clegg, C. Hardy and W. Nord (eds) *Handbook of Organization Studies*: London: Sage. pp. 218–256.

Calas, M. and Smircich, L. (1999) 'Past postmodernism? Reflections and tentative directions', *Academy of Management Review*, 24: 649–671.

Caldwell, N. and Coshall, J. (2000) 'Measuring brand associations for museums and galleries using repertory grid analysis', *Working Paper Series No. 6.* London: University of North London. pp. 1–11.

Callon, M. (1986) 'Some elements of a sociology of translation: domestication of the scallops and the fishermen of St. Brieuc Bay', in J. Law (ed.) *Power, Action, and Belief: A New Sociology of Knowledge.* London: Routledge and Kegan Paul.

Callon, M. (1999) 'Whose imposture?', *Social Studies of Science*, 29(2): 261–286.

Calori, R. (2000) 'Ordinary theorists in mixed industries', *Organization Studies*, 21(6): 1031–1059.

Calori, R. (2002) 'Essai: Real time/real space research; connecting action and reflection in organization studies', *Organization Studies*, 23(6): 877–884.

Campbell, D.T. and Fiske, D. (1959) 'Convergent and discriminant validation by the multitrait-multimethod matrix', *Psychological Bulletin*, 56: 81–105.

Canning, M. and O'Dwyer, B. (2003) 'A critique of the descriptive power of the private interest model of professional accounting ethics: an examination over time in the Irish context', *Accounting, Auditing and Accountability Journal*, 16(2): 159–185.

Capra, F. (1996) *The Web of Life*. New York: Doubleday.

Caputi, P. and Reddy, P. (1999) 'A comparison of triadic and dyadic methods of personal construct elicitation', *Journal of Constructivist Psychology*, 12(3): 253–264.

Caracelli, V.J. and Greene, J.C. (1997) 'Crafting mixed-method evaluation designs', in J.C. Greene and V.J. Caracelli (eds) *Advances in Mixed-method Evaluation: The Challenges and Benefits of Integrating Diverse Paradigms*: San Francisco, CA: Jossey-Bass. pp. 19–32.

Carlson, S. (1951) *Executive Behaviour: A Study of the Workload and the Working Methods of Managing Directors*. Stockholm: Strombergs.

Carr, A. (2000a) 'Critical theory and the management of change in organizations', *Journal of Organizational Change Management*, 13(3): 208–220.

Carr, A. (2000b) 'Critical theory and the psychodynamics of change: a note about organizations as therapeutic settings', *Journal of Organizational Change Management*, 13(3): 289–299.

Carr, A. and Hancock, P. (2003) *Art and Aesthetics at Work*. London: Palgrave.

Carson, P.P. and Carson, K.D. (1998) 'Theoretically grounding management history as a relevant and valuable form of knowledge', *Journal of Management History*, 4(1): 29–42.

Carter, C.R. (2000) 'Ethical issues in international buyer–supplier relationships: a dyadic examination', *Journal of Operations Management*, 18: 191–208.

Carter, P. and Jackson, N. (2004) 'For the sake of argument: towards an understanding of rhetoric as process', *Journal of Management Studies*, 41: 469–491.

Case, P. (1999) 'Remember re-engineering? The rhetorical appeal of a managerial salvation device', *Journal of Management Studies*, 36: 419–441.

Casey, C. (1995) *Work, Self and Society: After Industrialism*. London: Routledge.

Casey, D. and Pearce, D. (eds) (1977) *More Than Management Development: Action Learning at GECI*. Aldershot: Gower.

Cassell, C.M., Buehring, A., Symon, G. and Johnson, P. (2006) 'The role and status of qualitative research in the business and management field: an empirical study', *Management Decision*, 2: 290–303.

Cassell, C.M., Buehring, A., Symon, G., Johnson, P. and Bishop, V. (2005) 'Benchmarking good practice in qualitative management research'. Research report. Sheffield: University of Sheffield.

Cassell, C.M., Fitter, M.J., Fryer, D.F. and Smith, L. (1988) 'The development of computer applications by non-employed people in community settings', *Journal of Occupational Psychology*, 61(1): 89–102.

Cassell, C.M., Nadin, S.J., Gray, M. and Clegg, C.M. (2002) 'The use of HRM practices in small and medium-sized enterprises', *Personnel Review*, 31(6): 671–692.

Catterall, M. and Maclaran, P. (1997) 'Focus group data and qualitative analysis programs: coding the moving picture as well as the snapshots', *Sociological Research Online*, 2(1): http://www.socresonline.org.uk/socresonline/2/1/6.html.

Cavell, S. (1969) *Must we Mean What we Say?* New York: Charles Scribner.

Certeau De, M. (1984) *The Practice of Eeryday Life*. Berkeley: University of California Press.

Césaire, A. (1950) *Discourse on Colonialism*. New York: Monthly Review Press.

Chamberlayne, P., Bornat, J. and Wengraf, T. (eds) (2000) *The Turn to Biographical Methods in Social Science*. London: Routledge.

Chandler, A.D. (1964) *Strategy and Structure*. Cambridge, MA: MIT Press.

REFERENCES

Chandler, A.D. (1990) *Scale and Scope: The Dynamics of Industrial Capitalism*. Cambridge, MA: Belknap Press.

Chang, I. (1997) *The Rape of Nanking*. New York: Basic Books.

Charmaz, K. (2000/2003) 'Grounded theory: objectivist and constructivist methods', in N.K. Denzin and Y.S. Lincoln (eds) *Handbook of Qualitative Research* (2nd edn). London: Sage. pp. 509–535.

Charmaz, K. (2005) 'Grounded theory in the 21st century: applications for advancing social justice studies', in N.K. Denzin and Y.S. Lincoln (eds) *The Sage Handbook of Qualitative Research*. London: Sage.

Checkland, P. (1981) *Systems Thinking, Systems Practice*. London: John Wiley.

Checkland, P. and Holwell, S. (1998) *Information, Systems and Information Systems*. London: John Wiley.

Checkland, P. and Holwell, S. (2004) '"Classic" OR and "Soft" OR an asymmetric complementarity', in M. Pidd (ed.) *Systems Modelling: Theory and Practice*. London: John Wiley.

Checkland, P. and Poulter, J. (2006) *Learning for Action*. London: John Wiley.

Checkland, P. and Scholes, J. (1990/1999) *SSM in Action*. London: John Wiley.

Chell, E. (1998) 'Critical incident technique', in G. Symon and C. Cassel (eds) *Qualitative Methods and Analysis in Organizational Research: A Practical Guide*. London: Sage.

Chen, P. and Hinton, S.M. (1999) 'Realtime interviewing using the world wide web', *Sociological Research Online*, 4(3): www. socresonline.org.uk/4/3/chen.html.

Cheney, G., Christensen, T., Conrad, C. and Lair, D. (2005) 'Corporate rhetoric as organizational discourse', in D. Grant, C. Hardy, C. Oswick and L. Putnam (eds) *The Sage Handbook of Organizational Discourse*. London: Sage.

Cheyne, T.L. and Ritter, F.E (2001) 'Targeting audiences on the internet', *Communications of the ACM*, 44(4): 94–98.

Chia, R. (1999) 'A "rhizomic" model of organizational change and transformation: perspectives from a metaphysics of change', *British Journal of Management*, 10: 209–227.

Chia, R. (2002) 'Time, duration and simultaneity: rethinking process and change in organizational analysis,' *Organization Studies*, 23(6): 836–868.

Chia, R. (2004) 'Strategy as practice: reflections on the research agenda', *European Management Review*, 1(1): 29–34.

Chia, R. and Holt, R. (2006) 'Strategy as practical coping: a Heideggerian perspective', *Organization Studies*, 27(5): 635–655.

Chia, R. and Langley, A. (2004) 'The first Organization Studies Summer Workshop: theorizing process in organizational research' (call for papers), *Organization Studies*, 25(8): 1466.

Children and Young People's Unit (2001) *Learning to Listen: Core Principles for the Involvement of Children and Young People*. London: CYPU.

Chisholm, R.F. (1998) *Developing Network Organizations: Learning from Practice and Theory*. Reading, MA: Addison-Wesley.

Choi, T.Y., Dooley, K.J. and Rungtusanatham, M. (2001) 'Supply networks and complex adaptive systems: control versus emergence', *Journal of Operations Management*, 19(3): 351–366.

Christensen, L.T. (1995) 'Buffering organizational identity in the marketing culture', *Organization Studies*, 16(4): 651–672.

Clair, R.P. (1994) 'Resistance and oppression as a self-contained opposite: an organizational communication analysis of one man's story of sexual harassment', *Western Journal of Communication*, 58: 235–263.

Clapper, D.L. and Massey, A.P. (1996) 'Electronic focus groups: a framework for exploration', *Information & Management*, 30: 43–50.

Clark, P.A. (1972) *Action Research and Organisational Change*. London: Harper & Row.

Clark, T. and Mangham, I.L. (2004) 'From dramaturgy to theatre as technology: the case of corporate theatre', *Journal of Management Studies*, 41: 37–59.

Clarke, A. (1991) 'Social worlds/arenas theory as organizational theory', in D.R. Maines (ed.) *Social Organization and Social Process: Essays in the Honor of Anselm Strauss*. Hawthorn, NY: Aldine de Gruyter. pp. 119–158.

Clarke, A. (2005) *Situational Analysis: Grounded Theory After the Postmodern Turn*. London: Sage.

Clarke, J.S. (2007) *Seeing Entrepreneurship: Visual Ethnographies of Embodied Entrepreneurs*, unpublished PhD thesis, Leeds University Business School.

Clarke, I. and Mackaness, W. (2000) 'Management 'intuition': an interpretative account of structure and content of decision schemas using cognitive maps', *Journal of Management Studies*, 38: 147–172.

Clarke, I., Horita, M. and Mackaness, W. (2000) 'The spatial knowledge of retail decision makers: capturing and interpreting group insight using a composite cognitive map', *The International Review of Retail, Distribution and Consumer Research*, 10: 265–285.

Clarkson, G.P. and Hodgkinson, G.P. (2005) 'Introducing Cognizer™: a comprehensive computer pacag for the elicitation and analysis of cause maps', *Organizational Research Methods*, 8: 317–341.

Clegg, S. (1997) 'Foucault, power and organizations', in A. McKinlay and K. Starkey (eds) *Foucault, Management and Organization Theory: From Panopticon to Technologies of Self*. London: Sage. pp. 29–48.

Clegg, S. and Kornberger, M. (2003) 'Modernism, postmodernism, management and organization theory', *Research in the Sociology of Organizations*, 21: 57–89.

Clegg, S.R., Kornberger, M. and Rhodes, C. (2005a). 'Learning/becoming/organizing', *Organization*, 12(2): 147–167.

Clegg, S., Kornberger, M., Carter, C. and Rhodes, C. (2005b) 'For management?', *Management Learning*, 37: 7–27.

Clifford, J. (1986) 'Introduction: partial truths', in J. Clifford and G.E. Marcus (eds) *Writing Culture: The Poetics and Politics of Ethnography*. Berkeley and Los Angeles: University of California Press.

Coghlan, D. (1998) 'The interlevel dynamics of information technology', *Journal of Information Technology*, 13(2): 139–149.

Coghlan, D. and Pedler, M. (2006) 'Action learning dissertations: structure, supervision and examination', *Action Learning: Research & Practice*, 3(2): 127–140.

Collier, J. and Collier, M. (1986) *Visual Anthropology: Photography as a Research Method*. Albuquerque, NM: University of New Mexico Press.

Collins, D. and Rainwater, K. (2005) 'Managing change at Sears: a sideways look at a tale of corporate transformation', *Journal of Organizational Change Management*, 18(1): 16–30.

Collins, P. (1998) *Changing Ideals in Architecture*. Montreal: McGill-Queen's University Press.

Collinson, D. and Hearn, J. (1996) *Men as Managers, Managers as Men*. London: Sage.

Colville, I.D., Waterman, R.H. and Weick, K.E. (1999) 'Organizing and the search for E: excellence: making sense of the times in theory and practice', *Organization*, 6(1): 129–148.

Confucius (1979) 'The analects' (500 BC). Trans D.C. Lau. Hong Kong: Chinese University Press.

Cook, S.D.N. and Brown, J.S. (1999) 'Bridging epistemologies: the generative dance between organizational knowledge and organizational knowing', *Organization Science*, 10(4): 381–400.

Cooke, B. (2003) 'The denial of slavery in management studies', *Journal of Management Studies*, 40(8): 1895–1918.

Coomber, R. (1997) 'Using the internet for survey research', *Sociological Research Online*, 2(2): www.socresonline.org.uk/2/2/chen.html.

Cooper, R. (1976) 'The open field', *Human Relations*, 29(11): 999–1017.

Cooper, R. (1989) 'Modernism, postmodernism and organizational analysis 3: the contribution of Jacques Derrida', *Organization Studies*, 10: 479–502.

Cooper, R. (2005) 'Relationality', *Organization Studies*, 26(11): 1689–1710.

Cooperrider, D. (1990) 'Positive image, positive action: the affirmative basis of organizing', in S. Srivastva and D. Cooperrider (eds) *Appreciative Management and Leadership*. San Francisco, CA: Jossey-Bass. pp. 91–125.

Cooperrider D. and Srivastva, S. (1987) 'Appreciative inquiry in organizational life', *Research in Organizational Change and Development*, 1: 129–169.

Coopey, J., Keegan, O. and Elmer, N. (1998) 'Managers innovations and the structuration of organizations', *Journal of Management Studies*, 35: 264–284.

Cooren, F. (2004) 'The communicative achievement of collective minding: analysis of board meeting excerpts', *Management Communication Quarterly*, 17: 517–552.

REFERENCES

Cope, J. and Watts, G. (2000) 'Learning by doing: an exploration of experience, critical incidents, and reflection in entrepreneurial learning', *International Journal of Entrepreneurial Behaviour and Research*, 6(2): 104–124.

Corbin, J. and Strauss, A.L. (1990/1998) 'Grounded theory research: procedures, canons and evaluative criteria', *Qualitative Sociology*, 13: 3–21.

Cornelissen, J.P. (2004) 'What are we playing at? Theatre, organization and the use of metaphor', *Organization Studies*, 25: 705–726.

Cornelissen, J.P. (2005) 'Beyond compare: metaphor in organization theory', *Academy of Management Review*, 30(1): 751–764.

Coupland, C., Blyton, P. and Bacon, P. (2005) 'A longitudinal study of the influence of shop-floor work teams on expressions of "us" and "them"', *Human Relations*, 58: 1055–1081.

Covaleski, M., Dirsmith, M., Heian, J. and Samuel, S. (1998) 'The calculated and the avowed: techniques of discipline and struggles over identity in Big Six public accounting firms', *Administrative Science Quarterly*, 43: 293–327.

Coveney, P. and Highfield, R. (1996) *Frontiers of Complexity*. London: Faber and Faber.

Crabtree, B.F. and Miller, W.L. (1992) 'A template approach to text analysis: developing and using code-books', in B.F. Crabtree and W.L. Miller (eds) *Doing Qualitative Research*. Beverley Hills, CA: Sage.

Cragg, W. (2002) 'Business ethics and stakeholder theory', *Business Ethics Quarterly*, 12(2): 113–142.

Craib, I. (1995) 'Some comments on the sociology of emotions', *Sociology*, 29(1): 151–158.

Cressey, D. (1953) *Other Peoples' Money*. Glencoe, IL: Free Press.

Crowston, K. (1997) 'A coordination theory approach to organizational process design', *Organization Science*, 8: 157–175.

Crush, J. (1994) 'Scripting the compound: power and space in the South African mining industry', *Environment and Planning D: Society and Space*, 12(3): 301–324.

Cummings-Neville, R. (2000) *Boston Confucianism: Portable Tradition in the Late-modern World*. Albany, NY: State University of New York Press.

Cunliffe, A.L.(2001) 'Managers as practical authors: reconstructing our understanding of management practice', *Journal of Management Studies*, 38: 351–371.

Cunliffe, A.L. (2002) 'Social poetics: a dialogical approach to management inquiry', *Journal of Management Inquiry*, 11: 128–146.

Cunliffe, A.L. (2003) 'Reflexive inquiry in organization research: questions and possibilities', *Human Relations*, 56: 981–1001.

Currall, S.C. and Towler, A.J. (2003) 'Research methods in management and organizational research: toward integration of qualitative and quantitative techniques', in A. Tashakkori and C. Teddlie (eds) *Handbook of Mixed Methods in Social and Behavioral Research*. Thousand Oaks, CA: Sage. pp. 513–526.

Curran, J., Jarvis, R., Blackburn, R.A. and Black, S. (1993) 'Networks and small firms: constructs, methodological strategies, and some findings', *International Small Business Journal*, 11(2): 13–25.

Czarniawska, B. (1997) *Narrating the Organization: Dramas of Institutional Identity*. Chicago: University of Chicago Press.

Czarniawska, B. (1998) 'A narrative approach to organization studies', *Qualitative Research Methods Series* (Vol. 43). Thousand Oaks, CA: Sage.

Czarniawska, B. (1999) *Writing Management: Organisation Theory as a Literary Genre*. Oxford: Oxford University Press.

Czarniawska, B. and Sevón, G. (2003) 'Introduction: did the Vikings know how to organize?', in B. Czarniawska and G. Sevón (eds) *The Northern Lights: Organization Theory in Scandinavia*. Abstract. Libes. Stockholm, Oslo, Copenhagen: Copenhagen Business School Press. pp. 9–13.

Dachler, P.H. and Hosking, D.M. (1995) 'The primacy of relations in socially constructing organizational realities', in D.M. Hosking, P.H. Dachler and K. Gergen (eds), *Management and Organization: Relational Alternatives to Individualism*. Avebury: Aldershot. pp. 1–28.

Dalcher, D. and Drevin, L. (2003) 'Learning from information systems failures by using narrative and antenarrative methods', *Proceedings of SAICSIT*, pp. 137–142.

Dalton, M. (1959) *Men who Manage: Fusions of Feeling and Theory in Administration*. New York: Wiley.

Dalton, M. (1964) 'Preconceptions and methods in "Men who manage"', in P.E. Hammond (ed.) *Sociologists at Work: Essays on the Craft of Social Research*. New York: Basic Books.

Danieli, A. and Woodhams, C. (2005) 'Gaining access for researching sensitive subjects: the carrot or the stick?', Paper presented at Gender, Work and Organization, 4th International Interdisciplinary Conference, 22–24 June 2005, Keele.

Darso, L. (2004) *Artful Creation: Learning-Tales of Arts-in-Business*. Copenhagen: Samfundslitteratur.

Darwin, C. (1872/1955) *The Expression of Emotion in Man and Animals*. New York: Philosophical Library.

Davis, P.J. (2006) 'Critical incident technique: a learning intervention for organizational problem solving', *Development and Learning in Organizations*, 20(2): 13–16.

De Graaf, G. (2001) 'Discourse theory and business ethics: the case of bankers' conceptualizations of customers', *Journal of Business Ethics*, 31: 299–319.

De Vaus, D. (2001) *Research Design in Social Research*. London: Sage.

Dean, M. (1999) *Governmentality: Power and Rule in Modern Society*. Thousand Oaks, CA: Sage.

Deetz, S. (1996) 'Describing differences in approaches to organisation science: rethinking Burrel and Morgan and their legacy', *Organisation Science*, 7: 191–207.

Deetz, S.A. (1998) 'Discursive formations, strategized subordination and self-surveillance', in A. McKinlay and K. Starkey (eds) *Foucault, Management and Organization Theory*. London: Sage. pp. 151–172.

Delamont, S. (1976) 'Beyond Flanders' field: the relationship of subject-matter and individuality to classroom style', in M. Stubbs and S. Delamont (eds) *Explorations in Classroom Observation*. Chichester: Wiley. pp. 101–131.

Delanty, G. (1997) *Social Science: Beyond Constructivism and Realism*. Minneapolis, MN: University of Minnesota Press.

Delbridge, R. (1998) *Life on the Line in Contemporary Manufacturing: The Workplace Experience of Lean Production and the 'Japanese' Model*. Oxford: Oxford University Press.

Deleuze, G. and Guattari, F. (1987) *A Thousand Plateaus: Capitalism and Schizophrenia*. Trans B. Massumi. Minneapolis, MN: University of Minnesota Press.

Denning, S. (2001) *The Springboard: How Storytelling Ignites Action in Knowledge-era Organizations*, Woburn, MA: Butterworth-Heinemann.

Denning, S. (2005) *The Leader's Guide to Storytelling: Mastering the Art and Discipline of Business Narrative*. San Francisco, CA: Jossey-Bass.

Denyer, D. and Neely, A. (2004) 'Introduction to special issue: innovation and productivity performance in the UK', *International Journal of Management Reviews*, 5/6 (3&4): 131–135.

Denzin, N.K. (1971) 'The logic of naturalistic inquiry', *Social Forces*, 50: 166–82.

Denzin, N.K. (1978) *The Research Act: A Theoretical Introduction to Sociological Methods* (2nd edn). New York: McGraw-Hill.

Denzin, N.K. (1990) 'On understanding emotion: the interpretive-cultural agenda', in T.D. Kemper (ed.) *Research Agendas in the Sociology of Emotions*. Albany, NY: State University of New York Press.

Denzin, N.K. (1994) 'The art and politics of interpretation', in N.K. Denzin and Y.S. Lincoln (eds) *Handbook of Qualitative Research*. Thousand Oaks, CA: Sage.

Denzin, N.K. and Lincoln, Y.S. (2005) 'Introduction: the discipline and practice of qualitative research', in N.K. Denzin and Y.S. Lincoln (eds) *The Sage Handbook of Qualitative Research*. Thousand Oaks, CA: Sage.

Department of Health (UK) (1998) *Modernising Social Services: Promoting Independence, Improving Protection and Raising Standards* (CM4169). London: HMSO.

Department of Health (UK) (1999) *National Service Framework for Mental Health: Modern Standards and Modern Service Models*. London: Department of Health.

Department of Health (UK) (2000a) *A Quality Strategy for Social Care*. London: Department of Health.

Department of Health (UK) (2000b) *The NHS Plan: A Plan for Investment, a Plan for Reform*. London: Department of Health.

Department of Health (UK) (2001) *Research Governance Framework for Health and Social Care*. London: Department of Health.

Derrida, J. (1973) *Speech and Phenomena, and Other Essays on Husserl's Use of Signs*. Trans D. Allison. Evanston, IL: Northwestern University Press.

Derrida, J. (1976) *Of Grammatology*. Trans G. Spivak. Baltimore, MD: Johns Hopkins University Press.

Derrida, J. (1978/2001) *Writing and Difference*. Trans A. Bass. London: Routledge and Kegan Paul.

Dewey, J. (1922/1988) 'Human nature and conduct', in J.A. Boydston (ed.) *Middle Works 14*. Carbondale and Edwardsvillc, IL: Southern Illinois University Press.

Dewey, J. (1925/1984) 'The development of American pragmatism', in J.A. Boydston (ed.) *Later Works 2*. Carbondale and Edwardsvillc, IL: Southern Illinois University Press. pp. 3–21.

Dey, I. (2003) *Qualitative Data Analysis*. London: Sage.

Dey, I. (2004) 'Grounded theory', in C. Seale, G. Gobo, J.F. Gubrium and D. Silverman (eds) *Qualitative Research Practice*. London: Sage.

Dixon, N. (1997) 'More then just a task force', in M. Pedler (ed.) *Action Learning in Practice* (3rd edn). Aldershot: Gower Press. pp. 329–338.

Donaldson, L. (1996) *For Positivist Organization Theory: Proving the Hard Core*. London: Sage.

Donaldson, T. and Preston, L.E. (1995) 'The stakeholder theory of the corporation: concepts, evidence and implications', *Academy of Management Review*, 20(1): 65–91.

Donnellon, A. (1996) *Team Talk: The Power of Language in Team Dynamics*. Boston: Harvard Business School Press.

Doolin, B. (2003) 'Narratives of change: discourse, technology and organization', *Organization*, 10: 751–770.

Dougherty, D. (1992) 'A practice centred model of organizational renewal through product innovation', *Strategic Management Journal*, 13: S77–S96.

Dougherty, D. and Kunda, G. (1990) 'Photograph analysis: a method to capture organizational belief systems', in P. Gagliardi (ed.) *Symbols and Artefacts: Views of the Corporate Landscape*. Berlin: Walter De Gruyter.

Douglas, S.P. and Craig, C.S. (2006) 'On improving the conceptual foundations of international marketing research', *Journal of International Marketing*, 14(1): 1–22.

Dreyfus, H. (2006) 'Being and power: Heidegger and Foucault', available at http://ist-socrates.berkeley edu/~hdreyfus/html/paper_being.html [accessed: 9 June 2006].

Drori, I. (2000) *The Seam Line: Arab Workers and Jewish Managers in the Isaeli Textile Industry*. Stanford, CA: Stanford University Press.

Duberley, J., Mallon, M. and Cohen, L. (2006) 'Exploring career transitions: accounting for structure and agency', *Personnel Review*, 35(3): 261–296.

Duffy, F. (1997) *The New Office*. London: Conran Octopus.

Dunaway, D.K. and Baum, W.K. (eds) (1996) *Oral History: An Interdisciplinary Anthology* (2nd edn). Walnut Creek, CA: Altamira Press.

Duncombe, J. and Marsden, D. (1993) 'Love and intimacy – the gender division of emotion and "emotion work"', *Sociology*, 27(2): 221–241.

Duncombe, J. and Marsden, D. (1996) 'Can we research the private sphere? Methodological and ethical problems in the study of the role of intimate emotion in personal relationships', in L. Morris and E.S. Lyon (eds) *Gender Relations in Public and Private*. London: Macmillan.

Dunford, R. and Jones, D. (2000) 'Narrative in strategic change', *Human Relations*, 53(9): 1207–1226.

Durkheim, E. (1893/1964) *The Division of Labor in Society*. New York: Free Press.

Easterby-Smith, M. (1980) *How to Use Repertory Grids in HRD*. Bradford: MCB Publications.

Easterby-Smith, M. and Malina, D. (1999) 'Cross-cultural collaborative research: towards reflexivity', *Academy of Management Journal*, 42(1): 76–86.

Easterby-Smith, M., Thorpe, R. and Lowe, A. (1991/2002) *Management Research: An Introduction*. London: Sage.

Easton, G. (2002) 'Marketing: a critical realist approach', *Journal of Business Research*, 55: 103–109.

Easton, G., Easton, A. and Belch, M. (2003) 'An experimental investigation of electronic focus groups', *Information and Management*, 40: 717–727.

Eberle, T.S. (1995) 'Relational knowledge in organizational theory: an exploration into some of its implication', in D.-M. Hosking, P.H. Dachlerand and K. Gergen (eds), *Management and Organization: Relational Alternatives to Individualism*. Avebury: Aldershot. pp. 201–219.

Eco, U. (1984/1986) *Semiotics and the Philosophy of Language*. Bloomington: Indiana University Press.

Eden, C. (1988) 'Cognitive mapping: a review', *European Journal of Operational Research*, 36: 1–13.

Eden, C. (1989) 'Strategic options development and analysis – "SODA", in J. Rosenhead (ed.) *Rational Analysis in a Problematic World*. London: Wiley.

Eden, C. and Ackermann, F. (2001) 'SODA - the principles', in J. Rosenhead and J. Mingers (eds) *Rational Analysis in a Problematic World Revisited*. London: Wiley. pp. 21–42.

Eden, C., Ackermann, F. and Cropper, S. (1992). 'The analysis of causal maps', *Journal of Management Studies*, 29(3): 309–324.

Eden, C. and Huxham, C. (2002) 'Action research', in D. Partington (ed.) *Essential Skills for Management Research*. London: Sage. pp. 254–272.

Edvardsson, B. (1992) 'Service breakdowns: A study of critical incidents in an airline', *International Journal of Service Industry Management*, 3(4): 17–290.

Edvardsson, B. and Roos, I. (2001) 'Critical incident techniques: towards a framework for analysing the criticality of critical incidents', *International Journal of Service Industry Management*, 12(3): 251–268.

Edwards, D. (1997) *Discourse and Cognition*. London: Sage.

Edwards, T., Almond, P., Clark, I., Colling, T. and Ferner, A. (2005) 'Reverse diffusion in US multinationals: barriers from the American business system', *Journal of Management Studies*, 42(6): 1261–1286.

Eisenhardt, K.M. (1989a) 'Building theories from case study research', *Academy of Management Review*, 14: 532–550.

Eisenhardt, K.M. (1989b) 'Making fast strategic decisions in high velocity environments', *Academy of Management Journal*, 31(4): 543–576.

Elias, N. (1987) 'On human beings and their emotions: a process-sociological essay', *Theory, Culture and Society*, 4: 339–361.

Elkjaer, B. (2004) 'Organizational learning: the "third way"', *Management Learning*, 35(4): 419–434.

Elliot, C. (1999) *Locating the Energy for Change: An Introduction to Appreciative Inquiry*. Winnipeg, Canada: International Institute for Sustainable Development.

Elliott, J. (1991) *Action Research for Educational Change*. Buckingham: Open University Press.

Emirbayer, M. (1997) 'Manifesto for a relational sociology', *American Journal of Sociology*, 103(2): 281–317.

Emmanuel, A. (1972) 'Unequal exchange: a study of the imperialism of trade'. New York: Monthly Review Press.

Emmison, M. and Smith, P. (2000) *Researching the Visual: Images, Objects, Contexts and Interactions in Social and Cultural Inquiry*. London: Sage.

Empson, W. (1947) *Seven Types of Ambiguity* (Revised edn). London: Chatto and Windus.

Engels, F. (1880/1970) 'Socialism: utopian and scientific', in *Marx/Engels Selected Works*, (Vol. 3). London: Progress Publishers. pp. 95–151.

Engeström, Y. (1987) *Learning by Expanding. An Activity Theoretical Approach to Developmental Research*. Helsinki: Orienta Konsultit.

Engeström, Y. (1991) 'Developmental work research: reconstructing expertise through expansive learning', in M.I. Nurminen and G.R.S. Weir (eds) *Human Jobs and Computer Interfaces*. Amsterdam: Elsevier Science Publishers. pp. 265–290.

Engeström, Y., Virkkunen, J., Helle, M., Pihlaja, J. and Poikela, R. (1996) 'The change laboratory as a tool for transforming work', *Lifelong Learning in Europe*, 2: 10–17.

Erdem, F. and Satir, C. (2003) 'Features of organisational culture in manufacturing organisations: a metaphorical analysis', *Work Study*, 52(3): 129–135.

Erzberger, C. and Kelle, U. (2003) 'Making inferences in mixed methods: the rules of integration', in A. Tashakkori and C. Teddlie (eds) *Handbook of Mixed Methods in Social and Behavioral Research*. Thousand Oaks, CA: Sage. pp. 457–488.

Eskola, K. (1990) 'Literature and interpretive communities - literary communication: on relevant concepts and empirical applications in Finland', *Acta Sociologica*, 33(4): 359–371.

European Journal of Social Theory (2004) 7(3).

Evans, C. (2006) 'Repertory grids'. Available at: www.psyctc.org/grids/

Evans, C. and Carmichael, A. (2002) *User's Best Value: A guide to Good Practice in User Involvement in Best Value Reviews*. York: Joseph Rowntree Foundation, Wiltshire and Swindon Service Users' Network and the University of Bath.

Evans, R. (1997) *In Defence of History*. London: Granta.

Everitt, A., Hardiker, P., Littlewood, J. and Mullender, A. (1992) *Applied Research for Better Practice*. Basingstoke: Macmillan.

Fairclough, N. (1989) *Language and Power*. London: Longman.

Fairclough, N. (1992) *Discourse and Social Change*. Cambridge: Polity Press.

Fairclough, N. (1995) *Critical Discourse Analysis: The Critical Study of Language*. London: Sage.

Fairclough, N. and Hardy, G. (1997) 'Management learning as discourse', in J. Burgoyne and M. Reynolds (eds) *Management Learning: Integrating Perspectives in Theory and Practice*. London: Sage.

Fallon, G. and Brown, R.B. (2002) 'Focusing on focus groups: lessons from a research project involving a Bangladeshi community', *Qualitative Research*, 2(2): 195–208.

Fanon, F. (1952/1986) *Black Skins, White Masks*. London: Pluto Press.

Fanon, F. (1963) *The Wretched of the Earth*. London: Penguin.

Fay, B. (1996) *Contemporary Philosophy of Social Science: A Multicultural Approach*. Oxford: Blackwell.

Feldman, M.S. and Pentland, B.T. (2003) 'Reconceptualizing organizational routines as a source of flexibility and change', *Administrative Science Quarterly*, 48(March): 94–118.

Fergusson, F. (1961) 'Introduction', *Aristotle's Poetics*. Trans S.H. Butcher. New York: Hill and Wang.

Fern, E.F. (2001) *Advanced Focus Group Research*. Thousand Oaks, CA: Sage.

Fiedler, F.E. (1967) *A Theory of Leadership Effectiveness*. New York: McGraw-Hill.

Fielding, N. (1981) *The National Front*. London: Routledge and Kegan Paul.

Fielding, N. and Fielding, J. (1986) *Linking Data: The Articulation of Qualitative and Quantitative Methods in Social Research*. Beverly Hills, CA: Sage.

Finegold, M.A., Holland, B.M. and Lingham, T. (2002) 'Appreciative inquiry and public dialogue: an approach to community change', *Public Organization Review*, 2: 235–252.

Fineman, S. (ed.) (1993) *Emotion in Organizations*. London: Sage.

Fineman, S. (2000) 'Commodifying the emotionally intelligent', in S. Fineman (ed.) *Emotion in Organizations* (2nd edn). London: Sage.

Finlay, L. (2002) 'Negotiating the swamp: the opportunity and challenge of reflexivity in research practice', *Qualitative Research*, 2(2): 209–230.

Fiol, C.M. (2002) 'Intraorganizational cognition and interpretation', in J.A.C. Baum (ed.) *The Blackwell Companion to Organizations*. Oxford: Blackwell.

Fish, S. (1990) 'How to recognize a poem when you see one', in D. Bartholomae and A. Petrosky (eds) *Ways of Reading: An Anthology for Writers*. Boston, MA: Belford Books of St Martins Press.

Flanagan, J.C. (1954) 'The critical incident technique', *Psychological Bulletin*, 51: 327–358.

Fleetwood, S. (ed.) (1999) *Critical Realism in Economics: Development and Debate*. London: Routledge.

Flick, U. (1998) *An Introduction to Qualitative Research*. London: Sage.

Flood, R.L. (2001) 'The relationship of "systems thinking" to action research', in P. Reason and H. Bradbury (eds) *Handbook of Action Research*. London: Sage. pp. 133–144.

Flyvbjerg, B. (1998) *Rationality and Power: Democracy in Practice*. Chicago: University of Chicago Press.

Flyvbjerg, B. (2001) *Making Social Sciences Matter: Why Social Inquiry Fails and How it Can Succeed Again*. Cambridge: Cambridge University Press.

Flyvbjerg, B. (2003) 'Making organization research matter: power, values and *phronesis*', in B. Czarniawska and G. Sevón (eds) *The Northern Lights: Organization Theory in Scandinavia*. Abstract. Liber. Stockholm, Oslo, Copenhagen: Copenhagen Business School Press. pp. 357–381.

Flyvbjerg, B. (2004) 'Five misunderstandings about case-study research', in C. Seale, G. Gobo, J.F. Gubrium and D. Silverman (eds) *Qualitative Research Practice*. London: Sage.

Fontana, A. and Frey, J.H. (1994) 'Interviewing: the art of science', in N.K. Denzin and Y.S. Lincoln (eds) *Handbook of Qualitative Research*. Thousand Oaks, CA: Sage. pp. 361–376.

Ford, J. and Ford, L. (1995) 'The role of conversations in producing intentional change in organizations', *Academy of Management Review*, 20: 541–570.

Foreman, J. and Thatchenkery, T.J. (1996) 'Filmic representations for organizational analysis: the characterization of a transplant organization in the film *Rising Sun*', *Journal of Organizational Change Management*, 9(3): 44–61.

Foucault, M. (1972) *The Archaeology of Knowledge and the Discourse on Language*. Trans A.M. Sheridan Smith. New York: Pantheon Books.

Foucault, M. (1977) *Discipline and Punish: The Birth of the Prison*. London: Penguin.

Foucault, M. (1984) 'Des espaces autres', *Architecture-Mouvement-Continuité* [diacritics Spring 1986].

Fransella, F. (2004) *A Manual for Repertory Grid Technique* (2nd edn). Chichester: Wiley.

Frederick, W.C. (1998) 'Creatures, corporations, communities, chaos, complexity: a naturological view of the corporate social role', *Business and Society*, 37(4): 358–376.

Freeman, R.E. (1984) *Strategic Management: A Stakeholder Approach*. Boston, MA: Pitman.

Freeman, R.E. (1999) 'Divergent stakeholder theory', *Academy of Management Review*, 24(2): 233–236.

Freeman, R.E. and Phillips, R.A. (2002) 'Stakeholder theory: a libertarian defense', *Business Ethics Quarterly*, 12(3): 331–349.

Freud, S. (1921) S.E. Vol. XVIII. London: Hogarth Press.

Friedman, V.J., (2001) 'Action science: creating communities of inquiry in communities of practice', in P. Reason and H. Bradbury (eds) *Handbook of Action Research*. Thousand Oaks, CA: Sage.

Friedman, V.J. and Berthoin, A. (2005) 'Negotiating reality: a theory of action approach to intercultural competence', *Management Learning*, 36(1): 69–86.

Friedman, V.J. Razer, M. and Sykes, I. (2004) 'Towards a theory of inclusive practice', *Action Research* 2(2): 167–189.

Frost, P.J. and Stablein, R.E. (1992) *Doing Exemplary Research*. Newbury Park, CA: Sage.

Frost, P.J., Moore, L.F., Louis, M.R., Lundberg, C.C. and Martin, J. (eds) (1991) *Reframing Organizational Culture*. Newbury Park, CA: Sage.

Frye, N. (1957) *The Anatomy of Criticism*. Princeton, NJ: Princeton University Press.

Gabriel, Y. (1999) *Organizations in Depth*. London: Sage.

Gabriel, Y. (2000) *Storytelling in Organizations: Facts, Fictions and Fantasies*. Oxford: Oxford University Press.

Gadamer, H. (1989) *Truth and Method* (2nd edn). Trans by J. Weinsheimer and D.G. Marshall. New York: Crossroad.

Gagliardi, P. (ed.) (1990) *Symbols and Artifacts: Views of the Corporate Landscape*. Berlin: Walter de Gruyter.

Gagliardi, P. (1996) 'Exploring the aesthetic side of organizational life', in S. Clegg, C. Hardy and W. Nord (eds) *The Handbook of Organization Studies*. London: Sage. (2nd edn, 2006).

Galunic, D. and Eisenhardt, K. (2001) 'Architectural innovation and modular corporate forms', *Academy of Management Journal*, 44: 1229–1250.

Gammack, J. and Stephens, R.A. (1994) 'Repertory grid technique in constructive interaction', in C. Cassell and G. Symon (eds) *Qualitative Methods in Organizational Research*. London: Sage. pp. 72–90.

Gardiner, M. (1992) *The Dialogics of Critique*. London: Routledge.

Gardner, C. (2002) 'An exploratory study of bureaucratic, heroic, chaos, postmodern and hybrid story typologies of the expatriate journey'. Dissertation in Management, Department of Business Administration and Economics,

Garfinkel, H. (1967/1984) *Studies in Ethnomethodology*. Cambridge: Polity Press.

Garfinkel, H. (ed.) (1986) *Ethnomethodological Studies of Work*. London: Routledge and Kegan Paul.

Garfinkel, H. (1991) 'Respecification: evidence for locally produced, naturally accountable phenomena of order, logic, reason, meaning, method, etc. in and as of the essential haecceity of immortal ordinary society (I) – an announcement of studies', in G. Button (ed.) *Ethnomethodology and the Human Sciences*. Cambridge: Cambridge University Press.

Garfinkel, H. (2002) *Ethnomethodology's Program: Working Out Durkheim's Aphorism*. Anne Warfield Rawls (ed.). Lanham, Rowman & Littlefield Publishers.

Garfinkel, H. (2006) *Seeing Sociologically: The Routine Grounds of Social Action*. Anne Warfield Rawls (ed.). Boulder, CO: Paradigm Publishers.

REFERENCES

Gargiulo, T.L. (2002) *Making Stories: A Practical Guide for Organizational Leaders and Human Resource Specialists*. London/Westport, CN: Quorum Books.

Garrett, P.M. (2000) 'Responding to Irish "invisibility": anti-discriminatory social work practice and the placement of Irish children in Britain', *Adoption and Fostering*, 24(1): 23–34.

Garrett, P.M. (2003) *Remaking Social Work with Children and Families: A Critical Discussion on the 'Modernisation' of Social Care*. London: Routledge.

Gartner, W. and Birley, S. (2002) 'Introduction to special issue on qualitative methods in entrepreneurship', *Journal of Business Venturing*, 17: 387–395.

Garud, R. and Van de Ven, A.H. (1992) 'An empirical evaluation of the internal corporate venturing process', *Strategic Management Journal*, 13: S93–S109.

Gaver, W.W. (1991) 'Technology affordances', *Proceedings of CHI '91*, pp. 79–84. New Orleans: ACM Press.

Gaver, W.W. (1996) 'Affordances for interaction: the social is material for design', *Ecological Psychology* 8(2): 111–129.

Geertz, C. (1973) *The Interpretation of Cultures: Selected Essays*. New York: Basic Books.

Geertz, C. (2000) *Available Light: Anthropological Reflections on Philosophical Topics*. Princeton, NJ: Princeton University Press.

Gell-Mann, M. (1994) *The Quark and the Jaguar*. New York: Freeman.

Gephart, R.P. Jr. (1991) 'Succession, sensemaking, and organizational change: a story of a deviant college president', *Journal of Organizational Change Management*, 4: 35–44.

Gergen, K.J. (1994a) *Realities and Relationships: Soundings in Social Construction*. Cambridge, MA: Harvard University Press.

Gergen, K.J. (1994b) *Toward Transformation in Social Knowledge* (2nd edn). New York: Sage.

Gergen, K.J. (1999) *An Invitation to Social Construction*. London: Sage.

Geuss, R. (1981) *The Idea of a Critical Theory*. Cambridge: Cambridge University Press.

Ghauri, P. and Gronhaug, K. (2002) *Research Methods in Business Studies: A Practical Guide*. London: Prentice Hall.

Gherardi, S. (2000) 'Practice-based theorizing on learning and knowing in organizations', *Organization*, 7(2): 211–223.

Gherardi, S. (2006) *Organizational Knowledge: The Texture of Organizing*. London: Blackwell.

Ghoshal, S. (2005) 'Bad management theories are destroying good management practices', *Academy of Management Learning and Education*, 4(1): 75–91.

Gibbons, M.L., Limoges, C., Nowotney, S., Schwartman, S., Scott P. and Trow, M. (1994) *The New Production of Knowledge: The Dynamics of Science and Research in Contemporary Societies*. London: Sage.

Gibson, J.J. (1979) *The Ecological Approach to Visual Perception*. Boston: Houghton Mifflin Company.

Giddens, A. (1976) *New Rules of Sociological Method*. London: Hutchinson.

Giddens, A. (1979) *Central Problems in Social Theory: Action, Structure and Contradiction in Social Analysis*. London: Macmillan.

Giddens, A. (1984) *The Constitution of Society*. Oxford: Polity Press.

Giddens, A. (1987) *Social Theory and Modern Sociology*. Oxford: Polity Press.

Giddens, A. (1989) 'A reply to my critics', in D. Held and J.B. Thompson (eds) *Social Theory of Modern Societies: Anthony Giddens and His Critics*. Cambridge: Cambridge University Press.

Giddens, A. and Pierson, C. (1998) *Conversations with Anthony Giddens - Making Sense of Modernity*. Cambridge: Polity Press.

Gilbreth, F.B. (1911) *Motion Study: A Method for Increasing the Efficiency of the Workman*. New York: D. van Nostrand.

Gilchrist, A. (2000) 'The well-connected community: networking to the edge of chaos', *Community Development Journal*, 3(3): 264–275.

Gill, A. and Whedbee, K. (1995) 'Rhetoric', in T. Van Dijk (ed.) *Discourse: Structure and Process*. London: Sage.

Gill, J. and Johnson, P. (1991) *Research Methods for Managers*. London: Paul Chapman.

Gioia D.A. (2007) 'On Weick: an appreciation', *Organization Studies*, 27(11): 1709–1721.

Gioia, D.A., Thomas, J.B., Clark, S.M. and Chittipeddi, K. (1994) 'Symbolism and strategic change in academia: the dynamics of sensemaking and influence', *Organization Science*, 5(3): 363–383.

Giorgi, A. and Giorgi, B. (2003) 'Phenomenology', in J.A. Smith (ed.) *Qualitative Psychology: A Practical Guide to Research Methods*. London: Sage.

Girton, G.D. (1986) 'Kung Fu: toward a praxiological hermeneutic of the martial arts', in H. Garfinkel (ed.) *Ethnomethodological Studies of Work*. London: Routledge and Kegan Paul.

Glaser, B. (1978) *Theoretical Sensitivity*. Mill Valley, CA: Sociology Press.

Glaser, B.G. (1992) *Basics of Grounded Theory Research*. Mill Valley: Sociology Press.

Glaser, B.G. and Strauss, A.L. (1967) *The Discovery of Grounded Theory: Strategies for Qualitative Research*. Hawthorn, NY: Aldine de Gruyter.

Goffman, E. (1956/1959) *The Presentation of Self in Everyday Life*. Edinburgh: University of Edinburgh Social Sciences Research Centre.

Goffman, E. (1967) *Interaction Ritual: Essays in Face-to-Face Behaviour*. Garden City, NY: Doubleday.

Gioia, D. (2006) 'On Weick: an appreciation', *Organization Studies*, 27: 1709–1721.

Goldberg, J. and Markóczy, L. (2000) 'Complex rhetoric and simple games', *Emergence*, 2(1): 72–100.

Golembiewski, R.T. (1999) 'Fine-tuning appreciative inquiry: two ways of circumscribing the concept's value-added', *Organization Development Journal*, 17(3): 21–26.

Goodwin, B. and Saunders, P. (eds) (1989) *Theoretical Biology: Epigenetic and Evolutionary Order From Complex Systems*. Edinburgh: Edinburgh University Press.

Gopal, A. and Prasad, P. (2000) 'Understanding GDSS in symbolic context: shifting the focus from technology to interaction', *MIS Quarterly*, 24: 509–546.

Gordon, T. and Pease, A. (2006) 'RT Delphi: an efficient, "round-less" almost real-time Delphi method', *Technological Forecasting and Social Change*, 73: 321–333.

Gould, S.J. (1989) 'Punctuated equilibrium in fact and theory', *Journal of Social Biological Structure*, 12: 117–136.

Goulding, C. (2002) *Grounded Theory: A Practical Guide for Management, Business and Market Researchers*. London: Sage.

Granovetter, M. (1973) 'The strength of weak ties', *American Journal of Sociology*, 78(6): 1360–1380.

Grant, D., Keenoy, T. and Oswick, C. (eds) (1998) *Discourse and Organization*. London: Sage.

Greene, J.C. and Caracelli, V.J. (1997) 'Defining and describing the paradigm issues in mixed-method evaluation', in J.C. Greene and V.J. Caracelli (eds) *Advances in Mixed-Method Evaluation: The Challenges and Benefits of Integrating Diverse Paradigms*. San Francisco: Jossey-Bass. pp. 5–18.

Greenwood, D.J. and Levin, M. (2005) 'Reform of the social sciences and of universities through action research', in N.K. Denzin and Y.S. Lincoln (eds) *The Sage Handbook of Qualitative Research*. London: Sage.

Greenwood, M. and De Cieri, H. (2007) 'Stakeholder theory and the ethics of human resource management', in R. Pinnington (ed.) *Ethics in Human Resource Management and Employment Relations*. Oxford: Oxford University Press.

Grele, R. (1998) 'Movement without aim: methodological and theoretical problems in oral history', in R. Perks and A. Thompson (eds) *The Oral History Reader*. London and New York: Routledge.

Gremler, D.D. (2004) The critical incident technique in service research, *Journal of Service Research*, 7(1): 65–89.

Grint, K (1991/1998) *The Sociology of Work*. Oxford and Cambridge: Polity Press.

Guba, E. and Lincoln, Y.S. (1994) 'Competing paradigms in qualitative research', in N.K. Denzin and Y.S. Lincoln (eds) *Handbook of Qualitative Research*. Newbury Park, CA: Sage. pp. 105–117.

Guillén, M.F. (2006) *The Taylorized Beauty of the Mechanical: Scientific Management and the Rise of Modernist Architecture*. Princeton, NJ: Princeton University Press.

Guillet de Monthoux, P. (2004) *The Art Firm: Aesthetic Management and Metaphysical Marketing*. Stanford, CA: Stanford University Press.

Gummesson, E. (2000) *Qualitative Methods in Management Research*. London: Sage.

Habermas, J. (1971) *Toward a Rational Society: Student Protest, Science and Politics*. London: Heinemann.

REFERENCES

Habermas, J. (1987) *The Theory of Communicative Action, Vol. 2: The Critique of Functionalist Reason.* London: Heinemann.

Haken, H. (1983) *Laser Theory.* Berlin: Springer.

Hall, E.T. (1959) *The Silent Language.* New York: Doubleday.

Hall, E.T. (1966) *The Hidden Dimension: Man's Use of Space in Public and Private.* New York: Doubleday.

Hall, E.T. (1976) *Beyond Culture.* New York: Doubleday.

Halsey, A.H. (1972) *Educational Priority (Vol. 1: E.P.A. Problems and Policies).* London: HMSO.

Hamilton, P. (1997) 'Rhetorical discourse of local pay', *Organization,* 4: 229–254.

Hamilton, P. (2001) 'Rhetoric and employment relations', *British Journal of Industrial Relations,* 39: 433–449.

Hamilton, P. (2003) 'The saliency of synecdoche: the part and the whole of employment relations', *Journal of Management Studies,* 40: 1569–1585.

Hamilton, P. (ed.) (2005a) *Visual Research Methods* (4 vols). London: Sage.

Hamilton, P. (2005b) 'The enthymeme in naturally occurring talk: needing to state the un-stated', Paper presented at the Critical Management Studies Conference, Cambridge, UK.

Hammond, T. and Sikka, P. (1996) 'Radicalizing accounting history: the potential of oral history', *Accounting, Auditing and Accountability Journal,* 9(3): 79–97.

Haney, C., Banks, C. and Zimbardo, P. (1973) 'Interpersonal dynamics in a simulated prison', *International Journal of Criminology and Penology,* 1: 69–97.

Hänfling, O. (2000) *Philosophy and Ordinary Language.* London: Routledge.

Hänfling, O. (2002) *Whittgenstein and the Human Form of Life.* London: Routledge.

Hanley, B., Bradburn, J., Barnes, M., Evans, C., Goodare, H., Kelson, M., Kent, A., Oliver, S., Thomas, S. and Wallcraft, J. (2004) *Involving the Public in NHS, Public Health and Social Care: Briefing Notes for Researchers.* Eastleigh: Involve.

Hansemark, O.C. (1997) 'Objective versus projective measurement of need for achievement: the relation between TAT and CMPS', *Journal of Managerial Psychology,* 12(4): 280–289.

Harcourt, Bernard E. (2001) *Illusion of order: The False Promise of Broken Windows Policing.* Cambridge, MA: Harvard University Press.

Harland, C.M., Lamming, R.C. and Cousins, P.D. (1999) 'Developing the concept of supply strategy', *International Journal of Operations and Productions Management,* 19: 650–674.

Harper, D. (1994) 'On the authority of the image: visual methods at the crossroads', in N.K. Denzin and Y.S. Lincoln (eds) *Handbook of Qualitative Research.* Thousand Oaks, CA: Sage. pp. 403–412.

Harper, D. (2000) 'Reimagining visual methods: Galileo to *Neoromancer*', in N.K. Denzin and Y.S. Lincoln (eds) *Handbook of Qualitative Research* (2nd edn). Thousand Oaks, CA: Sage.

Harré, R. (1986) *Varieties of Realism.* Oxford: Basil Blackwell.

Harré, R. and Parrott, W.G. (eds) (1996) *The Emotions: Social, Cultural and Biological Dimensions.* London: Sage.

Harré, R. and Secord, P.F. (1972) *The Explanation of Social Behaviour.* Oxford: Blackwell.

Harris, C., Daniels, K. and Briner, R.B. (2003) 'A daily diary study of goals and affective well-being at work', *Journal of Occupational and Organizational Psychology,* 76(3): 401–410.

Harris E. (1999) 'Project risk assessment: a European field study', *British Accounting Review,* 31(3): 347–371.

Harris, G. and Attour, S. (2003) 'The international advertising practices of multinational companies: a content analysis study', *European Journal of Marketing,* 37(1/2): 154–168.

Harris, M. (1993) *Culture, People, Nature: An Introduction to General Anthropology.* New York: Harper Collins.

Harrison, C. and Young, L. (2005) 'Leadership discourse in action: a textual study of organizational change in a Canadian bank', *Journal of Business and Technical Communication,* 19: 42–77.

Harrison, J. (1997) 'Museums as agencies of neocolonialism in a postmodern world', *Studies in Cultures, Organizations and Societies,* 3: 41–65.

Hartman, J. (2004) 'Using focus groups to conduct business communication research', *Journal of Business Communication,* 41(4): 402–410.

Harwood, T.G. and Garry, T. (2003) 'An overview of content analysis', *The Marketing Review*, 3: 479–498.

Hassard, J. and Holliday, R. (eds) (1998) *Organization Representation: Work and Organization in Popular Culture*. London: Sage.

Hassard, J., Law J. and Lee, N. (1999) 'Introduction: actor-network theory and managerialism', *Organization*, 6: 387–391.

Hasu, M. (2000) 'Constructing clinical use: an activity-theoretical perspective on implementing new technology', *Technology Analysis and Strategic Management*, 12(3): 369–382.

Hatch, M.J. (1997) *Organization Theory: Modern, Symbolic and Postmodern Perspectives*. Oxford: Oxford University Press.

Hayes, J. (2006) *The Theory and Practice of Change Management* (2nd edn). Basingstoke: Palgrave.

Hayes, N. and Walsham, G. (2000) 'Competing interpretations of computer-supported cooperative work in organizational contexts', *Organization*, 7: 49–67.

Hayles, K.N. (2000) 'From chaos to complexity: moving through metaphor to practice', *Complexity and Chaos in Nursing*, 4. www.southernct.edu/scsu/chaos-nursing/chaos4.htm

Hazen, M.A. (1993) 'Towards polyphonic organization', *Journal of Organizational Change Management*, 6(5): 15–22.

Hazen, M.A. (1994) 'Multiplicity and change in persons and organizations', *Journal of Organizational Change Management*, 7(5): 72–81.

Healey, M.J. (1991) 'Obtaining information from businesses', in M.J. Healey, (ed.) *Economic Activity and Land Use*. Harlow: Longman.

Hearn, J. and Parkin, W. (1993) 'Organizations, multiple oppressions and postmodernism', in J. Hassard, and M. Parker (eds) *Postmodernism and Organizations*: London: Sage. pp. 148–161.

Heath, C. and Hindmarsh, J. (2002) 'Analyzing interaction: video, ethnography and situated conduct', in T. May (ed.) *Qualitative Research in action*. London: Sage.

Hedges, N. and Beynon, H. (1982) *Born to Work: Images of Factory Life*. London: Pluto Press.

Hegel, G.F. (1807/1910) *The Phenomenology of Mind*. Trans J.B. Baillie. New York: Macmillan.

Heidegger, M. (1927/1962) *Being and Time*. Trans J. Macquarrie and E. Robinson. New York: Harper & Row.

Heikkinen, H.L.T. (2002) 'Whatever is narrative research?' In R. Huttunen, H.L.T. Heikkinen and L. Syrjala (eds.), *Narrative Research: Voices of Teachers and Philosophers*. Jyvaskyla: SoPhi.

Held, D. and Thompson, J.B. (1989) *Social Theory of Modern Societies: Anthony Giddens and His Critics*. Cambridge: Cambridge University Press.

Heller, F. (ed.) (1986) *The Use and Abuse of Social Science*. London: Sage.

Heracleous, L. and Barrett, M. (2001) 'Organizational change as discourse: communicative actions and deep structures in the context of information technology implementation', *Academy of Management Journal*, 44: 755–778.

Heracleous, L. and Marshak, R.J. (2004) 'Conceptualizing organizational discourse as situated symbolic action', *Human Relations*, 57: 1285–1313.

Heritage, J. and Atkinson, J.M. (1984) 'Introduction', in J.M. Atkinson and J. Heritage (eds) *Structures of Social Action*: *Studies in Conversation Analysis*. Cambridge: Cambridge University Press.

Hillier, B. and Penn, A. (1991) 'Visible colleges: structure and randomness in the place of discovery', *Science in Context*, 4(1): 23–49.

Hine, C. (1995) 'Representations of information technology in disciplinary development: disappearing plants and invisible networks', *Science, Technology and Human Values*, 20: 65–85.

Hirschman, E.C. (1999) 'When expert consumers interpret textual products: applying reader-response theory to television programs', *Consumption, Markets and Culture*, 2(3): 259–310.

Hochschild, A.R. (1983) *The Managed heart: Commercialisation of Human Feeling*. Berkeley: University of California Press.

Hodgkinson, G.P. and Clarkson, G.P. (2005) 'What have we learned from almost thirty years of research on causal mapping?', in V.K. Narayanan and D.J. Armstrong (eds) *Causal Mapping for Information Systems and Technology Research: Approaches, Advances and Illustrations*. Hershey, PA: Idea Group Inc.

Hoffman, A. (1996) 'Reliability and validity in oral history', in D.K. Dunaway and W.K. Baum (eds) *Oral History: An Interdisciplinary Anthology* (2nd edn). Walnut Creek, CA: Altamira Press.

REFERENCES

Hofstede, G. (1984) *Culture's Consequences: International Differences in Work Related Values*, abridged edn. London: Sage.

Hofstede, G. (2001) *Culture's Consequences: Comparing Values, Behaviours, Institutions, and Organizations Across Nations*. London: Sage.

Hofstede, G. and Bond, M.H. (1988) 'The Confucius connection: from cultural roots to economic growth', *Organizational Dynamics*, 16(4): 5–21.

Holliday, R. (2000) 'We've been framed: visualising methodology', *Sociological Review*, 48(4): 504–521.

Holt, D.B. (1995) 'How consumers consume: a typology of consumption practices', *Journal of Consumer Research*, 22(1): 1–16.

Horkheimer, M. and Adorno, T. (1947) *The Dialectics of Enlightenment*. London: Verso.

Horn, R. (1983) *Trialectics: Towards a Practical Logic of Unity*. Lexington, May: Information Sources.

Horne, M. and Steadman Jones, D. (2001) *Leadership: The Challenge for All?* London: Institute of Management and Demos.

Horschild, A. (1998) 'The sociology of emotion as a way of seeing', in G. Bendelow and S. Williams (eds) *Emotions and Social Life: Critical Themes and Contemporary Issues*. London: Routledge.

Hosking, D.-M., Dachler, P.H. and Gergen, K. (1995) 'Preface', in D.-M. Hosking, P.H. Dachler and K.Gergen (eds), *Management and Organization: Relational Alternatives to Individualism*. Avebury: Aldershot. pp. x–xiii.

Howells, R. (2003) *Visual Culture*. Cambridge: Polity Press.

Huff, A.S. (1990) *Mapping Strategic Thought*. Chichester: Wiley.

Hull, R. (1999) 'Actor network and conduct: the discipline and practices of knowledge management', *Organization*, 6: 405–428.

Humphreys, L. (1970) *Tearoom Trade*. Chicago: Aldine Press.

Humphreys, M. Brown, A. and Hatch M.J. (2003) 'Is ethnography jazz?', *Organization*, 10: 5–31.

Hunt, S.D. (2003) *Controversy in Marketing Theory: For Reason, Realism, Truth, and Objectivity.* Armonk, NY: M.E. Sharpe.

Hunt, S.D. (2005) 'For truth and realism in management research', *Journal of Management Inquiry*, 14: 127–138.

Husserl, E. (1931/1962) *Ideas: General Introduction to Pure Phenomenology.* Trans W.R. Boyce Gibson. New York: Collier Books.

Hussey, J. and Hussey, R. (1997) *Business Research: A Practical Guide for Undergraduate and Postgraduate Students*. Basingstoke: Palgrave.

Hutchby, I. (2001) 'Technologies, texts and affordances', *Sociology*, 35(2): 441–456.

Hutchby, I. and Wooffitt, R. (1997) *Conversational Analysis*. Oxford: Blackwell.

Hutton, J., Bazalgette, J. and Reed, B. (1997) 'Organization-in-the-mind', in J. Neumann, K. Kellner and A. Dawson-Shepherd (eds) *Developing Organizational Consultancy*. London: Routledge.

Huxham, C. and Beech, N. (2003) 'Contrary prescriptions: recognizing good practice tensions in management', *Organization Studies*, 24(1): 69–93.

Huxham, C. and Vangen, S. (2005) *Managing to Collaborate: The Theory and Practice of Collaborative Advantage*. London: Routledge.

Iddings Bell, B. (1926) *Postmodernism and Other Essays*. New York: Morehouse Publishing Company.

IDeA (2004) *Prospects, Improvement and Development Agency Co-funded by Leadership Research and Development Ltd*. www.IdeA.org.uk

Imrie, B.C., Cadogan, J.W. and McNaugton, R. (2002) 'The service quality construct on a global stage', *Managing Service Quality*, 12(1): 10–18.

Isabella, L.A. (1990) 'Evolving interpretations as change unfolds: how managers construe key organizational events', *Academy of Management Journal*, 33(1): 7–41.

Iser, W. (1978) *The Act of Reading: A Theory of Aesthetic Response*. Baltimore, MD: Johns Hopkins University Press.

Jackson, S. (1993) 'Even sociologists fall in love: an exploration in the sociology of emotions', *Sociology*, 27(2): 201–220.

Jacobs, C.D. and Heracleous, L. (2006) 'Constructing shared understanding: the role of embodied metaphors in organisational development', *The Journal of Applied Behavioural Science*, 42(2): 207–226.

James, W. (1909/1996) *A Pluralistic Universe*. Lincoln, NB: University of Nebraska Press.

James, W. (1946) *Pragmatism: A New Name for Some Old Ways of Thinking; Together with Four Related Essays Selected From 'The Meaning of Truth'*. London: Longmans, Green & Co.

Jankowicz, A.D. (2005) *Business Research Projects*. London: Thomson.

Jaques, E. (1953) 'On the dynamics of social structure', *Human Relations*, 6(3): 3–24.

Jarzabkowski, P. (2004) 'Strategy as practice: recursiveness, adaptation, and practices-in-use', *Organization Studies*, 24(4): 529–560.

Jaworski, A. and Coupland, N. (1999) 'Perspectives on discourse analysis', in A. Jaworski and N. Coupland (eds) *The Discourse Reader*. London: Routledge.

Jenkins, M. (2002) 'Cognitive mapping', in D. Partington (ed.) *Essential Skills for Management Research*. London: Sage. pp. 181–196.

Jenkins, M. and Engels, F. (1964) *Frederick Engels in Manchester*. [With a portrait and facsimiles.] Manchester, Lancashire and Cheshire Communist Party.

Jenner, R.A. (1998) 'Dissipative enterprises, chaos, and the principles of lean organizations', *Omega: International Journal of Management Science*, 26(3): 397–407.

Jensen, D.F.N. (2006) 'Metaphors as a bridge to understanding educational and social contexts', *International Journal of Qualitative Research*, 5(1): www.ualberta.ca/~iiqm/backissues/5_1/ html/ Jensen.htm> (retrieved 1 September 2006).

Jeremy, D.J. (2002) 'Business history and strategy', in A. Pettigrew, H. Thomas and R. Whittington (eds) *Handbook of Strategy and Management*. London: Sage.

Jerimer, J. (1985) '"When the sleeper awakes": a short story extending themes in radical organization theory', *Journal of Management*, 11(2): 67–80.

Jessop, B. (2002) *The Future of the Capitalist State*. Cambridge: Polity Press.

Jick, T.D. (1979) 'Mixing qualitative and quantitative methods: triangulation in action', *Administrative Science Quarterly*, 24: 602–611.

Johnson, G. and Huff, A. (1997) 'Everyday innovation/everyday strategy', in G. Hamel, C.K. Pralahad, H. Thomas and D. O'Neal (eds) *Strategic Flexibility*. London: Wiley.

Johnson, G., Melin L. and Whittington R. (2003) 'Micro-strategy and strategising', *Journal of Management Studies*, 40(1): 3–20.

Johnson, P. and Cassell, C. (2001) 'Epistemology and work psychology: new agendas', *Journal of Occupational and Organizational Psychology*, 74(2): 125–143.

Johnson, P. and Duberley, J. (2000) *Understanding Management Research: An Introduction to Epistemology*. London: Sage.

Johnson, P. and Duberley, J. (2003) 'Reflexivity in management research', *Journal of Management Studies*, 40(5): 1279–1303.

Johnston, R. (1995) 'The determinants of service quality: satisfiers and dissatisfiers', *International Journal of Service Industry Management*, 6(5): 53–71.

Jones, T.M., Wicks, A.C. and Freeman, R.E. (2002) 'Stakeholder theory: the state of the art', in N.E. Bowie (ed.) *The Blackwell Guide to Business Ethics*. Oxford: Blackwell. pp. 19–37.

Jordan, T., Raubal, M., Gartrell, B. and Egenhofer, M.J. (1998) 'An affordance-based model of place in GIS', in T. Poiker and N. Chrisman (eds) *Eighth International Symposium on Spatial Data Handling*, Vancouver, Canada. pp. 98–109.

Jordanova, L. (2000) *History in Practice*. London: Arnold.

Kagan N., Schauble P., Resinikoff, A., Danish, S.J. and Kratwohl D.R. (1967) *Studies in Human Interaction*. East Lansing, MI: Educational Publishing Services, Michigan State University.

Kahn, C.H. (1979) *The Art and Thought of Heraclitus*. Cambridge: Cambridge University Press.

Kaler, J. (2002) 'Morality and strategy in stakeholder identification', *Journal of Business Ethics*, 39(1): 91–99.

Kaler, J. (2003) 'Differentiating stakeholder theories', *Journal of Business Ethics*, 46(1): 71–83.

Kameoka, A., Yokoo, Y. and Kuwahara, T. (2004) 'A challenge of integrating technology foresight and assessment in industrial strategy development and policy making', *Technological Forecasting and Social Change*, 71: 579–598.

Kan, M.M. and Parry, K.W. (2004) 'Identifying paradox: a grounded theory of leadership in overcoming resistance to change', *The Leadership Quarterly*, 15: 467–491.

Kane, P. (2004) *The Play Ethic: Living Creatively in the New Century.* London: Macmillan.

Kant, I. (1781/1900) *Critique of Pure Reason.* Introduction by translator, J.M.D. Meiklejohn and special introduction by Brant V.B. Dixon NY: The Colonial Press.

Kasanen, E., Lukka, K. and Siitonen, A. (1993) 'The constructive approach in management accounting research', *Journal of Management Accounting Research*, 5: 243–264.

Katz, A.M. and Shotter, J. (1996) 'Hearing the patient's "voice": towards a social poetics in diagnostic interviews', *Social Science Medicine*, 43: 919–931.

Kauffman, S.A. (1993) *Origins of Order: Self-organisation and Selection in Evolution.* Oxford: Oxford University Press.

Kaye, M. (1996) *Myth-makers and Story-tellers.* Sydney, NSW: Business and Professional Publishing.

Kearney, K.S and Hyle, A.E. (2004) 'Drawing out emotions: the use of participant-produced drawings in qualitative research', *Qualitative Research*, 4(3): 361–382.

Kelly, A., Lawlor, K. and O'Donohoe, S. (2005) 'Encoding advertisements: the creative perspective', *Journal of Marketing Management*, 21: 505–528.

Kelly, G.A. (1955a) *Principles of Personal Construct Psychology.* (Vols 1&2). New York: W.W. Norton.

Kelly, G.A. (1955b) *The Psychology of Personal Constructs.* New York: W. W. Norton.

Kelly, G.A. (1969) *Clinical Psychology and Personality.* New York: Wiley.

Kelly, M. (1990) 'Introduction', in M. Kelly (ed.) *Hermeneutics and Critical Theory in Ethics and Politics.* Cambridge, MA: MIT Press.

Kemper, T.D. (ed.) (1990) *Research Agendas in the Sociology of Emotions.* Albany, NY: State University of New York Press.

Kent, J., Williamson, E., Goodenough, T. and Ashcroft, R. (2002) 'Social science gets the ethics treatment: research governance and ethical review', *Sociological Research Online*, 7(4): www.socresonline. org.uk/7/4/ williamson.html.

Kerosuo, H. and Engeström, Y. (2003) 'Boundary crossing and learning in creation of new work practice', *Journal of Workplace Learning*, 15(7/8): 345–351.

Kiel, L.D. (1994) *Managing Chaos and Complexity in Government.* San Francisco, CA: Jossey-Bass.

Kilduff, M. (1993) 'Deconstructing organizations', *Academy of Management Review*, 18: 13–31.

Kilduff, M. and Kelemen, M. (2001) 'The consolations of organization theory', *British Journal of Management*, 12: S55–S59.

King, N. (1998) 'Template analysis', in G. Symon and C. Cassell (eds) *Qualitative Methods and Analysis in Organizational Research.* London: Sage.

King, N. (2004) 'Using templates in the thematic analysis of text', in C. Cassell and G. Symon (eds) *Essential Guide to Qualitative Methods in Organizational Research.* London: Sage.

Kitzinger, J. and Barbour, R.S. (1999) 'Introduction: the challenge and promise of focus groups', in J. Kitzinger and R.S. Barbour (eds) *Developing Focus Group Research: Politics, Theory and Practice.* London: Sage. pp. 1–20.

Klein, M. (1948) 'Mourning and its relation to manic depressive states', in J. Riviere (ed.) *Contributions to Psychoanalysis 1921–45.* London: Hogarth.

Klein, M. (1952) 'Notes on some schizoid mechanisms', in J. Riviere (ed.) *Contributions to Psychoanalysis 1921–45.* London: Hogarth.

Kluckhohn, F.R. and Strodtbeck, F.L. (1961) *Variations in Value Orientations.* New York: Peterson.

Knight, F. (1921) *Risk, Uncertainty and Profit.* Library of Economics and Liberty (retrieved 6 January 2006: www.econlib.org/library/ Knight/knRUP1.htm).

Kolakowski, L. (1972) *Positivist Philosophy.* Harmondsworth: Penguin.

Kolb, D.A. (1986) *Experiential Learning.* London: Prentice Hall.

Kozinets, R.V. (2002) 'The field behind the screen: using netnography for marketing research in online communities', *Journal of Marketing Research*, 39: 61–72.

Krippendorff, K. (2004) '*Content Analysis: An Introduction to its Methodology*' (2nd edn). Thousand Oaks, CA: Sage.

Kristeva, J. (1974/1984) *Revolution in Poetic Language.* Trans L. Roudiez. New York: Columbia University Press.

Kristiansen, M. and Bloch-Poulsen, J. (2004) 'Self-referentiality as a power mechanism', *Action Research*, 2(4): 371–388.

Krizanc, J. (with L.C. Shaine) (1989) *Tamara*. Mississauga: Ballantine Books.

Krueger, R.A. (1997a) *Moderating Focus Groups: Focus Group Kit 4*. London: Sage.

Krueger, R.A. (1997b) *Analyzing and Reporting Focus Group Results: Focus Group Kit 6*. London: Sage.

Krueger, R.A. and Casey, M.A. (2000) *Focus Groups*. Thousand Oaks, CA: Sage.

Kvale, S. (1996) *InterViews: An Introduction to Qualitative Research Interviewing*. Thousand Oaks, CA: Sage.

Kwan, K.M. and Tsang, E.W.K. (2001) 'Realism and constructivism in strategy research: a critical realist response to Mir and Watson', *Strategic Management Journal*, 22: 1163–1168.

Lachmann, L.M. (1977) *Capital, Expectations, and the Market Process: Essays on the Theory of the Market Economy*. Mission, KS: Sheed Andrews and McMeel, Inc.

Laird, J.D. and Apostoleris, N.H. (1996) 'Emotional self-control and self-perception', in R. Harré and W.G. Parrott (eds) *The Emotions: Social, Cultural and Biological Dimensions*. London: Sage.

Lakatos, I. and Feyerabend, P. (1999) *For and Against Method*. Chicago: University of Chicago Press.

Lakoff, G. (1987) *Women, Fire and Dangerous Things: What Categories Reveal About the Mind*. Chicago: University of Chicago Press.

Landau, S. (2001) *Dictionaries: The Art and Craft of Lexicography*. Cambridge: Cambridge University Press.

Langfield-Smith, K. (1992) 'Exploring the need for a shared cognitive map', *Journal of Management Studies*, 29: 349–368.

Langfield-Smith, K. and Wirth, A. (1992) 'Measuring differences between cognitive maps', *Journal of the Operational Research Society*, 43: 1135–1150.

Langley, A. (1999) 'Strategies for theorizing from process data', *Academy of Management Review*, 24(4): 691–710.

Langley, A. and Truax, J. (1994) 'A process study of new technology adoption in smaller manufacturing firms', *Journal of Management Studies*, 31(5): 619–652.

Larson, M.S. (1993) *Behind the Postmodern Facade: Architectural Change in Late-Twentieth-Century America*. Berkeley: University of California Press.

Latour, B. (1986) 'The powers of association', in J. Law (ed.) *Power, Action and Belief*. London: Routledge and Kegan Paul. pp. 261–277.

Latour, B. (1987) *Science in Action: How to Follow Scientists and Engineers Through Society*. Cambridge, MA: Harvard University Press.

Latour, B. (1992) 'Where are the missing masses?', in W. Bijker and J. Law (eds) *Shaping Technology/Building Society*. Cambridge, MA: MIT Press.

Latour, B. (1996) *Aramis, or the Love of Technology*. Trans C. Porter. Cambridge, MA: Harvard University Press.

Latour, B. (1999a) 'On Recalling ANT', in J. Law and J. Hassard (eds) *Actor Network Theory and After*. Oxford: Blackwell.

Latour, B. (1999b) *Pandora's Hope: Essays on the Reality of Science Studies*. Cambridge, MA: Harvard University Press.

Latour, B. (2005) *Reassembling the Social: An Introduction to Actor-network Theory*. Oxford: Oxford University Press.

Latour, B. and Woolgar, S. (1979) *Laboratory Life: The Social Construction of Laboratory Facts*. Beverly Hills, CA: Sage.

Laughlin, R. (1987) 'Accounting systems in organisational contexts: a case for critical theory', *Accounting, Organizations and Society*, 12(5): 479–502.

Laughlin, R. (1991) 'Environmental disturbances and organizational transitions and transformations', *Organization Studies*, 12(2): 209–232.

Laughlin, R. (1995) 'Empirical research in accounting: alternative approaches and a case for "middle range" thinking', *Accounting, Auditing and Accountability Journal*, 8(1): 63–87.

Laughlin, R. (2004) 'Putting the record straight: a critique of "methodology choices and the construction of facts": some implications from the sociology of knowledge', *Critical Perspectives on Accounting*, 15(2): 261–277.

REFERENCES

Laukannen, M. (1998) 'Conducting causal mapping research: opportunities and challenges', in C. Eden (ed.) *Managerial and Organizational Cognition*. London: Sage.

Lave, J. and Wenger, E. (1990/1991) *Situated Learning: Legitimate Peripheral Participation*. Cambridge: Cambridge University Press.

Law, J. (1999) 'After ANT: complexity, naming and topology', in J. Law and J. Hassard (eds) *Actor Network Theory and After*. Oxford: Blackwell. pp. 1–14.

Lawson, T. (1996) 'Developments in economic as realist social theory', *Review of Social Economy*, 54: 405–422.

Leach, C., Freshwater., K., Aldridge, J. and Sunderland, J. (2001) 'Analysis of repertory grids in clinical practice', *British Journal of Clinical Psychology*, 40(3): 225–248.

Learmonth, M. (1999) 'The National Health service manager, engineer and father? A deconstruction', *Journal of Management Studies*, 36: 999–1012.

Lee, N. and Hassard, J. (1999) 'Organization unbound: actor-network theory, research strategy and institutional flexibility', *Organization*, 6: 391–405.

Lee, T.W. (1999) *Using Qualitative Methods in Organizational Research*. London: Sage.

Lefebvre, H. (1991) *The Production of Space*. Oxford: Blackwell.

Legge, K. (1995) *Human Resource Management: Rhetorics and Realities*. Basingstoke: Macmillan.

Lenin, V.I. (1970) Imperialism: the highest stage of capitalism: A popular outline. *Selected Works* (Vol. 1). pp. 667–766. Online at: Lenin Internet Archive (marxists.org) 1999.

Leont'ev, A.N. (1978) *Activity, Consciousness, and Personality*. Englewood Cliffs, NJ: Prentice-Hall.

Leplin, J. (1984) *Scientific Realism*. Berkeley: University of California Press.

Leseure, M.J., Bauer, J., Birdi, K., Neely, A. and Denyer, D. (2004) 'Adoption of promising practices: a Systematic Review of the Evidence', *International Journal of Management Reviews*, 5/6(3&4): 169–190.

Levin, M.E. (1984) 'What kind of explanation is truth', in J. Leplin (ed.) *Scientific Realism*. Berkeley: University of California Press. pp. 124–139.

Levy, D. (1994) 'Chaos thoery and strategy: theory application and managerial implications,' *Strategic Management Journal*, 15(5) 167–178.

Levy, M. (2000) 'Sage of reason', *People Management*, 20(12): 24–26.

Lewin, K. (1946) 'Action research and minority problems', *Journal of Social Issues*, 2: 24–46.

Lewis, J. (2003) 'Design issues', in J. Ritchie and J. Lewis (eds) *Qualitative Research in Practice: A Guide for Social Science Students and Researchers*. London: Sage.

Lewis, M.W. and Grimes, A.J. (1999) 'Metatriangulation: building theory from multiple paradigms', *Academy of Management Review*, 24: 672–690.

Lewis, R. (1994) 'From chaos to complexity: implications for organizations', *Executive Development*, 7(4): 16–17.

Lichtenberg, G. (1800/1990) *The Waste Books*. New York: New York Review of Books.

Liddell, H.G., Scott, R. and Jones, H.S. (1940) *The Greek-English Lexicon*. Oxford: Oxford University Press.

Liff, S. and Steward, F. (2001) 'Community e-gateways: locating networks and learning for social inclusion', *Information, Communication and Society*, 4(3): 317-340.

Lincoln, Y.S. and Denzin, N.K. (1994) 'The fifth moment', in N.K. Denzin and Y.S. Lincoln (eds) *Handbook of Qualitative Research*. London: Sage.

Lincoln, Y.S. and Guba, E.G. (1985) *Naturalistic Enquiry*. Beverly Hills, CA: Sage.

Lincoln, Y.S. and Guba, E.G. (1989) 'Ethics: the failure of positivist science', *The Review of Higher Education*, 12(3): 221–240.

Linstead, S. and Höpfl, H. (eds) (2000) *The Aesthetics of Organization*. London: Sage.

Linstead, S.A. (ed.) (2004) *Organizational Theory and Postmodern Thought*. London: Sage.

Linstead, S.A. (2002a) 'Organization as reply: Henri Bergson and casual organization theory', *Organization*, 9(1): 95–111.

Linstead, S.A. (2002b) 'Organizational kitsch', *Organization*, 9(4): 657–682.

Linstone, H. and Turoff, M. (ed.) (1975) *The Delphi Method, Techniques and Applications*. Reading, MA: Addison-Wesley.

Lissack, M.R. (1999) 'Complexity: the science, its vocabulary, and its relation to organizations', *Emergence*, 1(1): 110–125.

Livingston, E. (1986) *The Ethnomethodological Foundations of Mathematics*. London: Routledge and Kegan Paul.

Locke, J. (1690/1988) *Essay Concerning Human Understanding*, Oxford: Clarendon Press.

Locke, K. (1996) 'Rewriting the discovery of grounded theory after 25 Years?', *Journal of Management Inquiry*, 5(3): 239–245.

Locke, K. (2000/2001) *Grounded Theory in Management Research*. London: Sage.

Locke, R. (1989) *Management and Higher Education Since 1940*. Cambridge: Cambridge University Press.

Lofland, J. and Lofland, L.H. (1995) *Analyzing Social Settings: A Guide to Qualitative Observation and Analysis*. Belmont, CA: Wadsworth .

Lofland, J. (1970) 'Interactionist imagery and analytic interruptus', in T. Shibutani (ed.) *Human Nature and Collective Behaviour: Papers in Honor of Herbert Blumer*. Englewood Cliffs, NJ: Prentice-Hall.

Lorenz, E. (1963) 'Deterministic nonperiodic flow', *Journal of the Atmospheric Sciences*, 20(2): 235–245.

Lorenz, E. (1993) *The Essence of Chaos*. London: UCL Press.

Luff, P., Hindmarsh, J. and Heath, C. (eds) (2000) *Workplace Studies: Recovering Work Practice and Informing System Design*. Cambridge: Cambridge University Press.

Luhmann, N. (1984/1995) *Social Systems*. Stanford, CA: Stanford University Press.

Luhmann, N. (2000) *Organisation and Entscheidung*. Wiesbaden: Westdeutscher Verlag.

Lupton, T. (1963) *On the Shop Floor*. London: Pergamon Press.

Lupton, T. (2000) Foreword in *Strategic Reward Systems*, R. Thorpe and G. Homan (eds). London: Financial Times-Prentice Hall. pp. xix–xxv.

Lyle, J. (2003) 'Stimulated recall: A report on its use in naturalistic research', *British Educational Research Journal*, 29(6): 861–878.

Lynch, M. (1990) 'The externalized retina: selection and mathematization in the visual documentation of objects in the life sciences', in M. Lynch and S. Woolgar (eds) *Representation in Scientific Practice*. Cambridge, MA: MIT Press.

Lynch, M. (1993) *Scientific Practice and Ordinary Action: Ethnomethodology and Social Studies of Science*. Cambridge: Cambridge University Press.

Lynch, M., Livingston, E. and Garfinkel, H. (1983) 'Temporal order in laboratory work', in K. Knorr-Cetina and M. Mulkay (eds) *Science Observed: Perspectives on the Social Study of Science*. London: Sage.

Lyotard, J.-F. (1979/1984) *The Postmodern Condition: A Report on Knowledge*. Manchester: Manchester University Press.

Mabey, C. and Thomson, A. (2000) 'The determinants of management development', *British Journal of Management*, 11: S3–S16.

Macbeth, D.K. (2002) 'Emergent strategy in managing cooperative supply chain Change', *International Journal of Operations and Production Management*, 22(7): 728–740.

MacCarthy, B.L. and Atthirawong, W. (2003) 'Factors affecting location decisions in international operations – a Delphi study', *International Journal of Operations and Productions Management*, 23: 794–818.

MacDougall, C. and Fudge, F. (2001) 'Planning and recruiting the sample for focus groups and in-depth interviews', *Qualitative Health Research*, 11(1): 117–126.

MacIntosh, R. and MacLean, D. (1999) 'Conditioned emergence: a dissipative structures approach to transformation', *Strategic Management Journal*, 20(4): 297–316.

MacIntosh, R. and MacLean, D. (2001) 'Conditioned emergence: researching change and changing research', *International Journal of Operations and Production Management*, 21(10): 1343–1357.

MacIntosh R., MacLean, D., Stacey, R. and Griffin, D. (eds) (2006) *Health Complexity and Organization: Readings and Conversations*. London: Routledge.

MacIntosh, R., MacLean, D. and Burns, H. (2007) 'Health in organization: toward a process-based view', *Journal of Management Studies*, 44(2): 206–221.

MacKinnon, E. (1979) 'Scientific realism: the new debates', *Philosophy of Science*, 46: 501–532.

REFERENCES

MacLean, D. and MacIntosh, R. (2002) 'One process, two audiences: on the challenges of management research', *European Management Journal*, 20(4): 383–392.

MacLean, D., MacIntosh, R. and Grant, S. (2002) 'Mode 2 management research', *British Journal of Management*, 13(3): 189–207.

Macpherson, A., and Holt, R. (2007) 'Knowledge, learning and small-firm growth: a systematic review of the evidence', *Research Policy*, 36(1), (2): 172–192.

Mandelbrot, B. (1977) *Fractals: Form, Chance and Dimension*. San Francisco, CA: Freeman.

Mangham, I.L. (ed.) (1987) *Organization Analysis and Development*. Chichester: Wiley.

Mangham, I.L. and Overington, M.A. (1987) *Organizations as Theatre: A Social Psychology of Dramatic Appearances*. Chichester: Wiley.

Manicas, P.T. (1987) *A History of Philosophy of the Social Sciences*. New York: Basil Blackwell.

Mann, C. and Stewart, F. (2000) *Internet Communication and Qualitative Research: A Handbook for Researching Online*. London: Sage.

Manson, S.M. (2001) 'Simplifying complexity: a review of complexity theory', *Geoforum*, 32: 405–414.

Manufacturing Visions (2005) 'Integrating diverse perspectives into Pan-European foresight', Group of authors, Fraunhofer Institute for System and Innovation Research, Karlsruhe, Germany.

March, J. (1991) 'Exploration and Exploitation in organizational learning', *Organization Science*, 2(1): 71–87.

Marcus, S. and Engels, F. (1974) *Engels, Manchester, and the Working Class*. London: Weidenfeld and Nicolson.

Marcuse, H. (1964) *One-dimensional Man: Studies in the Ideology of Advanced Industrial Society*. Boston, MA : Beacon Press.

Marcuse, H. (1993) 'A note on dialetic', in A. Arato and E. Gebhardt (eds) *The Essential Frankfurt School Reader*. New York: Continuum. pp. 444–451 (original work published 1960).

Markóczy, L. and Goldberg, J. (1995) 'A method for eliciting and comparing causal maps', *Journal of Management*, 21(2): 305–333.

Marshall, C. and Rossman, G.B. (1989) *Designing Qualitative Research*. London: Sage.

Marsick, V. and O'Neill, J. (1999) 'The many faces of action learning', *Management Learning*, 30(2): 159–176.

Martin, J. (1990) 'Deconstructing organizational taboos: the suppressions of gender conflict in organizations', *Organization Science*, 1(4): 339–359.

Martin, J., Feldman, M., Hatch, M.J. and Sitkin, S. (1983) 'The uniqueness paradox in organizational stories', *Administrative Science Quarterly*, 28: 438–453.

Martinko, M.J. and Gardner, W.L. (1984) 'The observation of high-performing educational managers: methodological issues and managerial implications', in J.G. Hunt, D. Hosking, C.A. Schriesheim and R. Steward (eds) *Leaders and Managers: International Perspectives on Managerial Behavior and Leadership*. New York: Pergamon. pp. 142–161.

Marwick, A. (2001) *The New Nature of History*. Basingstoke: Palgrave.

Marx, K. (1859/1970) 'A contribution to the critique of political economy', in K. Marx and F. Engels *Selected Works*. London: Lawrence and Wishart.

Marx, K. (1857/1973) *Grundisse*. Harmondsworth: Penguin.

Marx, K. (1867/1976) *Capital*. Harmondsworth: Penguin.

Matthews, D. (2000) 'Oral history, accounting history and an interview with Sir John Grenside', *Accounting, Business & Financial History*, 10(1): 57–83.

Maturana, H. (1981) 'Autopoiesis', in M. Zeleny (ed.) *Autopoiesis: A Theory of Living Organization* (Vol. 3) North Holland, NY: Columbia University Press.

Maxwell, J. and Loomis, D. (2003) 'Mixed method design: an alternative approach', in A. Tashakkori and C. Teddlie (eds) *Handbook of Mixed Methods in Social and Behavioral Research*. Thousand Oaks, CA: Sage. pp. 241–271.

May, R. (1973) *Man's Search for Himself*. New York: Dell.

May, T. (1997) *Social Research: Issues, Method and Process*. Milton Keynes: Open University.

Mayer, T.F. (1994) *Analytical Marxism*. London: Sage.

Mayhew, B.H. (1980) 'Structuralism versus individualism: part 1, shadowboxing in the dark', *Social Forces*, 59(2): 335–375.

McCall, G. and Simmons, J.L. (1978/1966) *Identities and Interactions*. New York: Free Press.

McCarthy, T. (1978) *The Critical Theory of Jürgen Habermas*. London: Hutchinson.

McClelland, D.C., Atkinson, J.W., Clark, R.A. and Lowell, E.L. (1953) *The Achievement Motive.* New York: Free Press.

McCloskey, D.N. (1995) 'Economics and the limits of scientific knowledge', in R.F. Goodman and W.R. Fisher (eds) *Rethinking Knowledge: Reflections Across the Disciplines*. Albany, NY: State University of New York Press.

McDougall, D. (1997) 'The visual in anthropology', in M. Banks and H. Morhpy (eds) *Rethinking Visual Anthropology*. London: New Haven Press.

McGaughey, S.L. (2004) 'Writing it up': Challenges of representation in qualitative research', in R. Marschan-Piekarri and C. Welch, C. (eds) *Handbook of Qualitative Research in International Business*. Cheltenham: Edward Elgar.

McGaughey, S.L. (2006) 'Reading as a method of inquiry: representations of the born global', *Management International Review*, 46(4): 461–480.

McHoul, A. and Rapley, M. (2005) 'Re-presenting culture and the self', *Theory and Psychology*, 15(4): 431–447.

McIntyre, A. (1985) *After Virtue: A Study in Moral Theory*. London: Duckworth.

McKelvey, B. (1999) 'Toward a Campbellian realist organization science', in J.A.C. Baum and B. McKelvey (eds) *Variations in Organization Science: In Honor of Donald T. Campbell*. Thousand Oaks, CA: Sage. pp. 383–411.

McKelvey, B. (2000) 'Complexity theory in organization science: seizing the promise or becoming a fad?', *Emergence*, 1(1): 5–32.

McKelvey, B. (2002) 'Model-centred organization science epistemology', in J.A.C. Baum (ed.) *Companion to Organizations*. Malden: Blackwell. pp. 752–780.

McLaren, M. (1997) 'Foucault and the subject of feminism', *Social Theory and Practice*, 23(1): 109–129.

McLaughlin, H. (2005) 'Young service users as co-researchers: methodological problems and possibilities', *Qualitative Social Work*, 4(1): 21–28.

McLaughlin, H. (2006a) *Understanding Social Work Research: Key Issues and Concepts*. London: Sage.

McLaughlin, H. (2006b) 'Involving young service users as co-researchers: possibilities, benefits and costs', *British Journal of Social Work*, 36: 1395–1410.

McLaughlin, H. and Thorpe, R. (1993) 'Action learning – a paradigm in emergence: the problems facing a challenge in traditional management education and development', *British Journal of Management* 4(1): 19–27.

McLaughlin, H., Brown, D. and Young, A. (2004) 'Consultation, community and empowerment: lessons from the deaf community', *Journal of Social Work*, 4(2): 153–165.

McMullin, E. (1984) 'A case for scientific realism', in J. Leplin (ed.) *Scientific Realism*. Berkeley: University of California Press. pp. 8–40

McNamee, S. (2000) 'The social poetics of relationally engaged research', in K. Deissler and S. McNamee (eds) *Philosophy in Therapy: The Social Poetics of Therapeutic Conversation (Phil und sophie auf der couch: Die soziale poesie therapeutischer gesprache)* Heidelberg: Carl-Auer-Systeme Verlag. pp. 146–156.

McNulty, T. (2002) 'Reengineering as knowledge management: a case of change in UK healthcare', *Management Learning* 33(4): 439–458.

McQuarrie, E. and McIntyre, S. (1988) 'Conceptual underpinnings for the use of group interviews in consumer research', *Advances in Consumer Research*, 15: 580–586.

Mead, G.H. (1934) *Mind, Self and Society.* Chicago: University of Chicago Press.

Mead, M. (1951) *Cultural Patterns and Technical Change*. Paris: UNESCO.

Mead, M. (1995) 'Visual anthropology in a discipline of words', in P. Hockings (ed.) *Principles of Visual Anthropology* (2nd edn). New York: Mouton de Gruyter.

Mead, R. (2005) *International Management: Cross-cultural Dimensions*. Oxford: Blackwell.

Meckler, M. and Baillie, J. (2003a) 'The truth about social construction in administrative science', *Journal of Management Inquiry*, 12: 273–284.

REFERENCES

Meckler, M. and Baillie, J. (2003b) 'You can't handle the truth: a response to Gioia and Lounsbury', *Journal of Management Inquiry*, 12: 299–303.

Meeuwsen, H. (1991) 'Variables affecting perceptual boundaries in bipedal stair slimbing', *Perceptual and Motor Skills* 72(2): 539–543.

Menzies Lyth, I. (1959) 'A case study in the functioning of social systems as a defence against anxiety', *Human Relations*, 16(13): 95–121.

Merleau-Ponty, M. (1988) *In Praise of Philosophy and other Essays*. Trans J. Wild et al. Evanston, IL: Northwestern University Press.

Merton, R. (1968) *Social Theory and Social Structure*. New York: Free Press.

Merton, R. and Kendall, P. (1946) 'The focused interview', in *American Journal of Sociology*, 51: 541–557.

Merton, R., Fiske, M. and Kendall, P. (1956) *The Focused Interview: A Manual of Problems and Procedures*. Glencoe, IL: Free Press. (See also Merton, R., Fiske, M. and Kendall, P. (1990) *The Focused Interview: A Manual of Problems and Procedures* (2nd edn). New York: Free Press.)

Meyer, A.D. (1982) 'Adapting to environmental jolts', *Administrative Science Quarterly*, 27: 515–537.

Meyer, A.D. (1991) 'Visual data in organizational research', *Organization Science*, 2(2): 218–236.

Miettenen, R. and Virkkunen, J. (2005) 'Epistemic objects, artifacts and organizational change', *Organization*, 12(3): 437–456.

Miles, M. and Huberman, A. (1994a) *Qualitative Data Analysis: A Source Book of New Methods* (2nd edn). London: Sage.

Miles, M. and Huberman, A. (1994b) *Qualitative Data Analysis: An Expanded Sourcebook*. Thousand Oaks, CA and London: Sage.

Milgram, S. (1963) 'A behavioral study of obedience', *Journal of Abnormal and Social Psychology*, 67: 371–378.

Mill, J.S. (1874) *A System of Logic*. London: Longman Green.

Miller, P. (2003) 'Management and accounting', in T.M. Porter and D. Ross (eds) *The Cambridge History of Science, Vol. 7: The Modern Social Sciences*. Cambridge: Cambridge University Press. pp. 565–576.

Miller, P. and Rose, N. (1997) 'Mobilising the consumer: assembling the subject of consumption', *Theory, Culture and Society*, 14: 1–36.

Miller, R. L. (2000) *Researching Life Stories and Family Histories*. London: Sage.

Mintzberg, H. (1970) 'Structured observation as a method to study managerial work', *Journal of Management Studies*, 7(1): 87–104.

Mintzberg, H. (1973) *The Nature of Managerial Work*. New York: Harper & Row.

Mintzberg, H. (2004) *Managers Not MBAs*. London: Finanacial Times, Prentice Hall.

Mintzberg, H., Raisinghani, D. and Theoret, A. (1976) 'The structure of unstructured decision processes', *Adminsitrative Science Quarterly*, 21(2): 246–275.

Mir, R., Mir, A. and Wong, D.J. (2006) 'Diversity: the cultural logic of global capital?', in A.Konrad, P. Prasad and J. Pringle (eds) (2006) *Handbook of Workplace Diversity*. Thousand Oaks, CA: Sage. pp. 167–188.

Mitchell, J.C. (1983) 'Case and situational analysis', *Sociological Review*, 31(2): 187–211.

Mitchell, R.K. (1997) 'Oral history and expert scripts: demystifying the entrepreneurial experience', *International Journal of Entrepreneurual Research and Behaviour*, 3(2): 122–139.

Mitchell, R.K., Agle, B.R. and Wood, D.J. (1997) 'Towards a theory of stakeholder identification and salience: defining the principle of who and what really counts', *Academy of Management Review* 22(4): 853–886.

Moenaert, R. and Caeldries, F. (1996) 'Architectural redesign, interpersonal communication, and learning in R&D', *Journal of Product Innovation Management*, 13: 296–310.

Mohr, L.B. (1982) *Explaining Organizational Behavior*. San Francisco, CA: Jossey-Bass.

Moingeon, B. and Edmondson, A. (1996) *Organizational Learning and Competitive Advantage*. Thousand Oaks, CA: Sage.

Molloy, E. and Whittington, R. (2005) 'Practices of organizing: inside and outside the processes of change', in *Advances in Strategic Management* (Vol. 22).

Monaco, J. (2000) *How to Read a Film: The World of Movies, Media, and Multimedia* (3rd edn). New York and Oxford: Oxford University Press.

Monin, N. and Monin, D.J. (2005) 'Hijacking the fairytale: genre blurring and allegorical breaching in management literature', *Organization*, 12(4): 511–528.

Monin, N., Barry, D. and Monin, D.J. (2003) 'Toggling with Taylor: a different approach to reading in management text', *Journal of Management Studies*, 40: 377–401.

Montoya-Weiss, M.M., Massey, A.P. and Clapper, D.L. (1998) 'On-line focus groups: conceptual issues and a research tool', *European Journal of Marketing*, 32: 713–723.

Moon, Y. (1998) 'Impression management in computer-based interviews: the effects of input modality, output modality, and distance', *Public Opinion Quarterly*, 62: 610–622.

Moore, G.E. (1903) 'The refutation of idealism', *Mind* 12: 433-453. Reprinted in G.E. Moore (ed.) (1922) *Philosophical Studies*. London: Trench, Trubner, and Co.

Morgan, C.D. and Murray, H.A. (1935) 'A method for investigating fantasies: the thematic appreciation test', *Archives of Neurological Psychiatrists*, 34: 289–306.

Morgan, D.L. (1988) 'Focus groups as qualitative research', *Qualitative Research Methods Series 16*. London: Sage.

Morgan, D.L. (1996) 'Focus groups', *Annual Review of Sociology*, 22: 129–52.

Morgan, D.L. (1997) *Focus Groups as Qualitative Research*. Thousand Oaks, CA: Sage.

Morgan, D.L. and Krueger, R.A. (1997) *The Focus Group Kit* (Vols 1–6). London: Sage.

Morgan, G. (1980) 'Paradigms, metaphors and puzzle solving in organizational theory', *Administrative Science Quarterly* 25: 605–622.

Morgan, G. (1983) 'More on metaphor: why we cannot control tropes in administrative science', *Administrative Science Quarterly* 28: 601–607.

Morgan, G. (1986/1997) *Images of Organisation*. Newbury Park, CA: Sage.

Morgan, G. (1996) 'Is there anything more to be said about metaphor?', in D. Grant and C. Oswick (eds) *Metaphor and Organizations*. London: Sage. pp. 227–240.

Morgan, S. (2001) 'Electronic interviews in organizational research', Paper presented at the BPS Wessex and Wight Branch Centenary Event: Psychology and the Internet: A European Perspective, Farnborough, UK.

Morgan, S. and Symon, G. (2004) 'Electronic interviews', in C. Cassell and G. Symon (eds) *Essential Guide to Qualitative Methods in Organizational Research*. London: Sage.

Morse, J.M. (1994) 'Emerging from the data: the cognitive process of analysis in qualitative enquiry', in J.M. Morse (ed.) *Critical Issues in Qualitative Research Methods*. London: Sage.

Mueller, F., Sillence, J., Harvey, C. and Howorth, C. (2003) 'A rounded picture is what we need: rhetorical strategies, arguments and the negotiation of change in a UK hospital trust', *Organization Studies*, 25: 75–93: 191–207.

Mulhall, S. (2001) *Inheritance and Originality: Wittgenstein, Heidegger and Kierkegaard*. Oxford: Clarendon Press.

Mumby, D. (1987) 'The political function of narrative in organizations', *Communication Monographs*, 54: 113–127.

Mumby, D. (1994) 'Review of cultures in organizations' (book by J. Martin), *Academy of Management Review*, 19(1): 156–159.

Mumby, D. and Putnam, L. (1992) 'The politics of emotion: a feminist reading of bounded rationality', *Academy of Management Review*, 17(3): 465–486.

Munier, F. and Ronde, P. (2001) 'The role of knowledge codification in the emergence of consensus under uncertainty: empirical analysis and policy implications', *Research Policy*, 30: 1537–1551.

Munslow, A. (1997) *Deconstructing History*. London: Routledge.

Nadin, S. and Cassell, C.M. (2004) 'Matrices analysis', in C. Cassell and G. Symon (eds) *Essential Guide to Qualitative Methods in Organizational Research*. London: Sage.

Nadkarni, S. and Shenoy, P. (2004) 'A causal mapping approach to constructing Bayesian networks', *Decision Support Systems*, 38: 259–281.

Neimeyer, R.A., Anderson, A. and Stockton, L. (2001) 'Snakes versus ladders: a validation of laddering technique as a measure of hierarchical structure', *Journal of Constructivist Psychology*, 14(2): 85–105.

Newton, T. (2002) 'Creating the new ecological order?: Elias and actor-network theory', *Academy of Management Review*, 27: 523–540.

REFERENCES

Ng, W. and de Cock, C. (2002) 'Battle in the boardroom: a discursive perspective', *Journal of Management Studies*, 39(1): 23–49.

Nicolini, D., Gherardi, S. and Yanow, D. (eds) (2003) *Knowing in Organizations: A Practice-based Approach*. Armonk, NY: M.E. Sharpe.

Niece, J.M. and Trompeter, G.M. (2004) 'The demise of Aurthur Andersen's one-firm concept: a case study in corporate governance', *Business and Society Review*, 109(2): 183–207.

Nietzsche, F. (1885/1969) *Thus Spoke Zarathustra*. London: Penguin.

Nieuwenburg, P. (2004) 'The agony of choice: Isaiah Berlin and the phenomenology of conflict', *Administration and Society*, 35(1): 683–700.

Niiniluoto, I. (1999) *Critical Scientific Realism*. Oxford: Oxford University Press.

Nkomo, S.M. (1992) 'The emperor has no clothes: rewriting "race" in organizations', *Academy of Management Review*, 17(3): 487–513.

Norman, D. (1988) *The Design of Everyday Things*. New York: Doubleday.

Norris, F.M., Jones, H.G. and Norris, H. (1970) 'Articulation of the conceptual structure in obsessional neurosis', *British Journal of Social and Clinical Psychology*, 9: 264–274.

North, D.C. (1990) *Institutions, Institutional Change and Economic Performance*. Cambridge: Cambridge University Press.

Nossiter, V. and Biberman, G. (1990) 'Projective drawings and metaphor: analysis of organisational culture', *Journal of Managerial Psychology*, 5(3): 13–16.

O'Connor, E.S. (2000) 'Plotting the organization: The embedded narrative as a construct for studying change', *The Journal of Applied Behavioral Science*, 36(2): 174–192.

Obholzer, A. and Roberts, V.Z. (eds) (1994) *The Unconscious at Work: Individual and Organisational Stress in the Human Services*. London: Routledge.

O'Connor, E. (2002) 'Storied business: typology, intertextuality, and traffic in entrepreneurial narrative', *The Journal of Business Communication*, 39(1): 36–54.

O'Connor, H. and Madge, C. (2001) 'Cyber-mothers: online synchronous interviewing using conferencing softwares', *Sociological Research Online*: www.socresonline.org.uk/5/4/o%27connor.html.

O'Dwyer, B., Unerman J. and Bradley, J. (2005) Perceptions on the emergence and future development of corporate social disclosure in Ireland: engaging the voices of non-governmental organisations', *Accounting, Auditing and Accountability Journal*, 18(1): 14–43.

O'Hara, S., Bourner T. and Webber T. (2004) 'Self managed action learning: theory and practice', *Action Learning: Research and Practice*, 1(1): 29–42.

Olivero, N. and Lunt, P. (2004) 'Privacy versus willingness to disclose in e-commerce exchanges: the effect of risk awareness on the relative role of trust and control', *Journal of Economic Psychology*, 25: 243–262.

Ollman, B. (1976) *Alienation: Marx's Conception of Man in Capitalist Society*. Cambridge: Cambridge University Press.

O'Neill, J. (1998) 'Rhetoric, science and philosophy', *Philosophy of the Social Sciences*, 28: 205–225.

Ong, A. (1987) *Spirits of Resistance and Capitalist Description: Factory Women in Malaysia*. Albany, NY: State University of New York Press.

O'Regan, N., Ghobadian, A. and Sims, M. (2006) 'Fast tracking innovation in manufacturing SMEs', *Technovation*, 26: 251–261.

Orlikowski, W. (1993) 'Case tools as organizational change: investigating incremental and radical changes in systems development', *MIS Quarterly*, 17: 309–341.

Orlikowski, W. (2000) 'Using technology and constituting structures: a practice lens for studying technology in organisations', *Organization Science*, 11(4): 404–428.

Ortner, S.B. (1984) 'Theory in anthropology since the sixties', *Comparative Studies in Sociology and History*, 26: 126–166.

Ortony, A. (1975) 'Why metaphors are necessary and not just nice', *Educational Theory*, 25(1): 45–53.

Osborne, J. (1996) 'Beyond constructivism', *Science Education*, 80(1): 53–82.

Osland, J. and Bird, A. (2000) 'Beyond sophisticated stereotyping: cultural sensemaking in context', *Academy of Management Executive*, 149(1): 65–79.

Oswick, C. and Montgomery, J. (1999) 'Images of an organisation: the use of metaphor in a multinational company', *Journal of Organisational Change Management*, 12(6): 501–523.

Oswick, C., Anthony, P., Keenoy, T., Mangham, I.L., and Grant, D. (2000) 'A dialogic analysis of Organizational learning', *Journal of Management Studies*, 37(6): 887–102.

Oswick, C., Keenoy, T. and Grant, D. (2001) 'Editorial dramatizing and organizing: acting and being', *Journal of Organizational Change Management*, 14(3): 218–224.

Oswick, C., Keenoy, T. and Grant, D. (2002) 'Metaphor and analogical reasoning in organization theory: beyond orthodoxy', *Academy of Management Review*, 27: 294–303.

Oswick, C., Putnam, L. and Keenoy, T. (2005) 'Tropes, discourse and organizing', in D. Grant, C. Hardy, C. Oswick and L. Putnam (eds) *The Sage Handbook of Organizational Discourse*. London: Sage.

Oxford Dictionary (2001) 'Practice, practise, practising' in *Oxford Dictionary*. Oxford: Oxford University Press. p. 702.

Øyen, E. (1990) 'The imperfections of comparisons', in E. Øyen (ed.) *Comparative Methodology*. London: Sage.

Paget, M.A. (1995) 'Narrative and sociology', in J. Van Maanen (ed.) *Representation in Ethnography*. Thousand Oaks, CA: Sage.

Palmer, I. and Dunford, R. (1996) 'Conflicting uses of metaphors: reconceptualizing their use in the field of organizational change', *Academy of Management Review*, 21(3): 691–717.

Palmer, R.E. (1969) *Hermeneutics: Interpretation Theory in Schleiermacher, Dilthey, Heidegger, and Gadamer*. Evanston, IL: Northwestern University Press.

Parasuraman, A., Zeithaml, V.A. and Berry, L.L. (1988) 'SERVQUAL: a multiple-item scale for measuring consumer perceptions of service quality', *Journal of Retailing*, 64(1): 12–40.

Parker, J. (2006) 'Beyond caring: organizational change and identity in healthcare', unpublished PhD thesis, De Montfort University, Leicester, UK.

Parkin, M. (2004) *Tales for Change: Using Storytelling to Develop People and Organizations*. London/Sterling, VA: Kogan Page.

Parry, J. (2003) 'Making sense of executive sensemaking: a phenomenological case study with methodological criticism', *Journal of Health Organization and Management*, 19(4/5): 378–394.

Parry, K. (1999) 'Enhancing adaptability: leadership strategies to accommodate change in local government settings', *Journal of Organizational Change Management*, 12(2): 134–156.

Parry, K.W. (1998) 'Grounded theory and social process: a new direction for leadership research', *Leadership Quarterly*, 9: 85–106.

Pawson, R. and Tilley, N. (1997) *Realistic Evaluation*. London: Sage.

Payne, S.L and Carlton, J.M. (2002) 'Towards a managerial practice of stakeholder engagement: developing multi-stakeholder learning dialogues', *Journal of Corporate Citizenship*, 6: 37–52.

Pedler, M., Burgoyne, J.G. and Brook, C. (2005) 'What has action learning learned to become?', *Action Learning: Research & Practice*, 2(1): 49–68.

Penn, A., Desyllas, J. and Vaughan, L. (1999) 'The space of innovation: interaction and communication in the work environment', *Environment and Planning B: Planning and Design*, 26(2): 193–218.

Penrose, E. (1959) *The Theory of the Growth of the Firm*. New York: John Wiley & Sons.

Penrose, R. (1989) *The Emperor's New Mind*. New York: Oxford University Press.

Pentland, B. (1999) 'Building process theory with narrative: from description to explanation', *Academy of Management Review*, 24(4): 711–724.

Peppet, S. and Moffitt, M. (2006) 'Learning how to learn to negotiate', in Schneider and Honeyman (eds), *The Negotiator's Fieldbook*. Chicago, IL: American Bar Association Books.

Perelman, C. (1987) *The New Rhetoric and the Humanities*. Dordrecht, Holland: D. Reidel.

Perks, R. (1999) 'Oral history websites', *Oral History*, 27(2): 87–89.

Perrow, C. (1986) *Complex Organizations*. New York: Random House.

Pesqueux, Y. (1999) 'Discussing the company: model, metaphor and image', *Management Decision*, 37(10): 817–824.

Peters, T.J. and Waterman, R.H. (1982) *In Search of Excellence*. New York: Harper & Row.

REFERENCES

Petticrew, M. and Roberts, H. (2006) *Systematic Reviews in the Social Sciences*. Oxford: Blackwell.

Pettigrew, A.M. (1990) 'Longitudinal field research on change: theory and practice', *Organization Science*, 1(3): 267–292.

Pettigrew, A.M. (1992) 'The character and significance of strategy process research', *Strategic Management Journal*, 13: 5–16.

Pfeffer, J. (1995) 'Morality, reproducibility and the persistence of styles of theory', *Organization Science*, 6(6): 680–686.

Phillips, N. (1995) 'Telling organizational tales: on the role of narrative fiction in the study of organization', *Organization Studies*, 16(4): 625–649.

Phillips, N. and Hardy, C. (2002) *Discourse Analysis: Investigating Processes of Social Construction*, Thousand Oaks, CA: Sage.

Phillips, R. (1997) 'Stakeholder theory and a principle of fairness', *Business Ethics Quarterly*, 7(1): 51–66.

Phillips, R. (1999) 'On stakeholder delimitation', *Business and Society* 38(1): 32–34.

Phillips, R. (2003) *Stakeholder Theory and Organizational Ethics*. San Francisco, CA: Berrett-Koehler.

Phillips, R., Freeman, R.E. and Wicks, A.C. (2003) 'What stakeholder theory is not', *Business Ethics Quarterly*, 13(4): 479–502.

Piaget, J. (1972) *Psychology and Epistemology: Towards a Theory of Knowledge*. London: Allen Lane.

Pickering, A. (1995) *The Mangle of Practice: Time, Agency and Science*. Chicago: University of Chicago Press.

Pinder, C. and Bourgeois, W. (1982) 'Controlling tropes in administrative science', *Administrative Science Quarterly*, 27: 641–652.

Pink, S. (2001) *Doing Visual Ethnography: Images, Media and Representation in Research*. London: Sage.

Piore, C. (2006) 'Qualitative research: does it fit in economics?', *European Management Review*, 3(1): 17–23.

Pittaway, L., Robertson, M., Munir, K., Denyer, D. and Neely, A. (2004) 'Networking and innovation: a systematic review of the evidence', *International Journal of Management Reviews*, 5/6 (3/4): 137–168.

Podmore, F. (1906/1971) *Robert Owen: A Biography*. New York: Haskell House Publishers.

Polkinghorne, D. (1995) 'Narrative configuration in qualitative analysis', in J. Hatch and R. Wisniewski (eds) *Life History and Narrative*. London: Falmer Press.

Polkinghorne, D. (1997) 'Reporting qualitative research as practice', in W.G. Tierney and Y.S. Lincoln (eds) *Representation and the Text: Reframing the Narrative Voice*. Albany, NY: State University of New York Press.

Polkinghorne, D.E. (1998) *Natrrative Knowing and the Human Sciences*. Albany, NY: State of New York University Press.

Pollner, M. (1991) 'Left of ethnomethodology: the rise and decline of radical reflexivity', *American Sociological Review*, 56: 370–380.

Popper, K. (1945) *The Open Society and its Enemies* (Vols. 1 & 2) London: Routledge.

Popper, K. (1963) *Conjectures and Refutations: The Growth of Scientific Knowledge*. London: Routledge.

Popper K. (1968) *The Logic of Scientific Discovery* (3rd edn). London: Hutchinson.

Portelli, A. (1998) 'Oral history as genre', in M. Chamberlain and P. Thompson (eds) *Narrative and Genre*. London: Routledge.

Potter, J. (1996) *Representing Reality: Discourse, Rhetoric and Social Construction*. London: Sage.

Potter, J. and Weatherall, M. (1987) *Discourse and Social Psychology: Beyond Attitudes and Behaviour*. London: Sage.

Pozzebon, M. (2004) 'The influence of a structurationist perspective on strategic management research', *Journal of Management Studies*, 41(2): 247–272.

Pozzebon, M. and Pinsonneault, A. (2005) 'Challenges in conducting empirical work using structuration theory: learning from IT research', *Organization Studies*, 26(9): 1353–1376.

Prasad, A. (ed.) (2003) *Postcolonial Theory and Organizational Analysis: A Critical Engagement*. Basingstoke and New York: Palgrave.

Prasad, A. (2005) 'The jewel in the crown: postcolonial theory and workplace diversity', in A. Konrad, P. Prasad, and J. Pringle (eds) *Handbook of Workplace Diversity*. Thousand Oaks, CA: Sage. pp. 95–120.

Prasad, A. and Prasad, P. (2002) 'Otherness at large: identity and difference in new globalized land-scapes', in I. Aalito and A. Mills (eds) *Gender, Identity and the Culture of Organizations*. London and New York: Routledge.

Prasad, P. (2005) *Crafting Qualitative Research: Working in the Postpositivist Traditions*. Armonk, NY: M.E. Sharpe.

Prasad, P. and Mills, A.J. (1997) 'From showcase to shadow: understanding the dilemmas of workplace diversity', in P. Prasad, P., Mills, A.J. Elmes, M. and Prasad, A. (eds) *Managing the Organizational Melting Pot: Dilemmas of Workplace Diversity*. Thousand Oaks, CA: Sage.

Prigogine, I. (1996) *The End of Certainty*. New York: Free Press.

Prigogine, I. and Stengers, I. (1984) *Order Out of Chaos: Man's New Dialogue with Nature*. New York: Bantam.

Prins, S. (2002) 'Guidelines for the evaluation of ethnographic visual media: historical background', *American Anthropologist*, 104(1): 303–305.

Propp, V.J. (1928/1968) *Morphology of the Folktale*. Austin, TX: University of Texas Press.

Prosser, J. (ed.) (1998) *Image-based Research: A Sourcebook for Qualitative Researchers*. London: Falmer Press.

Pugh, R. (2003) 'Considering the countryside: is there a case for rural social work?', *British Journal of Social Work*, 33(1): 67–86.

Puonti, A. (2004) 'Searching for synchrony: negotiating schedules across organizations involved in investigating economic crime', *Public Management Review*, 6(1): 55–75.

Putnam, H. (1990) *Realism with a Human Face*. Cambridge, MA: Harvard University Press.

Putnam, H. (1999) *The Threefold Cord: Mind, Body, and World*. New York: Columbia University Press.

Putnam, R.W. (1990) 'Putting concepts to use: re-educating professionals for organizational learning'. Unpublished doctoral dissertation, Harvard University, Cambridge, MA.

Putnam, R.W. (1991) 'Recipes and reflective learning', in D.A. Schön (ed.) *The Reflective Turn*. New York: Teachers College Press.

Quinn, R. (1988) *Beyond Rational Management: Mastering the Paradoxes and Competing Demands of High Performance*. San Francisco, CA: Jossey-Bass.

Rabinow, P. (1999) *French DNA: Trouble in Purgatory*. Chicago: University of Chicago Press.

Radcliffe, D. (2004) *Video and Audio Media in Qualitative Research* [On-Line Booklet]. Available at: www.don.ratcliffs.net/video/

Raelin, J. (1999) 'The action dimension in management: diverse approaches to research, teaching and development', *Management Learning*, 30(2): 115–125.

Raelin, J. (2000) *Work-based Learning*. Upper Saddle River, NJ: Prentice-Hall.

Rafaeli, A. and Sutton, R. (1991) 'Emotional contrast strategies as lessons of social influence: lessons from criminal interrogators and bill collectors', *Academy of Management Journal*, 34: 749–775.

Raimond, P. (1993) *Management Projects: Design, Research and Presentation*. London: Chapman and Hall.

Rallis, S.F. and Rossman, G.B. (2003) 'Mixed methods in evaluation contexts: a pragmatic framework', in A. Tashakkori and C. Teddlie (eds) *Handbook of Mixed Methods in Social and Behavioral Research*. Thousand Oaks, CA: Sage. pp. 491–512.

Ramirez, R. (1991) *The Beauty of Social Organization*. Munich: Accedo.

Raskin, J.D. (2001) 'On relativism in constructivist psychology', *Journal of Constructivist Psychology*, 14(3): 285–313.

Reason, P. and Bradbury, H. (2001) *Handbook of Action Research: Participative Inquiry and Practice*. London: Sage.

Reckwitz, A. (2002) 'Toward a theory of social practices: a development in cultural theorizing', *European Journal of Social Theory*, 5(2): 243–263.

Reddiford, S. (1996) 'Drawn into change', *Management Development Review*, 9(5): 37–40.

Reed, M.I. (1997) 'In praise of duality and dualism: rethinking agency and structure in organizational analysis', *Organization Studies*, 18(1): 21–42.

Reissman, C.K. (1993) *Narrative Analysis*. Newbury Park, CA: Sage.

REFERENCES

Rescher, N. (1996a) *Complexity: A Philosophical Overview*. New York: Transaction Publishers.

Rescher, N. (1996b) *Process Metaphysics: An Introduction to Process Philosophy*. Albany NY: SUNY.

Revans, R.W. (1971) *Developing Effective Managers*. New York: Praeger.

Revans, R.W. (1980) *Action Learning: New Techniques for Managers*. London: Blond & Briggs.

Revans, R.W. (1982) *The Origins and Growth of Action Learning*. Bromley: Chartwell Bratt.

Revans, R.W. (1983/1998) *ABC of Action Learning*. London: Lemos and Crane.

Reynolds, M. (1999) 'Grasping the nettle: possibilities and pitfalls of a critical management pedagogy', *British Journal of Management*, 10(2): 171–184.

Reynolds, M. and Vince, R. (2004) 'Critical management education and action-based learning: synergies and contradictions', *Academy of Management Learning and Education*, 3(4): 442–457.

Richardson, J. and McKenna, S. (2006) 'Exploring relationships with home and host countries: a study of self-directed expatriates', *Cross-cultural Management*, 13(1): 6–22.

Richardson, L. (1990) *Writing Strategies: Reaching Diverse Audiences* (Qualitative Research Methods No. 21). Newbury Park, CA: Sage.

Richardson, L. (1993) 'Poetics, dramatics, and transgressive validity: the case of the skipped line', *The Sociological Quarterly*, 34(3): 695–710.

Richardson, L. and St Pierre, E.A. (2005) 'Writing: a method of inquiry', in N.K. Denzin and Y.S. Lincoln (eds) *The Sage Handbook of Qualitative Research*. Thousand Oaks, CA: Sage.

Ricœur, P. (1981) *Hermeneutics and the Human Sciences*, ed. and trans. J. Thompson. Cambridge: Cambridge University Press.

Rigg, C. and Trehan, K. (2004) 'Reflections on working with critical action learning', *Action Learning: Research and Practice*, 1(2): 149–165.

Riley, M., Wood, R., Clark, M., Wilkie, E. and Szivas, E. (2000) *Researching and Writing Dissertations in Business and Management*. London: Thomson.

Roberts, B. (2002) *Biographical Research*. Buckingham: Open University Press.

Roberts, H. (2004) 'Health and social care', in S. Fraser, J. Lewis, S. Ding, M. Kellett and C. Robinbson (eds) *Doing Research with Children and Young People*. London: Sage/Open University.

Roberts, J. (1996) 'Management education and the limits of technical rationality: the conditions and consequences of management practice?', in R. French and C. Grey (eds) *Rethinking Management Education*. London: Sage. pp. 54–75.

Robinson, W.S. (1951) 'The logical structure of analytic induction', *American Sociological Review*, 16: 812–18.

Robson, C. (1993/2002) *Real World Research: A Resource for Social Scientists and Practitioner-researchers*. Oxford: Blackwell.

Robson, S. (1989) 'Group discussions', in S. Robson and A. Foster (eds.), *Qualitative Research in Action*. London: Edward Arnold. pp. 24–36.

Roethlisberger, F.J. and Dickson, W.J. (1939) *Management and the Worker*. Cambridge, MA: Harvard University Press.

Romm, C.T. and Pliskin, N. (1997) 'Playing politics with e-mail: a longitudinal conflict-based analysis', in A.S. Lee, J. Lieberau and J.I. DeGross (eds); (1997) *Information Systems and Qualitative Research: Proceedings of the IFIP Conference*. London: Chapman and Hall.

Ronan, W.W. and Latham, G.P. (1974) 'The reliability and validity of the critical incident technique: a closer look', *Studies in Personnel Psychology*, 6(1): 53–64.

Ropo, A., Eriksson, P. and Hunt, J.G. (1997) 'Reflections on conducting processual research on management and organizations', *Scandinavian Journal of Management*, 13(4): 331–335.

Rorty, R. (1980) *Philosophy and the Mirror of Nature*. Oxford: Blackwell.

Rorty, R. (1982) *Consequences of Pragmatism*. Minneapolis, MN: University of Minnesota Press.

Rorty, R. (1989) *Contingency, Irony and Solidarity*. New York: Cambridge University Press.

Rose, G. (2001) *Visual Methodologies: An Introduction to the Interpretation of Visual Materials*. London: Sage.

Rosenblatt, L.M. (1978) *The Reader, the Text, the Poem: The Transactional Theory of the Literary Work*. Place, IL: Southern Illinois University Press.

Rosenhan, D.I. (1973) 'On being sane in insane places', *Science*, 179: 350–358.

Rosenhead, J. (1998) 'Complexity theory and management practice', *Science as Culture* (human-nature.com/science-as-culture/rosenhead.html).

Roth, G.L and Kleiner, A. (1998) 'Organizational reflection: Developing organizational memory through learning histories', *Organizational Dynamics*, Winter, Vol. 27(2): 43–60.

Roy, D. (1958) 'Banana time: job satisfaction and informal interaction', *Human Organization*, 18: 158–168.

Rudolph, J.W., Simon, R., Dufresne, R.L. and Raemer, D.B. (2006) There's no such thing as "non-judgmental" debriefing: a theory and method for debriefing with good judgment', *Simulation in Healthcare*, 1: 49–55.

Runciman, W. (1983) *A Treatise on Social Theory* (Vol. 1). Cambridge: Cambridge University Press.

Russell, B. (1929) *Our Knowledge of the External World*. New York: The New American Library.

Saari, E. and Miettinen R. (2001) 'The dynamics of change in research work: constructing a new research area in a research group', *Science, Technology, Human Values*, 26(3): 300–321.

Sacks, H. (1992) *Lectures on Conversations* (Vols 1 & 2). G. Jefferson (ed.). Oxford: Basil Blackwell.

Sacks, H., Schegloff, E.A. and Jefferson, G.H. (1974) 'The simplest systematics for the organization of turn-taking', *Language*, 50: 697–735.

Said, E.W. (1978) *Orientalism*. New York: Vintage Books.

Samra-Fredericks, D. (2003) 'Strategizing as lived experience and strategists' everyday efforts to shape strategic direction', *Journal of Management Studies*, 40(1): 141–174.

Samra-Fredericks, D. (2004) 'Managerial elites making rhetorical and linguistic 'moves' for a moving (emotional) display', *Human Relations*, 57: 1103–1144.

Sandberg, J. (2000) Understanding human competence at work: an interpretative approach', *Academy of Management Journal*, 43: 9–25.

Sandelands, L.E. and Boudens, C.J. (2000) 'Feeling at work', in S. Fineman (ed.) *Emotion in Organizations*, (2nd edn). London: Sage.

Sanjek, R. (1990) 'A vocabulary for fieldnotes', in R. Sanjek *Fieldnotes: The Making of Anthropology*. New York: Cornell University Press.

Saunders, M., Lewis, P. and Thornhill, A. (2003) *Research Methods for Business Students*.

Saussure, F. de (1916/1966/1971/1983) *Course in General Linguistics*. Trans R. Harris, C. Bally and A. Sechehaye, A (eds). London: Duckworth (1916/1983) and New York: McGraw-Hill (1966).

Sawyer, R.K. (2002) 'Nonreductive individualism: Part I – supervenience and wild disjunction', *Philosophy of the Social Sciences*, 32(4): 537–559.

Sayer, A. (1992) *Methods in Social Science: A Realist Approach* (2nd edn). London: Routledge.

Sayer, A. (1999) *Realism and Social Science*. London: Sage.

Scapens, R.W. (2004) 'Doing case study research', in C. Humphrey and B. Lee (eds) *The Real Life Guide to Accounting Research*. Oxford: Elsevier. pp. 257–279.

Scarry, E. (1985) *The Body in Pain: The Making and Unmaking of the World*. New York: Oxford University Press.

Schaefer, D.R. and Dillman, D.A. (1998) 'Development of a standard e-mail methodology: results of an experiment', *Public Opinion Quarterly*, 62: 378–397.

Schatzki, T. (2001) 'Social science in society', *Inquiry*, 45: 119–138.

Schatzki, T. (2002) *The Site of the Social - a Philosophical Account of the Constitution of Social Life and Change*. University Park, PA: The Pennsylvania State University Press.

Schatzki, T. (2005a) 'The sites of organizations', *Organization Studies*, 26(3): 465–484.

Schatzki, T. (2005b) 'On interpretive social inquiry', *Philosophy of the Social Sciences*, 35(2): 231–249.

Schatzki, T., Knorr-Cetina, K. and von Savigny, E. (2001) *The Practice Turn in Contemporary Social Theory*. London: Routledge.

Scheer, J. (2006) 'Computer programs for the analysis of repertory grids: the psychology of personal constructs', available at: www.pcp-net.de/info/comp-prog.html, PA (The PCP Info Center, Hamburg).

Scheffler, I. (1982) *Science and Subjectivity* (2nd edn). Indianapolis: Hackett.

REFERENCES

Schendel, D. (1992) 'Fundamental themes in strategy process research', *Strategic Management Journal*, 13: S1–S13.

Schlackman, B. (1989) 'An historical perspective,' in S. Robson and A. Foster (eds) *Qualitative Research in Action*. London: Edward Arnold. pp. 15–23.

Schmitt, R. (2000) 'Notes towards the analysis of metaphor', *Forum: Qualitative Social Research* [online]: http:// qualitative-research.net/fqs (accessed 5 August 2006).

Schoenfelder, J.B. and Harris, P. (2002) 'Brand asset intelligence in high-tech consumer markets', *Proceedings of the Academy Of Marketing Conference*, Nottingham University Business School, Nottingham.

Schoenfelder, J.B. and Harris, P. (2004) 'High-tech corporate branding: lessons for market research in the next decade', *Qualitative Market Research, An International Journal*, 7(2): 91–99.

Scholl H.J. (2004) 'Involving salient stakeholders', *Action Research*, 2(3): 277–304.

Schön, D.A. (1983) *The Reflective Practitioner: How Professionals Think in Action*. New York: Basic Books.

Schön, D.A. (1993) 'Generative metaphor: a perspective on problem-setting in social policy', in A. Ortony (ed.) *Metaphor and Thought*. Cambridge: Cambridge University Press.

Schram, Sanford F. and Caterino, B. (eds) (2006) *Making Political Science Matter: Debating Knowledge, Research, and Method*. New York: New York University Press.

Schreyogg, G. and Hopfl, H. (2005) 'Theatre and organization', *Organization Studies*, 25(5).

Schur, D. (1998) *The Way of Oblivion*. London: Harvard University Press.

Schutz, A. (1967) *The Phenomenology of the Social World*. Trans G. Walsh. Evanston, IL: Northwestern University Press.

Scott, G.M. (2000) 'Critical technology management issues of new product development in high-tech companies', *Journal of Product Innovation Management*, 17: 57–77.

Scott, L.M. (1994) 'The bridge from text to mind: adapting reader-response theory to consumer research', *Journal of Consumer Research*, 21: 461–480.

Scottish Executive (2002) *Research Governance Framework for Health and Community Care*. Edinburgh: The Scottish Executive.

Seale, C. (2004) 'Quality in qualitative research', in C. Seale, G. Gobo, J.F. Gubrium and D. Silverman (eds) *Qualitative Research Practice*. London: Sage.

Searle, J. (1995) *The Construction of Social Reality*. New York: Free Press.

Searle, J. (2005) 'What is an institution', *Journal of Institutional Economics*, 1(1): 1–22.

Secrist, C., de Koeyer, I., Bell, H. and Fogel, A. (2002) 'Combining digital video technology and narrative methods for understanding infant development', *Forum: Qualitative Social Research* [Online], 3(2): www.qualitative-research.net/fqs-texte/2-02/2-02secristetal-e.html

Seidl, D. and Becker, K.H. (eds.) (2005) *Niklas Luhmann and Organizaiton Studies*. Copenhagen: Copenhagen Business School Press.

Selwyn, N. and Robson, K. (1998) 'Using e-mail as a research tool', *Social Research Update*. Available at: www.soc.surrey.ac.uk/sru/SRU21.html (accessed 11 January 2005).

Semler, R. (1993) *Maverick: The Success Story Behind the World's Most Unusual Workplace*. London: Century.

Senge, P. (1990) *The Fifth Discipline*. New York: Doubleday.

Seo, M.G. and Creed, W.E.D. (2002) 'Institutional contradictions, praxis and institutional change: a dialectical perspective', *Academy of Management Review*, 27(2): 222–247.

Shackle, G.L.S. (1972) *Epistemics and Economics: A Critique of Economic Doctrines*. New Brunswick, NJ: Transaction.

Shapiro, E. and Carr, A. (1991) *Lost in Familiar Places: Creating New Connections Between the Individual and Society*. New Haven, CT: Yale University Press.

Sharrock, W. and Randall, D. (2004) 'Ethnography, ethnomethodology and the problem of generalisation in design', *European Journal of Information Systems*, 13(3): 186–194.

Shenhav, Y. (1999) *Manufacturing Rationality: The Engineering Foundations of the Managerial Revolution*. Oxford: Oxford University Press.

Sherry, J.F. and Shouten, J.W. (2002) 'A role for poetry in consumer research', *Journal of Consumer Research*, 29: 218–234.

Shin, T. (1998) 'Using Delphi for a long-range technology forecasting, and assessing directions of future R&D activities: the Korean exercise', *Technological Forecasting and Social Change*, 58: 125–154.

Shotter, J. (1975) *Images of Man in Psychological Research*. London: Methuen.

Shotter, J. (1993) *Conversational Realities: Constructing Life Through Language*. London: Sage.

Shotter, J. (1996) 'Living in a Wittgensteinian world: beyond theory to a poetics of practices', *Journal for the Theory of Social Behaviour*, 26: 293–311.

Shrum, W., Duque, R. and Brown, T. (2005) 'Digital video as research practice: methodology for the millennium', *Journal of Research Practice* [Online] 1(2): http://jrp.icaap.org/content/v1.1/ shrum.html.

Siegel, H. (1983) 'Brown on epistemology and the new philosophy of science', *Synthese*, 56(1): 61–89.

Siegel, H. (1987) *Relativism Refuted*. Dordrecht, Netherlands: Reidel.

Siegel, L., Siegal, L.C., Capretta, P.J., Jones, R.L. and Berkowitz, H. (1963) 'Students' thoughts during class: a criterion for educational research', *Journal of Educational Psychology*, 54(1): 44–51.

Sievers, B. (2007) 'Pictures from below the surface of the university: the social photo-matrix as a method for understanding organizations in depth', in M. Reynolds and R. Vince (eds) *Experiential Learning and Management Education*. Oxford: Oxford University Press.

Sillence, J. (2002) 'A model of the strength and appropriateness of argumentation in organizational contexts', *Journal of Management Studies*, 39: 585–618.

Sillence, J. (2005) 'A contingency theory of rhetorical congruence', *Academy of Management Review*, 30: 608–621.

Silverman, D. (1993) *Interpreting Qualitative Data: Methods for Analysis Talk, Text and Interaction*. London: Sage.

Silverman, D. (2000) *Doing Qualitative Research: A Practical Handbook*. London: Sage.

Simsek, Z. and Veiga, J.F. (2000) 'The electronic survey technique: an integration and assessment', *Organizational Research Methods*, 3: 92–114.

Sköldberg, K. (1998) 'Heidegger and organization: notes towards a new research programme', *Scandinavian Journal of Management*, 14: 77–102.

Slinger, G. (1999) 'Spanning the gap: the theoretical principles that connect stakeholder policies to business performance', *Corporate Governance: An International Review*, 7(2): 136–151.

Smircich, L., Calás, M. and Morgan, G. (1992a) 'New intellectual currents in organization and management theory', *Academy of Management Review*, 17: 404–406.

Smircich, L., Calás, M. and Morgan, G. (1992b) 'Afterward/after words: open(ing) spaces', *Academy of Management Review*, 17: 607–611.

Smith, A. (1776) *An Inquiry into the Nature and Causes of the Wealth of Nations*. London: Metheun and Co. Ltd, Edwind Cannan (ed) (1904) 5th edn.

Smith, B. nd Smith, D. (1995) *The Cambridge Companion to Husserl*. Cambridge: Cambridge University Press.

Smith, D. (1996) 'Keeping a strategic dialogue moving', availabe at: www.actiondesign.com/ resources/theory/ksdm.html

Smith, H.W. (1975) *Strategies of Social Research: The Methodological Imagination*. London: Prentice Hall.

Smith, J.A. and Dunworth, F. (2003) 'Qualitative methodology', in J. Valsiner and K. Connolly (eds) *Handbook of Developmental Psychology*. London: Sage.

Smith, R., Monaghan, M. and Broad, B. (2002) 'Involving young people as coresearchers: facing up to the methodological issues', *Qualitative Social Work*, 1(2): 191–207.

Sokal, A. and Bricmont, J. (1998) *Intellectual Impostures: Postmodern Philosophers' Abuse of Science*. London: Profile Books.

Sorensen, P.E., Yaeger, T.F. and Bengtsson, U. (2003a) 'The promise of Appreciative inquiry: a 20-year review', OD ', OD cultures in organizations' (book by J. Martin), *Academy of Management Review*, 19(1): 156–159.

Sorensen, P.E., Yaeger, T.F. and Bengtsson, U. (2003b) 'The promise of appreciative inquiry: a 20-year review', *OD Practitioner*, 35(4): 15–21.

Spender, J.C. (1998) 'The dynamics of individual and organizational knowledge', in C. Eden and J.C. Spender (eds) *Managerial and Organizational Cognition: Theory, Methods and Research*. London: Sage. pp. 13–39.

Srivastva, S. and Cooperrider, D. (1990) *Appreciative Management and Leadership: The Power of Positive Thought and Action in Organizations*. San Francisco, CA: Jossey-Bass.

Stacey, R.D. (2001) *Complex Responsive Processes in Organizations*. London: Routledge.

Stacey, R.D. (2003) *Strategic Management and Organisational Dynamics: The Challenge of Complexity*. Harlow: FT/Prentice Hall.

Stacey, R.D. and Griffin, D. (2005) *A Complexity Perspective on Researching Organizations*. London: Routledge.

Stacey, R.D., Griffin, D. and Shaw, P. (2002) *Complexity and Management: Fad or Radical Challenge to Systems Thinking*. London: Routledge.

Stake, R.E. (2000) 'Case studies', in N.K. Denzin and Y.S. Lincoln (eds) *Handbook of Qualitative Research*. London: Sage.

Starr, L. (1996) 'Oral history', in D.K. Dunaway and W.K. Baum (eds) *Oral History: An Interdisciplinary Anthology* (2nd edn). Walnut Creek, CA: Altamira Press.

Steedman, P. (1991) 'On the relations between seeing, interpreting and knowing', in F. Steier (ed.) *Research and Reflexivity*. London: Sage.

Steier, F. (1995) 'Reflexivity, interpersonal communication and interpersonal communication research', in W. Leeds-Hurwitz (ed.) *Social Approaches to Communication*. New York: Guilford Press.

Steinhauser, K.E., Clipp, E.C., McNeilly, M., Christakis, N.A., McIntyre, L.M. and Tulsky, J.A. (2000) 'In search of a good death: observations of patients, families, and providers', *Annals of Internal Medicine*, 132(10): 825–832.

Sternberg, E. (1997) 'The defects of stakeholder theory', *Corporate Governance: An International Review*, 5(1): 3–10.

Stevens, C. (1998) 'Realism and Kelly's pragmatic constructivism', *Journal of Constructivist Psychology*, 11(4): 283–307.

Stewart, D.W, Shamdasani, P.N. and Rook, D.W. (1990/2006) *Focus Groups Theory and Practice* (2nd edn). London: Sage.

Stewart, V. and Mayes, J. (1997–2006) 'Enquire within', www.enquirewithin.co.nz/ ENQUIRE WITHIN®. New Zealand and USA.

Stewart, V. and Stewart, A. (1981) *Business Applications of Repertory Grid*. Maidenhead: McGraw-Hill.

Stickland, F. (1998) *The Dynamics of Change: Insights into Organisational Transition from the Natural World*. London: Routledge.

Stiles, D.R. (2004) 'Pictorial representation', in C. Cassell and G. Symon (eds) *Essential Guide to Qualitative Methods in Organizational Research*. London: Sage.

Stokes, D. (2000) 'Entrepreneurial marketing: a conceptualisation from qualitative research', *Qualitative Market Research: An International Journal*, 3(1): 47–54.

Stoney, C. and Winstanley, D. (2001) 'Stakeholding: confusion or utopia? Mapping the conceptual terrain', *The Journal of Management Studies*, 38(5): 603–626.

Strangleman, T. (2004) 'Ways of (not) seeing work: the visual as a blind spot in WES?', *Work, Employment and Society*, 18(1): 179–192.

Strati, A. (1992) 'Aesthetic understanding of organizational life', *Academy of Management Review*, 17: 568–81.

Strati, A. (1999) *Organization and Aesthetics*. London: Sage.

Strati, A. and Guillet de Monthoux, P. (eds) (2002) 'Organizing aesthetics'. Special issue. *Human Relations*, 57(7).

Strauss, A. and Corbin, J. (1990/1998) *Basics for Qualitative Research: Techniques and Procedures for Developing Grounded Theory*. London and Thousand Oaks, CA: Sage.

Strauss, A.L. (1993) *Continual Permutations of Action*. Hawthorn, NY: Aldine de Gruyter.

Strecker, I. (1997) 'The turbulence of images: on imagery, media and ethnographic discourse', *Visual Anthropology*, 9: 207–227.

Stueber, K.R. (2006) 'How to structure a social theory? A critical response to Anthony King's the structure of social theory', *Philosophy of the Social Sciences*, 36(1): 95–104.

Stumfp, S. and McDonnell, J. (2003) 'Using repertory grids to test data quality and experts' hunches', Paper presented at 4th International Workshop on Theory and Applications of Knowledge Management (TAKMA, 03), Prague.

Sturdy, A.J. (2003) 'Knowing the unknowable?: a discussion of methodological and theoretical issues in emotion research and organisational studies', *Organization*, 10(1): 81–105.

Styhre, A. (2002) 'Non-linear change in organizations: organization change management informed by complexity theory', *Leadership and Organization Development Journal*, 23(6): 343–351.

Suddaby, R. and Greenwood, R. (2005) 'Rhetorical strategies of legitimacy', *Administrative Science Quarterly*, 50: 35–67.

Summerfield, P. (1998) 'They didn't want women back in that job! The Second World War and the construction of gendered work histories', *Labour History Review*, 63(1): 83–104.

Suppe, F. (1977) *The Structure of Scientific Theories* (2nd edn). Chicago: University of Illinois Press.

Symon, G. (2000) 'Everyday rhetoric: argument and persuasion in everyday life', *European Journal of Work and Organizational Psychology*, 9: 477–488.

Symon, G. (2005) 'Exploring resistance from a rhetorical perspective', *Organization Studies*, 26: 1641–1663.

Tan, F.B. (1999) 'Exploring business: IT alignment using the repertory grid', paper presented at 10th Australasian Conference on Information Systems, Australia.

Tannen, D. (ed.) (1988) *Linguistics in Context: Connecting Observation and Understanding* (Vol. XXIX). Advances in Discourse Processes Series. Norwood, NJ: Ablex Publishing.

Tashakkori, A. and Teddlie, C. (eds) (2003) *Handbook of Mixed Methods in Social and Behavioral Research*. Thousand Oaks, CA: Sage.

Taylor, C. (1995) *Philosophical Arguments*. Cambridge, MA: Harvard University Press.

Taylor, F.W. (1903) 'Shop management', in *Scientific Management*. Westport, CT: Greenwoods.

Taylor, F.W. (1911) *The Principles of Scientific Management*. New York: W.W. Norton.

Terkel, S. (1975) *Working*. Harmondsworth: Penguin.

Tetenbaum, T. (1998) 'Shifting paradigms: from Newton to chaos', *Organizational Dynamics*, 26(4): 21–32.

Teune, H. (1990) 'Comparing countries: lessons learned', in E. Øyen (ed) *Comparative Methodology*. London: Sage.

Thom, R. (1975) *Structural Stability and Morphogenesis*. New York: Addison-Wesley.

Thomas, W.I. and Thomas, D.S. (1928) *The Child in America: Behavior Problems and Programs*. New York: Knopf.

Thompson, P. (1998) 'The voice of the past: oral history', in R. Perks and A. Thomson (eds), *The Oral History Reader*. London/New York: Routledge.

Thompson, P. (2000) *The Voice of the Past* (3rd edn). Oxford: Oxford University Press.

Thomson, A., Storey, J., Mabey, C., Farmer, E. and Thomson, R. (1997) *A Portrait of Management Development*. London: Institute of Management.

Thorpe, R. and Cornelisson, J. (2003) 'Visual media and the construction of meaning', in D. Holman and R. Thorpe (eds) *Management and Language*. London: Sage.

Thorpe, R., Holt, R. and Gold, J. (2004) 'The mature entrepreneur', Paper presented at the Academy of Management Conference, New Orleans.

Thorpe, R., Holt, R., Macpherson, A. and Pittaway, L. (2005) 'Knowledge within small and medium sized firms: a systematic review of the evidence', *International Journal of Management Reviews*, 7(4): 257–281.

Tichy, G. (2004) 'The over-optimism among experts in assessment and foresight', *Technological Forecasting and Social Change*, 71: 341–368.

Toiviainen, H. (2003) 'Learning across levels: Challenges of collaboration in a small-firm network', Doctoral dissertation. University of Helsinki, Department of Education. Helsinki: Helsinki University Press.

Toker, U. (2006) 'Workspaces for knowledge generation: facilitating innovation in university research centers', *Journal of Architectural and Planning Research*, 23(3): 181–199.

REFERENCES

Tolman, E.C. (1948) 'Cognitive maps in rats and men', *Psychological Review*, 55: 189–208.

Torbert, W. (1976) *Creating a Community of Inquiry*. London: John Wiley.

Torbert, W. (2000) 'The challenge of creating a community of inquiry among scholar-consultants critiquing one another's theories-in-practice', in F. Sherman and W. Torbert (eds) *Transforming Social Inquiry, Transforming Social Action*. Norwell, MA: Kluwer Academic Publishers.

Torbert, W. and Associates (2004) *Action Inquiry: The Secret of Timely and Transforming Leadership*. San Francisco, CA: Berrett-Koehler.

Tranfield, D. and Starkey, K. (1998) 'The nature of social organisation and promotion of management research: towards policy', *British Journal of Management*, 9(4): 341–353.

Tranfield, D.R., Denyer, D. and Smart, P. (2003) 'Towards a methodology for developing evidence-informed management knowledge by means of systematic review', *British Journal of Management*, 14: 207–222.

Trapp-Fallon, J.M. (2002) 'Searching for rich narratives of tourism and leisure experience: how oral history could provide an answer', *Tourism and Hospitality Research*, 4(4): 297–305.

Truss, C., Gratton, L., Hope-Hailey, V., McGovern, P. and Stiles, P. (1997) 'Soft and hard models of human resource management: a reappraisal', *Journal of Management Studies*, 34: 53–73.

Tsoukas, H. (1989) 'The validity of idiographic research explanations', *Academy of Management Review*, 14(4): 551–561.

Tsoukas, H. (1991) 'The missing link: a transformational view of metaphors in organizational science', *Academy of Management Review*, 16: 566–585.

Tsoukas, H. (1993) 'Analogical reasoning and knowledge generation in organization theory', *Organization Studies*, 14: 323–346.

Tsoukas, H. (1996) 'The firm as a distributed knowledge system: a constructionist approach', *Strategic Management Journal*, 17: 11–25.

Tsoukas, H. (2005) 'Afterword: why language matters in the analysis of organisational change', *Journal of Organisational Change Management*, 18(1): 96–104.

Tsoukas, H. and Chia, R. (2002) 'On organizational becoming: rethinking organizational change', *Organization Science*, 13(5): 567–582.

Tsoukas, H. and Vladimirou, E. (2001) 'What is organizational knowledge?', *Journal of Management Studies*, 38: 973–993.

Tu, W.M. (1985) *Confucian Thought: Selfhood as Creative Transformation*. Albany, NY: State University of New York Press.

Tu, W.M. (1989) 'The rise of industrial East Asia: the role of Confucian values', *Copenhagen Papers*, 4: 81–97.

Tu, W.M. (1991) 'A Confucian perspective on the rise of industrial East Asia', in S. Krieger (ed.) *Confucianism and the Modernization of China*. Berlin: Hase & Koehler. pp. 29–41.

Tu, W.M. (1994) (ed.) *The Living Tree: The Changing Meaning of Being Chinese Today*. Stanford, CA: Stanford University Press.

Tuhiwai Smith, L. (1999) *Decolonizing Methodologies: Research and Indigenous Peoples*. London: Zed Books.

Tulin, M.F. (1997) 'Talking organization: possibilities for conversational analysis in organizational behavior research', *Journal of Management Inquiry*, 6: 101–119.

Turner, B.A. (1976) 'The organizational and interorganizational development of disasters', *Administrative Science Quarterly*, 21: 378–397.

Turner, B.A. (ed.) (1990) *Organizational Symbolism*. Berlin: deGruyter.

Turner, S. (1994) *The Social Theory of Practices*. Cambridge: Polity Press.

Udehn, L. (2001) *Methodological Inidividualism: Background, History and Meaning*. New York: Routledge.

Usunier, J-C. (1998) *International and Cross-Cultural Management Research*, London: Sage Publications.

Van Aken, J.E. (2004) 'Management research based on the paradigm of the design sciences: the quest for field-tested and grounded technological rules', *Journal of Management Studies*, 41: 219–245.

Van Buren, H. (2001) 'If fairness is the problem, is consent the solution? Integrating ISCT and stakeholder theory', *Business Ethics Quarterly*, 11(3): 481–499.

Van de Rijt, J. and Santema, S. (2001) 'Strategy disclosure in Dutch annual reports', *European Management Journal*, 19(1): 101–108.

Van de Ven, A.H. (1992) 'Suggestions for studying strategy process: a research note', *Strategic Management Journal*, 13: S169–S188.

Van de Ven, A.H. and Poole, M.S. (1990) 'Methods for studying innovation in the Minnesota innovation research program', *Organization Science*, 1(3): 313–335.

Van de Ven, A.H. and Poole, M.S. (1995) 'Explaining development and change in organizations', *The Academy of Management Review* 20(3): 510–540.

Van de Ven, A. and Poole, M.S. (2005) 'Alternative approaches for studying organizational change', *Organization Studies*, 26(9): 1377–1404.

Van Maanen, J. (1988) *Tales of the Field*. Chicago: Chicago University Press.

Van Maanen, J. (ed.) (1995a) *Representation in Ethnography*. Thousand Oaks, CA: Sage.

Van Maanen, J. (1995b) 'Style as theory', *Organization Science*, 6(1): 135–143.

Vickers, M.H. (2002) 'Illness, work and organization: postmodernism and antenarratives for the reinstatement of voice', working paper, University of Western Sydney, Sydney, Australia.

Vidgen, R. and McMaster, T. (1996) 'Black boxes, non-human stakeholders and the translation of IT', in W. Orlikowski, G. Walsham, M. Jones and J. DeGross (eds) *Information Technology and Changes in Organizational Work*. London: Chapman and Hall.

Vince, R. (1995) 'Working with emotions in the change process: using drawings for team diagnosis and development', *Organisations and People*, 2(1): 11–17.

Vince, R. and Broussine, M. (1996) 'Paradox, defence and attachment: accessing and working with emotions and relations underlying organizational change', *Organization Studies*, 17(1): 1–21.

Vince, R. and Martin, L. (1993) 'Inside action learning: an exploration of the psychology and politics of the action learning model', *Management Education and Development*, 24(3): 205–215.

Vischer, J. (1999) 'Will this open space work?', *Harvard Business Review*, 77(May–June): 28–36.

Von Glasersfeld, E. (1987) *The Construction of Knowledge: Contributions to Conceptual Semantics*. Seaside, CA: Intersystems Publications.

Von Glasersfeld, E. (2002) *Radical Constructivism*. London: Routledge.

Vyakarnam, S., Bailey, A., Myers, A. and Burnett, D. (1997) 'Towards an understanding of ethical behaviour in small firms', *Journal of Business Ethics*, 16(15): 1625–1636.

Vygotsky, L. (1979) *Mind in Society: The Development of Higher Psychological Processes*. Cambridge, MA: Harvard University Press and Cambridge University Press.

Vygotsky, L.S. (1986) *Thought and Language*. Translated and newly revised by Alex Kozulim. Cambridge, MA: The MIT Press.

Waddington, K. and Fletcher, C. (2005) 'Gossip and emotion in nursing and healthcare organizations', *Journal of Health Organization and Management*, 19(4/5): 378–394.

Walsh, J.P. (1995) 'Managerial and organizational cognition: notes from a trip down memory lane', *Organization Science*, 6(3): 280–321.

Walsham, G. (1993) *Interpreting Information Systems in Organizations*. Cambridge: John Wiley.

Walter, J.B. (1996) 'Computer-mediated communication: Impersonal, interpersonal, and hyperpersonal interaction. *Communication Research*, 23: 3–43.

Wang, S. (1996) 'A dynamic perspective of differences between cognitive maps', *Journal of the Operational Research Society*, 47: 538–549.

Wansink, B. (2003) 'Using laddering to understand and leverage a brand's equity', *Qualitative Market Research: An International Journal*, 6(2): 111–118.

Warnaby, G. and Yip, K.M. (2005) 'Promotional planning in UK regional shopping centres: an exploratory study', *Marketing Intelligence and Planning*, 23(1): 43–57.

Watkins, K.E. and Marsick, V.J. (1999) *Facilitating Learning Organizations: Making Learning Count*. London: Grover.

Watson, T. (1994a) 'Managing, crafting and researching: words, skill and imagination in shaping management research', *British Journal of Management*, 5: 77–87.

Watson, T. (1994b/2001) *In Search of Management: Culture, Chaos and Control in Managerial Work* (2nd edn). London: Routledge and Thomson.

Watson, T. (1995a) 'Shaping the story: rhetoric, persuasion and creative writing in organisational ethnography', *Studies in Cultures, Organisations and Society*, 1: 301–311.

Watson, T. (1995b) 'In search of HRM: beyond the rhetoric and reality distinction or the case of the dog that didn't bark', *Personnel Review*, 24: 6–16.

Watson, T. (1995c) 'Rhetoric, discourse and argument in organizational sense making: a reflexive tale', *Organization Studies*, 16: 805–821.

Watson, T. (2007) 'Identity work, managing and researching', in A. Pullen, N. Beech and D. Sims (eds) *Researching Identity: Concepts and Methods*. London: Routledge.

Watzlawick, P. (ed.) (1984) *The Invented Reality: How Do We Know What We Believe We Know?* New York: Norton & Co.

Weaver, G.R. and Gioia, D.A. (1994) 'Paradigms lost: incommensurability vs structuration inquiry', *Organization Studies*, 15(4): 565–590.

Webb, E.J. Campbell, D.T., Schwartz, R.D. and Sechrest, L. (1966) *Unobtrusive Measures: Nonreactive Research in the Social Sciences*. Chicago, IL: Rand McNally.

Weber, M. (1972) *Basic Concepts of Sociology*, translated by H.P. Secher. Secaucus: Citadel.

Weick, K.E. (1968) 'Systematic observational methods', in G.Lindzey and E. Aronson (eds) *Handbook of Social Psychology, Vol. 2*, (2nd edn). Reading, MA: Addison-Wesley.

Weick, K.E. (1969/1979) *The Social Psychology of Organizing* (2nd edn). Reading, MA: Addison-Wesley.

Weick, K.E. (1989) 'Theory construction as disciplined imagination', *Academy of Management Review*, 14: 516–531.

Weick, K.E. (1995) *Sensemaking in Organizations*. Thousand Oaks, CA: Sage.

Weick, K.E. (1998) 'Improvization as a mindset for organizational analysis', *Organization Science*, 9: 543–555.

Weick, K.E. (1999) 'Theory construction as disciplined reflexivity: tradeoffs in the 90s', *Academy of Management Review*, 24: 797–806.

Weick, K.E., Sutcliffe, K.M. and Obstfeld, D. (2005) 'Organizing and the processes of sensemaking', *Organization Science*, 16(4): 409–421.

Weinstein, K. (1995) *Action Learning: A Journey in Discovery and Development*. London: HarperCollins.

Weiss, H. and Brief, T. (2001) 'Affect at work: an historical perspective', in R. Payne and C.L. Cooper (eds) *Emotions at Work*. Chichester: Wiley.

Wenger, E. (1998) *Communities of Practice: Learning, Meaning, and Identity*. Cambridge: Cambridge University Press.

Wheatley, M.J. (1992) *Leadership and the New Science: Learning About Organization from an Orderly Universe*. San Francisco, CA: Berrett- Koehler.

Whitehead, A.N (1920) The Concept of Nature. Cambridge: The University Press.

Whitehead, A.N. (1927) Symbolism: Its Meaning and Effect. New York: Fordham University Press.

Whitehead, A.N. (1929a) *The Function of Reason*. Princeton, NJ: Princeton University Press.

Whitehead, A.N. (1929b/1978) *Process and Reality: An Essay in Cosmology*. D.R. Griffin and D.W. Sherburne (eds). New York: Macmillan and The Free Press.

Whitehead, A.N. (1933) *Adventures of Ideas*. New York: The Free Press.

Whitfield, K. and Strauss, G. (eds) (1998) *Researching the World of Work: Strategies and Methods in Studying Industrial Relations*. Ithaca, NY and London: ILR Press.

Whittington, R. (2003) 'The work of strategizing and organizing: for a practice perspective', *Strategic Organization*, 1(1): 117–124.

Whittington, R. (2006) 'Completing the practice turn in strategy research', *Organization Studies*, 27(5): 613–634.

Whitty, M.T. and Carr, A.N. (2006) 'New rules in the workplace: applying object–relations theory to explain problem internet and email behaviour in the workplace', *Computers in Human Behavior*, 22: 235–250.

Whyte, W.F. (1955) *Street Corner Society*. Chicago: University of Chicago Press.

Whyte, W.F. (1991) *Participatory Action Research*. Newbury Park, CA: Sage.

Wicks, A.C. and Freeman, R.E. (1998) 'Organization studies and the new pragmatism: positivism, anti-positivism, and the search for ethics', *Organization Science*, 9(2): 123–140.

Wieland, G.F. (1981) *Improving Health Care Management*. Ann Arbor, MI: Health Administration Press.

Wieland, G.F., Leigh, G.F. and Leigh, H. (eds) (1971) *Changing Hospitals: a Report on the Hospital Internal Communications Project*. London: Tavistock.

Wilkins, A. (1983) 'Organizational stories as symbols which control the organization', in L. Poindy, G. Morgan, P. Forst and T. Dandridge (eds) *Organizational Symbolism*. Greenwich, CT: JAI Press. pp. 81–92.

Williams, R.J., Douglas Barret, J. and Brabston, M. (2000) 'Managers' business school education and military service: possible links to corporate criminal activity', *Human Relations*, 53(5): 691–712.

Williams, S.J. and Bendelow, G.A. (1998) 'Introduction – emotions in social life: mapping the socio-logical terrain', in S. Williams and G. Bendelow (eds) *Emotions and Social Life: Critical Themes and Contemporary Issues*. London: Routledge.

Willig, C. (2001) *Introducing Qualitative Research in Psychology*. Buckingham: Open University Press.

Willis, V. (2004) 'Inspecting cases: prevailing degrees of action learning using Revans' theory and rules of engagement as standard', *Action Learning: Research and Practice*, 1(1): 11–27.

Willmott, H. (1993a) 'Breaking the paradigm mentality', *Organization Studies*, 14(5): 681–719.

Willmott, H. (1993b) 'Strength is ignorance, slavery is freedom: managing culture in modern organi-zations', *Journal of Management Studies*, 30(4): 515–552.

Willmott, H. (1994) 'Management education: provocations to a debate', *Management Learning*, 25(1): 105–36.

Willmott, H. (1997) 'Critical management learning', in J. Burgoyne and M. Reynolds (eds) *Management Learning: Integrating Perspectives in Theory and Practice*. London: Sage. pp. 161–176.

Willmott, H. (2000) 'From knowledge to learning', in D. Knights, P. Thompson and H. Willmott (eds) *Managing Knowledge: Critical Investigations of Work and Learning*. London: Macmillan. pp. 216–222.

Witherspoon, R. and Cannon, M. (2004) 'Coaching leaders in transition', in A. Buono (ed.) *Creative Consulting: Innovative Perspectives on Management Consulting*. Greenwich, CT: Information Age Publishing.

Wittgenstein, L. (1953) *Philosophical Investigations*. Oxford: Blackwell.

Wittgenstein, L. (1972) *On Certainty*. Trans G.E.M. Anscombe and G.H. von Wright. New York: Harper & Row.

Wittgenstein, L. (1980) *Remarks on the Philosophy of Psychology* (Vols I & II). Oxford: Blackwell.

Wolfram Cox, J. and Hassard, J. (2005) 'Triangulation in research methods: a critique and re-presentation', *Organization*, 12: 109–133.

Wong, A. and Sohal, A. (2003) 'A critical incident approach to the examination of customer relationship management in a retail chain: an exploratory study', *Qualitative Market Research: An International Journal*, 6(4): 248–262.

Wood, M. (2002) 'Mind the gap: a processual reconsideration of organizational knowledge', *Organization*, 9: 151–171.

Wood, M. (2005) 'The fallacy of misplaced leadership', *Journal of Management Studies*, 42(6): 1101–1121.

Wood, M. and Ferlie, E. (2003) 'Journeying from Hippocrates with Bergson and Deleuze', *Organization Studies*, 24(1): 47–68.

Woolgar, S. (1988) 'Reflexivity is the ethnographer of the text', in S. Woolgar, (ed) *Knowledge and Reflexivity*. London: Sage.

Wortham, S. (1999) 'The heterogeneously distributed self', *Journal of Constructivist Psychology*, 12(2): 153–172.

Wright, M. Filatotchev, I., Hoskisson, R.E. and Peng, M.W. (2005) 'Strategy research in emerging economies: challenging the conventional wisdom', *Journal of Management Studies*, 42(1): 1–34.

REFERENCES

Yanamanadram, V. and White, L. (2006) 'Switching barriers in business-to-business services: a qualitative study', *International Journal of Service Industry Management*, 17(2): 158–192.

Yao, X.-Z. (2000) *An Introduction to Confucianism*. Cambridge: Cambridge University Press.

Yauch, C.A. and Steudel, H.J. (2003) 'Complementary use of qualitative and quantitative cultural assessment methods', *Organizational Research Methods*, 6: 465–481.

Yin, R. (1994) *Case Study Research* (2nd edn). Thousand Oaks, CA: Sage.

Young, M.D. (1996) 'Cognitive mapping meets semantic networks', *Journal of Conflict Resolution*, 40: 395–414.

Young, R.Y.C. (2001) *Postcolonialism: An Historical Introduction*. Oxford and Malden: Blackwell.

Zald, M.N. (1993) 'Organization studies as a scientific and humanistic enterprise: toward a reconceptualization of the foundations of the field', *Organization Science*, 4(4): 513–528.

Zaner, R. (1970) *The Way of Phenomenology*. New York: Pegasus.

Zbaracki, M. (1998) 'The rhetoric and reality of total quality management', *Administrative Science Quarterly*, 43: 602–636.

Zemke, R. (1999) 'Don't fix the company', *Training*, 36(6): 26-34.

Zhilin, Y. and Xiang, F. (2004) 'Online service quality dimensions and their relationships with satisfaction: a content analysis of customer reviews of securities brokerage services', *International Journal of Services Industries Management*, 15(3): 302–327.

Zhuge, H. and Shi, X. (2001) 'Communication cost of cognitive co-operation for distributed team development', *The Journal of Systems and Software*, 57: 227–233.

Zuboff, S. (1988) *In the Age of the Smart Machine: The Future of Work and Power*. New York: Basic Books.

Index

Note: Page numbers in bold refer to the main dictionary entry for that subject, or if under an author, authorship of a main dictionary entry. The letter 'f' after a page number denotes a figure; 't' denotes a table.

INDEX